ROYAL HISTORICAL SOCIETY

GUIDES AND HANDBOOKS
No. 14

SCOTTISH HISTORY SOCIETY

FOURTH SERIES
VOLUME 23

SCOTTISH TEXTS AND CALENDARS
AN ANALYTICAL GUIDE TO SERIAL
PUBLICATIONS

ROYAL HISTORICAL SOCIETY

GUIDES AND HANDBOOKS
ISSN 0080–4398

MAIN SERIES

1. *Guide to English commercial statistics 1696–1782.* By G. N. Clark and Barbara M. Franks. 1938.
2. *Handbook of British chronology.* Edited by F. M. Powicke, Charles Johnson and W. J. Harte. 1939. 2nd edition, edited by F. M. Powicke and E. B. Fryde, 1961. 3rd edition, edited by E. B. Fryde, D. E. Greenway, S. Porter and I. Roy, 1986.
3. *Medieval libraries of Great Britain. A list of surviving books.* Edited by N. R. Ker. 1941. 2nd edition, 1964.
4. *Handbook of dates for students of English history.* Edited by C. R. Cheney. 1945. Reprinted, 1982.
5. *Guide to the national and provincial directories of England and Wales, excluding London, published before 1856.* By Jane E. Norton. 1950.
6. *Handbook of oriental history.* Edited by C. H. Philips. 1951.
7. *Texts and Calendars. An analytical guide to serial publications.* By E. L. C. Mullins. 1958. Reprinted (with corrections), 1978.
8. *Anglo-Saxon Charters. An annotated list and bibliography.* By P. H. Sawyer. 1968.
9. *A Centenary Guide to the publications of the Royal Historical Society 1868–1968 and of the former Camden Society 1838–1897.* By Alexander Taylor Milne. 1968.
10. *Guide to the local administrative units of England.* Volume I. *Southern England.* By Frederic A. Youngs, Jr. 1979. 2nd edition, 1981.
11. *Guide to bishops' registers of England and Wales. A survey from the middle ages to the abolition of episcopacy in 1646.* By David M. Smith. 1981.
12. *Texts and Calendars II. An analytical guide to serial publications 1957–1982.* By E. L. C. Mullins. 1983.
13. *Handbook of Medieval Exchange.* By Peter Spufford, with the assistance of Wendy Wilkinson and Sarah Tolley. 1986.

SUPPLEMENTARY SERIES

1. *A Guide to the papers of British Cabinet Ministers, 1900–1951.* Compiled by Cameron Hazlehurst and Christine Woodland. 1974.
2. *A Guide to the reports of the U.S. Strategic Bombing Survey. I Europe. II The Pacific.* Edited by Gordon Daniels. 1981.

SCOTTISH TEXTS AND CALENDARS

AN ANALYTICAL GUIDE
TO SERIAL PUBLICATIONS

BY

DAVID AND WENDY B. STEVENSON

LONDON
ROYAL HISTORICAL SOCIETY
EDINBURGH
SCOTTISH HISTORY SOCIETY
1987

First published 1987
by The Royal Historical Society and
The Scottish History Society

Royal Historical Society ISBN 0 86193 111 4
Scottish History Society ISBN 0 906245 08 7

British Library Cataloguing in Publication Data

Stevenson, David, *1942–*
    Scottish texts and calendars: an
    analytical guide to serial publications.
    — (Royal Historical Society guides and
    handbooks; no. 14)
    — (Scottish History Society;
    ser. 4, no. 23)
    1. Scotland—History—Sources—
    Bibliography
    I. Title   II. Stevenson, Wendy B.
    III. Series
    016.9411   Z2061

ISBN 0-86193-111-4
ISBN 0-906-245-08-7

Printed in Great Britain by St Edmundsbury Press, Bury St Edmunds, Suffolk

PREFACE

This book is primarily intended to form a companion volume to two works produced by E. L. C. Mullins for the Royal Historical Society's 'Guides and Handbooks' series: *Texts and calendars. An analytical guide to serial publications* (1958) and *Texts and calendars II. An analytical guide to serial publications 1957–1982* (1983). Mullins described the first of these works as 'an analytical guide to printed texts and calendars relating to English and Welsh history issued in general collections or in series by a public body or private society'. However, the work was also planned to form a catalogue of a section of the Royal Historical Society Library which, though defined in similar terms to those quoted above, was in fact rather more extensive than they suggest, in that the Library included texts and calendars published by official bodies relating to Scotland (and some relating to Ireland) as well as English and Welsh ones. Thus, in both of Mullins' invaluable works, 'Part 1: Official Bodies' includes works relating to Scotland, while parts 2–5, concerned with publications of private societies, are limited in coverage to England and Wales. The present work, designed as a Scottish supplement to Mullins' works, is therefore limited to private societies; listings of Scottish works produced by official bodies should be sought in Mullins. The only exception to this is that a few Scottish official publications omitted by Mullins, or published since his second work appeared, are listed in an Appendix.

Thus it might be argued that Mullins' works contain a degree of inconsistency in their coverage (British for official publications but English and Welsh for private ones) through trying to be two things at once (general reference work and library guide). It may be that the same strains are apparent in the present work. As well as being designed as a supplement to Mullins, it is also intended to update and partly replace two older Scottish reference works: C. S. Terry, *A catalogue of the publications of Scottish historical and kindred clubs and societies, and of the volumes*

*relevant to Scottish history issued by His Majesty's Stationery Office,
1780–1908* (1909), and C. Matheson, *A catalogue of the publications of Scottish historical and kindred clubs and societies . . .
1908–1927* (1928). The replacement of Terry and Matheson
offered by the present volume is however incomplete in that—

1. As explained above, the present work does not list official
   publications.
2. The present work is limited to listing series mainly concerned
   with primary sources, and thus omits the listing of contents
   of series and periodicals consisting of secondary works which
   Terry and Matheson included.
3. The detailed bibliographical information they contained as to
   pagination, size of volumes, illustrations, etc., has been
   omitted.
4. No attempt has been made to continue Terry's policy of
   including such items as the annual reports, rules, and lists of
   members of societies—though those he listed do appear in
   the present work.

In compensation for these omissions, however, the present work
offers much more information than Terry and Matheson as to
the contents of the works listed. They were primarily concerned
to catalogue, leaving titles to speak for themselves (however
inadequately). The present work, being an analytical guide,
seeks as far as is possible in brief entries, to elucidate the
contents of the works listed.

The compilers have to admit some inconsistency in the choice
of series for inclusion. The general policy has been to seek to be
inclusive rather than exclusive. In some instances, in which a
large portion of the publications in a series are not relevant (e.g.,
2, 17, 19, 35, 41), only relevant works are listed. Series **4** and **8**,
being the inventions of booksellers rather than genuine private
societies, and having no emphasis on Scottish sources, might
well have been omitted, but have been included for the sake of
completeness as they were catalogued by Terry. The purely
literary and linguistic publishing societies would have been
excluded by strict adherence to Mullins' criteria, but are
included here both because they are listed in Terry and
Matheson, and because a high proportion of their publications
consist of important historical sources. Two further series
perhaps require special pleading to justify their inclusion. 'Bute
Scottish Record Series' (**7**) is a title created here to describe the
series of volumes printed and circulated privately by the 4th

Marquis of Bute and his successor. Being the productions of an individual rather than a society they should, strictly speaking, not appear in the present work. But they form a clearly-defined series of great value which it is hard to find listed anywhere else. Though the Roxburghe Club (**17**) has a Scottish name it is essentially English—and literary at that. But a significant proportion of its publications consists of sources relating to Scottish (primarily Jacobite) history, and these have been listed. Both cases for inclusion rest on expediency rather than principle, but it is hoped the compilers may be indulged here as the inclusion of these series should add to the usefulness of the work as a reference tool.

In general the forms of entry and index used in this volume follow Mullins, though there are some minor differences. For those not familiar with Mullins, entries take the form of a title entry followed (indented and in smaller type) by an analytical entry. In some instances the title entry conveys so much information that it stands alone, no analytical entry being thought necessary.

Titles are copied strictly from title pages, except that capitalization has been standardized and punctuation added where necessary for clarity. Phrases such as 'Edited by' or 'with introduction and notes by' are copied from the title page, but names of editors, etc., are standardized by giving a single Christian name and other initials before the surname; titles such as 'Rev.' or 'Dr' are omitted, along with details of qualifications, offices held, etc. Where no editor's name appears on the title page, this is added silently if the editor can be identified from the volume itself. If, however, the indentification has been made from other sources, the editor's name appears in square brackets. In some cases of publications for which no editor can be identified with certainty, but which carry the name of the person presenting the volume to the club or society, the presenter's name is included in the title entry. Those who thus presented volumes were frequently, but not invariably, their editors. Dates of publication are those that appear on the volumes, though it is clear in some cases that they are incorrect.

Full titles are given, except in a few instances in which excessively long ones have been slightly shortened. Where works consist of several volumes which are listed separately, title entries after the first are often shortened, the editor's name being omitted if it is the same as in the previous volume or volumes. It is assumed that pagination is continuous in works issued in several 'parts', separate in each volume of works produced in several 'volumes'. But where, as frequently happens, clubs and societies do not adhere to this distinction between parts and volumes this is commented on in the analytical entry.

In the numbering of items within a series (at the start of title entries), for most series the numbering of Terry and Matheson has been adopted and, where necessary, continued. Elsewhere the official numbering of the issuing body has usually been adopted. Divergences from these practices are explained and justified in footnotes on the first pages of entries for the series concerned. The references in the right-hand margins opposite each title entry are solely for purposes of cross-referencing and indexing, taking the form of a number in bold denoting the series, followed (after a full point) by the number of that item within the series. These forms of reference are *not* intended to replace the Terry and Matheson numbering, or official club numbering, for general reference purposes.

The analytical entries that follow the title entries are intended to supplement the latter, and thus title and analytical entries should be read together; information clearly given in the title entry is not repeated in the analytical entry. Thus the information in the analytical entry depends to a considerable extent on how informative the title of the work is; the intention is to give as much information as is possible in a few lines about the type of documents printed, the form of publication (full transcripts assumed unless otherwise stated), and the subjects or topics they are mainly concerned with. The language of the documents printed is the same as the language of the title of the item, unless otherwise stated. The problem of whether or not Scots and English should be held to constitute separate languages and, if so, of how to classify borderline cases, has been solved by the crude expedient of ignoring it. Thus if a title is in English, it has not been thought necessary to comment on the fact that the documents or literary works in the volume are in Scots, and the term English is sometimes used to refer to documents some of which may be in Scots. This will doubtless offend some, but in many cases the decision on whether to describe, say, a series of letters as being in Scots or English would be an arbitrary one. In general it may safely be assumed that documents up to the seventeenth century written in Scotland and by Lowland Scots in their vernacular will be in Scots, but that in the course of that century a transition to standard English is made—except in some literary works in which Scots is revived in the eighteenth century.

In analytical entries 'contains' refers to all the documents in the item, 'includes' singles out items of particular interest. 'Also' is used, firstly, to introduce references calling attention to documents whose presence is unexpected (as they lie outside the description of contents suggested in the item title); and secondly to introduce references to a work having been published by other bodies as well as by that under which it is listed.

In *Texts and calendars II* Mullins extended the analytical entries to include detailed comment on secondary material in items listed (introductions, appendices, etc.), but the present work follows the first of his two works in limiting comment to source material. Items which are listed without an analytical entry and which do not include any mention of sources in their titles are secondary works, not containing texts or calendars.

In miscellany-type volumes the main title entry is followed by the titles of individual sections (indented and in smaller type), each of which is followed by its analytical entry in square brackets. These section titles are taken either from the list of contents of the volume, or from the title pages of the sections, depending on which is most informative.

For those not familiar with the Scottish publishing clubs and societies and their specializations, the following list of 'specialities' not obvious from the titles of series may be useful:

Aberdeenshire and the North East, **2, 22, 36–38**
Ecclesiastical (Episcopalian), **22, 39**
         (presbyterian), **43**
Highlands, **13, 23**
Indexes, inventories, etc., **29–30, 44**
Jacobites, **17**
Legal history, **40**
Literature and language, **3, 12, 18, 20, 23, 31–34** (and, to a
   certain extent), **1, 6**
Northern Isles, **42**
Pamphlet reprints, **4, 8**
Renfrewshire, **16**

In the case of series which are still being added to, works have been included which were published up to the end of 1985. This is a highly appropriate end date for a guide to Scottish source publications, as it means that the guide marks a hundred years of work by the most prolific Scottish publishing club of the century, the Scottish History Society. We are most grateful to the Publications Committee of the Royal Historical Society and to the Council of the Scottish History Society for arranging that the volume should appear as a joint publication of the two bodies.

In compiling the present work a secure foundation was provided by the catalogues of Terry and Matheson. Working through these volumes has confirmed their high standard of accuracy and comprehensiveness, though some minor errors have needed correction, and the following items which they omitted but which were published before 1927 should be noted: **9**.1; **11**.38–41; **15**.51, 80; **16**.10–15. In addition, a troublesome urban ghost raised by Terry is here exorcised (**21**.11).

The other essential foundation for the present work is provided by the two works by Mullins. They have provided us with an inspiration and a splendid model to follow. Without the first of Mullins' works to set an example, work on the compilation of the present work would probably not have been undertaken.

We also owe our thanks to those secretaries of publishing societies, librarians and archivists who have responded so willingly to our pleas for help on a number of points.

For the meticulous preparation of drafts and the final typescript we are very much in the debt of Margaret Croll of the Centre for Scottish Studies, University of Aberdeen, and we wish also to thank the Centre for allowing this use of its resources which has made our task much easier than it would otherwise have been. Finally, Charles Sandford Terry was Professor of History in Aberdeen when he compiled his catalogue. Cyril Matheson produced his successor to Terry while Assistant to the Professor of History in Aberdeen. It is a past and a present member of the Department of History, University of Aberdeen, who now offer this work as a partial replacement for their catalogues. It is pleasant thus to continue a worthy local tradition.

CONTENTS

1.	Abbotsford Club	1
2.	Aberdeen University Studies	7
3.	Association for Scottish Literary Studies	9
4.	Aungervyle Society	11
5.	Ayrshire and Wigtonshire (later Ayrshire and Galloway) Archaeological Association	14
6.	Bannatyne Club	17
7.	Bute Scottish Record Series	39
8.	Clarendon Historical Society	41
9.	Dumfriesshire and Galloway Natural History and Antiquarian Society, Record Text Publications	44
10.	Glasgow University, Department of Scottish History, Occasional Papers	45
11.	Grampian Club	46
12.	Hunterian Club	52
13.	Iona Club	54
14.	Literary and Antiquarian Society of Perth, Transactions	56
15.	Maitland Club	57
16.	New Club	72
17.	Roxburghe Club	75
18.	Rymour Club	79
19.	St Andrews University Publications	80
20.	Scotish Literary Club	82
21.	Scottish Burgh Records Society	83
22.	Scottish Clergy Society	90
23.	Scottish Gaelic Texts Society	91
24.	Scottish History Society, First Series	93
25.	Scottish History Society, Second Series	104
26.	Scottish History Society, Third Series	108
27.	Scottish History Society, Fourth Series	116
28.	Scottish Local History Group	120
29.	Scottish Record Society, Old Series	122
30.	Scottish Record Society, New Series	132
31.	Scottish Text Society, Old Series	134

CONTENTS

32. Scottish Text Society, New Series   139
33. Scottish Text Society, Third Series   143
34. Scottish Text Society, Fourth Series   147
35. Society of Antiquaries of Scotland   149
36. Spalding Club   150
37. New Spalding Club   158
38. Third Spalding Club   165
39. Spottiswoode Society   169
40. Stair Society   173
41. Sutherland Association   181
42. Viking Society for Northern Research, Old Lore
        Series   182
43. Wodrow Society   183

APPENDIX

44. Royal Commission on the Ancient and
        Historical Monuments of Scotland, Inventories   189
45. Scottish Record Office   192
Index   193

1. ABBOTSFORD CLUB

Place of publication: Edinburgh

1. Ancient mysteries from the Digby manuscripts. Preserved in the Bodleian Library, Oxford. Edited by Thomas Sharpe. 1835.   **1.1**

Verse. English mystery plays from a ms. compiled by 'Jhan Parfre' in 1512. Contains 'Candlemas day', 'The conversion of Saul', 'Mary Magdalene' and 'A morality'. **1.10** below contains the completion of the last of these, and is often bound in at the end of **1.1**.

2. The presentation in the temple, a pageant, as originally represented by the corporation of weavers in Coventry. Now first printed from the books of the company. [Edited by Thomas Sharpe.] 1836.   **1.2**

Verse. In a version 'nevly translate be Robert Croo', 1534. Also extracts from the weavers' accounts relating to performances, 1523–1607.

3. Compota domestica familiarum de Bukingham et d' Angouleme, MCCCCXLIII, LII, LXIII. Quibus annexae expensae cujusdam comitis in itinere, MCCLXXIII. [Edited by William B. D. D. Turnbull.] 1836.   **1.3**

Household books of Humphrey, Duke of Buckingham, 1443–4; of Jean d'Orléans, Earl of Angoulême, 1452; and of Anne, Dowager Duchess of Buckingham, 1463–4; and fragments of a roll of the expenses of an unknown earl travelling from Darlington to Usk, Monmouthshire, 1274.

4. The romances of Rouland and Vernagu, and Otuel. From the Auchinleck manuscript. [Edited by William B. D. D. Turnbull.] 1836.   **1.4**

The Auchinleck ms. is a compilation of Middle English verse, first half of 14th century. Also a fragment of 'The romance of Alexander', from the same ms.; and an extract (Latin) from the history of Charlemagne erroneously attributed to Turpin, Archbishop of Reims, on which 'Rouland and Vernagu' is based.

5. Account of the monastic treasures confiscated at the dissolution of the various houses in England. By Sir John Williams, knight, late master and treasurer of the jewels to His Majesty King Henry VIII. [Edited by William B. D. D. Turnbull.] 1836.   **1.5**

Account, dated 1551, of property received by Williams and others on the king's behalf, 1537–45.

6. Historical memoirs of the reign of Mary Queen of Scots, and a portion of the reign of King James the Sixth. By [John, 7th] Lord Herries. [Edited by Robert Pitcairn.] 1836.

1.6

1542–71. From an 18th century ms. which is an abridged copy of part of Herries' lost 'An abridgement of the Scotishe historie, from the first foundation untill our tyms'. This was dated 1656 and originally continued the narrative to 1631. Also miscellaneous docs. (partly French) relating to the Scots College in Paris; and letters of the 5th (d. 1603) and 6th (d. 1631) Lords Herries, 1567, 1608.

7. Ecclesiastical records. Selections from the minutes of the presbyteries of St Andrews and Cupar, MDCXLI–MDCXCVIII. Edited by George R. Kinloch. 1837.

1.7

St Andrews, 1641–98; Cupar, 1646–60.

8. Ecclesiastical records. Selections from the minutes of the synod of Fife, MDCXI–MDCLXXXVII. [Edited by George R. Kinloch.] 1837.

1.8

1611–36, 1639–57, 1662–88.

9. State papers, and miscellaneous correspondence of Thomas, Earl of Melros. Edited by James Maidment. 2 vols. 1837.

1.9

Mainly from Balfour of Denmylne mss. Pagination continuous.
i : [1599–1620.]
ii: [1620–5, and additional letters, 1614–15.]

10. Mind, will, and understanding: a morality. From the Macro ms. in the possession of Hudson Gurney. [Edited by William B. D. D. Turnbull.] 1837.

1.10

Verse. The Macro ms. comprises a complete text of 'A morality', part of which was printed in **1.1**. Only the concluding sections, not included in the former volume, are here transcribed. **1.10** is frequently bound in at the end of **1.1**.

11. Miscellany of the Abbotsford Club. Edited by James Maidment. Vol. i: 1837.

1.11

Selection from the papers of the family of Boyd of Kilmarnock, MCCCCLXVIII–MDXC.
Dispute between the abbot and convent of Lindores and the inhabitants of Newburgh, MCCCIX. [Latin. For an English abstract see **24.42**.]
Burlesque sermon of the fifteenth century. [From a 15th century ms. written in North West England.]
Verses and letter from Mr John Edmestoun to King James VI. [Letter 15 Nov. 1607.]
Account of the last moments of Queen Anne of Denmark, 27th March 1619. [Copy of a letter.]

The trial of Mungo Murray for assaulting Thomas Sydserf, comedian, IV and XI June MDCLXIX. [Before the Court of Justiciary in Edinburgh.]

Brevis narratio martyrii venerabilis sacerdotis Thomae Maxfeildij, qui passus est Londini in Anglia 11° die Julij anni praesentis 1616.

Epistolae virorum clarorum ad Jacobum Sextum, Britanniae Regem. [Letters from Cornelius Van Drebbel, George Carleton (Bishop of Chichester), John Cameron, and Father John Barnes; the last is dated Paris 1625.]

Virorum doctorum epistolae. [Letters from Meric Casaubon to a bishop (undated); and from Launcelot Andrewes (Bishop of Winchester) to Peter du Moulin, 1618.]

Joannis Hoskyns supplicatio ad regem. [Verse. 1615. Hoskins had been imprisoned in the Tower of London since 1614 for remarks made in the English parliament on James VI and I's Scottish favourites.]

Trials for witchcraft, sorcery, and superstition, in Orkney. [Trials of 1624, 1633, 1640 and 1643 in the sheriff court, and an examination before the kirk session of Sanday, 1633.]

True relation of my Lord of Warwick's passage. [An account, evidently by Robert Rich, Earl of Warwick, of a near escape from capture by Spanish ships off Lisbon while on a privateering expedition, 1627.]

Award by James the Sixth as to the succession to the barony of Sanquhar. [Following on the execution of Robert, 6th Lord Sanquhar, in London in 1612.]

Letters by King James VI to the Countess Dowager of Angus. [c. 1593]

Letters of Thomas Lord Ellesmere, lord high chancellor of England. [To James VI and I, 1608 and (with the Duke of Lennox) 1615; and to John Murray, 1614 and 1616.]

Letters and papers relative to the history of Great Britain during the reign of James I. From the Balfour mss. [1614–24, and several undated.]

Letters and papers relative to Irish matters. From the Balfour mss. [1604–24, and several undated.]

Satire against Scotland. [1617. The second printed edition (1649) attributes authorship to James Howell, but it is more likely to be the work of Sir Anthony Weldon.]

Answer to the satire. [Reply to the above, in the form of a letter.]

The complaint of the muses upon Sir William Alexander. [Verse. By James VI and I, c. 1616–18.]

Memoir of John Geddy. By Robert Mylne, junior. [Geddy was a late 17th century Scottish writer on bee keeping.]

Correspondence between George Ridpath and the Rev. Robert Wodrow. [1706–19.]

Account of the discussion in parliament as to the losses of [Daniel] Campbell of Shawfield. [In a letter from George Drummond to James Erskine, Lord Grange, 5 Mar. 1726.]

12. **Arthour and Merlin: a metrical romance. Now first edited from the Auchinleck ms. [Edited by William B. D. D. Turnbull.] 1838.**   1.12

The ms. dates from the first half of the 14th century. Also a fragment of a verse 'Life of Merlin'.

13. **Letters and state papers during the reign of King James the**   1.13

Sixth. Chiefly from the manuscript collections of Sir James Balfour of Denmyln. Edited by James Maidment. 1838.

c. 1578–1625. Some Latin and French. Also papers of John Lindsay of Menmuir, from the Balcarres mss.

14. Inventaire chronologique des documents relatifs à l'histoire d'Ecosse conservés aux archives du royaume à Paris. Suivi d'une indication sommaire des manuscrits de la bibliotheque royale. [Edited by J. B. Alexandre T. Teulet, jnr.] 1839. **1.14**

French and Latin. Documents in the 'Inventaire', 1263–1666; those in the 'Indication sommaire' relate to 791–1624. A corrected set of pp. 113–20 was issued after the volume was bound.

15. Davidis Humii de familia Humia Wedderburnensi liber. Presented by John Miller. 1839. **1.15**

Written by David Hume of Godscroft in 1611.

16. Ecclesiastical records. Selections from the registers of the presbytery of Lanark, MDCXXIII–MDCCIX. Presented by John Robertson. 1839. **1.16**

17. Jacobite correspondence of the Atholl family, during the rebellion, MDCCXLV–MDCCXLVI. From the originals in the possession of James Erskine of Aberdona. Edited by J. Hill Burton and David Laing. 1840. **1.17**

Also other Atholl letters and miscellaneous Jacobite papers, 1715–52.

18. The romances of Sir Guy of Warwick, and Rembrun his son. Now first edited from the Auchinleck ms. Edited by William B. D. D. Turnbull. 1840. **1.18**

Verse. The ms. dates from the first half of the 14th century. Also fragments of another version of 'Sir Guy' from a ms. of Sir Thomas Phillips.

19. Le roman des aventures de Fregus, par Guillaume le Clerc, trouvère du treizième siècle. Publié, pour la première fois. Edited by Francisque Michel. 1841. **1.19**

Anglo-Norman verse romance.

20. The legend of St Katherine of Alexandria. Edited, from a manuscript in the Cottonian Library, by James Morton. 1841. **1.20**

Verse. 12th century, probably based on an Anglo-Saxon original.

21. Liber conventus S. Katherine Senensis prope Edinburgum. [Edited by James Maidment.] 1841. **1.21**

Constitutions, charters etc. of the nunnery of Sciennes, 1512–88.

22. The chartularies of Balmerino and Lindores. Now first printed from the original mss. in the Library of the Faculty of Advocates. [Edited by William B. D. D. Turnbull.] 1841.

1.22

> The two sections are paginated separately.
> Liber Sancte Marie de Balmorinach. [14th century cartulary, containing charters, late 12th–14th centuries. Also miscellaneous docs., early 13th century–1617, 1789.]
> Liber Sancte Marie de Lundoris. [Early 16th century transcript of miscellaneous docs., late 12th–early 16th centuries. Also miscellaneous docs., late 12th century–1402. For another cartulary see 24.42.]

23. Extracta e variis cronicis Scocie. From the ancient manuscript in the Advocates Library at Edinburgh. Now first printed. Edited by William B. D. D. Turnbull. 1842.

1.23

> From a ms. compiled in the early 16th century, possibly by Alexander Myln (d. 1548), with annotations and additions up to 1575 evidently by Sir William Sinclair of Roslin.

24. Memoirs of Sir Ewen Cameron of Locheill, chief of the Clan Cameron. With an introductory account of the history and antiquities of that family and of the neighbouring clans. [Edited by James Macknight.] 1842.

1.24

> Sir Ewen lived 1629–1719. The memoirs, by John Drummond, were completed in the 1730s, but the account of the life of Sir Ewen is only taken up to the 1690s. Also an account of Sir Ewen's death, evidently by the same author; and miscellaneous docs., 1622–1747. Also issued as 15.61.

25. Liber officialis Sancti Andree: curie metropolitane Sancti Andree in Scotia sententiarum in causis consistorialibus que extant. Presented by J. H. Forbes, Lord Medwyn. 1845.

1.25

> Extracts, sometimes abridged, from three mss. containing the decisions of the ecclesiastical courts of the archdiocese of St Andrews and the archdeaconry of Lothian. All cases concerning marriage, divorce and legitimacy are included, and a selection of others, 1513–53. Also miscellaneous docs., 1420–1559.

26. A garden of grave and godlie flowers, by Alexander Gardyne. The theatre of Scotish kings, by Alexander Garden, professor of philosophy. Together with miscellaneous poems, by John Lundie, professor of humanity in the University of Aberdeen. Edited by William B. D. D. Turnbull. 1845.

1.26

> The poems of Garden (Gardyne), advocate, are reprinted from editions published in Edinburgh in 1609 and 1709 respectively. The description of the author as 'professor of philosophy' in the latter is inaccurate. Lundie's poems (partly Latin) all or mainly date from the 1630s, and are taken from his ms. The three sections have separate paginations.

27. The buke of the order of knyghthood. Translated from the French, by Sir Gilbert Hay, knight. From the manuscript in the library at Abbotsford. Edited by Beriah Botfield. 1847.

> Late 15th century translation. The book is the second of three works translated by Hay, the others being 'The buke of batailles' and 'The buke of the governance of princes'; the vol. contains extracts from and summaries of these.

1.27

28. Sire Degarré. A metrical romance of the end of the thirteenth century. [Edited by David Laing.] 1849.

> An English romance from the Auchinleck ms., which dates from the first half of the 14th century.

1.28

29. A penni worth of witte: Florice and Blauncheflour: and other pieces of ancient English poetry selected from the Auchinleck manuscript. Edited by David Laing. 1857.

> Ten poems in all. Also a description of the Auchinleck ms., which dates from the first half of the 14th century, and an account of its contents.

1.29

30. Memoirs of the insurrection in Scotland in 1715. By John, Master of Sinclair. From the original manuscript in the possession of the Earl of Rosslyn. With notes, by Sir Walter Scott, bart. Edited by James Macknight. 1858.

> 1708–16. Sinclair d. 1750.

1.30

31. Oppressions of the sixteenth century in the islands of Orkney and Zetland: from original documents. Edited by David Balfour. 1859.

> 1575–92. Also complaints of Orkneymen, 1420s (Latin), from Thormodo Torfaeo, *Rerum Orcadensium historiae*, Copenhagen 1697; and extracts from rentals, 1502–1600. Also issued as **15.77**.

1.31

32. Stephen Hawes. The conversion of swerers: A joyfull medytacyon to all Englonde of the coronacyon of Kynge Henry the Eyght. Edited by David Laing. 1865.

> The 'Conversion' is from the 1509 and 1551 editions and an undated edition, the 'Joyful 1 medytacyon' from the *c.* 1510 edition.

1.32

33. Abbotsford Club. A list of the members; the rules; and a catalogue of books printed for the Abbotsford Club since its institution in 1833. Edited by David Laing. 1866.

1.33

34. [Abbotsford garlands. By William B. D. D. Turnbull.] 2 numbers. 1836–7.

> Poems on Club publications.

1.34

2. ABERDEEN UNIVERSITY STUDIES*

Place of publication: Aberdeen.

39. A catalogue of the publications of Scottish historical and kindred clubs and societies, and of the volumes relative to Scottish history issued by His Majesty's Stationery Office, 1780–1908. With a subject index. By Charles S. Terry. 1909.

2.1

Also issued for general sale. This work and Terry's *An index to the papers relating to Scotland described or calendared in the Historical Mss. Commission's reports* (1908) were both continued in Cyril Matheson, *A catalogue of the publications of Scottish historical and kindred clubs and societies . . . 1908–1927* (1928).

40. Aberdeen friars. Red, Black, White, Grey. Preliminary calendar of illustrative documents. Compiled by Peter J. Anderson. 1909.

2.2

1211–1790.

67. Bishop Gilbert Burnet as educationist, being his Thoughts on education, with notes and life of the author by John Clarke. 1914.

2.3

Written *c*. 1668. From the first edition, London 1761.

93. Epistolare in usum ecclesiae cathedralis Aberdonensis. Edited by Bruce M'Ewen, with introduction by Francis C. Eeles. 1924.

2.4

Epistolary (service book containing epistles) written in Antwerp, 1527. Includes notes on the bishops of Aberdeen, on gifts to the cathedral, etc.

95. The alba amicorum of George Strachan, George Craig, Thomas Cumming. By James F. K. Johnstone. 1924.

2.5

Includes extracts from these autograph books—Strachan, 1599–1609; Craig, 1602–5; and Cumming, 1611–19.

---

*Only publications relevant to this vol. are listed here, and, to avoid repetition, the twenty-three New Spalding Club vols. which were also issued in the Aberdeen University Studies series have been omitted here and only listed under the former body. See **36**.21–43.

100. Last leaves of traditional ballads and ballad airs. Collected in Aberdeenshire by the late Gavin Greig, and edited, with an introductory essay, collations, and notes, by Alexander Keith. 1925.   2.6

> Extracts from collection by Greig, d. 1914. Appears in Matheson, *Catalogue*, as Buchan Club, B.

113. Philosophical orations of Thomas Reid. Delivered at graduation ceremonies in King's College, Aberdeen, 1753, 1756, 1759, 1762. Edited, with an introduction, from the Birkwood ms. by Walter R. Humphries. 1937.   2.7

> Latin.

114. Ewen MacLachlan's Gaelic verse. Comprising a translation of Homer's Iliad books I–VIII and original compositions. Edited by John MacDonald. 1937.   2.8

> MacLachlan lived 1773–1822.

122. James Beattie's London diary, 1773. Edited with an introduction and notes by Ralph S. Walker. 1946.   2.9

> 23 Apr.–30 Sept. 1773. Beattie, poet and philosopher, lived 1735–1803. Also extracts from Beattie's day book, 1773, relating to his expenditure.

145. The Gordon's Mill Farming Club, 1758–1764. By J. H. Smith. 1962.   2.10

> Includes extensive extracts from the club's minute book.

3. ASSOCIATION FOR SCOTTISH LITERARY STUDIES

Place of publication: Edinburgh.

1. The three perils of man. War, women and witchcraft. By 3.1
James Hogg. Introduction, textual notes and glossary by
Douglas Gifford. 1972.
Novel. From the first edition, 1822.

2. The poems of John Davidson. Edited by Andrew Turnbull. 3.2
vol. i. 1973.
Davidson lived 1857–1909.

3. The poems of John Davidson. . . . Vol. ii. 1973. 3.3
Pagination continuous with vol. i.

4. Poems by Allan Ramsay and Robert Fergusson. Edited by 3.4
Alexander M. Kinghorn and Alexander Law. 1974.
Selections. Ramsay d. 1758, Fergusson d. 1774.

5. The member: an autobiography. By John Galt. Edited by Ian 3.5
A. Gordon. 1975.
Novel. From the first edition, 1832.

6. Poems and prose. By William Drummond of Hawthornden. 3.6
Edited by Robert H. MacDonald. 1976.
Selections. For other editions of the poems see 15.18 and 32.3, 4.

7. Peter's letters to his kinsfolk. By John Gibson Lockhart. 3.7
Edited by William Ruddick. 1977.
Novel. Selections from the second edition (which claims to be the third), 1819.

8. Selected short stories. By John Galt. Edited by Ian A. 3.8
Gordon. 1978.
Written 1832–6.

9. Selected political writings and speeches. By Andrew Fletcher 3.9
of Saltoun. Edited by David Daiches. 1979.
From the London 1732 edition of Fletcher's *Political works*.

10. Scott on himself. A selection of the autobiographical   3.10
writings of Sir Walter Scott. Edited by David Hewitt. 1981.
  Scott d. 1832.

11. The party-coloured mind. Prose relating to the conflict of   3.11
church and state in seventeenth century Scotland. Edited by
David Reid. 1982.
  Extracts.

12. Selected stories and sketches. By James Hogg. Edited by   3.12
Douglas S. Mack. 1982.
  First published 1819–31.

13. The jewel. By Sir Thomas Urquhart of Cromarty. Edited   3.13
with an introduction and commentary by R. D. S. Jack and R. J.
Lyall. 1983.
  From the first edition, London 1652, of *Ekskubalauron; or, the discovery of a
  most exquisite jewel* . . . The work includes an appeal for release from prison
  in London and a proposal for a universal language. Also passages omitted
  from the *Jewel* but printed in *Logopandecteision* (1653); and letters by
  Urquhart, 1648–55.

14. Ringan Gilhaize, or the covenanters. By John Galt. Edited   3.14
by Patricia J. Wilson. 1984.
  Novel. From the first edition, 1823, with a few corrections from Galt's ms.

15. Selected short stories of the supernatural. By Margaret   3.15
Oliphant. Edited by Margaret K. Gray, 1985.
  First published 1876–96.

4. AUNGERVYLE SOCIETY*

Place of publication: Edinburgh.

1. Aungervyle Society reprints. First series. [Edited by Edmund M. Goldsmid.] 1881–2.   **4.1**

Flagellum Parliamentarium; being sarcastic notices of nearly 200 members of the first Parliament after the Restoration (A.D. 1661 to A.D. 1678). From a contemporary ms. in the British Museum. 1881. (1). [Compiled 1671–2; sometimes attributed to Andrew Marvell.]

A journey into England in the year MDXCVIII. By Paul Hentzner. Being a translation of part of his Itinerary. Edited by Horace Walpole. 1881. (2). [The *Itinerary* was first published at Nuremberg in 1612, and Walpole's edition of these extracts at Strawberry Hill in 1757.]

A garland of old historical ballads. 1600–1752. I. Marie Hamilton. II. Robert Oig. III. Willy and Mary. 1881. (3).

Fragments of ancient poetry collected in the Highlands of Scotland, and translated from the Gaelic or Erse language. 1760. Being a reprint of the first Ossianic publication of James Macpherson. 1881. (4).

The romance of Octavian, Emperor of Rome. Abridged from a manuscript in the Bodleian Library (circa 1250). By the Rev. J. J. Coneybeare, and edited with additional notes by Edmund M. Goldsmid. 1882. (5). [Coneybeare's edition was first published in 1809.]

The imprisonment & death of King Charles I. Related by one of his judges. Being extracts from the memoirs of Edmund Ludlow, the regicide, with a collection of original papers relating to the trial of the king. 1882. (6). [From the third edition of Ludlow, Edinburgh 1751.]

2. Aungervyle Society reprints. Second series. [Edited by Edmund M. Goldsmid.] 1884.   **4.2**

The Indian game of chess: by Sir William Jones, president of the Asiatic Society of Bengal. And the Burmha game of chess compared with the Indian, Chinese, and Persian games. By Captain Hiram Cox. (Reprinted from 'Asiatic researches'). 1883. (7). [Jones d. 1794; Cox's work is dated 1799.]

---

*Publications were originally issued in separate parts (which do not always correspond to the individual items), and had two paginations so the items could either be bound separately, or with each series forming a single vol. (for which title pages were supplied). Terry treated each item as a separate vol., but each series is catalogued here as a single miscellany vol., with Terry's original numbering appearing in brackets after the item title entries.

A key to 'Epics of the ton'. 1883. (8). [A key to the satirical poem (second edition, revised, London 1807) by Lady Anne Hamilton.]

Proper lessons for the Tories, to be read throughout the year. . . . 1883. (9). [From London 1716 edition.]

London and the countrey carbonadoed, and quartred into seruall characters. By Donald Lupton. 1883. (10). [From London 1632 edition.]

The mystery of the good old cause briefly unfolded. In a catalogue of such members of the late Long Parliament, that held places, both civil and military, contrary to the self-denying ordinance of April 3, 1645. Together with the sums of money and lands which they divided among themselves during their sitting (at least such as were disposed of by them publicly). 1883. (11). [From London 1660 edition.]

The impeachment of James, Lord Strange, son and heire apparant of William, Earle of Derby. By the Commons of England, of high treason. 1883. (12). [From London 1642 edition.]

A chronological table of the principal dramatic works that have been publicly performed in France, from A.D. 1200 to A.D. 1800. By Edmund M. Goldsmid. Pt. 1. 1883. (13). [1200–1599.]

Two political squibs. (1660–1690). 1883. (14). [Verse. 'The ghost', 1660; 'An epitaph on the Duke of Grafton', 1690.]

The hermit of Warkworth. A Northumberland ballad. In three fits or cantos. By Thomas Percy. 1883. (15). [From London 1771 edition.]

'We pity the plumage but forget the dying bird'. An address to the people on the death of the Princess Charlotte. By the Hermit of Marlow. 1883. (16). [From first edition, 1817. Radical tract by Percy Bysshe Shelley.]

The passionate remonstrance made by his holiness in the conclave at Rome: upon the late proceedings, and great covenant of Scotland, etc. With a reply of Cardinall de Barbarini in the name of the Roman clergy. Together with a letter of intelligence from the apostolic nuntio (now residing in London) to Pope Vrban the 8. 1884. (17). [Satire. From Edinburgh 1641 edition.]

A discovery of the Barmudas: otherwise called the Ile of Divels. By Sir Thomas Gates, Sir George Sommers, and Captayne Newport. With diuers others. Set forth for the loue of my country. And also for the good of the plantation in Virginia. By Sil. Jourdan. 1884. (18). [From London 1610 edition.]

The Russian invasion of Poland in 1563. Being a translation of a contemporary account in Latin. Published at Douay. 1884. (19). [From an Italian news sheet of 1563.]

Kisses: being fragments and poetical pieces on the kiss. 1884. (20). [From appendix of the 1803 edition of Johannes Secundus (d. 1536), *Basia*.]

A marriage trivmphe solemnized in an epithalamivm, in memorie of the happie nuptials betwixt the high and mighty Prince Count Palatine and the most excellent Princesse the Lady Elizabeth. Written by Thomas Heywood. 1884. (21). [From London 1613 edition.]

3. Aungervyle Society reprints. Third series. [Edited by Edmund M. Goldsmid.] 1884–6. 4.3

[Title pages of individual parts call this the New series.]

The nauigation and vyages of Lewis Wertomannus, in the yeere of our Lord 1503. 1884–5. (22). [By Lodovico de Varthema. Translated into English by Richard Eden, and reprinted from Eden's *The history of trauayle in the West and East Indies*, London 1577.]

A description of May. From Gawin Douglas, Bishop of Dunkeld. By Francis Fawkes, A.M. 1885. (23). [Verse description of the Isle of May prefixed to book 12 of Douglas' translation of the *Aeneid* (for which see **6.67**). From the London 1752 edition of the *Description*.]

A call from death to life, being an account of the sufferings of Marmaduke Stephenson, William Robinson and Mary Dyer, in New England, in the year 1659. 1886. (24). [Stephenson and Robinson were executed as Quakers in 1659, Dyer in 1660. From London 1660 edition.]

The statesman's progress, or a pilgrimage to greatness. Delivered under the similitude of a dream. By John Bunyan. 1886. (25). [An anonymous parody of Bunyan's *Pilgrim's progress*, the statesman satirised being Sir Robert Walpole. From the London 1741 edition.]

4. Aungervyle Society reprints. Fourth series. [Edited by Edmund M. Goldsmid.] 1886.
4.4

Londoni quod reliquum, or Londons remains. 1886. (26). [Latin, with English translation. From London 1667 edition.]

The last advice of Charles the First to his son. 1886. (27). [1648. From Sir William Sanderson's *Compleat history of the life and raigne of King Charles*, 1658.]

The peasant of Auburn, and other poems, attributed to J. Coombe, D.D., circa 1786. 1887. (28). [Poems by *Thomas* Coombe.]

Gypsies: some curious investigations, collected, translated, or reprinted from various sources, concerning this peculiar race. By J. Watts de Peyster. 1887. (29).

The prize of wisdom, a dialogue between Anacreon and Aristotle. From the French of M. de Fontenelle. 1887. (30). [From London 1777 edition.]

A lesson in biography; or how to write the life of one's friend, being an extract from the life of Dr Pozz, in ten volumes, folio, written by James Bozz, esq. By Alexander Chalmers. 1887. (31). [Satire on Boswell's *Life of Johnson*. From London 1798 edition.]

A full and true account of the dreadful and melancholy earthquake, which happened between twelve and one o'clock in the morning, on Thursday the 5th of April, 1750. Ascribed to Paul Whitehead. 1887. (32). [A satire in the form of a letter signed 'A.B.'. From London 1798 edition.]

A remembrance of the wel imployed life, and godly end, of G. Gascoigne, esq. 1886. (33). [Verse. By George Whetston. George Gascoigne d. 1577. From London 1577 edition.]

5. Explanatory notes of a pack of Cavalier playing cards, temp. Charles II. Forming a complete political satire of the Commonwealth. By Edmund M. Goldsmid. 1886.
4.5

Also issued in **8.2**.

5. AYRSHIRE AND WIGTONSHIRE (later AYRSHIRE AND GALLOWAY) ARCHAEOLOGICAL ASSOCIATION*

Place of publication: Edinburgh.

1. Archaeological and historical collections relating to the   5.1
counties of Ayr and Wigton. Vol. i. 1878.

> Collections towards a history of the monastery of Kilwinning. [15th century
> life of St Wynnyn (Latin); the office of St Wynnyn, from the *Breviarium
> Aberdonense* (for which see **6**.99); and charters and other docs., *c.*
> 1202–1616 (Latin, with English abstracts).]
> Proceedings of the gild court of Ayr. Edited by Thomas Dickson. [Latin.
> 1428–34.]

2. Archaeological and historical collections. . . . Vol. ii. 1880.   5.2

> Collections relating to the parish of Tarbolton. By W. S. Cooper. [Extracts
> (some Latin) and abstracts from miscellaneous docs., 12th century– 1749.]
> Extracts from ms. correspondence at Craufurdland Castle. Edited by
> J. R. H. Craufurd of Craufurdland. [Letters, 1747-50, 1756, mainly
> between John W. Craufurd of Craufurdland and the 16th Earl of
> Sutherland.]
> Selections from family papers at Lanfine. Edited by R. Gairdner.
> [Miscellaneous docs., 1687–1741, some relating to James Brown (minister
> of St Mungo's, Glasgow), d. 1714.]

3. Archaeological and historical collections. . . . Vol. iii. 1882.   5.3

> The Boyd papers. [Mainly Latin, with English translations or abstracts.
> Charters and miscellaneous docs., 1466–1581.]

4. Archaeological and historical collections. . . . Vol. iv. 1884.   5.4

> Military report on the districts of Carrick, Kyle, and Cunningham, with
> reference to the possibility of the occupation of that portion of Scotland by
> an English army. Prepared by an English official between the years 1563
> and 1566. Edited by R. B. Armstrong.
> The Logan charter. Charter by Uchtred, son of Fergus, Lord of Galloway.
> Edited by Sir Herbert Maxwell. [Latin, with English translation, *c.* 1166.]
> Corshill baron-court book. Edited by John Shedden-Dobie. [1666–1719.]

---

*Vols. i–vii of the *Collections* (5.1–7) consist mainly of secondary articles on
archaeological and antiquarian topics. These are not listed here, the entries being
confined to items containing docs. Vols. viii and ix (5.8–9) each contain only a single
item, as listed.

5. Archaeological and historical collections relating to Ayrshire and Galloway. Vol. v. 1885.   5.5

Letters by John fifth Earl of Cassillis to the laird of Barnbarroch, 1600–1615. Edited by R. Vans Agnew of Barnbarroch. [Letters to Sir John Vaus, c. 1600–c. 1615.]

Glenluce Abbey. Edited by David Henry. [Mainly Latin, with English abstracts. Charters and miscellaneous docs., 1560–77.]

6. Archaeological and historical collections. . . . Vol. vi. 1889.   5.6

Valuation of the shire of Wigtown, made in 1667. Edited by Sir Herbert Maxwell. [With alterations and annotations up to 1721.]

Mason's protocol book. Abstracts. Edited by John Shedden-Dobie. [1576–93. By John Mason.]

Notorial note-book of John Mason, clerk of the burgh of Ayr. 1582–1612. Edited by John Shedden-Dobie. [1582–96, 1612. Mainly relating to Ayr and Ayrshire. Also some minutes of the burgh court of Ayr, 1554.]

7. Archaeological and historical collections. . . . Vol. vii. 1894.   5.7

Selections from some papers in possession of the Countess of Stair. Edited by the Hon. Hew Dalrymple. [1597–1746. Mainly letters to 1st, 2nd and 3rd Lords Bargany.]

Protocol book of Robert Broun. Edited by Walter MacLeod. [Latin, with English translations, and English. 1612–16. Mainly relating to Ayr and Ayrshire.]

8. Archaeological and historical collections. . . . Vol. viii. 1894.   5.8

Protocol book of Robert Broun, continued. [Edited by Walter MacLeod. Latin, with English abstracts. 1616–17. Mainly relating to Ayr and Ayrshire.]

9. Archaeological and historical collections. . . . Vol. ix. 1895.   5.9

Protocol book of Robert Broun, continued. [Edited by Walter MacLeod. Latin, with English abstracts. 1618–20. Mainly relating to Ayr and Ayrshire.]

10. Archaeological and historical collections. . . . Vol. x. The five great churches of Galloway: forming the concluding volume of the collections of the Ayr and Galloway Archaeological Association. Drawings by David MacGibbon and Thomas Ross. Edited by the Hon. Hew H. Dalrymple. 1899.   5.10

Drawings of abbeys of Sweetheart, Dundrennan and Glenluce, the collegiate church of Lincluden and the priory of Whithorn.

11. Mvnimenta fratrvm predicatorvm de Are. Charters of the Friars Preachers of Ayr. Edited by Robert W. Cochran-Patrick. 1881.   5.11

Latin, with English translations or abstracts, and English. 1242–1614. Also extracts from exchequer rolls, 1329–77; and miscellaneous docs., 1477, and 1666. Spine reads *Archaeological and historical collections of Ayr and Wigton.*

12. Charters of the royal burgh of Ayr. Edited by W. S. Cooper. 1883.   5.12

Latin, with English translations or abstracts, and English. Charter, and miscellaneous docs., *c.* 1202–1715. Spine reads *Archaeological and historical collections of Ayr and Wigton.*

13. Charters of the abbey of Crosraguel. Edited by F. C. Hunter Blair. 2 vols. 1886.   5.13

Latin, with English translations or abstracts, and English. Charters and miscellaneous docs.
i : [1225–1569.]
ii: [1570–1656.]

14. Correspondence of Sir Patrick Waus of Barnbarroch, knight, parson of Wigtown; first almoner to the queen; senator of the College of Justice; lord of Council, and ambassador to Denmark. Edited from the original documents by Robert Vans Agnew. 2 pts. 1887.   5.14

Some Latin. Letters and miscellaneous docs.
Pt. 1: 1540–1584.
Pt. 2: 1584–1597.

15. Muniments of the royal burgh of Irvine. 2 vols. 1890–1.   5.15

Latin, with English translations or abstracts, and English.
i : [Charters etc. 1205–1761.]
ii: [Miscellaneous docs., 1472–1783; council book, 1664–8; and extracts from accounts, 1600–1745.]

6. BANNATYNE CLUB

Place of publication: Edinburgh, unless otherwise stated.

1. Vitae Dvnkeldensis ecclesiae episcoporvm, a prima sedis fvndatione, ad annvm MDXV. Ab Alexandro Myln, eivsdem ecclesiae canonico, conscriptae. Edited by Thomas Thomson. 1823.

6.1

Early 16th century (Myln d. 1548), covering *c.* 1127–*c.* 1516. For English translations see **14.1** and (part only) **25.10**. An improved text (edited by Cosmo Innes) was published in 1831, with *Editio altera, cui accedit appendix cum nominum et locorum indice* added to the title. The 1831 edition has an appendix of accounts (Latin) of Myln as Dean of Christianity of Angus, 1511–13, and as master of the bridge works at Dunkeld, 1513–14; and of Thomas Brown as master of the bridge works, 1515–16. For an abbreviated translation of the accounts, see **25.10**. Extra copies of the appendix were printed for binding in with the 1823 edition.

2. Poems by Sir David Murray of Gorthy. Presented by Thomas Kinnear. 1823.

6.2

From the first editions, *The tragicall death of Sophonisba* and *Caelia. Containing certaine sonets*, both London 1611, and *A paraphrase of the CIV psalme*, Edinburgh 1615. See notes in **6.118**.

3. The buke of the howlat. By Holland. [Edited by David Laing.] 1823.

6.3

Verse. Composed 1453 or 1454 by Sir Richard Holland. Satire, probably directed against James Kennedy, Bishop of St Andrews, praising the Douglases. See notes in **6.118**. Revised and reissued as **16.6**. For another edition see **31.13**.

4. Teares for the death of Alexander Earle of Dunfermeling, lord chancellar of Scotland. Presented by James Maidment. 1823.

6.4

Verse. From first edition, Edinburgh 1622. Attributed to John Lyoun of Auldbar.

4A. The poems of George Bannatyne, MDLXVIII. [Edited by David Laing.] 1824.

6.5

The date is that of the ms.

5. Discovrs particvlier d'Ecosse: escrit par commandement et ordonnance de la royne dovariere et regente, par Messires Iacques Makgill clerc du registre, et Iean Bellenden clerc de la iustice, XI Ianvier MDLIX. Presented by Thomas Thomson. 1824.   **6.6**

> A report dealing with the patrimony of the crown, the courts and the law of treason in Scotland, compiled by James McGill of Nether Rankeilor and John Bellenden of Auchnoul on the orders of the regent, Mary of Lorraine, for the use of Mary Queen of Scots. For another edition see **40**.37.

6. Robene and Makyne, and The testament of Cresseid; by Robert Henryson. [Edited by George Chalmers.] 1824.   **6.7**

> Verse. Composed late 15th century. 'Robene' is printed from the Bannatyne ms. of 1568, 'Cresseid' from the Edinburgh 1593 edition.

7. Report by Thomas Tucker upon the settlement of the revenues of excise and customs in Scotland. A.D. MDCLVI. Presented by Sir John A. Murray. 1824.   **6.8**

> Report to the commissioners for appeals and regulating the excise. Also printed in **21**.13.

8. Etchings, chiefly of views in Scotland. By John Clerk of Eldin. MDCCLXXIII–MDCCLXXIX. 1825.   **6.9**

> See **6**.101 for an enlarged edition.

9. Auld Robin Gray; a ballad. By the Right Honourable Lady Anne Barnard, born Lady Anne Lindsay of Balcarras. Presented by Sir Walter Scott. 1825.   **6.10**

> The authoress d. 1825.

10. Recit de l'expedition en Ecosse, l'an MDXLVI et de la battayle de Muscleburgh. Par le Sieur Berteville, au Roy Edouard VI. Presented by David Constable. 1825.   **6.11**

> By Sir John Berteville. Battle of Pinkie.

11. Hectoris Boetii Murthlacensium et Aberdonensium episcoporum vitae, iterum in lucem editae. Presented by Henry Cockburn and Thomas Maitland. 1825.   **6.12**

> From the first edition, Paris 1522. For an English translation see **37**.13.

12. An apology for Sir James Dalrymple of Stair, president of the Session. By himself. Presented by William Blair. 1825.   **6.13**

> From first edition, Edinburgh 1690. See notes in **6**.118.

13. The historie and life of King James the Sext: being an account of the affairs of Scotland, from the year 1566, to the year   **6.14**

1596; with a short continuation to the year 1617. Edited by Thomas Thomson. 1825.

Attributed to John Colville (see **6**.107), but may not be the work of a single author.

14. The discoverie and historie of the gold mynes in Scotland. By Stephen Atkinson: written in the year MDCXIX. Presented by Gilbert L. Meason. 1825.

6.15

Also miscellaneous docs., 16th and 17th centuries.

15. Letters of John Grahame of Claverhouse, Viscount of Dundee, with illustrative documents. Edited by George Smythe. 1826.

6.16

1678–89.

16. De vita et morte Roberti Rollok, academiae Edinburgenae primarii, narrationes; auctoribus Georgio Robertson, et Henrico Charteris. Edited by John Lee. 1826.

6.17

Robertson's life of Rollock (d. 1599) is from the first edition, Edinburgh 1599, Charteris' from a ms. Also includes verse epitaphs on Rollock. See notes in **6**.118.

17. The palice of honour. By Gawyn Douglas, Bishop of Dunkeld. Presented by John G. Kinnear. 1827.

6.18

Verse. Composed *c*. 1501. From the Edinburgh 1579 edition.

18. Memoirs of his own life. By Sir James Melville of Halhill. MDXLIX–MDXCIII. From the original manuscript. Edited by Thomas Thomson. 1827.

6.19

Melville d. 1617. Also issued as **15**.21 dated 1833.

19. The Bannatyne miscellany; containing original papers and tracts, chiefly relating to the history and literature of Scotland. Edited by Sir Walter Scott and David Laing. Vol. i. 1827.

6.20

Pt. 1: A proposal for uniting Scotland with England, addressed to King Henry VIII, by John Elder, clerke, a reddshanke. [1542.]
The progress of the regent of Scotland, with certain of his nobility, June 1568. [Also contains letter of Sir William Dury to the Earl of Leicester, 1 July 1568, with which the 'progress' of the Earl of Moray was enclosed.]
An account of a pretended conference held by the regent, Earl of Murray, with the Lord Lindsay, and others, January 1570. [A forgery, indicating that the regent intended to dethrone James VI. From Richard Bannatyne's journal (see **6**.54) and other mss.]
An opinion of the present state, faction, religion, and power of the nobility of Scotland, 1583. [Attributed to an English agent.]
Instructions from Henry III, King of France, to the Sieur de la Mothe Fenelon, ambassador at the court of Scotland, 1583. [French.]

The heads of a conference between King James VI and Sir Francis Walsingham, September 1583.

Notes presented by Mr John Colville, to Lord Hunsdon, 1584.

The manner and form of the examination and death of William Earl of Gowrye, May 1584.

The apology of Mr Patrick Galloway, minister of Perth, when he fled to England, 1585.

Relation by the Master of Gray, concerning the surprise of the king at Stirling, November 1585.

The application of three several discourses delivered on occasion of the Gowrye conspiracy, August 1600. I. By Mr Patrick Galloway, at the Cross at Edinburgh. II. By Mr William Cowper, at Edinburgh. III. By Mr Patrick Galloway, at Glasgow.

Narrative by Mr Robert Bruce, one of the ministers of Edinburgh, concerning his troubles in the year 1600.

Pt. 2: Edinburgi regiae Scotorum urbis descriptio, per Alexandrum Alesium Scotum, S.T.D., 1550. [Alesius (or Alan) had left Scotland in 1532. From Sebastian Munster's *Cosmographia*, Basle 1550.]

Elegy on Sir Robert Kerr, of Cessford, first Earl of Roxburghe, 1650. [Verse. By S.M.]

A relation of the imprisonment and examination of James Cathkin, bookseller, June 1619. [Examination before the English Privy Council.]

Letter from Robert of Dunhelm, monk of Kelso, to the prior and convent of Tynemouth, 1257. [Latin. Account of the discovery of the bodies of Malcolm III and his son Edward.]

Reasons against the reception of King James's metaphrase of the psalms, 1631. [Probably by David Calderwood.]

Declaration in the court of the Superintendent of Fife, 1561, upon the articles and sentence against Sir John Borthwick, knight, by Cardinal Beaton, 1540. [Partly Latin. From minutes of St Andrews kirk session, for which see 24.4.]

A diary of the expedition of King Edward I into Scotland, 1296. [Two versions are printed, from a contemporary ms. (French) and an early 16th century English translation. For another version see 6.50.]

Extracts from the obituary of the Rev. Robert Boyd of Trochrig, principal of the college of Edinburgh, 1609–1625. [French. Notes by Boyd on the deaths of friends, as transcribed by Robert Wodrow in 1701.]

Poems by Sir Robert Ayton. [Collected from various printed editions. Ayton lived 1570–1638. For other editions see 11.38 and 34.1.]

Letters of Florentius Volusenus. [Latinised version of a Scots name, perhaps Wilson or Williamson. Letters to Thomas Cromwell, 1531 or 1532 (English), to John Starkey, 1535 (Latin), and from Cardinal Sadoleto, 1546 (Latin).]

Meditation faite par Marie Royne d'Escosse et Dovairiere de France, 1572. [Verse. Reprinted from a work by John Leslie, Bishop of Ross, Paris 1574.]

Letters of John Earl of Gowrye, 1595. [To James VI and Mr John Malcolm.]

19A. The Bannatyne miscellany. . . . [Edited by David Laing.]   6.21
Vol. ii. 1836.

Strena ad Jacobum V Scotorum regem, de suscepto regni regimine, 1528. [Verse, with English translation. From the first edition, Edinburgh 1530s?]

Historia miraculose fundationis monasterii Sancte Crucis prope Edinburgh, 1128. Historia fundationis prioratus Insule de Traile. Nomina abbatum monasterii Sancte Crucis. Inventarium jocalium, etc. 'magni altaris eiusdem monasterii, Oct. 1493. [First three items taken from a 13th or 14th century ms. Also extracts (English) from papers concerning case of commendator and convent of Holyrood against provost and magistrates of Edinburgh, 1560s.]

Negotiations of the Scottish commissioners at Nottingham, September 1484.

Oratio Scotorum ad regem Ricardum tertium pro pace firmanda inter Anglos et Scotos. By Archibald Whytelaw, 12 Sept. 1484.

List of contributions to the senators of the College of Justice. [1583–91.]

A survey of the castle and town of Edinburgh, January 1573. Journal of the siege of the castle of Edinburgh, April and May 1573. [Second item from Holinshed's *Chronicles*, 1577 and 1586 editions.]

The opinion of George Buchanan concerning the reformation of the University of St Andrews, 1563. [Also printed in **31.12**.]

Testamentum domini Jacobi de Douglas domini de Dalkeith militis, 30 Sept. 1390. Testamentum ejusdem, 19 Dec. 1392.

The spectakle of luf, translated from the Latin by G. Myll, at St Andrews, 1492. [Also printed in **32.14**.]

Catalogus librorum manuscriptorum, e bibliotheca D. Joannis Ducis de Lauderdale, 1692. [Auction catalogue.]

The quair of jelousy, a poem by James Auchinleck, written about the year 1480. [Attribution to Auchinleck not certain. Also printed in **19.2** and **33.4**.]

Collection of the wills of printers and booksellers in Edinburgh between the years 1577 and 1687. [1577–1717]

An obituary from the rental book of the preceptory of St Anthony, near Leith, 1526. [Latin. Obits, 1439–1528. Also list of benefactors (English). Also printed in **11.14**.]

Collection of papers relating to the 'Theatrum Scotiae' and 'History and present state of Scotland', by Captain John Slezer, 1693–1707. [1695–c. 1700.]

Collection of papers relating to the geographical description, maps, and charts of Scotland, by John Adair, F.R.S., geographer for the kingdom of Scotland, 1686–1723. [1692–1723.]

Urbis Edinburgi descriptio, per Davidem Buchananum, circa A.D. 1648.

19B. The Bannatyne miscellany. . . . Edited by David Laing. Vol. iii. 1855.   6.22

Two ancient records of the bishopric of Caithness, from the charter-room at Dunrobin. With a prefatory notice, by Cosmo Innes. [Latin. Charter of constitution of the cathedral at Dornoch by Bishop Gilbert de Moravia (1222 or 1223–1245); and charter of Bishop Archibald Herok, 1275, relating to controversy between him and the Earl of Sutherland.]

Extracts from a manuscript volume of chronicles, in the possession of the Right Hon. Lord Panmure. [Mainly Latin. Ms. *c.* 1460. Includes extracts from 'The chronycle of Scotland in a part' on the origins of the Scots (another version of which is printed in **32.14**); and from 'Nomina regum Scotorum', which ends with Robert III.]

Diploma of Thomas, Bishop of Orkney and Zetland, and the chapter of Kirkwall, addressed to Eric King of Norway, respecting the genealogy of William Saint Clair, Earl of Orkney. With a translation by Dean Thomas Guild, monk of Newbattle, 1554. [Latin. 1440s, not 1406 as dated in the texts printed, and evidently addressed to King Eric's successor, Christopher. From the ms. vol. detailed in the preceding item.]

Extract from Thorm. Torfaei Orcades. [Latin. From Thomodo Torfaeo's *Orcades*, 1697 and 1715. Investiture of Earl of Orkney at Copenhagen, 1434.]

The testament of Alexander Suthyrland of Dunbeath, at Roslin Castle, 15th November 1456.

The testament of Sir David Synclar of Swynbrocht knycht, at Tyngwell, 10th July 1506.

The diary of John Lesley, Bishop of Ross, April 11–October 16, 1571. [Partly Latin.]

The preface by Henry Charteris to his edition of Henry's Wallace, printed at Edinburgh, 1594.

A catalogue of the bishops of Orkney, 1112–1477. By Professor Munch, of Christiania.

Notes by Professor Munch on the extracts from the Panmure manuscripts in the present volume.

The testament of Richard Lawson, bookseller and merchant-burgess of Edinburgh, 1622.

The progress of my Lord Walden's journey in Scotland, in August 1614. [Theophilus Howard, later Earl of Suffolk.]

Carta Jacobi tertii Regis Scotorum, de tenemento terre cum orto murato in burgo de Edinburgh, concess. David de Dalrympill, 15 Octobris 1471.

Proceedings of the commissioners of the kirk, at a meeting held at Edinburgh, in July 1627.

An account of the foundation of the Leightonian Library. By Robert Douglas, Bishop of Dunblane. [Bishop Robert Leighton left his library to Dunblane on his death in 1684; Douglas' account was written 1691 but ends in 1688.]

Letters relating to the Leightonian Library, Dunblane, 1703–1710.

Letters of assedation to Agnes Countess of Bothwell; and other deeds connected with the Hepburns Earls of Bothwell, and the Hepburns of Waughton, 1520–1564. [Transcripts and extracts, partly Latin. 1485–1586.]

A Godly exhortation, as set forth by John [Hamilton] Archbishop of St Andrews, commonly styled 'The twopenny faith', 1559. [From first edition, 1559.]

A plan of the city of St Andrews, from an original drawing by James Gordon, A.M., minister of Rothiemay, 1642.

The contract with James de Witte, painter, for the portraits of the kings of Scotland in the palace of Holyrood; and the accompt for portraits, by Godfrey Kneller, of King Charles II and his brother James Duke of York, 1684.

Extracts from 'The richt way to the kingdome of hevine', by John Gau, printed at Malmoe, in Sweden, 1533. [Also printed in **31.8**.]

22

An advertisement and general queries for the description of Scotland, by Sir Robert Sibbald, M.D., his majesties geographer for Scotland, 1682. [1680s.]

Proposals by Walter Gibson, merchant in Glasgow, to persons who wish to transport themselves to America, 1684. [From a broadside.]

Advertisement to all tradesmen and others, who are willing to transport themselves into the province of East-New-Jersey in America, 1684. [From a broadside.]

Extracts from the acts and proceedings of the presbytery of Haddington, relating to Dr Gilbert Burnet, and the library of the kirk of Salton, 1664–1669. [1664–74.]

Letters of Patrick Earl of Bothwell, and articles which he undertook to maintain at the appointment of the King of France, 1548–1549.

Additional extracts relating to the Earls of Bothwell and the Master of Hailes. [Partly Latin. 1509–71.]

The retour and royal warrant of taxation of the lands in the sheriffdom of Edinburgh, in the year 1479.

20. Chronicum coenobii Sanctae Crucis Edinburgensis, iterum in lucem editum. Presented by Robert Pitcairn. 1828.   6.23

The Holyrood chronicle. Superseded by **26.30**, which see for details.

21. Thomae Dempsteri historia ecclesiastica gentis Scotorum: sive, de scriptoribus Scotis. Editio altera. Edited by David Irving. 2 vols. 1829.   6.24

Biographical dictionary of Catholic writers. From first edition, 1627.
i : [A–G.]
ii: [H–W.]

22. Extract from the despatches of M. Courcelles, French ambassador at the court of Scotland. MDLXXXVI–MDLXXXVII. Edited by Robert Bell. 1828.   6.25

Also letters of Henry III and M. Brulart to Courcelles.

23. Siege of the castle of Edinburgh. MDCLXXXIX. Presented by Robert Bell. 1828.   6.26

Narrative by Father David Burnet, from a ms. of 1691, with other papers 1688–91. See notes in **6.118**.

24. Letters from the Lady Margaret Kennedy to John, Duke of Lauderdale. 1828.   6.27

1660s, with miscellaneous letters, late 16th–late 17th centuries. Spine reads *Lady Margaret Burnet's letters*, and the list of errata directs that *Kennedy* on the title page and running heads be changed to *Burnet* (as the writer of the letters subsequently married Gilbert Burnet). Copies issued for general sale appeared under the title *Letters from Lady Margaret Burnet. . . .* This appears as a second title page in the Bannatyne Club copies.

25. The history of the troubles and memorable transactions in   **6.28**
Scotland and England, from MDCXXIV to MDCXLV. By John
Spalding. Edited by James Skene. 2 vols. 1828–9.

   Also issued as **15.20**. For a better edition see **36**.21, 23.
   i : [1624–41.]
   ii: [1642–5.]

26. Papers relative to the marriage of King James the Sixth of   **6.29**
Scotland, with the Princess Anna of Denmark; A.D.
MDLXXXIX. And the form and manner of her majesty's
coronation at Holyroodhouse, A.D. MDXC. Presented by
James T. G. Craig. 1828.

   Partly Latin. Includes Andrew Melville's *Stephaniskion ad Scotiae regem
   habitum in coronatione reginae* (verse), from the first edition, Edinburgh 1590.

27. A diary of the proceedings in the Parliament and Privy   **6.30**
Council of Scotland May 21, MDCC–March 7, MDCCVII. By
Sir David Hume of Crossrigg, one of the senators of the College
of Justice. Presented by John Hope. 1828.

28. Memoirs of his own life and times. By Sir James Turner.   **6.31**
MDCXXXII–MDCLXX. From the original manuscript. [Edited
by Thomas Thomson.] 1829.

   1632–63, 1666–70. Also Turner's 'Bishop [Henry] Guthry's observations of
   the late rebellion observed'; and letters to Turner, 1672–82.

29. Les affaires du Conte de Boduel. L'an MDLXVIII.   **6.32**
Presented by Henry Cockburn and Thomas Maitland. 1829.

   Narrative by the Earl of Bothwell of events leading to his flight from
   Scotland, 1567, written in Denmark. Also related docs., 1567–71 (partly
   Danish, with English translation, and Latin). See notes in **6**.118.

30. Papers relative to the regalia of Scotland. Presented by   **6.33**
William Bell. 1829.

   1621–1818. Includes Sir George Ogilvie's *A true account of the preservation of
   the regalia*, from the 1701 edition.

31. The history of the house of Seytoun to the year MDLIX. By   **6.34**
Sir Richard Maitland of Lethington, knight. With the con-
tinuation, by Alexander Viscount Kingston, to MDCLXXXVII.
Edited by John Fullarton. Glasgow. 1829.

   Also 'Collections upon the life of Alexander Seaton, Dominican freir,
   confessor to King James the Fifth, and afterwards chaplain to the Duke of
   Suffolk, in England. By the Rev. Robert Wodrow, minister of Eastwood',
   from a ms. dated 1729. Also issued as **15**.1.

32. Descrittione del regno di Scotia di Petruccio Ubaldini.   **6.35**
Presented by Andrew Coventry. 1829.

From the first edition, Antwerp 1588. Largely taken from Hector Boece's *Scotorum regni descriptio*.

33. Letters from Archibald, Earl of Argyll, to John, Duke of Lauderdale. [Edited by Sir George Sinclair and Charles K. Sharpe.] 1829.

    6.36

1663–70. Also letters of Sir Andrew Ramsay of Abbotshall to Lauderdale, 1663–7. Also issued for general sale.

34. The diary of Mr James Melvill. 1556–1601. [Edited by George R. Kinloch.] 1829.

    6.37

For another edition see 43.3.

35. Memorials of George Bannatyne. MDXLV – MDCVIII. 1829.

    6.38

Memoir of George Bannatyne. By Sir Walter Scott.
Extracts from the 'memoriall buik' of George Bannatyne. [Notes on births and deaths of members of his family, 1512–1606, and on papers concerning his properties, 1553–1601. See 24.16 for another transcript.]
An account of the contents of George Bannatyne's manuscript. 1568. By David Laing.
Appendix. [Includes notes on Bannatyne and his family; transcripts of family testaments, 1603–38; poems by Bannatyne from the 1568 ms.; etc.]

36. The anatomie of humors, and The passionate sparke of a relenting minde. By Simion Grahame. Presented by Robert Jameson. 1830.

    6.39

From the first editions, the *Anatomie* (prose and verse), Edinburgh 1609, and the *Passionate sparke* (verse), London 1604. See notes in 6.118.

37. A relation of proceedings concerning the affairs of the Kirk of Scotland, from August 1637 to July 1638. By John [Leslie] Earl of Rothes. Edited by David Laing. 1830.

    6.40

A composite account of events compiled by the covenanters. Also a number of related documents.

38. The history of Scotland, from the death of King James I, in the year MCCCCXXXVI, to the year MDLXI. By John Lesley, Bishop of Ross. [Edited by Thomas Thomson.] 1830.

    6.41

1437–1561. English version, completed by 1571 (before publication of the first edition (Latin), Rome 1578). Also issued for general sale. For a translation of the Latin edition see 31.4.

39. Memoirs of the affairs of Scotland. By David Moysie. MDLXXVII–MDCIII. From early manuscripts. [Edited by James Dennistoun.] 1830.

    6.42

1577–98, 1600, 1603. Also miscellaneous docs., 1596–9. Also issued as 15.3.

40. Trial of Duncan Terig alias Clerk, and Alexander Bane Macdonald, for the murder of Arthur Davis, sergeant in General Guise's regiment of foot. June, A.D. MDCCLIV. Presented by Sir Walter Scott. 1831.

6.43

> Before the Court of Justiciary.

41. Hymns and sacred songs, by Alexander Hume. Reprinted from the edition of Waldegrave, 1599. Presented by John G. Kinnear. 1832.

6.44

> Also contains Hume's prose 'Ane afold admonitioun to the ministerie of Scotland. By a deing brother', written *c.* 1607–9. See notes in **6.118**. Hume's works were also printed as **31.23**, and the 'Admonitioun' in **43.11**.

42. Ancient criminal trials in Scotland; compiled from the original records and mss., with historical illustrations, etc. By Robert Pitcairn. 3 vols. in 7 parts. 1833.

6.45

> Mainly from justiciary records, with many related docs. printed in notes and appendices. The covering dates for the various vols. and pts. refer to trials held in these years; many of the related docs. fall outside these dates, and vol. iii pt. 2 has docs. relating to trials dealt with in earlier pts. The work was originally issued in ten parts (dated 1829–33) with title pages reading *Criminal trials and other proceedings before the High Court of Justiciary in Scotland.* . . . On completion new title pages were issued, all dated 1833. Those for volumes for general sale were titled *Criminal trials in Scotland, from A.D. MCCCCLXXXVIII to A.D. MDCXXIV. Embracing the entire reigns of James IV and V, Mary Queen of Scots, and James VI. Compiled from the original records and mss. With historical illustrations and notes.* . . . These sets are usually bound as 3 vols. in 4, vol. i being divided into 2 pts., or as 3 vols. in 6, all three vols. being in two pts. Some of these general sale sets have been inserted in runs of the Bannatyne and Maitland Club (the work was also issued as **15.19**) publications, but the sets originally intended for the clubs had title pages reading as indicated at the opening of this entry, and instructions were issued for binding them as follows:
> i. pt. 1: 1488–1542 [Original pt. 9 and 1st section of pt. 10. Paginated 1*–325*.]
> i. pt. 2: 1543–1584. [2nd section of original pt. 10 and 1st section of original pt. 1. Paginated 327*–513* and 1–112.]
> i. pt. 3: 1584–1596. [2nd section of original pt. 1 and all original pt. 2. Paginated 113–400.]
> ii. pt. 1: 1596–1600. [Original pt. 3 and 1st section of pt. 4. Paginated 1–304.]
> ii. pt. 2: 1600–1609. [2nd section of original pt. 4 and all original pt. 5. Paginated 305–604.]
> iii. pt. 1: 1609–1615. [Original pt. 6 and 1st section of pt. 7. Paginated 1–360.]
> iii. pt. 2: 1615–1624. [2nd section of original pt. 7, all pt. 8, and 3rd section of pt. 10, including general index. Paginated 361–746.]

43. A diurnal of remarkable occurrents that have passed within the country of Scotland since the death of King James the

6.46

Fourth till the year MDLXXV. From a manuscript of the
sixteenth century, in the possession of Sir John Maxwell of
Pollock, baronet. Edited by Thomas Thomson. 1833.

> 1557–75, evidently written by a contemporary living in Edinburgh, the
> earlier sections being compiled from other sources. Also issued as 15.23.
> There is a separate undated *Index to the Diurnal of occurrents. Prepared by
> A. G. Scott and other collaborators. Also glossary.*

44. Collection of ancient Scottish prophecies, in alliterative   6.47
verse: reprinted from Waldegrave's edition, MDCIII. [Edited by
David Laing, with a preface by Thomas Thomson.] 1833.

> Collated with the Edinburgh 1615 edition.

45. Memoirs of the war carried on in Scotland and Ireland.   6.48
MDCLXXXIX–MDCXCI. By Major General Hugh Mackay,
commander in chief of his majesty's forces. With an appendix of
original papers. [Edited by James M. Hog, Patrick F. Tytler and
Adam Urquhart.] 1833.

> Comprises memoirs of the war in Scotland, 1689–90 (English), and of the
> campaign in Ireland, 1691 (French); and letters from Mackay to William III
> and the Earl of Portland, 1690 (French) from a ms. of 1702. Also issued as
> 15.22. See 6.56 for a biography of Mackay.

46. The buik of the most noble and vailzeand conquerour   6.49
Alexander the Great. [Edited by David Laing.] 1831.

> Verse romance. From the first edition, Edinburgh *c.* 1580. By John Barbour
> (d. 1395). 6.118 prints David Laing's preface written for the Club edition but
> omitted. See 32.12, 17, 21, 25 for another edition.

47. Instrumenta publica sive processus super fidelitatibus et   6.50
homagiis Scotorum domino regi Angliae factis, A.D. MCCXCI
–MCCXCVI. [Edited by Thomas Thomson.] 1834.

> Spine reads *The ragman rolls, 1291–6.* Also 'Itineraire de Roy Edward en
> Escoce, A.D. MCCXCVI', for which see also 6.20.

48. Letters and papers relating to Patrick Master of Gray,   6.51
afterwards seventh Lord Gray. [Edited by Thomas Thomson.]
1835.

> 1515–1608.

49. Chronica de Mailros, e codice unico in bibliotheca   6.52
Cottoniana servato, nunc iterum in lucem edita. Notulis
indiceque aucta. Edited by Joseph Stevenson. 1835.

> *c.* 731–1270, from a late 13th century ms. Based on English sources up to the
> mid-12th century, thereafter an independent contemporary Scottish chronicle.
> Also 'Chronicon rythmicum', 741–1093, added to the same ms. in the early
> 14th century.

50. Philotus; a comedy. Reprinted from the edition of Robert Charteris. Presented by John W. Mackenzie [with a preface by David Irving.] 1835.

6.53

> Verse. From the first edition, Edinburgh 1603, collated with 1612 edition. Also 'Barnaby Rich's tale of Phylotus and Emelia' from 1583 (?) and 1606 editions of *Rich his farewell to militarie profession*. For another edition of *Philotus* see 33.4.

51. Memorials of transactions in Scotland, A.D. MDLXIX – MDLXXIII. By Richard Bannatyne, secretary to John Knox. Edited by Robert Pitcairn. 1836.

6.54

> Also a number of docs. appended to the *Memorials* in the mss., 1572–81; miscellaneous docs. 1570s; and the testaments of Knox, 1572, and Bannatyne, 1605. Also issued for general sale.

52. A diary of public transactions and other occurrences, chiefly in Scotland, from January 1650 to June 1667. By John Nicoll. Edited by David Laing. 1836.

6.55

53. The life of Lieut.-General Hugh Mackay, commander in chief of the forces in Scotland, 1689 and 1690. By John Mackay of Rockfield. 1836.

6.56

> Originally intended to be prefixed to 6.48. Also letters (mainly by Hugh Mackay), 1689–90. Also issued for general sale.

54. Excerpta e libris domicilii domini Jacobi Quinti Regis Scotorum. MDXXV–MDXXXIII. Presented by J. Henry Mackenzie (Lord Mackenzie), Robert Graham and James Mackenzie. 1836.

6.57

55. Davidis Buchanani de scriptoribus Scotis libri duo, nunc primum editi. Edited by David Irving. 1837.

6.58

> Printed from a ms. dated 1627. Also Buchanan's testament, 1652.

56. Liber Sancte Marie de Melros. Munimenta vetustiora monasterii Cisterciensis de Melros. [Edited by Cosmo Innes.] 2 vols. 1837.

6.59

> From cartularies and original charters. Pagination continuous.
> i : [David I–1306.]
> ii: [Robert I–James VI, with some earlier and undated charters.]

57. The seven sages, in Scotish metre. By John Rolland of Dalkeith. Edited by David Laing. 1837.

6.60

> From the first edition, Edinburgh 1578. The work is dated 1560. See notes in 6.118. For another edition see 33.3.

58. Registrum episcopatus Moraviensis, e pluribus codicibus consarcinatum circa A.D. MCCCC. Cum continuatione diplo-

6.61

matum recentiorum usque ad A.D. MDCXXIII. [Edited by Cosmo Innes.] 1837.

Transcripts, partly abridged. From cartularies etc., covering mid-12th century to 1623. Includes a rental of the bishopric, 1565.

59. Ancient Scotish melodies, from a manuscript of the reign of King James VI. With an introductory enquiry illustrative of the history of the music of Scotland. By William Dauney. 1838.

6.62

From the Skene ms. of tunes arranged for the lute, 1615–35, partly compiled by John Skene of Hallyards. Also extracts from the treasurers' and other accounts relating to music, 1474–1642. Also issued as 15.44 and to other subscribers.

60. Catalogue of the library at Abbotsford. [By John G. Cochrane.] 1838.

6.63

Library of Sir Walter Scott (d. 1832). Also issued as 15.46.

61. Syr Gawayne; a collection of ancient romance-poems, by Scotish and English authors, relating to that celebrated knight of the round table, with an introduction, notes, and a glossary. By Sir Frederic Madden. London. 1839.

6.64

From 15th and 16th century mss.

62. De arte logistica Joannis Naperi Merchistonii baronis, libri qui supersunt. Edited by Mark Napier. 1839.

6.65

A treatise on mathematics. John Napier d. 1617. Also issued as 15.48.

63. Ferrerii historia abbatum de Kynlos: una cum vita Thomae Chrystalli abbatis. [Edited by William D. Wilson, with a preface by James P. Muirhead.] 1839.

6.66

John Ferrerius completed his work in 1537. Also a charter of William I, and a rental of the abbey, c. 1574.

64. The Aeneid of Virgil translated into Scottish verse. By Gawin Douglas, Bishop of Dunkeld. [Edited by George Dundas.] 2 vols. 1839.

6.67

The translation was made 1512–13. Pagination continuous. See notes in 6.118. For another edition see 33.26, 28, 29, 31.

65. Chronicon de Lanercost. MCCI – MCCCXLVI. E codice Cottoniano nunc primum typis mandatum. Edited by Joseph Stevenson. 1839.

6.68

Written in the north of England, and covers events in both England and Scotland. It has no real connection with Lanercost. Also many illustrative docs. Also issued as 15.47.

66. Historical observes of memorable occurrents in church and   **6.69**
state, from October 1680 to April 1686. By Sir John Lauder of
Fountainhall. Edited by Adam Urquhart and David Laing.
1840.

> Originally issued with title page reading *Historical selections from the*
> *manuscripts of Sir John Lauder.* . . . Vol. i. 1837, but the new title was
> substituted in 1840. Also an account of the Convention of Estates, 1678, and
> other papers, some added (with the index) in 1840.

67. Correspondance diplomatique de Bertrand de Salignac de la   **6.70**
Mothe Fénélon, ambassadeur de France en Angleterre de 1568 à
1575. Publiée pour la première fois sur les manuscrits conservés
aux archives du Royaume. [Edited by J. B. Alexandre T.
Tuelet.] 7 vols. Paris and London. 1838–40.

> Vols. have the above as a second title page, with a first title reading *Recueil*
> *des dépêches, rapports, instructions et mémoires des ambassadeurs de France en*
> *Angleterre et en Écosse pendant le XVIᵉ siècle . . . publiés . . . sous la direction de*
> *M. Charles Purton Cooper.* These were the only vols. of Cooper's work ever
> published. See notes in **6.118**. Also issued for general sale.
> i : Années 1568 et 1569.   v : Années 1572–1573.
> ii : Année 1569.   vi : Années 1574–1575.
> iii: Années 1570–1571.   vii: Années 1568–1575. [In fact 1569–75.]
> iv: Années 1571–1572.

68. Roman de la Manekine, par Philippe de Reimes, trouvère   **6.71**
du treizième siècle. Publié par Francisque Michel. Paris. 1840.

> In fact written by Philippe de Beaumanoir, seigneur de Remi, d. 1296. See
> notes in **6.118**.

69. Liber cartarum prioratus Sancti Andree in Scotia. E registro   **6.72**
ipso in archivis baronum de Panmure hodie asservato. [Edited
by Thomas Thomson.] 1841.

> 12th–15th centuries.

70. Liber cartarum Sancte Crucis. Munimenta ecclesie Sancte   **6.73**
Crucis de Edwinesburg. [Edited by Cosmo Innes.] 1840.

> Mainly from original charters, 12th to late 16th centuries. Also stent rolls of
> Holyrood, 1578, 1630; warrants of Charles II and James VII, 1671–87; etc.

71. Memoirs   touching   the   revolution   in   Scotland,   **6.74**
MDCLXXXVIII–MDCXC. By Colin Earl of Balcarres.
Presented to King James II at St Germains, MDCXC. [Edited
by Lord Lindsay.] 1841.

72. Correspondence of George Baillie of Jerviswood. MDCCII–   **6.75**
MDCCVIII. Edited by [Gilbert Elliot] Earl of Minto. 1842.

73. The letters and journals of Robert Baillie, A.M., principal of the University of Glasgow, MDCXXXVII–MDCLXII. Edited from the author's manuscripts, by David Laing. 3 vols. 1841–2.   **6.76**

> A 'Memoir of the life and writings of Robert Baillie' was issued with vol. iii. It was intended that it be re-bound in vol. i, but it frequently remains in vol. iii. The volumes were also issued for general sale.
> i : [1637–41. Also miscellaneous papers, 1633–9.]
> ii : [1642–6. Also miscellaneous papers, 1639–46.]
> iii: [1647–62. Also miscellaneous papers, 1647–61.]

74. Registrum de Dunfermelyn. Liber cartarum abbatie Benedictine S. S. Trinitatis et B. Margarete regine de Dunfermelyn. [Edited by Cosmo Innes.] 1842.   **6.77**

> Transcript, partly abridged. 12th to 16th centuries. Also rental of the abbey, 1561 (English); and lists of contents of 'Registra infeodacionum et alienationum', 1555–1611.

75. Registrum episcopatus Glasguensis: munimenta ecclesie metropolitane Glasguensis, a sede restaurata seculo ineunte XII, ad reformatam religionem. Edited by Cosmo Innes. 2 vols. 1843.   **6.78**

> Also issued as **15.63**.
> i : [c. 1116–1403. Also miscellaneous docs.]
> ii: [1413–1581. Also charters, 12th to 16th centuries.]

76. A diary of the public correspondence of Sir Thomas Hope of Craighall, bart., 1633–1645. From the original, in the library at Pinkie House. [Edited by Thomas Thomson.] 1843.   **6.79**

> Ms. is titled 'Nott of the pacquetts and letteris sent and resavit from court'. Also two letters by Hope, 1638.

77. Leven and Melville papers. Letters and state papers chiefly addressed to George Earl of Melville, secretary of state for Scotland, 1689–1691. From the originals in the possession of the Earl of Leven and Melville. Edited by William L. Melville. 1843.   **6.80**

78. Liber ecclesie de Scon. Munimenta vetustiora monasterii Sancte Trinitatis et Sancti Michaelis de Scon. Presented by William Smythe. 1843.   **6.81**

> c. 1114–1570. Also rental of the abbey, 1561; an abstract of a vol. of feus, 1584–6; and extracts from books of assignation of Thirds of Benefices, 1594–1608. Also issued as **15.64**.

79. The accounts of the great chamberlains of Scotland, and some other officers of the crown, rendered at the exchequer. Edited by Thomas Thomson. 3 vols. 1817.   **6.82**

Latin. Printed 1817, but published as Bannatyne Club vols. in 1841 (vols. i–ii) and 1845 (vol. iii and preface to vol. i). Some copies of vol. ii have a title page dated 1836.
i : [1326–70, with extracts from rolls, 1263–6 and 1288–90.]
ii : [1371–1406.]
iii: [1406–53. The accounts after 1437 were added in 1845.]

80. Horn et Rimenhild. Recueil de ce qui reste des poëmes relatifs à leurs aventures composés en François, en Anglois et en Écossois dans les treizième, quatorzième, quinzième et seizième siècles. Publié d'après les manuscrits de Londres, de Cambridge, d'Oxford et d'Edinburgh, par Francisque Michel. Paris. 1845.   **6.83**

French and Scots romances.

81. Acts and proceedings of the General Assemblies of the Kirk of Scotland, from the year MDLX. Collected from the most authentic manuscripts. Edited by Thomas Thomson. 3 parts. 1839–45.   **6.84**

Commonly known as 'The booke of the Universall Kirk of Scotland', which is the title of the principal source (early 17th century) used for 1560–1616. Additions to this have been made from other sources, especially the works of David Calderwood. Also issued as **15.50**. For an appendix vol. see **15.51**.
Pt. 1: [1560–77.]
Pt. 2: [1578–92.]
Pt. 3: [1593–1618. With preface, and papers relating to the registers of the General Assembly, 1593–1834.]

82. Liber S. Marie de Calchou. Registrum cartarum abbacie Tironensis de Kelso. 1113–1567. Edited by Cosmo Innes. 2 vols. 1846.   **6.85**

Pagination continuous.

83. Liber S. Marie de Dryburgh. Registrum cartarum abbacie Premonstratensis de Dryburgh. Edited by William Fraser. 1847.   **6.86**

Mid-12th to late 14th centuries, from a 16th century cartulary. Also charters, rentals, tax rolls, etc., *c.* 1170–1634.

84. Carte monialium de Northberwic. Prioratus Cisterciensis B. Marie de Northberwic munimenta vetusta que supersunt. Edited by Cosmo Innes. 1847.   **6.87**

Late 12th century–1544. Also a rental of the nunnery, *c.* 1550; abridged charters, 1525–51; and extracts from the protocol book of Robert Lauder, 1543–62 (partly English).

85. Liber insule missarum. Abbacie canonicorum regularium B. Virginis et S. Johannis de Inchaffery registrum vetus: premissis quibusdam comitatus antiqui de Stratherne reliquiis. [Edited by Cosmo Innes.] 1847.   **6.88**

c. 1200–14th century, with abridgements of charters late 12th century–1618. Also rental, 1563; tax roll 1630; extracts from the charge of the temporality of kirklands, 1590s; and an act of Parliament in favour of Sir Robert Murray of Abercairnie, 1696. For texts of originals of many of the charters see **24.56**.

86. Liber S. Thome de Aberbrothoc. Edited by Cosmo Innes   **6.89** and Patrick Chalmers. 2 pts. 1848–56.

> Separate pagination. Also issued to other subscribers.
> Pt. 1: Registrorum abbacie de Aberbrothoc pars prior. Registrum vetus munimentaque eidem coetanea complectens. 1178–1329.
> Pt. 2: Registrorum abbacie de Aberbrothoc pars altera. Registrum nigrum necnon libros cartarum recentiores complectens. 1329–1536. [Also extracts from accounts of collector of Thirds of Benefices, 1561, from the books of assumption of Thirds (a rental) 1561, and from charge of temporality of kirklands, 1590s; and charters, late 12th century–1438.]

87. Historical notices of Scotish affairs, selected from the   **6.90** manuscripts of Sir John Lauder of Fountainhall, bart., one of the senators of the College of Justice. Edited by David Laing. 2 vols. 1848.

> Pagination continuous.
> i : 1661–1683.
> ii: 1683–1688.

88. The ancient sculptured monuments of the county of Angus;   **6.91** including those at Meigle in Perthshire, and one at Fordoun in the Mearns. Presented by Patrick Chalmers. 1848.

> Plates, with notes.

89. Registrum S. Marie de Neubotle. Abbacie Cisterciensis   **6.92** Beate Virginis de Neubotle chartarium vetus. Accedit appendix cartarum originalium, 1140–1528. Edited by Cosmo Innes. 1849.

> Also extracts from accounts of collector of Thirds of Benefices, 1561; from books of assumption of Thirds (a rental), 1561; and from the charge of the temporality of kirklands, 1590s.

90. The Darien papers: being a selection of original letters and   **6.93** official documents relating to the establishment of a colony at Darien by the Company of Scotland trading to Africa and the Indies. 1695–1700. Edited by John H. Burton. 1849.

91. Descriptive catalogue of impressions from ancient Scottish   **6.94** seals, royal, baronial, ecclesiastical, and municipal, embracing a period from A.D. 1094 to the Commonwealth. Taken from

original charters and other deeds preserved in public and private archives. By Henry Laing. 1850.

Also issued as **15.70** and for general sale. A *Supplemental descriptive catalogue of ancient Scottish seals* by Henry Laing was published in 1866.

92. Original letters relating to the ecclesiastical affairs of Scotland, chiefly written by, or addressed to, His Majesty King James the Sixth, after his accession to the English throne. Edited by David Laing. 2 vols. 1851.

6.95

Pagination continuous.
i : [1603–14.]
ii: [1614–25.]

93. The history of the Church of Scotland. By John Spottiswood, Archbishop of St Andrews. [Edited by Mark Napier and Michael Russell.] 3 vols. 1850.

6.96

From the ms. prepared for the press by Spottiswoode, and the first edition, London 1655; the preface is dated 1639. Also issued as **39.7**. The Spottiswoode Society title pages (dated 1847–51) appear as second title pages in Bannatyne Club copies; they identify the editor as Michael Russell, though vols. ii–iii were edited by Mark Napier.
i : [203–1560.]
ii : [1561–96.]
iii: [1596–1625.]

94. Registrum honoris de Morton. A series of ancient charters of the earldom of Morton with other original papers. Edited by Thomas Thomson, Alexander Macdonald and Cosmo Innes. 2 vols. 1853.

6.97

Latin and English.
i : Original papers. [Miscellaneous docs., 1529–1607, and charters etc. early 13th century–1578.]
ii: Ancient charters. [Cartularies and charters, mid 12th–late 16th centuries; and abridgements of great seal charters, 1439–1507.]

95. Thomas Thomson, esq., advocate, president of the Bannatyne Club. By David Laing. 1853.

6.98

A brief life of Thomson accompanying a portrait of him engraved from a painting by Robert S. Lauder.

96. Breviarium Aberdonense. Edited by William Blew. 2 pts. London. 1854.

6.99

Reprinted from the first edition, Edinburgh 1509–10. A preface by David Laing, issued in 1855, contains part of *Compassio Beate Marie*, from the Edinburgh *c.* 1520 edition. Also issued as **15.72**, **36.41**, and for other subscribers.
1: Pars hyemalis
2: Pars estiva.

97. Origines parochiales Scotiae. The antiquities, ecclesiastical   6.100
and territorial, of the parishes of Scotland. Edited by Cosmo
Innes, James B. Brichan and others. 2 vols. in 3. 1850–5.

> i: [Diocese of Glasgow.]
> ii. pt 1: [Dioceses of Argyll and the Isles.]
> ii. pt. 2: [Dioceses of Ross and Caithness, with additions to dioceses of
> Argyll and the Isles.]

98. A series of etchings chiefly of views in Scotland. By John   6.101
Clerk of Eldin, esq., MDCCLXXIII–MDCCLXXIX. With
additional etchings and facsimiles from his drawings. Edited by
David Laing. 1855.

> Includes the etchings in 6.9.

99. Memoir of Thomas Thomson, advocate. By Cosmo Innes.   6.102
1854.

> Thomson d. 1852, having been president of the Bannatyne Club since 1832.

100. The Black Book of Taymouth. With other papers from the   6.103
Breadalbane charter room. Edited by Cosmo Innes. 1855.

> The Black Book of Taymouth. [A genealogical history of the Campbells of
> Glenorchy, compiled by William Bowie, 1598, with additions to 1648.]
> The chronicle of Fortirgall. [Latin and English. By James MacGregor, Dean
> of Lismore and vicar of Fortingall, d. 1551, with additions to 1579.]
> Duncan Laideus' *alias* Makgregouris testament. [16th century anticlerical
> poem.]
> The buke of bandis of manrent seruice, calpis. . . . [1488–1681.]
> Portions of rentals, court books, household books and inventories of
> Breadalbane. [1582–1642. Also roll of fencible men, 1638; and feu charters
> and tacks, 1550–1703.]
> Letters from the charter room at Taymouth, 1570–1619.

101. Letters from Roundhead officers written from Scotland   6.104
and chiefly addressed to Captain Adam Baynes, July MDCL–
June MDCLX. Edited by John Y. Akerman. 1856.

102. Registrum episcopatus Brechinensis cui accedunt cartae   6.105
quamplurimae originales. Edited by Patrick Chalmers and
Cosmo Innes. 2 vols. Aberdeen. 1856.

> i : Registrum. [Mid 12th century–1553.]
> ii: Appendix cartarum. [Latin and English. Late 12th century–1674. Also
> rentals and acounts, 1462–85, 1574, 1689; and tax roll of shire of Forfar,
> 1613.]

103. Vita Sancti Columbae: auctore Adamnano monasterii   6.106
Hiensis abbate. Edited by William Reeves. Dublin. 1857.

> Late 7th century. As published for the Irish Archaeological and Celtic
> Society, and including its title page reading *The life of St Columba, founder of
> Hy; written by Adamnan.* . . .

104. Original letters of Mr John Colville 1582–1603. To which is added, his Palinode, 1600. With a memoir of the author. Edited by David Laing. 1858.   **6.107**

> *The palinod* from the first edition, Edinburgh 1600. Also contains miscellaneous docs., 1513–1602.

105. Registrum cartarum ecclesie Sancti Egidii de Edinburgh. A series of charters and original documents connected with the church of St Giles, Edinburgh. MCCCXLIV–MDLXVII. Edited by David Laing. 1859.   **6.108**

> 1344–1648.

106. A catalogue of the graduates in the faculties of arts, divinity, and law, of the University of Edinburgh, since its foundation. By David Laing. 1858.   **6.109**

> 1587–1858. Also lists of principals, regents and professors, 1583–1858. Also issued for general sale.

107. Papiers d'état, pièces et documents inédits ou peu connus relatifs à l'histoire de l'Écosse au XVIe siècle, tirés des bibliothèques et des archives de France, et publiés pour le Bannatyne Club D'Édimbourg, par J. B. Alexandre T. Teulet. 3 vols. Paris. 1852–60.   **6.110**

> See **6.**123 for a revised edition.
> i : [1515–61.]
> ii : [1561–87.]
> iii: [1563–87, 1599–1603.]

108. Tracts by Dr Gilbert Skeyne, medicinar to his majesty. Edited by William F. Skene. 1860.   **6.111**

> Reprinted from the first editions of *Ane breve descriptiovn of the pest*, Edinburgh 1568, and *Ane breif descriptioun of the qualiteis and effectis of the well of the woman hill besyde Abirdene*, Edinburgh 1580.

109. Registrum domus de Soltre, necnon ecclesie collegiate S. Trinitatis prope Edinburgh, etc. Charters of the hospital of Soltre, of Trinity College, Edinburgh, and other collegiate churches in Mid-Lothian. Edited by David Laing. 1861.   **6.112**

> Latin and English. Trinity College and hospital of Soutra (annexed to Trinity, 1460), mid 12th century–1612; other churches, 1406–1531.

110. Tracts by David Fergusson, minister of Dunfermline, MDLXIII–MDLXXII. Edited by John Lee. 1860.   **6.113**

> From the first editions of *Ane answer to ane epistle written by Renat Benedict to John Knox*, Edinburgh 1563; *Ane sermon preichit befoir the regent and nobilitie*, St Andrews 1572; and *Epistola Renati Benedicti verbi Dei professoris ad Johannem Knox*, 1561. Also Fergusson's testament, 1598.

111. Inuentaires de la royne descosse douairiere de France. 6.114
Catalogues of the jewels, dresses, furniture, books and paintings
of Mary Queen of Scots. 1556–1569. Edited by Joseph
Robertson. 1863.

> Inventories, 1556–78.

112. The works of John Knox; collected and edited by David 6.115
Laing. 6 vols., 1846–64.

> All vols. (except v) also contain miscellaneous docs. Vols. i and ii were issued
> by the Bannatyne Club and also as **43**.12. Vols. iii–vi are uniform with i and ii
> and were made available to members of the two bodies, but were not
> published by them.
> i : [History of the Reformation in Scotland, books 1 and 2, 1494–1559.]
> ii : [Ditto, books 3 and 4, 1559–67.]
> iii: [Miscellaneous works, 1548–54.]
> iv : [Ditto, 1554–8.]
> v : [Ditto, 1558–60.]
> vi: [Ditto, 1562–72, including letters relating to the Reformation in
> Scotland, mainly by Knox, 1559–72. Also several works not by, or not
> entirely by, Knox, including the *Book of Common Order*, from the
> Edinburgh 1564 edition, and the *Psalms* in metre, from the Edinburgh
> 1565 edition.]

113. Concilia Scotiae. Ecclesiae Scoticanae statuta tam pro- 6.116
vincialia quam synodalia quae supersunt. MCCXXV–MDLIX.
Edited by Joseph Robertson. 2 vols. 1866.

> Also miscellaneous related docs. *c.* 700–1563. **24**.54 comprises an English
> translation of the statutes and miscellaneous docs.

114. Royal letters, charters, and tracts, relating to the coloniza- 6.117
tion of New Scotland, and the institution of the order of knight
baronets of Nova Scotia, 1621–1638. Edited by David Laing.
1867.

> 1621–61. The four tracts are reprinted from the first editions, London and
> Edinburgh 1620–5.

115. Adversaria. Notices illustrative of some of the earlier works 6.118
printed for the Bannatyne Club. By David Laing. 1867.

> Notes on **6**.2, 3, 13, 17, 26, 32, 39, 44, 49, 60, 67, 70, 71. Also a pamphlet on
> the Gowrie conspiracy, *A short discourse of the good ends of the higher
> providence. . . .*, from the first edition, Edinburgh 1600.

116. The Bannatyne Club. Lists of members and the rules, with 6.119
a catalogue of the books printed for the Bannatyne Club since its
institution in 1823. By David Laing. 1867.

> There are also several earlier catalogues of Bannatyne Club publications.

117. Album of the Bannatyne Club. 3 numbers. 1825–54. 6.120

> Containing lists of works suggested or considered for publication by the club.

118. [Bannatyne garlands.] 10 numbers. [*c*. 1823]–1848. 6.121

All consist of poems on club and antiquarian topics except—
No. 9: Two Bannatyne garlands from Abbotsford. 1848. [Two ballads,
'Captain Ward and the Rainbow' and 'The reever's penance'.]
No. 10: Tears on the death of Evander. Occasioned by the lamentable losse
of the truelie noble and generous, Sir George Swynton, knight. . . . By
George Lauder. 1848. [Verse. From the first edition, The Hague 1630.]

WORKS RELATIVE TO BUT NOT PART OF THE CLUB'S SERIES

A. Notices relative to the Bannatyne Club, instituted in 6.122
February, MDCCCXXIII. Including critiques on some of its
publications. Edited by James Maidment. 1836.

Reviews, etc.

B. Relations politiques de la France et de l'Espagne avec 6.123
l'Écosse au XVIe siècle. Papiers d'état, pièces et documents
inédits ou peu connus tirés des bibliothèques et des archives de
France. Publiés par J. B. Alexandre T. Teulet. New edition. 5
vols. Paris. 1862.

An expansion of **6.110**.
i : Correspondances françaises, 1515–1560.
ii :   „   „   1559–1573.
iii: „   „   1575–1585. [In fact 1576–85.]
iv: „   „   1585–1603.
v : Correspondances espagnoles 1562–1588. [In fact 1563–87.]

C. Fasti Ecclesiae Scoticanae: the succession of ministers in the 6.124
parish churches of Scotland, from the Reformation, A.D. 1560,
to the present time. By Hew Scott. 3 vols. in 6 parts. 1866–71.

Superseded by new edition, 8 vols., 1915–50,
i.   pt. 1: Synod of Lothian and Tweedale.
i.   pt. 2: Synods of Merse and Teviotdale, Dumfries, and Galloway.
ii. pt. 1: Synod of Glasgow and Ayr.
ii. pt. 2: Synods of Fife, and Perth and Stirling.
iii. pt. 1: Synods of Argyll, Glenelg, Moray, Ross, Sutherland and Caithness,
Orkney, and Zetland.
iii. pt. 2 : Synods of Aberdeen, and Angus and Mearns.

D. Correspondence of Sir Robert Kerr, first Earl of Ancram, 6.125
and his son William, third Earl of Lothian. Edited by David
Laing. 2 vols. 1875.

Continuous pagination. Also issued as **17.9** and for general sale.
i : 1616–1649.
ii: 1649–1667. [Also additional letters, 1625–67; psalms in English verse by
Ancram, 1624; letters of John Donne and Drummond of Hawthornden to
Ancram; and accounts for books and paintings purchased for Lothian,
1643–9.]

7. BUTE SCOTTISH RECORD SERIES*

Place of publication: Edinburgh (though this is not always stated).

1. Rothesay parish records. The session book of Rothesay, 1658–1750. Transcribed and edited by Henry Paton. 1931.
    7.1

    Minutes, 1658–61, 1685–8, 1691–1750; notes of a few baptisms, 1673–94; and record of appointment of a schoolmaster, 1680.

2. Kingarth parish records. The session book of Kingarth, 1641–1703. Transcribed and edited by Henry Paton. 1932.
    7.2

    Minutes, 1641, 1648–51, 1664–86, 1691–1700, with additions and variations from draft minutes, 1669–86, 1691–1703. Also notes of a few marriages, 1648–9, 1672–86, and baptisms, 1648–50.

3. Penninghame parish records. The session book of Penning-hame. Vol. i: 1696–1724. Transcribed and edited by Henry Paton. 1933.
    7.3

    Minutes, 1696–1724, and accounts of collection and distribution of the poors' money. Includes a valuation of the parish, 1704.

4. Penninghame parish records. . . . Vol. ii: 1724–1749. . . . 1933.
    7.4

    Minutes, 1724–47, and accounts of collection and distribution of the poors' money, 1724–49.

5. Wigtown parish records. The session book of Wigtown, 1701–1745. Transcribed and edited by Henry Paton. 1934.
    7.5

    Minutes and accounts of the poors' money.

6. Rothesay town council records, 1653–1766. Transcribed by Mary B. Johnston. [Vol. i: 1653–1688.] 1935.
    7.6

    The dates for vol. contents appear on the spine only. Minutes, 1654–88.

7. Rothesay town council records, 1653–1766. . . . [Vol. ii: 1689–1766.] 1935.
    7.7

---

*These volumes were printed for private circulation by John, 4th Marquis of Bute, and on the title pages of 7.1–13 it is stated that they were edited or transcribed 'for' or 'at the instance of' the Marquis. The volumes bear no formal series title or numbering.

The dates for vol. contents appear on the spine only. The vol. lacks a title page, and is paginated continuously with vol. i. Minutes, 1689–1766; burgh charters, 1401, 1584 (Latin, with English translations); list of hearths, 1693; mail (rental) books, 1642, 1659, 1689; and designation of glebe, 1596 (from presbytery minutes, 1658).

8. Dundonald parish records. The session book of Dundonald, 1602–1731. Transcribed and edited by Henry Paton. 1936.   7.8

Minutes, 1602–12, 1628–43, 1702–13, 1717–20, 1724–6, 1729–31.

9. Court book of the regality of Broughton and the burgh of the Canongate, 1569–1573. Transcribed by Marguerite Wood. 1937.   7.9

10. Kirkcudbright town council records, 1576–1604. Transcribed by Mary B. Johnston and Catherine M. Armet. 1939.   7.10

Minutes.

11. Minnigaff parish records. The session book of Minnigaff, 1694–1750. Transcribed and edited by Henry Paton. 1939.   7.11

Minutes, 1694–6, 1699–1710, 1718–50; draft minutes, 1699–1701, 1740; accounts of collections and poors' money, 1695–1737.

12. Kirkcudbright sheriff court deeds, 1623–1675. Transcribed by Mary B. Johnston and Catherine M. Armet. 1939.   7.12

Calendar.

13. Kirkcudbright sheriff court deeds, 1676–1700. Transcribed by Catherine M. Armet. Vol. i. 1953.   7.13

Calendar. 1676–93.

14. Kirkcudbright sheriff court deeds, 1676–1700. . . . Vol. ii. 1953.   7.14

Calendar. 1693–1700. Pagination continuous with vol. i.

15. Kirkcudbright town council records, 1606–1658. Transcribed by John, IV Marquis of Bute and Catherine M. Armet. Vol. i. 1958.   7.15

Minutes, 1606–29.

16. Kirkcudbright town council records, 1606–1658. . . . Vol. ii. 1958.   7.16

Minutes, 1629–58. Pagination continuous with vol. i.

8. CLARENDON HISTORICAL SOCIETY*

Place of publication: Edinburgh.

1. **The Clarendon Historical Society's reprints. Series I. [Edited by Edmund M. Goldsmid.] 1882–1884.**   8.1

The wicked wayes of the cruell Cavaliers. 1644. 1882. (1). [From *A copie of the king's message sent by the Duke of Lenox* . . ., London 1644.]

Two extracts from The Mercurius Caledonius of January 8th, 1661. 1882. (2). [On proclamation of Charles II in Edinburgh, and the funeral of the Marquis of Montrose.]

The devill and the Parliament, or, the Parliament and the devill: a contestation between them for the precedencie. 1882. (3). [From 1648 edition.]

Cheriton fight (March 29th, 1644), being Sir William Balfour's account of the battle in a letter to the Earl of Essex. 1882. (4). [From *Sir William Balfores letter of March 30. 1644*. . ., London 1644.]

Scotiae numisma: or, ancient Scotish coins: their real and proportional value; with some observations on the prices of provisions in Scotland in ancient times, to which is added a notice of Scotish monastic institutions at the period of the Reformation (1738). 1883. (5). [By D. Webster. From *c.* 1738 edition.]

A miraculous victory obtained by the Right Honorable Ferdinando Lord Fairfax, against the army under the command of the Earl of Newcastle at Wakefield in Yorkshire. . . . 1883. (6). [From London 1643 edition.]

A letter from a gentleman in Boston, to Mr George Wishart, one of the ministers of Edinburgh, concerning the state of religion in New-England. 1883. (7). [From Edinburgh 1742 edition.]

A brief discovery of the true mother of the pretended Prince of Wales, known by the name of Mary Grey. . . . By William Fuller. 1883. (8). [From London 1696 edition.]

A letter from the Right Honourable Ferdinando, Lord Fairfax, to His Excellency Robert, Earle of Essex. . . . 1883. (9). [Relating the raising of the siege of Hull, 1643. From London 1643 edition.]

The remonstrance of the state of the kingdom: to which is added the petition

---

* Publications were originally issued in separate parts (which do not always correspond to the individual items), and had two paginations so the items could either be bound separately or with each series forming a single vol. (for which title pages were supplied). Terry treated each item as a separate vol., but each series is catalogued here as a single miscellany vol., with Terry's original numbering appearing in brackets after the item title entries. Terry's numbering for the new and third series is continuous as he failed to realize that there was a separate third series.

41

of the House of Commons which accompanied it. 1883. (10). [From London 1641 edition.]

A historical enquiry concerning Henry Hudson, his friends, relatives, and early life, his connection with the Muscovy Company and discovery of Delaware Bay. Abridged from the work of John Meredith Read, Jr. . . . and edited by Edmund Goldsmid. 1883. (11). [From Albany, New York, 1866 edition.]

A letter from an English traveller at Rome to his father. (1721). Now first printed. 1884. (12). [Describes meetings with James Stuart, the Old Pretender. Ascribed to William Godolphin, Marquis of Blandford. Printed in 1721, and reprinted in **39**.3.]

A king and no king: or, the best argument for a just title. Being the present case of Great Britain, briefly consider'd in a seasonable address to the people. 1884. (13). [From London 1716 edition.]

Considerations upon a printed sheet entitled The speech of the late Lord Russel to the sheriffs: together with the paper delivered by him to them, at the place of execution, on July 21, 1683. 1884. (14). [From London 1683 edition.]

The closing days about Richmond; or, the last days of Sheridan's cavalry. By H. Edwin Tremain. 1884. (15).

The rebellion of 1715. Gathering clouds: being a contemporary account of the events immediately preceding the rebellion. 1884. (16). [Extracts from *The present state of Europe, or historical and political monthly mercury*, 1715.]

The rebellion of 1715. The storm: being a contemporary account of the rebellion. 1884. (17). [Extracts as in preceding item, 1715–16.]

Colchesters teares: affecting & afflicting city & country, dropping from the sad face of a new warr threatning to bury in her own ashes that woful town. . . . 1884. (18). [From London 1648 edition.]

2. The Clarendon Historical Society's reprints. Series II. [Edited by Edmund M. Goldsmid.] 1884–6. 8.2

[Title pages of individual parts call this the New Series.]

The journal of King Edward's reign, written with his own hand. From the original in the Cotton Library (Nero *c*. 10). 1884. (1). [1537–49.]

Lex talionis; or, a declaration against Mr Challener, the crimes of the times and the manners of you know whom. 1885. (2). [Royalist tract, against Thomas Chaloner. From 1647 edition.]

Gallienus redivivius; or, murther will out, etc., being a true account of the de-Witting of Glencoe, Gaffney, etc. 1885. (3). [From the Edinburgh 1695 edition.]

The several declarations made in council concerning the birth of the Prince of Wales. (4). [From the London 1688 edition.]

Memoirs of the Chevalier de St George, with some private passages of the life of the late King James II. 1712. Never before published. 1885. (5). [From London 1712 edition.]

A faithful memorial of that remarkable meeting of many officers of the army in England, at Windsor Castle, in the year 1648. 1885. (6). [From London 1659 edition.]

A dialogue between a Whig and a Jacobite upon the subject of the late rebellion and the execution of the rebel lords, etc. 1715–16. 1885. (7). [From London 1716 edition.]

An account of the execution of Mary, Queen of Scots. 1886. (8). [Letter dated 11 Feb. 1587 from Robert Wyngfield to William Cecil, Lord Burghley. From London 1752 edition.]

Twenty lookes over all the Round-heads that ever lived in the world. 1886. (9). [From 1643 edition.]

The memoirs of George Leyburn. Being a journal of his agency for Prince Charles in Ireland in the year 1647. 1886. (10). [From London 1722 edition.]

The character of a modern Whig, or an alamode true loyal Protestant. 1886. (11). [From London 1681 edition.]

A letter from his excellencie the Lord General Monck, and the officers under his command, to the parliament in the name of themselves and the souldiers under them. 1886. (12). [From London 1660 edition.]

Explanatory notes of a pack of Cavalier playing cards, temp. Charles II. Forming a complete political satire of the Commonwealth. By Edmund M. Goldsmid. 1886. (16). [A supplement to the second series. Also issued as 4.5]

3. The Clarendon Historical Society's reprints. Series III. [Edited by Edmund M. Goldsmid.] 1886–8.

8.3

Seditious preachers, ungodly teachers. 1887. (13). [Denunciation of the ministers ejected from the Church of England under the 1662 act of uniformity. From London 1709 edition.]

The massacres of Saint Bartholomew. 1888. (2). [Late 19th century anti-Catholic tract.]

An ordinance appointing commissioners for approbation of publique preachers. 1889. (15). [From 1653 edition.]

9. DUMFRIESSHIRE AND GALLOWAY NATURAL HISTORY AND ANTIQUARIAN SOCIETY

Place of publication: Dumfries, unless otherwise stated.

RECORDS OF THE WEST MARCHES

1. An introduction to the history of Dumfries. By Robert Edgar. Edited with an introduction and extensive annotations by R. C. Reid. 1915.   9.1

> Written *c.* 1746 by the clerk of the incorporated trades of Dumfries, and printed from a ms. of 1791. Also charters and other papers relating to Dumfries (some Latin), mid-12th century–1709; burgh accounts, 1590–1, 1612–13, 1627–8, 1633–4, 1662–3; and burgh customs accounts, 1578, 1580.

2. The Bell family in Dumfriesshire. By James Steuart. 1932.   9.2

3. The Upper Nithsdale coalworks from Pictish times to 1925. Compiled by J. C. I. McConnel. Gillingham, Dorset. 1962.   9.3

> Includes extracts from the reminiscences of the compiler's grandmother, John [*sic*] Anne McConnel, d. 1917, and father, James Irving McConnel, d. 1957.

RECORD TEXT PUBLICATIONS

1. 1980. Vol. i.   9.4

> Girthon memorials. An alphabetical index of the memorials in the Old Churchyard of Girthon. By W. James Wolffe.
> Cassillis estate rental 1614/1615. Transcribed by A. E. Truckell from a ms. in the Nithsdale District Archives.
> A Dumfries rental for 1674. Transcribed by A. E. Truckell. [Burgh stent roll.]
> The Dumfries burgess lists. By A. E. Truckell. [Lists of burgesses entered '1644–1727 and 1724–present'.]

10. GLASGOW UNIVERSITY, DEPARTMENT OF SCOTTISH HISTORY, OCCASIONAL PAPERS

Place of publication: Glasgow.

1. James I, 1424–1437. By Archibald A. M. Duncan. 1976.   **10.1**

A revised 2nd edition of the essay was published in 1984 with the title *James I, King of Scots, 1424–1437*.

2. Formulary E. Scottish letters and brieves, 1286–1424. Edited   **10.2**
by Archibald A. M. Duncan. 1976.

Latin, with brief English abstracts. From a late 15th century ms.

11. GRAMPIAN CLUB

Place of publication: London, unless stated otherwise.

1. Scotland social and domestic. Memorials of life and manners in North Britain. By Charles Rogers. 1869.   **11.1**

2. The Jacobite lairds of Gask. By T. L. Kington Oliphant. 1870.   **11.2**
   Oliphants of Gask. Includes many miscellaneous docs., 18th century.

3. Monuments and monumental inscriptions in Scotland. By Charles Rogers. 2 vols. 1871–2.   **11.3**

4. Registrum monasterii S. Marie de Cambuskenneth. A.D. 1147–1535. Edited by Sir William Fraser. Edinburgh. 1872.   **11.4**
   Transcript of original charters, mid 12th–early 16th centuries, made in 1535.

5. Genealogical collections concerning the Scottish house of Edgar. With a memoir of James Edgar, private secretary to the Chevalier St George. Edited by a committee of the Grampian Club. 1873.   **11.5**
   Includes many extracts from docs.

6. Estimate of the Scottish nobility during the minority of James the Sixth. With preliminary observations by Charles Rogers. 1873.   **11.6**
   By Alexander Hay (later Lord Easter Kennet), 1577. Also other lists of the nobility, 1584–1602.

7. Boswelliana. The commonplace book of James Boswell. With a memoir and annotations by Charles Rogers and introductory remarks by the Right Honourable Lord Houghton. 1874.   **11.7**
   Late 1770s–early 1780s.

8. Liber protocollorum M. Cuthberti Simonis notarii publici et scribae capituli Glasguensis, A.D. 1499–1513. Also rental book of diocese of Glasgow, A.D. 1509–1570. Edited by Joseph Bain and Charles Rogers. 2 vols. 1875.   **11.8**

i: [Rental book (Latin, with English translations, and English); the will of Archbishop James Beaton, 1603 (French, with English translation); and English abstracts of the protocols in vol. ii.]

ii: [Liber protocollorum. Simon's protocols relate to the diocese of Glasgow. Also some anon. protocols relating mainly to Ayrshire, especially Irvine.

9. Three Scottish reformers. Alexander Cunningham, fifth Earl of Glencairn, Henry Balnaves of Halhill and John Davidson, minister of Prestonpans. With their poetical remains and Mr Davidson's 'Helps for young scholars in Christianity'. Edited, with memoirs, by Charles Rogers. 1876. **11.9**

Late 16th–early 17th centuries. *Helps* reprinted from the Edinburgh 1602 edition. Also issued by the English Reprint Society, 1874.

10. Leaves from my autobiography. By Charles Rogers. 1876. **11.10**

Rogers was born in 1825. Also issued for general sale. Stated in **11.19** not to be a Club publication, but the Club's name appears on the title page of some copies. Second edition 1896.

11. Life of George Wishart, the Scottish martyr. With his translation of the Helvetian Confession, and a genealogical history of the family of Wishart. By Charles Rogers. 1876. **11.11**

The Confession is reprinted from **43.11**.

12. The charters of the priory of Beauly. With notices of the priories of Pluscardine and Ardchattan and of the family of the founder, John Byset. By Edmund C. Batten. 1877. **11.12**

Charters (Latin, with English abstracts), 1231–1568; miscellaneous docs. (Latin and English), 13th–19th centuries.

13. Genealogical memoirs of the family of Sir Walter Scott, bart., of Abbotsford. With a reprint of his Memorials of the Haliburtons. By Charles Rogers. 1877. **11.13**

Memorials from Edinburgh 1824 edition. Also issued by the Royal Historical Society (A. T. Milne, *Centenary Guide* (1968), p. 137).

14. Historical notices of St Anthony's monastery, Leith, and Rehearsal of events which occurred in the North of Scotland from 1635 to 1645 in relation to the National Covenant. Edited from a contemporary ms. By Charles Rogers. 1877. **11.14**

Includes obits, 1439–1528, and list of benefactors (both also printed in **6.21**); forms of prayer and absolution; and regulations etc., all from the 'Rentale buke' of St Anthony's Hospital and Newhaven (Latin, with English translations); and an early 17th century inventory of South Leith kirk session writs relating to St Anthony's, 1444–1606. The 'Rehearsal' is by 'a friend of Dr Alexander's, at Aberdeen', perhaps Dr John Alexander himself.

15. Register of the collegiate church of Crail. With introductory   **11.15**
remarks by Charles Rogers. 1877.

    Calendar. Charters, inventories, etc., 1499–1555.

16. Genealogical memoirs of John Knox and of the family of   **11.16**
Knox. By Charles Rogers. 1879.

    Also issued by the Royal Historical Society (Milne, *Centenary Guide*, p. 137).

17. Rental book of the Cistercian abbey of Cupar-Angus, with   **11.17**
the breviary of the register. Edited by Charles Rogers. 2 vols.
1879–80.

    Also issued by the British Topographical Society, with both vols. dated 1880.
    i: [Rental book (English, partly translated from Latin), 1443–1536; and
       register (Latin), 12th–15th centuries, from a 17th century abbreviated
       transcript. Also rental, 1562; and inventory of jewels, 1296.]
    ii: [Register of tacks, 1539–59; rental, 1542; extracts from accounts of Thirds
       of Benefices, 1563; miscellaneous charters, 12th century–1609 (Latin, with
       English abstracts); and extracts from a 1724 inventory of Lord Balmerino's
       writs, 1492–1618.]

18. Chartulary of the Cistercian priory of Coldstream. With   **11.18**
relative documents. Edited by Charles Rogers. 1879.

    Transcript of original charters, 12th–early 15th centuries, made in 1434
    (Latin, with English abstracts); relative charters and docs., 12th century–
    1538 (Latin and French, mainly with English abstracts).

19. The Grampian Club for editing and printing works in   **11.19**
Scottish history and antiquities. Patron H.R.H. the Prince of
Wales. President his Grace the Duke of Athole, K.T. 1879.

    Lists of Grampian Club publications, and of vols. not in the Club series but
    issued by the Club's secretary (Charles Rogers) and supplied by him to
    members; lists of members and office holders; and the laws of the Club.

20. History of the Chapel Royal of Scotland. With the register of   **11.20**
the Chapel Royal of Stirling. Including details in relation to the
rise and progress of Scottish music and observations respecting
the Order of the Thistle. By Charles Rogers. Edinburgh. 1882.

    Register (Latin), 1501–37. Also transcripts and extracts of miscellaneous
    docs. (Latin and English), 1407–1692.

21. Social life in Scotland from early to recent times. By Charles   **11.21**
Rogers. 3 vols. Edinburgh. 1884–6.

22. The book of Wallace. By Charles Rogers. 2 vols. Edinburgh.   **11.22**
1889.

    i : [Genealogies of Wallaces.]
    ii: [William Wallace (d. 1305) and the War of Independence.]

23. The book of Robert Burns. Genealogical and historical   **11.23**
memoirs of the poet, his associates and those celebrated in his
writings. By Charles Rogers. 3 vols. Edinburgh. 1889–91.

> i: [Includes 'Verses on the memory of Burns', by the Rev. Henry Duncan
> (1774–1846).]
> iii: The lineage of the poet, by Charles Rogers. The life of the poet, by J. C.
> Higgins. [Includes 'Manual of religious belief', by the poet's father
> William; and Burns' commonplace books, 1783–c. 1789.]

WORKS RELATIVE TO BUT NOT PART OF THE CLUB'S SERIES*

A. Genealogical chart of the family of Bain, Co. Haddington.   **11.24**
Compiled from original and authentic sources by Charles
Rogers. 1871.

B. The Scottish branch of the Norman house of Roger. With a   **11.25**
genealogical sketch of the family of Playfair. By Charles Rogers.
1872.

> See **11.28**.

C. The staggering state of Scottish statesmen from 1550 to 1650.   **11.26**
By Sir John Scot of Scotstarvet, with a memoir of the author and
historical illustrations by Charles Rogers. Edinburgh. 1872.

> Scotstarvet lived 1585–1670. Based on the Edinburgh 1754 edition. Also
> Walter Goodal's 'A short account of the officers of state, and other great
> officers in Scotland', from the same edition.

D. Memorials of the Strachans, baronets of Thornton, Kin-   **11.27**
cardineshire, and of the family of Wise of Hillbank, formerly
Wyse of Lunan, in the county of Forfar. By Charles Rogers.
[1873.]

> See **11.31**.

E. The Scottish house of Roger. With notes respecting the   **11.28**
families of Playfair and Haldane of Bermony. By Charles Rogers.
Second edition. Edinburgh. 1875.

> **11.25** is regarded as forming the first edition.

F. Genealogical memoirs of the family of Robert Burns and of   **11.29**
the Scottish house of Burnes. By Charles Rogers. 1877.

> Issued by the Royal Historical Society, but not listed in Milne, *Centenary
> Guide*.

---

* Vols. O–R (**11.38–41**) are not in Terry's *Catalogue*, but are listed in **11.19** as supplied
to members. Vol. A is listed by Terry but does not appear in **11.19**.

G. Memorials of the Earl of Stirling and of the house of Alexander. By Charles Rogers. 2 vols. Edinburgh. 1877.   **11.30**

> Vol. ii includes charters, 1621 and 1625, and the first Earl of Stirling's 'Anacrisis; or, a censure of poets ancient and modern', *c*. 1634.

H. Memorials of the Scottish families of Strachan and Wise. By Charles Rogers. 1877.   **11.31**

> Revised second edition of **11.27**.

I. Genealogical memoirs of the Scottish house of Christie, compiled from family papers and the public records. By Charles Rogers. 1878.   **11.32**

> Issued by the Royal Historical Society (see Milne, *Centenary Guide*, p. 137).

J. Genealogical memoirs of the families of Colt and Coutts. By Charles Rogers. 1879.   **11.33**

> Issued by the Royal Historical Society and the Cottonian Society (see Milne, *Centenary Guide*, p. 137).

K. The Earl of Stirling's register of royal letters relative to the affairs of Scotland and Nova Scotia from 1615 to 1635. [Edited by Charles Rogers.] 2 vols. Edinburgh. 1885.   **11.34**

> i : [1615–29.]
> ii: [1630–5.]

L. Four Perthshire families. Roger, Playfair, Constable and Haldane of Barmony. By Charles Rogers. Edinburgh. 1887.   **11.35**

M. Memorials of the Scottish family of Glen. By Charles Rogers. Edinburgh. 1888.   **11.36**

N. Memorials of the Scottish house of Gourlay. By Charles Rogers. Edinburgh. 1888.   **11.37**

O. The poems of Sir Robert Aytoun, secretary to the queens of James VI and Charles I. With a memoir, from original sources, by Charles Rogers. 1871.   **11.38**

> English and Latin. Rogers' edition was first published in 1844. Ayton lived 1570–1638. See **6.20** and **34.1** for other editions.

P. The poetical remains of King James the First of Scotland. With a memoir and an introduction to the poetry by Charles Rogers. Edinburgh. 1873.   **11.39**

Q. Life and songs of the Baroness Nairne, with a memoir, and poems of Caroline Oliphant the Younger. Edited by Charles Rogers. Edinburgh. 1869. 11.40

Carolina Oliphant, Lady Nairne, lived 1766–1845, her niece Caroline 1807–31. Second edition, enlarged, 1869; third edition, 1872.

R. Memorials and recollections of the Very Reverend Edward Bannerman Ramsay, LL.D., F.R.S.E., Dean of Edinburgh. By Charles Rogers. 1873. 11.41

Ramsay d. 1872. Includes letters of Ramsay to Rogers.

12.   HUNTERIAN CLUB

Place of publication: [Glasgow.]

1. The Bannatyne Manuscript. Compiled by George Bannatyne. 1568. 4 vols. 1896.   **12.1**

> Verse. Originally issued in 11 pts., 1873–1901. Pts. 8–11 should form vol. i, pts. 1–7 should form vols. ii–iv (pagination continuous), but sets arranged differently retaining the original title pages occur. For another edition see **32.22, 23, 26** and **33.5**.

2. The poetical works of Alexander Craig of Rose-Craig. 1604–31. Now first collected. Edited by David Laing. 1873.   **12.2**

> From first editions, 1604–31.

3. Sir Thomas Overburies vision. By Richard Niccols. 1616. With introduction by James Maidment. 1873.   **12.3**

> Verse. From the first edition, 1616.

4. The poetical works of Patrick Hannay, A.M. MDCXXII. With a memoir of the author. Edited by David Laing. 1875.   **12.4**

> From the first edition, London 1622.

5. A theatre of Scottish worthies: and the lyf, doings, and deathe of William Elphinston, Bishop of Aberdeen. By Alexander Garden, advocate, Aberdeen. 1878.   **12.5**

> Verse. From the first editions, Aberdeen *c*. 1626 and 1619 respectively.

6. The complete works of Samuel Rowlands, 1598–1628. Now first collected. 3 vols. 1880.   **12.6**

> Mainly verse. From the first editions, 1598–1628 and 1682. Pagination separate for each item. See also **12.8**.

7. The complete works of Thomas Lodge (1580–1623?). Now first collected. 4 vols. 1883.   **12.7**

> Partly verse. Mainly from first editions *c*. 1580–*c*. 1623. Pagination separate for each item.

8. Aue Caesar. God saue the king. By Samuel Rowlands. Reprinted from the unique original 1603. 1886.   **12.8**

> Verse. Usually bound in **12.6**, vol. i, in accordance with new page of contents issued with **12.9**.

9. Concluding part of the Hunterian Club issues. Containing   **12.9**
several notices of the club, complete list of the works issued to
members, complete list of the works arranged in the proper
order for binding, reprinted page of contents for vol. i of
Rowland's works. 1902.

Includes details of the sixty-eight individual parts in which the works were
originally issued.

13. IONA CLUB

Place of publication: Edinburgh.

1. Collectanea de rebus Albanicis, consisting of original papers **13.1**
and documents relating to the history of the Highlands and
Islands of Scotland. Edited by the Iona Club. 1847.

> Original documents. Communicated by Donald Gregory.
> Documents illustrative of the history of Icolmkill and the bishoprick of the
> Isles. [c. 1561–81. Concluded below.]
> Documents illustrative of the custom of fosterage in the Highlands. [1641,
> 1665.]
> Miscellaneous documents. [1508–1610. Include John Elder's proposal for
> uniting England and Scotland, 1542, and rolls of Highland clans,
> landlords, etc., 1587 and 1594. Concluded below.]
> Genealogies of the Highland clans, extracted from ancient Gaelic mss. With
> translation and notes, by William F. Skene. [From a ms. of c. 1450.
> Concluded below.]
> Extracts from the Norse sagas, illustrative of the early history of the north of
> Scotland, and of the influence of the Norwegian pirates upon its
> inhabitants. Translated, with notes, by William F. Skene. [Concluded
> below.]
> The Gaelic poem 'A eolcha Albain uile', written circiter A.D. 1057, and
> edited from the Codex Stowensis, no. XLI; with a translation and note by
> William F. Skene.
> Original documents continued. Communicated by Donald Gregory.
> Contracts of friendship, bonds of maintenance and manrent, and other
> similar documents. [1467–1587. Concluded below.]
> Documents illustrative of the history of the fisheries in the West Highlands
> and Isles. [1566–1635.]
> Documents illustrative of the state of education, religion, and morals, in
> the dioceses of the Isles and Argyle, in the reigns of James VI and Charles
> I. [1607–31.]
> Documents illustrative of the history of the Clan Gregor. [1603–13.]
> Documents connected with the succession to the estates possessed by
> William Macleod of Dunvegan, who died in the year 1553. [1553–72.]
> Documents connected with the general intercourse of trade between the
> Highlands and Lowlands, and more particularly the trade of cattle-dealing
> in the Highlands and Isles. [1565–1622.]
> Miscellaneous documents continued. [1528–1613.]
> Documents illustrative of the history of Icolmkill and the bishoprick of the
> Isles. [1588–1635. Continued from above.]

Documents connected with the preservation of game, woods, etc. in the Highlands and Isles. [1584–1628.]

Contracts of friendship, bonds of maintenance and manrent, and other similar documents. [1572–1673. Continued from above.]

Extracts from the Irish annalists, illustrative of the early history of the Highlands of Scotland. With a literal English translation by William F. Skene. [502–1153.]

Fragment of a manuscript history of the Macdonalds, written in the reign of Charles II. From the Gregory collections. [With notes by William F. Skene.]

Extracts from the Norse sagas concluded. Translated by William F. Skene. Genealogies of the Highland clans, extracted from ancient Gaelic mss. With translation and notes by William F. Skene. [c. 1450–c. 1550. Continued from above.]

Notices of the Highland dress and armour, collected from various sources, and arranged for the transactions of the Iona Club, collected by Donald Gregory and Willaim F. Skene.

14. LITERARY AND ANTIQUARIAN SOCIETY OF PERTH, TRANSACTIONS

Place of publication: Perth.

1. Vol. i. 1827.

Copies of papers relative to a projected translation of the University of St Andrews to the city of Perth, in the years 1697 and 1698.

The lives of the bishops of Dunkeld. [Translation (early 18th century) from the Latin, for which see **6**.1. For another translation see **25**.10. Written early 16th century by Alexander Myln, and covers *c*. 1127–*c*. 1516.]

Scotland's teares. By William Lithgow. [Verse. Written on the death of James VI and I.]

Summary of the evidence on the Gowrie conspiracy, with plans of Gowrie House. [1600.]

List of lands and baronies contained in the seizin of James, Master of Gowrie. [Abstract. 11 April 1584.]

Gift of Donald M'Donald, as a perpetual servant, to the Earl of Tullibardine. December 5, 1701. [By the commissioners of justiciary of the south district, for securing the peace of the Highlands.]

Lithograpahic copies and descriptions of three ivory Pali tablets, with inscriptions in massy gold, found in the temple of Rangoon.

The history of Scottish affaires, particularly during the reign of Charles I, by Mr James Wilson, burgher of Dumfries. Begun the Calends of May, 1654. [In spite of the title page's claims as to the 'impartiall labour and faithful study and diligence' of Wilson, the ms. is a version of the memoirs of Henry Guthry, Bishop of Dunkeld (1600?–1676), which circulated widely in manuscript before being published London 1702 (second edition Glasgow 1748).]

Museum of the Literary and Antiquarian Society of Perth. [Catalogue.]

15.   MAITLAND CLUB

Place of publication: Edinburgh, unless otherwise stated.

1. The history of the house of Seytoun to the year MDLIX. By Sir Richard Maitland of Lethington, knight. With the continuation, by Alexander Viscount Kingston, to MDCLXXXVII. Edited by John Fullarton. Glasgow. 1829.
    Also issued as **6.34**, which see for details.

15.1

2. Histoire de la guerre d'Ecosse: pendant les campagnes 1548 et 1549. Par Jean de Beaugué. [Edited by Joseph Bain.] 1830.
    From the first edition, Paris 1556.

15.2

3. Memoirs of the affairs of Scotland. By David Moysie. MDLXXVII–MDCIII. From early manuscripts. [Edited by James Dennistoun.] 1830.
    Also issued as **6.42**, which see for details.

15.3

4. The poems of Sir Richard Maitland, of Lethingtoun, knight. With an appendix of selections from the poems of Sir John Maitland, Lord Thirlestane, and of Thomas Maitland. [Edited by Joseph Bain.] Glasgow. 1830.
    Sir Richard d. 1586; Sir John *d.* 1595; Thomas d. 1572.

15.4

5. Register of ministers, exhorters and readers, and of their stipends, after the period of the Reformation. Presented by Alexander Macdonald. 1830.
    Probably compiled by Mr John Gray, *c.* 1567–73. Also related docs., 1566; and extracts from the books of assignations of stipends, 1576.

15.5

6. Babell; a satirical poem, on the proceedings of the General Assembly in the year MDCXCII. Presented by George R. Kinloch. 1830.
    By Dr Archibald Pitcairne.

15.6

7. The diary of Mr John Lamont of Newton. 1649–1671. [Edited by George R. Kinloch.] 1830.
    Sometimes referred to as *The chronicle of Fife*, the title given to an edition published in 1810. Also memoranda by Moncreiff of Carnbee, 1566–1606.

15.7

8. A chronicle of the kings of Scotland, from Fergus the First, to James the Sixth, in the year MDCXI. Presented by John W. Mackenzie. 1830.   **15.8**

> Early 17th century ms. Up to 1561 the work is a translation by David Chalmers of a French history first published in Paris in 1572; 1561–73 is an abridgement and translation of George Buchanan's *Rerum Scoticarum historia*; 1573–1611 is evidently an original anonymous work.

9. Clariodus; a Scotish metrical romance. Printed from a manuscript of the sixteenth century. [Edited by David Irving.] 1830.   **15.9**

10. The chronicle of Perth; a register of remarkable occurrences, chiefly connected with that city, from the year 1210 to 1668. Presented by James Maidment. 1831.   **15.10**

> Sometimes referred to as Mercer's chronicle, though John Mercer was the author of only a few entries in this composite work. Also extracts from the kirk session minutes of Perth, 1577–1632; and a transcript of the trial of David Roy, cook, before Perth sheriff court in 1601.

11. Registrum metellanum. Vol. i. 1831.   **15.11**

> A list of mss., drawing attention to them and suggesting their suitability for publication by the Maitland Club. No other vols. issued.

12. Descriptions of the sheriffdoms of Lanark and Renfrew, compiled about MDCCX, by William Hamilton of Wishaw. With illustrative notes and appendices. Edited by John Dillon and John Fullarton. Glasgow. 1831.   **15.12**

> Also testament of James Law, Archbishop of Glasgow, 1632; other descriptions of the shires, *c.* 1650–1720; and charters and other docs., *c.* 1116–1517 (mainly Latin). Also issued for general sale and as **16.3** (dated 1878).

13. Inventory of the ornaments, reliques, jewels, vestments, books, etc. belonging to the cathedral church of Glasgow, MCCCCXXXII. With observations on the catalogue of books. Edited by John Dillon. Glasgow. 1831.   **15.13**

> Latin. Also charters concerning vestments and the office of sacristan, 1293–1459.

14. Notices and documents illustrative of the literary history of Glasgow during the greater part of last century. Edited by William J. Duncan. Glasgow. 1831.   **15.14**

> Notes on Glasgow printers, 17th and 18th centuries; and docs., 1713–76, mainly relating to Robert and Andrew Foulis.

15. The moral fables of Robert Henryson. Reprinted from the edition of Andrew Hart. [Edited by David Irving.] Glasgow. 1832.

15.15

From Edinburgh 1621 edition.

16. Burgh records of the city of Glasgow, MDLXXIII–MDLXXXI. Edited by John Smith. Glasgow. 1832.

15.16

Extracts from court and council records and accounts. Also charter to Glasgow University, 1572 (Latin). An index to the vol. was issued in 1834.

17. Registrum monasterii de Passelet. Cartas privilegia conventiones aliaque munimenta complectens a domo fundata A.D. MCLXIII usque ad A.D. MDXXIX ad fidem codicis ms. in bibliotheca facultatis juridicae Edinensis servati nunc primum typis mandatum. [Edited by Cosmo Innes.] 1832.

15.17

Paisley Abbey. Early 16th century ms. Also issued as **16**.1 dated 1877.

18. The poems of William Drummond of Hawthornden. [Edited by Thomas Maitland.] 1832.

15.18

From various editions, 1616–1711, and mss. Also the prose 'A cypresse grove'. For other editions see **3**.6 and **32**.3, 4.

19. Ancient criminal trials in Scotland; compiled from the original records and mss., with historical illustrations etc. By Robert Pitcairn. 3 vols. in 7 pts. 1833.

15.19

Also issued as **6**.45 (which see for details) and for general sale. Terry, *Catalogue*, incorrectly gives Maitland Club sets the title used for the general sale sets.

20. The history of the troubles and memorable transactions in Scotland and England, from MDCXXIV to MDCXLV. By John Spalding. Edited by James Skene. 2 vols. 1828–9.

15.20

Also issued as **6**.28, which see for details. For a better edition see **36**.21, 23.

21. Memoirs of his own life. By Sir James Melville of Halhill. MDXLIX–MDXCIII. From the original manuscript. Edited by Thomas Thomson. 1833.

15.21

Also issued as **6**.19 (dated 1827), which see for details.

22. Memoirs of the war carried on in Scotland and Ireland. MDCLXXXIX–MDCXCI. By Major General Hugh Mackay, commander in chief of his majesty's forces. With an appendix of original papers. [Edited by James M. Hog, Patrick F. Tytler and Adam Urquhart.] 1833.

15.22

Also issued as **6**.48, which see for details.

23. A diurnal of remarkable occurrents that have passed within the country of Scotland since the death of King James the Fourth till the year MDLXXV. From a manuscript of the sixteenth century, in the possession of Sir John Maxwell of Pollok, baronet. Edited by Thomas Thomson. 1833.

15.23

> Also issued as **6.46**, which see for details.

24. Cartularium comitatus de Levenax ab initio seculi decimi tertii usque ad annum MCCCXCVIII. Ad fidem apographi in bibliotheca facultatis juridicae Edinensis servati cum aliis mss. collati. Edited by James Dennistoun. 1833.

15.24

> Earldom of Lennox. Late 12th century–*c*. 1398, from 18th century transcripts of the cartulary. Also additional charters, early 13th century–1400, 1680.

25. Miscellany of the Maitland Club. Consisting of original papers and other documents illustrative of the history and literature of Scotland. [Edited by James Dennistoun and Alexander Macdonald. Vol. i, pt. 1.] 1833.

15.25

> The library of Mary Queen of Scots, and of King James the Sixth. [1576–1602.]
> The archearis of our Soverane Ladyis Gaird. MDLXII–MDLXVII. [Accounts of payments to Mary Queen of Scots' bodyguard.]
> Contract of marriage betwixt Alexander Ogilvy of Boyne, and Mary Bethune, daughter of Robert Bethune of Creich, May 3, 1566.
> Extracts from the registers of the presbytery of Glasgow, from November 1592 to March 1601.
> Extracts from the buik of the general kirk of Edinburgh, in the years 1574 and 1575.
> Extracts from the registers of the kirk session of the burgh of Stirling, from November 1597 to December 1600.
> Obligation by John Earl of Cassillis, to make certain payments to his brother Hugh Kennedy of Brunston, upon his taking the laird of Auchindrain's life, Sept. 4 1602. [John Muir of Auchindrain was suspected of murdering Sir Thomas Kennedy of Cullean.]
> Letter from King James VI to the Privy Council of Scotland, and proclamation by the Privy Council, anent the robes of earls, judges, magistrates, churchmen, advocates, clerks of the Session and signet, in the years 1606 and 1610.
> The household account of Ludovick Duke of Lennox when commissioner to the Parliament of Scotland in the year 1607.
> Indenture of a horse race betwixt the Earls of Morton and Abercorn and the Lord Boyd, dated at Hamilton, Aug. 15 1621.

25A. Miscellany of the Maitland Club. . . . Vol. i, [pt. 2.] 1834.

15.26

> Letters from Henry II king of France to his cousin Mary Queen Dowager of Scotland, MDXLV–MDLIV. [French. See also note at end of **15.53**.]
> Letters of Mary Queen of Scots during her residence in France to her mother Mary the Queen Dowager of Scotland. [French. 1558–9.]

Act for sequestrating the quenis majesties person, and detening the same in the hous and place of Lochlevin, xvi Jun. MDLXVII.

Royal letters and other original documents addressed to the lairds of Barnbarroch. MDLIX–MDCXVIII. [Vaus or Waus of Barnbarroch.]

Cathologus librorum quos vir eximius et beate memorie magister Clemens Litill Edinburgene ecclesie et ministris ejusdem obiens legavit et consecravit. MDLXXX.

Inventories of buikis in the colleges of Sanctandrois, MDLXXXCIII–MDCXII. [Partly Latin.]

The testament and lettir will of Mr John Johnstoun ane of the principall maisters of the New College of St Androis, anno MDCXI.

De jure prelationis nobilium Scotiae—a memorial of the writes and evidents produced be sundry earles and lords before the commissioners deput be the kings majesty anent the precedency and priority of dignitie, anno MDCVI. [Also 'Decreit anent the ranking and placeing of the nobilitie of Scotland in thair ordour in Parliaments and Generall Counselis. V Martii MDCVI'.]

Extracts from the registers of the presbytery of Glasgow, from November 1603 to August 1626.

Extracts from the register of the kirk session of Cambusnethan, from April 1636 to September 1695.

Extracts from the register of the kirk session of Humbie, from October 1644 to April 1655.

Extracts from the register of the kirk session of Stirling, from May 1601 to November 1649.

Petition for a toleration to the stang, with the proceedings of the regality court of Huntly thereon, January 1734. [Traditional punishment for wife-beating.]

26. Miscellaneous papers, principally illustrative of events in the reigns of Queen Mary and King James VI. Edited by William J. Duncan. Glasgow. 1834.   15.27

Carta Gulielmi Gordon, episcopi Aberdonensis, de receptione magistri Joannis Watsoun, in sacris literis licentiati, in canonicum ecclesie de Aberdene. IX Julii MDXLVII. [From a copy dated 1550.]

Inuentaires des ornaments d'eglise receus du secretain de la chapelle de Strellin, 1562, et des habillements et aultres choses enuoyes a la royne d'Escosse, tant durant le temps qu'elle estoict a Lochlin que depuys, commensant en Jullet, 1567.

Private letters to James Betoun, Archbishop of Glasgow, while ambassador at the court of France, principally from his servants in Scotland, MDLXIX–MDLXXXVIII.

Letter from Sir William Maitland of Lethingtoun to James Betoun, Archbishop of Glasgow, XXVIII August MDLXXI. [Also a related discharge, 1571 (French).]

Testament de Jacques de Betoun, Archevesque de Glasco, embassadeur pour le roy Descosse, en France, les jours le vingt troisieme et le vingt quatriesme davril, mil sixcens troys.

Relatio incarcerationis et martyrii P. Joannis Ogilbei. 1615. [Reprinted from first edition, Douai 1615. Also other papers relating to Ogilvie.]

Escriptura de fundacion y dotacion del seminario de colegeales seglares Escoceses en la villa de Madrid, X de Mayo MDCXXVII.

Ane copie of the testament of Coronel William Semple, X February MDCXXXIII.

[All items in this volume are from transcripts of documents formerly in the archives of the Scots College in Paris. Also documents relating to the college's archives, 1716–97; inventory of jewels of the chapel royal at Stirling, 1505 (Latin); and other papers relating to the chapel, 1501 and 1562.]

27. Records of the burgh of Prestwick in the sheriffdom of Ayr. MCCCCLXX–MDCCLXXXII. With an appendix and illustrative notes. Edited by John Fullarton. Glasgow. 1834. **15.28**

1470–1616, 1693, 1726–82. Appendix, 1446, 1487–9, 1540, 1600, 1730 (some Latin).

28. Illustrations of Scottish history, from the twelfth to the sixteenth century; selected from unpublished manuscripts in the British Museum, and the Tower of London. Edited by Joseph Stevenson. Glasgow. 1834. **15.29**

Latin and English. Contents listed in Terry, *Catalogue*.

29. The works of George Dalgarno of Aberdeen. Edited by Thomas Maitland. 1834. **15.30**

Ars signorum, vulgo character universalis et lingua philosophica from the first edition, London 1661; *Didascalocophus, or the deaf and dumb mans tutor, to which is added a discourse of the nature and number of double consonants*, from the first edition, Oxford 1680.

30. The works of Sir Thomas Urquhart of Cromarty, knight. Reprinted from the original editions. [Edited by Thomas Maitland.] 1834. **15.31**

Some verse. From 1641–53 editions. Includes epigrams, and works on mathematics, the genealogy of the Urquharts, and a universal language.

31. History of Mary Queen of Scots; a fragment; translated from the original French of Adam Blackwood. [Edited by Alexander Macdonald.] 1834. **15.32**

c. 1565–87. Blackwood's work was first published 1587, and the translation dates from *c.* 1600.

32. Collections upon the lives of the reformers and most eminent ministers of the church of Scotland. By the Rev. Robert Wodrow, minister of the Gospel at Eastwood. Edited by William J. Duncan. 2 vols. in 3 pts. Glasgow. 1834–48. **15.33**

Wodrow d. 1734.

i: [John Erskine of Dun, John Spottiswoode, John Willock, John Winram, Bishop John Carswell, Bishop Alexander Gordon, Robert Pont, James Boyd of Trochrig, Archbishop George Gladstanes, and related docs., 1559–1638 (some Latin).]

ii. pt. 1: [Robert Boyd of Trochrig.]
ii. pt. 2: [David Wemyss, John Cameron, and docs. relating to Robert Boyd, 1596–1650 (mainly Latin).]

33. Certane tractatis for reformatioun of doctryne and maneris in Scotland. By Niniane Winzet. MDLXII–MDLXIII. [Edited by David Laing.] 1835.   15.34

From the first edition, Edinburgh 1562. Also (from first editions) *The last blast of the trompet of Godis worde aganis the vsurpit auctoritie of Iohne Knox*, Edinburgh 1562; *The buke of four scoir thre questions*, Antwerp 1563; and *Vincentivs Lirinensis of the natioun of Gallis*, Antwerp 1563. The last of these is a translation of 'Commonitorium pro Catholicae fidei antiquate et universitate' by Vincentius (5th century). For another edition of these works see **31.10**.

34. Reports on the state of certain parishes in Scotland, made to his majesty's commissioners for plantation of kirks, etc. in pursuance of their ordinance dated April XII, MDCXXVII. From the originals preserved in His Majesty's General Register House. [Edited by Alexander Macdonald.] 1835.   15.35

35. Letters to King James the Sixth from the queen, Prince Henry, Prince Charles, the Princess Elizabeth and her husband Frederick King of Bohemia, and from their son Prince Frederick Henry. From the originals in the Library of the Faculty of Advocates. [Edited by Alexander Macdonald.] 1835.   15.36

Facsimiles. Also extracts from accounts of the treasurers of Scotland, 1593–1603.

36. Papers relative to the royal guard of Scottish archers in France. From original documents. [Edited by Alexander Macdonald.] 1835.   15.37

French and English. Concerning origins and privileges of the guard, *c.* 1611–12. Also *L'Escosse Francoise* from Paris 1608 edition (a history of the alliances between Scotland and France from 777); and docs. relating to Scots privileges in France, 1642–3.

37. The Cochrane correspondence regarding the affairs of Glasgow, MDCCXLV–VI. Edited by James Dennistoun. Glasgow. 1836.   15.38

Correspondence of Andrew Cochrane, who was provost during the Jacobite occupation of the burgh. Also miscellaneous docs., 1714–49.

38. Catalogue of the works printed for the Maitland Club, instituted March, MDCCCXXVIII. With lists of the members and rules of the Club. 1836.   15.39

39. Index to a private collection of notices entitled Memorabilia of the city of Glasgow, selected from the minute-books of the burgh. MDLXXXVII–MDCCL. By John Smith. 1836.   15.40

Smith completed the private printing of his *Memorabilia* in 1835. It contains extracts 1550–60 from Ayr burgh records as well as the Glasgow extracts. A supplement by Alexander Macdonald has extracts from Crail, Culross and Edinburgh burgh records.

40. Scalacronica: by Sir Thomas Gray of Heton, knight. A chronicle of England and Scotland from A.D. MLXVI to A.D. MCCCLXII. Now first printed from the unique manuscript. With an introduction and notes. Edited by Joseph Stevenson. 1836.   15.41

French. Mid-14th century. Also extracts from the pre-1066 section of the chronicle; and English notes made by John Leyland from the chronicle.

41. Selections from unpublished manuscripts in the College of Arms and the British Museum illustrating the reign of Mary Queen of Scotland, MDXLIII–MDLXVIII. Edited by Joseph Stevenson. Glasgow. 1837.   15.42

42. The life and death of King James the First of Scotland. Edited by Joseph Stevenson. 1837.   15.43

Chronicon Jacobi Primi Regis Scottorum. [From a late 15th century ms. Includes two 15th century poems.]
The dethe of the Kynge of Scotis. [Evidently a translation by John Shirley, d. 1456, of a Latin account.]

43. Ancient Scotish melodies, from a manuscript of the reign of King James VI. With an introductory enquiry illustrative of the history of the music of Scotland. By William Dauney. 1838.   15.44

Also issued as **6.62**, which see for details.

44. Sir Beves of Hamtoun: a metrical romance. Now first edited from the Auchinleck ms. [Edited by William B. D. D. Turnbull.] 1838.   15.45

Early 14th century ms.

45. Catalogue of the library at Abbotsford. [By J. G. Cochrane.] 1838.   15.46

Sir Walter Scott's library. Also issued as **6.63**.

46. Chronicon de Lanercost. MCI–MCCCXLVI. E codice Cottoniano nunc primum typis mandatum. Edited by Joseph Stevenson. 1839.   15.47

Also issued as **6.68**, which see for details.

47. De arte logistica Joannis Naperi Merchistonii baronis libri qui supersunt. Edited by Mark Napier. 1839.   15.48

John Napier d. 1617. Also issued as **6.65**.

48. The Scottish metrical romance of Lancelot du Lak. Now   **15.49**
first printed from a manuscript of the fifteenth century,
belonging to the university of Cambridge. With miscellaneous
poems from the same volume. Edited by Joseph Stevenson.
1839.

> See **32.2** for another edition.

49. Acts and proceedings of the General Assemblies of the Kirk   **15.50**
of Scotland, from the year MDLX. Collected from the most
authentic manuscripts. Edited by Thomas Thomson. 3 parts.
1839–45.

> Also issued as **6.84**, which see for details.

49A. Appendix to the booke of the Universall Kirk of Scotland: **15.51**
containing historical illustrations of the proceedings of the
church of Scotland, from the years MDXCVII–MDCIII. Edited
by Thomas Thomson. 1845.

> Material printed for inclusion in **15.50** but omitted. Instead it was issued to
> members of the Maitland Club with the above title page, paginated 931–
> 1161, with index paginated 1–61. The vol. is not listed in Terry, *Catalogue*.

50. Letters to the Argyll family, from Elizabeth Queen of   **15.52**
England, Mary Queen of Scots, King James VI, King Charles I,
King Charles II, and others. From originals preserved in the
General Register House. Edited by Alexander Macdonald. 1839.

> Letters, 1520–1685. Also miscellaneous docs., 1472–1588.

51. Miscellany of the Maitland Club. Consisting of original   **15.53**
papers and other documents illustrative of the history and
literature of Scotland. [Edited by James Dennistoun and
Alexander Macdonald.] Vol. ii. 1840.

> Pt. 1: Acts of the Parliament and of the Privy Council of Scotland, relative to
> the establishing and maintaining of schools, from the year MCCCCXCVI
> to the year MDCXCVI.
> Appendix—Extracts from the accounts of the common good of various
> burghs in Scotland relative to payments for schools and schoolmasters,
> between the years 1557 and 1634.
> Extracts from original letters of George Earl of Morton to his son James
> Lord Aberdour, as to proceedings in Parliament relative to the Porteous
> mob, 1736. [Letters, 1737.]
> Acts, statutes and other proceedings of the provost, bailies and council of
> the burgh of Edinburgh, from the year MDXXIX to the year MDXXXI.
> Letter from Mr Zachary Boyd to Mr Patrick Lindsay, Archbishop of
> Glasgow, XXVIII Jan. MDCXXXVII.
> Bands of friendship by Scott of Balwery, Orrok of that Ilk, and Boswell of
> Glasmont, to the laird of Raith etc., from the year MDIX to the year
> MDLVI. [Also two letters of James V, 1533, 1541; and a protection by
> Mary Queen of Scots, 1556 (Latin).]

Acts and statutes of the lawting, sheriff, and justice courts, within Orkney and Zetland, from the year MDCII to the year MDCXLIV.

List of the parishes and islands within the earldom of Orkney and lordship of Zetland (exclusive of the bishoprick of Orkney), and certificate of the number of examinable persons in each parish and island, heads of familys, days services, etc. February 1748.

Journal from Kirkwall to Edinburgh. [17th or 18th century. Routes, mileages and prices of ferries.]

Documents relative to the printers of some early Scottish newspapers, etc. from the year MDCLXXXVI to the year MDCCV. [Concerning censorship.]

Pt. 2: Extracts from the records of the burgh of the Canongate near Edinburgh, MDLXI–MDLXXXVIII. [Partly Latin.]

Royal letters and instructions and other documents from the archives of the Earls of Wigton, MDXX–MDCL. [Mainly 1640s, concerning the activities of the Marquis of Montrose and other royalists.]

Excerpts from the household book of my Lord Archbishop of St Andrews from 1663 to 1666. [Archbishop James Sharp.]

Appendix—Note by Mr Dennistoun, regarding the letters of Henry II, printed in vol. i of the Miscellany. [See 15.26.]

52. Rob Stene's dream, a poem. Printed from a manuscript in the Leightonian Library, Dunblane. Edited by William Motherwell. Glasgow. 1836.

15.54

A satire directed against John Maitland, Lord Thirlestane, *c.* 1591, by a member of James VI's household.

53. Narrative of Charles Prince of Wales' expedition to Scotland in the year 1745. By James Maxwell of Kirkconnell. Presented by Walter Buchanan. 1841.

15.55

1745–6. Maxwell was an officer in the Jacobite army.

54. Documents illustrative of Sir William Wallace, his life and times. Edited by Joseph Stevenson. 1841.

15.56

Latin, French and English.

55. The historie of the Kirk of Scotland. Edited by B. Botfield. 2 pts. 1842.

15.57

An extra title page allows binding in a single vol. See **43.4** for better texts of these works.

Pt. 1: Containing The historie of the kirk, MDLVIII–MDCXXXVII. By John Row, minister at Carnock. The Coronis; being a continuation of The historie. By William Row, minister at Ceres. [The 'Coronis' is in fact also by John Row, minister at Carnock.]

Pt. 2: Containing a supplement of The historie of the kirk, MDCXXXVII–MDCXXXIX. By John Row, principal of King's College, Aberdeen. Additional illustrations of The historie. By William Row, minister at Ceres.

56. Notices of original unprinted documents, preserved in the Office of the Queen's Remembrancer and Chapter-House, Westminster, illustrative of the history of Scotland. Edited by Joseph Stevenson. 1842.   **15.58**

> Documents respecting the affairs of Scotland during the reign of Edward I preserved in the Office of Queen's Remembrancer. [c. 1298–c. 1306.]
> Documents respecting the affairs of Scotland during the reign of Henry VIII. Contained in a volume preserved in the Chapter House, Westminster.

57. Miscellany of the Maitland Club. Consisting of original papers and other documents illustrative of the history and literature of Scotland. [Edited by James Dennistoun and Alexander Macdonald.] Vol. iii. 1843.   **15.59**

> Pt. 1: Acts and orders of the Privy Council of Scotland against the Clangregour, and information anent the state of the Highlands and Isles. MDCX–MDCXXI.
> Order of the king and lords of the Privy Council of Scotland, anent the election of the principal, and regents of the College of Glasgow; and for halding of the common table within the said college, etc. Aug. MDCII.
> The address of the provest, baillies, town council and citizens of the city of Glasgow to King William and Queen Mary upon their majestys accession to the throne. 1 Feb. MDCXC.
> Bond of association by the chancellor, rector, principal, dean of faculty, professors of theology and philosophy, students and others belonging to the University of Glasgow. MDCXCVI. [In support of William II.]
> Establishment for the pay of his majesty's standing forces in the kingdom of Scotland. 16 June 1684.
> Establishment for the pay of her majesty's standing forces in the kingdom of Scotland. 15 May 1702.
> Extracts from the registers of the Privy Council of Scotland, and other papers connected with the method and manner of ryding the Scottish Parliament. MDC–MDCCIII.
> Acts of the Parliament of Scotland for settling the orders in the Parliament House. MDCLXII–MDCCVI.
> Lists of fees and pensions granted to the officers of state and other servants of the crown etc. in Scotland. MDCLXVII–MDCXCIX.
> Letters from Mary Queen of Scots, to Sir Robert Melvill; and other papers from the archives of the Earl of Leven and Melville. MDLXV–MDLXVIII.
> Register of vestments, jewels, and books for the choir, etc. belonging to the College of St Salvator in the university of St Andrews, circa A.D. MCCCCL.
> Pt. 2: Extracts from the register of the kirk session of the city and parish of St Andrews. MDLIX–MDLXIII. [See 24.4.]
> Account of the expenses of certain dogs sent to the King of Denmark, and requests by King James VI to the Earl of Mar for 'terrieres or earth dogges'. MDXCIX–MDCXXIV.
> Letters from Christian Countess of Devonshire to Thomas second Earl of Haddington and to William seventh Earl of Morton about the year 1639.

The compt of James Murray of Kilbabertoun maister of wark to our soverane lord of the haill expensis maid upoun building and reparatiounes within and about his majesties castell of Stirling. MDCXXVIII–MDCXXIX. [Largely relating to painting done by Valentine Jenkin.]

Declarations by the clergy and nobility of Scotland and by the barons and commissioners of burghs against the National Covenant and the Solemn League and Covenant. Jul. MDCLXXXI.

List of Popish parents and their children in various districts of Scotland as given in to the lords of the Privy Council and to the commission of the General Assembly. MDCCI–MDCCV.

Accounts of the burning of the villages of Auchterarder, Muthill, Crieff, Blackford, Dalreoch and Dunning, about the beginning of the year 1716. [By Jacobite forces.]

Commission by the meeting of the estates to Sir Alexander Leslie to be general of all the Scots forces. MDCXL.

The testament testamentar and inventar of the guidis and geir etc. pertening to umquhile George Heriot jeweler to the kingis majestie. MDCXXIV.

58. The Coltness collections, MDCVIII–MDCCCXL. Edited by James Dennistoun. 1842.   **15.60**

> Memorials of the Stewarts of Allanton, Coltness, and Goodtrees, by Sir Archibald Stewart Denham of Coltness and Westshield, bart. MDCVIII–MDCXCVIII. [Sir Archibald d. 1773.]
>
> A journey in England, Holland and the Low Countries, by Mrs Calderwood of Polton, born Miss Steuart of Coltness. MDCCLVI.
>
> Memoir of Sir James Steuart Denham, bart., of Coltness and Westshield, compiled for the Lady Frances Steuart, his disconsolate widow. MDCCXIII–MDCCLXXX. [By Andrew Kippis.]
>
> Family notices. [Genealogical notes, 1630–1840.]

59. Memoirs of Sir Ewen Cameron of Locheill, chief of the Clan Cameron. With an introductory account of the history and antiquities of that family and of the neighbouring clans. [Edited by James Macknight.] 1842.   **15.61**

> Also issued as **1.24**, which see for details.

60. Analecta: or, materials for a history of remarkable providences; mostly relating to Scotch ministers and Christians. By the Rev. Robert Wodrow, minister of the Gospel at Eastwood. [Edited by Mathew Leishman.] 4 vols. 1842–3.   **15.62**

> Notes and anecdotes, often based on oral evidence, relating to the late 16th and 17th centuries as well as to contemporary events.
>
> i : [1701–11. Also extracts from Wodrow's diary, 1697–1701.]
> ii : [1712–23.]
> iii: [1723–8.]
> iv : [1728–31.]

61. Registrum episcopatus Glasguensis: munimenta ecclesie metropolitane Glasguensis, a sede restaurata seculo ineunte XII, ad reformatam religionem. Edited by Cosmo Innes. 2 vols. 1843. **15.63**

Also issued as **6**.78, which see for details.

62. Liber ecclesie de Scon. Munimenta vetustiora monasterii Sancte Trinitatis et Sancti Michaelis de Scon. Presented by William Smythe. 1843. **15.64**

Also issued as **6**.81, which see for details.

63. Registrum episcopatus Aberdonensis. Ecclesie cathedralis Aberdonensis regesta que extant in unum collecta. Edited by Cosmo Innes. 2 vols. 1845. **15.65**

Also issued as **36**.13, 14.
i : [1062–1559.]
i: [*c.* 1180–1566.]

64. Papers illustrative of the political condition of the Highlands of Scotland, from the year MDCLXXXIX to MDCXCVI. Presented by John Gordon. Glasgow. 1845. **15.66**

Not all the docs. relate to the Highlands.

65. Liber collegii nostre Domine. Registrum ecclesie B.V. Marie et S. Anne infra muros civitatis Glasguensis, MDXLIX. Accedunt munimenta fratrum predicatorum de Glasgu, domus Dominicane apud Glasguenses carte que supersunt. MCCXLIV–MDLIX. Edited by Joseph Robertson. Glasgow. 1846. **15.67**

Cartulary of Our Lady College, Glasgow, dated 1549, of docs., 1516–49; charters relating to the Glasgow Blackfriars, 1244–1559. Also charters relating to lands and houses in Glasgow, late 12th century–1567; and miscellaneous docs., 1550–98.

66. Memorials of Montrose and his times. Edited by Mark Napier. 2 vols. 1848–50. **15.68**

i [1615–42.]
ii: [1640–50.]

67. Miscellany of the Maitland Club. Consisting of original papers and other documents illustrative of the history and literature of Scotland. Edited by Joseph Robertson. Vol. iv, pt. 1. Glasgow. 1847. **15.69**

In festo Sancti Kentigerni episcopi quod extra dyocesin eius celebratur in crastino octaue Epiphanie ad missam officium. A.D. 1492. [From the Arbuthnott missal.]

Brevis descriptio regni Scotie, circa A.D. 1296. [Notes by an Englishman on the northern part of Scotland.]

Observations of Mr Dioness Campbell, Deane of Limerick, on the West Isles of Scotland. A.D. 1596.

Descriptive catalogue of the state papers and other historical documents preserved in the archives at Hamilton Palace. A.D. 1309–A.D. 1759.

Register of the provincial synod of Glasgow and Ayr. A.D. 1687–A.D. 1690.

Demission by Dr Robert Leighton, of his charge of the diocese of Glasgow. A.D. 1674.

68. Descriptive catalogue of impressions from ancient Scottish **15.70** seals, royal, baronial, ecclesiastical, and municipal, embracing a period from A.D. 1094 to the Commonwealth. Taken from original charters and other deeds preserved in public and private archives. By Henry Laing. 1850.

Also issued as **6.94**, which see for details, and for general sale.

69. Deeds instituting bursaries, scholarships, and other founda- **15.71** tions, in the College and University of Glasgow. [Edited by William Thomson.] 1850.

Latin and English. 1576–1849. Also issued for general sale.

70. Breviarium Aberdonense. Edited by William Blew. 2 pts. **15.72** Aberdeen. 1854.

Also issued as **6.99**, which see for details, and **36.41**.

71. Selections from the family papers preserved at Caldwell. **15.73** Presented by William Mure of Caldwell. 2 pts. in 3. Glasgow. 1854.

Also issued as **16.7** (dated 1883–5).
Pt. 1: MCCCCXCVI–MDCCCLIII. [Miscellaneous papers.]
Pt. 2, vol. i : MDCCXXXIII–MDCCLXIV. [Correspondence and miscellaneous papers of Baron William Mure.]
Pt. 2, vol. ii: MDCCLXV–MDCCCXXI. [Ditto, 1765–76, and correspondence and miscellaneous papers of Baron Mure's son, William Mure, 1777–1821.]

72. Munimenta alme Universitatis Glasguensis: Records of the **15.74** University of Glasgow from its foundation till 1727. Edited by Cosmo Innes. 4 vols. Glasgow. 1854.

i : Privileges and property. [1451–1744.]
ii : Statutes and annals. [1451–1727.]
iii : Lists of members—internal economy. [1475–1746.]
[iv]: Preface—supplemental lists—indices. [1559–1730.]

73. Notices from the local records of Dysart. Edited by William **15.75** Muir. Glasgow. 1853.

1510–1697.

74. Topographical account of the district of Cunningham, Ayrshire. Compiled about the year 1600, by Mr Timothy Pont. With notes and an appendix. Edited by John Fullarton. Glasgow. 1858.   **15.76**

> Also extracts from testaments, 1547–1659; and from Irvine customs books, 1724–88.

75. Oppressions of the sixteenth century in the islands of Orkney and Zetland. From original documents. Edited by David Balfour. 1859.   **15.77**

> Also issued as 1.31, which see for details.

76. Reports of the Maitland Club, from 1834–1845.   **15.78**

> See also **15.80** below.

77. Autographs of members of the Maitland Club. With notices of contributions etc.   **15.79**

> A unique vol. in the British Library, with the title page in ms. by John Smith, secretary of the Club, dated 2 May 1836. The ms. signatures are mainly on printed papers concerning elections to the Club dated 1835–6, with ms. notices as to contributions added by Smith.

78. History of the Maitland Club.   **15.80**

> This title appears on the spine of a unique vol. in the British Library. Inside is a ms. note dated 2 May 1836 by John Smith, secretary of the Club, reading 'The contents of this volume form a history of the Maitland Club'. The contents consist of printed rules, reports, papers concerning elections to the club, etc., 1828–35. This vol. is not listed in Terry, *Catalogue*.

16. NEW CLUB*

Place of publication: Paisley.

1. Registrum monasterii de Passelet: artas privilegia conven-   **16.1**
tiones aliaque munimenta complectens a domo fundata A.D.
MCLXIII usque ad A.D. MDXXIX. [Edited by Cosmo Innes.]
1877.

>   Reissue of **15.**17 (which see for details) with a new title page.

2. The abbey of Paisley, from its foundation till its dissolution,   **16.2**
with notices of the subsequent history of the church, and an
appendix of illustrative documents. By J. Cameron Lees. 1878.

>   Includes transcripts and abstracts of miscellaneous docs. (Latin and English),
>   13th century–1665, including rental, 1460.

3. Descriptions of the sheriffdoms of Lanark and Renfrew. By   **16.3**
William Hamilton of Wishaw. [Edited by John Dillon and John
Fullarton.] 1878.

>   Reissue of **15.**12 (which see for details) with new title page and a few
>   additional notes.

4. Cantus, songs and fancies, to three, four, of [sic] five parts,   **16.4**
both apt for voices and viols. With a brief introduction to musick
as taught in the musick-school of Aberdeen. Reproduced by
photo-lithography for the New Club series. 1879.

>   From third edition, Aberdeen 1682 (first edition 1662). Collected and printed
>   by John Forbes (d. 1675).

5. An etymological dictionary of the Scottish language. . . . By   **16.5**
John Jamieson. A new edition, carefully revised and collated,
with the entire supplement incorporated, by John Longmuir and
David Donaldson. 4 vols. 1879–82.

---

* **16.**10–15 are produced by the same publisher as earlier vols., and are uniform with
them, but do not state that they belong to the Club series. However, Terry, *Catalogue*,
lists 10–13 as Club vols., and states that 'Occasional volumes are still issued to surviving
members'.

From the first edition, Edinburgh 1808, and the supplement, Edinburgh 1825. A supplement to the New Club edition was issued in 1887: *Supplement to Jamieson's Scottish dictionary, with memoir, and introduction, by David Donaldson.*

6. The buke of the howlat. Edited by David Donaldson and David Laing. 1882.

16.6

Reissue of **6**.3 (which see for details) with new title page and additional notes and collations. Also an article on the Maitland Club, from *The Scots Times*, 19 Sept. 1829.

7. Selections from the family papers preserved at Caldwell. Presented by William Mure of Caldwell. 2 pts. in 3. 1883–5.

16.7

Reissue of **15**.73 (which see for details) with new title pages.

8. The Black Book of Paisley and other manuscripts of the Scotichronicon. With a note upon John de Burdeus or John de Burgundia, otherwise Sir John Mandeville, and the pestilence. By David Murray. 1885.

16.8

Notes on the 15th century ms., not a transcript. Sir John d. 1372. Also miscellaneous docs. (Latin and English), 16th century.

9. Caledonia: or, a historical and topographical account of North Britain from the most ancient to the present times, with a dictionary of places, chorographical and philological. By George Chalmers. 8 vols. 1887–1902.

16.9

i–vi: [From the incomplete first edition, 3 vols., Edinburgh 1807–24. Pagination continuous in vols. i–ii, iii–iv, and v–vi.]
vii : From the hitherto unpublished mss. in the Advocates' Library.
viii: [Index.]

10. Kilmacolm. A parish history 1100–1898. By James Murray. 1898.

16.10

Includes poll tax roll, 1695.

11. Eastwood. Notes on the ecclesiastical antiquities of the parish. By George Campbell. 1902.

16.11

12. Kilbarchan. A parish history. By Robert D. MacKenzie. 1902.

16.12

Includes poll tax roll, 1695; and (in a supplement) signatures on the parish's Solemn League and Covenant, 1648.

13. A history of the county of Renfrew from the earliest times. By William M. Metcalfe. 1905.

16.13

Includes a few extracts from and abstracts of miscellaneous docs., 1386–1490, 1665–early 18th century.

14. A history of the parish of Neilston. By David Pride. 1910.   **16.14**

Includes poll tax roll, 1695; and *Fowler's Neilston, Barrhead, Grahamston and neighbourhood directory for 1830*. Not in Matheson, *Catalogue*.

15. Pollokshaws. Village and burgh, 1600–1912. With some   **16.15**
account of the Maxwells of Pollok. By Andrew M'Callum. 1925.

Not in Matheson, *Catalogue*.

17.   ROXBURGHE CLUB*

Place of publication: London, unless otherwise stated.

7. Newes from Scotland, declaring the damnable life of Doctor Fian, a notable sorcerer, who was burned at Edenbrough in Ianuarie last, 1591. Presented by H. Freeling. 1816.

   17.1

> From London 1591 edition. John Cunningham, or 'Dr Fian', was accused of sorcery intended to bring about the death of James VI.

22. Ceremonial at the marriage of Mary Queen of Scotts with the Dauphin of France. Presented by William Bentham. 1818.

   17.2

> French. From *Discours du grand et magnifique triumphe, fait au mariage de tresnoble et magnifique Prince François de Vallois Roy Dauphin. . . .*, Rouen 1558.

45. Proceedings in the court-martial, held upon John, Master of Sinclair, captain-lieutenant in Preston's Regiment, for the murder of Ensign Schaw of the same regiment, and Captain Schaw, of the Royals, 17th October 1708. With correspondence respecting that transaction. [Edited by Sir Walter Scott.] Edinburgh. 1828.

   17.3

> The letters are to and from Sir John Schaw, the brother of the murdered men, 1708–10.

59. The decline of the last Stuarts. Extracts from the despatches of British envoys to the secretary of state. Edited by Philip H. Stanhope, Lord Mahon. 1843.

   17.4

> 1749–88.

65. La vraie cronique d'Escoce. Pretensions des Anglois a la couronne de France. Diplome de Jacques VI Roi de la Grand Bretagne. Drawn from the Burgundian Library by Robert Anstruther. 1847.

   17.5

---

* Though the Club is an English body, its publications are not listed in Mullins, *T & C*, as the majority of them are of a literary nature. But the publications contain a substantial number of volumes of historical sources relating to Scotland, and these are listed here, together with publications relating to Stuart and Jacobite history, though these are not all specifically Scottish. The numbering is that adopted by the Club: see N. Barker, *The publications of the Roxburghe Club, 1814–1962* (1964).

The three items are paginated separately. The 'Cronique' and 'Pretensions' are narratives ending in 1463 and the late 15th century respectively. The 'Diplome' is a historical account of Franco-Scottish relations, pre–1603.

90. Ruthven correspondence. Letters and papers of Patrick Ruthven, Earl of Forth and Brentford, and his family: A.D. 1615–A.D. 1662. With an appendix of papers relating to Sir John Urry. Edited, from the original mss., by William D. Macray. 1868.   **17.6**

The papers relating to Urry and his family are dated 1609–1709.

92. Correspondence of Colonel N. Hooke, agent from the court of France to the Scottish Jacobites, in the years 1703–1707. Edited, from transcripts in the Bodleian Library, by William D. Macray. Vol. i. 1870.   **17.7**

Partly French. 1703–5. The transcripts contain marginal notes by Nathaniel Hooke himself.

95. Correspondence of Colonel N. Hooke. . . . Vol. ii. 1871.   **17.8**

Partly French. 1706–7. Also answers by Hooke to questions on the state of Scotland, 1710; petition of Major General Thomas Buchan to Louis XIV; and list of papers relating to Hooke.

100. Correspondence of Sir Robert Kerr, first Earl of Ancram, and his son William, third Earl of Lothian. Edited by David Laing. Edinburgh. 2 vols. 1875.   **17.9**

Also issued as **6.125**, which see for details.

106. A tract on the succession to the crown (A.D. 1602). By Sir John Harington, kt., of Kelston. Printed for the first time from a manuscript in the chapter library at York, and edited with notes and an introduction by Clements R. Markham. 1880.   **17.10**

Supporting the succession of James VI to the English throne. Includes a letter from James to Harington, 1591.

116. Basilicon doron: or, his majesty's instructions to his dearest sonne, Henry the prince. Written by King James I. Reprinted from the excessively rare privately-printed edition of Edinburgh, 1599. . . . Edited by Charles Edmonds. 1887.   **17.11**

120. Stuart papers relating chiefly to Queen Mary of Modena and the exiled court of King James II. Printed from official copies of the originals, with facsimiles, under the superintendence of Falconer Madan. 2 vols. 1889.   **17.12**

French. Pagination continuous.
i : Letters of Mary of Modena, 1689–1715; papers relating to Queen Henrietta Maria, 1625–69; miscellaneous papers, 1685–1715.

ii: Miscellaneous letters and papers, 1670–1702, *c*. 1766; accounts of cures of diseases by the touch or prayers of James II, compiled 1702–3; and memoirs relating to Mary of Modena and her children, 1711–13.

126. Memoirs of the life of Sir John Clerk of Penicuik, baronet, baron of the Exchequer, extracted by himself from his own journals, 1676–1755. From the manuscript in Penicuik House with introduction and notes by John M. Gray. 1895.   17.13

The text is taken from **24.13**, which see for details.

126A. Memoirs of the secret services of John Macky, esq., during the reigns of King William, Queen Anne, and King George I. Including, also, The true secret history of the rise, promotions, etc. of the English and Scots nobility; officers, civil, military, naval, and other persons of distinction, from the Revolution. In their respective characters at large; drawn up by Mr Macky, pursuant to the direction of Her Royal Highness the Princess Sophia. Published from his original manuscript as attested by his son Spring Macky, esq. [1895.]   17.14

This work is included with no. 126 above in a single vol., but has its own title page and pagination. From London 1733 edition. The Memoirs deal largely with the 1690s, and were compiled in 1723. Also the will of Gilbert Burnet, 1711–14; Burnet's epitaph; Burnet's 'Resolution of two important cases of conscience'; and letters from Princess Sophia to John Macky, 1703–6 (French, with English translations).

140. The Gowrie conspiracy. Confessions of George Sprot. Edited by Andrew Lang. 1902.   17.15

1608. Also forged letters relating to the conspiracy; testament of Robert Logan of Restalrig; and a narrative account of the conspiracy, 1600.

165. The letters of Thomas Burnet to George Duckett, 1712–1722. Edited by D. Nicol Smith. Oxford. 1914.   17.16

Thomas was the son of Gilbert Burnet, but he lived in England and these letters contain nothing relating to the family's Scottish origins. Also letter of Thomas Burnet to the Duke of Newcastle about the treatment of his father's family, 1734; and Thomas' will, 1748.

168. The Melvill book of roundels. Edited, with an introduction, by Granville Bantock and H. Orsmond Anderton. 1916.   17.17

Ms. compiled in 1612 by David Melville, whose younger brother James (best known for his *Diary*, see **43.3**) composed one of the roundels.

173. Correspondence of the Scots commissioners in London, 1644–1646. Edited by Henry W. Meikle. Edinburgh. 1917.   17.18

Abridged transcripts and calendars. Also instructions to the commissioners.

181. Papers of devotion of James II. Being a reproduction of the ms. in the handwriting of James the Second now in the possession of Mr B. R. Townley Balfour. With an introduction by Godfrey Davies. Oxford. 1925. **17.19**

> Also extracts of the explanation of Anne, Duchess of York, of why she became a Catholic, *c.* 1670.

199. English bards and Scotch reviewers. By Lord Byron. Edited by Sir John Murray. 1936. **17.20**

> Verse. Facsimile of the fourth edition, 1811, with ms. notes by Byron, 1816.

206. The history of the rebellion in the years 1745 and 1746. From a manuscript now in the possession of Lord James Stewart-Murray. Edited by Henrietta Tayler. Oxford. 1944. **17.21**

> A detailed contemporary narrative of the '45, which includes an appendix of miscellaneous docs., 1743–7. Also a letter by John Gordon of Glenbuchat to James Stuart, the Old Pretender, 1738; and an order by Sir John Cope, Sept. 1745.

209. A Jacobite miscellany. Eight original papers on the rising of 1745–1746. Edited, with introduction and notes, by Henrietta Tayler. Oxford. 1948. **17.22**

> Memoria istorica per l'anno 1744. [Italian, with English translation. Account of Prince Charles Edward's journey from Rome to Paris in 1744, in two letters by James Murray, Lord Dunbar.]
>
> Two letters from Magdalen Pringle written during the occupation of Edinburgh by the prince, September–October 1745.
>
> Manuscript account of the expedition to Scotland. From July 1745 to April 1746. By Sir John Macdonald. In French.
>
> Istoria di sua Altezza Reale, il Principe Carlo Edoardo Stuart di Galles. [Italian, with English translation. From the Milan 1760 edition. An account of the prince's escape from Scotland in 1746 based on *Ascanius; or the young adventurer*, which was first printed London 1746.]
>
> The prince's own account of a part of his wanderings. [As written down in 1746 by Richard Warren and Archibald Cameron.]
>
> A portion of the diary of David, Lord Elcho, 1721–87. [1744–6.]
>
> The loss of the *Prince Charles*. [French. Letter by Captain George A. Talbot of the French navy narrating the loss of his ship, 1746.]
>
> Letters of Flora Macdonald. [1774, 1789. Also her accounts written in 1789 of her part in the escape of Prince Charles, 1746, and of her and her family's sufferings as loyalists in the American War of Independence.]

18.   RYMOUR CLUB*

Place of publication: Edinburgh.

1. Miscellanea of the Rymour Club, Edinburgh. Vol. i. 1906–11.   **18.**1
Poems, traditional ballads and rhymes, etc.

2. Miscellanea. . . . Vol. ii. 1912–19.   **18.**2
Ditto.

3. Transactions (formerly Miscellanea) of the Rymour Club,   **18.**3
Edinburgh. Vol. iii. 1928.
Ditto. Secondary material includes 'Inception and history of the Rymour
Club' and 'The Rymour and his rhymes', both by John Geddie. The latter
was also issued separately, Edinburgh 1920.

---

* Numbering altered from the two incompatible systems used by Terry and Matheson.

19. ST ANDREWS UNIVERSITY PUBLICATIONS*

Place of publication: St Andrews.

7. The statutes of the faculty of arts and the faculty of theology at the period of the Reformation. Edited with introduction and notes by Robert K. Hannay. 1910.   **19.1**

Latin. University of St Andrews theology statutes 1560, arts 1570.

8. The kingis quair and The quare of jelusy. Edited with introduction, notes, appendix and glossary, by Alexander Lawson, 1910.   **19.2**

Verse. The text of James I's 'The kingis quair', is given in two versions, as in the ms. and 'as criticism would amend' it. Also contains James' 'A ballad of good counsel'. See also **31.1** and **32.1** for other editions of 'The kingis quair'; and **6.21** and **33.4** for 'The quare of jelusy' (doubtfully attributed to James Auchinleck).

30. An old St Andrews music book (Cod. Helmst. 628). Published in facsimile, with an introduction by James H. Baxter. 1931.   **19.3**

A collection of 14th century mss.

31. Copiale prioratus Sanctiandree. The letter-book of James Haldenstone, Prior of St Andrews (1418–1443). Transcribed and edited, with an appendix of documents illustrating Scottish history from 1378 to 1450, by James H. Baxter. 1930.   **19.4**

Mainly Latin, with brief English abstracts. Includes leases and legal docs. as well as letters.

50. Two students at St Andrews, 1711–1716. Edited from the Delvine papers by W. Croft Dickinson. 1952.   **19.5**

Letters to John Mackenzie of Delvine from his student sons Alexander, Kenneth and Thomas, and from James Morice, the tutor of Kenneth and Thomas, 1707–16; Morice's accounts, 1712–16; and 'Ane account of the diet of the bursars of St Leonard's College, c. 1731.

---

*Only publications relevant to this volume are listed.

54. Letters of John Johnston, *c*. 1565–1611, and Robert Howie, **19.6**
c. 1565–1645. Collected and edited by James K. Cameron. 1963.

   Mainly Latin. Letters of two Scots theologians, 1586–1611. Also miscellaneous related letters, 1588–1611.

56. Acta facultatis artium Universitatis Sanctandree, 1413–   **19.7**
1588. Edited by Annie I. Dunlop. 1964.

   Also issued (in 2 vols.) as **26.54–5** which see for details.

20.   SCOTISH LITERARY CLUB

Place of publication: Edinburgh.

1. The works of Adam Petrie, the Scotish Chesterfield.   **20.1**
MDCCXX–MDCCXXX. Now first collected. Edited by
Thomas G. Stevenson. 1877.

> *Rules of good deportment, or of good breeding* from first edition, Edinburgh
> 1720; *Rules of good deportment for church-officers; or, friendly advice to them*
> from first edition, Edinburgh 1730.

2. Metrical history of the honourable families of the name of   **20.2**
Scot and Elliot in the shires of Roxburgh and Selkirk. In two
parts. Gathered out of ancient chronicles, histories, and
traditions of our fathers. Compiled by Captain Walter Scot of
Satchells, Roxburghshire. With prefatory notices. Edited by
Thomas G. Stevenson. 1892.

> Largely verse. From second edition, Edinburgh 1776 (first edition,
> Edinburgh 1688).

21. SCOTTISH BURGH RECORDS SOCIETY

Place of publication: Edinburgh, unless otherwise stated.

1. Ancient laws and customs of the burghs of Scotland. Vol. i: **21.1**
A.D. 1124–1424. Edited by Cosmo Innes. 1868.
> Latin, with English translations. Continued in **21.25**.

2. Extracts from the records of the burgh of Edinburgh. A.D.   **21.2**
1403–1528. Edited by Sir James D. Marwick. 1869.
> Mainly from council registers; includes abstracts of charters and other docs.,
> *c.* 1124–1527; and tables of tolls and customs, 12th century? and 1468.

3. Extracts . . . Edinburgh. A.D. 1528–1557. . . . 1871.   **21.3**
> Mainly from council registers; includes extracts from accounts, 1552–6; and
> acts of parliament, 1535.

4. Extracts . . . Edinburgh. A.D. 1557–1571. . . . 1875.   **21.4**
> From council registers.

5. Extracts . . . Edinburgh. A.D. 1573–1589. . . . 1882.   **21.5**
> From council registers. Continued in **21.43**.

6. Index to Extracts from the records of the burgh of   **21.6**
Edinburgh. A.D. 1403–1589. And a glossary of peculiar words.
1892.
> Index by David Donaldson.

7. Charters and other documents relating to the city of   **21.7**
Edinburgh. A.D. 1143–1540. Edited by Sir James D. Marwick.
1871.
> Mainly Latin, with English translations and abstracts, *c.* 1143–1540.

8. Extracts from the council register of the burgh of Aberdeen.   **21.8**
1625–1642. Edited by John Stuart. 1871.
> Continued from **36.19**.

9. Extracts . . . Aberdeen. 1643–1747. . . . 1872.   **21.9**

10. Charters and documents relating to the burgh of Peebles,   **21.10**
with extracts from the records of the burgh. A.D. 1165–1710.
Edited by William Chambers. 1872.

Charters and other docs., *c.* 1165–1641 (mainly Latin with English translations); extracts mainly from council registers, 1456–1710; and extracts from burgh accounts, 1554–1661.

11. Extracts from the records of the burgh of Glasgow. [vol. i:] A.D. 1573–1642. Edited by Sir James D. Marwick. Glasgow. 1876.   21.11

Mainly from council registers, 1573–1613, 1623–30, 1636–42; includes extracts from burgh accounts, 1573–1641.

12. Extracts . . . Glasgow. [vol. ii:] A.D. 1630–1662. . . . Glasgow. 1881.   21.12

Mainly from council registers, 1630–6, 1641–62; includes other docs., 1608–41; and extracts from burgh accounts, 1630–4, 1641–62.

13. Miscellany of the Scottish Burgh Records Society. . . . Edited by Sir James D. Marwick. 1881.   21.13

Report by Thomas Tucker upon the settlement of the revenues of excise and customs in Scotland, A.D. MDCLVI. [Also printed in **6.8.**]
Register containeing the state and condition of every burgh within the kingdom of Scotland, in the year 1692. [Compiled on the orders (1691) of the Convention of Royal Burghs. Also printed in **21.55.**]
Setts of the royal burghs of Scotland. [Compiled on the orders (1708) of the Convention of Royal Burghs and submitted 1709–*c.* 1713. The reports often include extracts from earlier docs., and alterations made to burgh constitutions up to 1822 have been added.]
[Also excerpt from the civil list for Scotland, 1655, relating to customs and excise officials; and docs. relating to the communication of trade to burghs of barony and regality, 1676–7.]

14. Charters and other documents relating to the city of Glasgow. [Vol. i:] A.D. 1175–1649. Pt. 1. Edited by Sir James D. Marwick. Glasgow. 1897.   21.14

Abstracts, and a few transcripts, early 12th century–1648.

15. Charters . . . Glasgow. [Vol. i:] A.D. 1175–1649. Pt. 2. . . . Edinburgh. 1894.   21.15

Transcripts (mainly Latin with English translations) and abstracts. Pagination separate from pt. 1.

16. Extracts . . . Glasgow. [Vol. iii:] A.D. 1663–1690. Edited by Sir James D. Marwick and Robert Renwick. Glasgow. 1905.   21.16

Mainly from council registers: includes rentals of burgh lands, 1590 and *c.* 1657; and extracts from burgh accounts, 1662–90.

17. Charters . . . Glasgow. Vol. ii: A.D. 1649–1707. With appendix A.D. 1434–1648. Edited by Sir James D. Marwick and Robert Renwick. Glasgow. 1906.   21.17

Transcripts (some Latin with English translations) and abstracts.

18. Charters and documents relating to the collegiate church
and hospital of the Holy Trinity, and the Trinity Hospital,
Edinburgh. A.D. 1460–1661. Edited by Sir James D. Marwick.
1871.   **21.18**

> Transcripts (mainly Latin with English translations) and abstracts. Also
> issued by the Lord Provost, Magistrates and Council of Edinburgh.

19. Extracts . . . Glasgow. [Vol. iv:] A.D. 1691–1717. . . .
Glasgow. 1908.   **21.19**

> Mainly from council registers: includes a few miscellaneous docs., 1593,
> 1704–16.

20. The River Clyde and the Clyde burghs. The city of Glasgow
and its old relations with Rutherglen, Renfrew, Paisley,
Dumbarton, Port-Glasgow, Greenock, Rothesay, and Irvine. By
Sir James D. Marwick. Glasgow. 1909.   **21.20**

> Also tables of revenue of the Clyde Navigation Trust, 1700–1908; of customs
> revenue, 1796–1908; and of number and tonnage of ships arriving at
> Glasgow, 1828–1908.

21. Edinburgh guilds and crafts. A sketch of the history of
burgess-ship, guild brotherhood, and membership of crafts in
the city. By Sir James D. Marwick. 1909.   **21.21**

> Includes many extracts from sources.

[22. The old laws of Scotland relating to the burghs, in
continuation of the volume of Ancient laws and customs, A.D.
1124–1424.]   **[21.22]**

> A 'ghost'. No vol. with the above title was ever published, but Terry,
> *Catalogue*, printed this entry in advance of publication to describe the vol.
> which later appeared as *Ancient laws and customs* . . . vol. ii (see **21.25** below).
> Matheson, *Catalogue*, assigned the vol. as published a new no., 25, thus
> failing to note that Terry had already numbered it 22.

23. Extracts . . . Glasgow. [Vol. v:] A.D. 1718–38. With
charters and other documents, A.D. 1708–38. Edited by Robert
Renwick. Glasgow. 1909.   **21.23**

> Mainly from council registers; includes charters and other docs., 1594–1738.
> Printed for the Corporation of Glasgow but also issued as a Society vol.

24. Extracts from the records of the burgh of Peebles, 1652–
1714. With appendix, 1367–1665. Edited by Robert Renwick.
Glasgow. 1910.   **21.24**

> Mainly from council registers; includes charters, 1367–1439 (Latin with
> English translations); and extracts from burgh accounts, 1651–65.

25. Ancient laws and customs of the burghs of Scotland. Vol. ii: **21.25**
A.D. 1424–1707. Edited by Robert Renwick. 1910.

Part Latin, with English translations. Acts of parliament relating to burghs.
See **21.1** for vol. i.

26. The history of the collegiate church and hospital of the Holy **21.26**
Trinity, and the Trinity Hospital, Edinburgh, 1460–1661. By
Sir James D. Marwick. 1911.

27. Extracts . . . Glasgow, with charters and other documents. **21.27**
Vol. vi: A.D. 1739–59. Edited by Robert Renwick. Glasgow.
1911.

Mainly from council registers. **21.11, 12, 16, 19** and **23** were retrospectively
held to constitute vols. i-v. Continued in **21.36**.

WORKS UNIFORM WITH BUT NOT PART OF THE SOCIETY'S SERIES★

A. Charters, writs, and public documents of the royal burgh of **21.28**
Dundee, the hospital, and Johnston's Bequest: 1292–1880, with
inventory of the town's writs annexed. Edited by William Hay.
Dundee. 1880.

Partly Latin, with English translations. Printed by order of the Provost,
Magistrates, and Town Council.

B. Charters and other documents relating to the royal burgh of **21.29**
Stirling. A.D. 1124–1705. Edited by Robert Renwick. Glasgow.
1884.

Partly Latin, with English translations. Transcripts, excerpts and abstracts,
c. 1124–1705. Includes extracts from council registers, 1561–4, 1595–7.
Printed for the Provost, Magistrates, and Council of the Burgh of Stirling.

C. Extracts from the records of the royal burgh of Stirling. A.D. **21.30**
1519–1666. With appendix, A.D. 1295–1666. Edited by Robert
Renwick. Glasgow. 1887.

Mainly from council registers; includes abstracts from protocol books,
1470–1596; and rental of burgh lands, 1652. Printed for the Glasgow
Stirlingshire and Sons of the Rock Society.

★ Terry, *Catalogue*, listed the 'Uniform' and 'Convention of Royal Burghs' (see p. 89
below) groups of vols. separately, but assigned a single continuous series of reference
letters (A to N) to them. Matheson, *Catalogue*, began a new series of reference numbers
for each group of vols. As these two systems cannot be reconciled they are here partly
replaced, as follows: Terry A to H remain unchanged; I to Q were listed by Matheson as
1 to 9; a to f were listed by Terry as I to N; and g to h were listed by Matheson as 1 to 2.

D. Extracts . . . Stirling. A.D. 1667–1752. With Appendix, A.D. 1471–1752. . . . Glasgow. 1889.   21.31

    Mainly from council registers; includes abstracts from protocol books, 1471–80; extracts from guildry records, 1592–1747; and from burgh accounts, 1634–1752. Printed for the Glasgow Stirlingshire and Sons of the Rock Society.

E. Extracts from the records of the royal burgh of Lanark. With charters and documents relating to the burgh. A.D. 1150–1722. Edited by Robert Renwick. Glasgow. 1893.   21.32

    Mainly from council registers, 1488–1722; includes charters (some Latin with English translations), and abstracts of charters and other docs., c. 1150–1719.

F. Edinburgh records. The burgh accounts. Vol. i: I. Bailies' accounts, 1544–1566. II. Town treasurers' accounts, 1552–1567. Edited by Robert Adam. With preface by Thomas Hunter. 1899.   21.33

    Printed for the Lord Provost, Magistrates and Council.

G. Edinburgh records. The burgh accounts. Vol. ii: dean of guild's accounts, 1552–1567. . . . 1899.   21.34

    Printed for the Lord Provost, Magistrates and Council.

H. Charters and documents relating to the burgh of Paisley (1163–1665) and extracts from the records of the town council (1594–1620). Edited, with an introduction, by W. M. Metcalfe. Paisley. 1902.   21.35

    Charters and docs. (partly Latin, with English translations), 1158–1690.

I. Extracts from the records of the burgh of Glasgow, with charters and other documents. Vol. vii: A.D. 1760–80. Edited by Robert Renwick. Glasgow. 1912.   21.36

    Extracts and abstracts, mainly from council registers; includes miscellaneous docs., 1725–49. Printed (like **21.37–41** below) for the Corporation of Glasgow. Continues **21.27**.

J. Extracts . . . Glasgow. . . . Vol. viii: A.D. 1781–95. . . . Glasgow. 1913.   21.37

    Mainly from council registers.

K. Extracts . . . Glasgow. . . . Vol. ix: A.D. 1796–1808. . . . Glasgow. 1914.   21.38

    Mainly from council registers.

L. Extracts . . . Glasgow. . . . Vol. x: A.D. 1809–1822. . . . Glasgow. 1915.   21.39

    Mainly from council registers.

M. Extracts . . . Glasgow. . . . Vol. xi: A.D. 1823–1833. . . .   **21.40**
Glasgow. 1916.

Mainly from council registers.

N. Abstract of charters and documents relating to the city of   **21.41**
Glasgow, A.D. 1833–1872. Compiled by Robert Renwick.
Glasgow. 1917.

Also table of customs' rates chargeable at Glasgow, from the 1677 edition.

O. The Stirling guildry book. Extracts from the records of the   **21.42**
merchant guild of Stirling. A.D. 1592–1846. Edited by W. B.
Cook and David B. Morris. Stirling. 1916.

Printed for the Glasgow Stirlingshire and Sons of the Rock Society.

P. Extracts from the records of the burgh of Edinburgh, A.D.   **21.43**
1589 to 1603. Edited by Marguerite Wood and Robert K.
Hannay. 1927.

1562, 1589–1603. Mainly from council registers and burgh accounts;
includes miscellaneous docs. Published (like **21.44–51** below) for the
Corporation of the City of Edinburgh. Continues **21.5**.

Q. Extracts . . . Edinburgh. 1604 to 1626. Edited by Marguerite   **21.44**
Wood. 1931.

Mainly from council registers; includes extracts from burgh accounts; and
miscellaneous docs., 1364, 1600–27 (partly Latin and French).

R. Extracts . . . Edinburgh. 1626 to 1641. . . . 1936.   **21.45**

Mainly from council registers.

S. Extracts . . . Edinburgh. 1642 to 1655. . . . 1938.   **21.46**

Mainly from council registers; includes extracts from burgh accounts,
1641–55.

T. Extracts . . . Edinburgh. 1655 to 1665. . . . 1940.   **21.47**

Mainly from council registers; includes extracts from burgh accounts,
1649–61; and miscellaneous docs., 1580–1664.

U. Extracts . . . Edinburgh. 1665 to 1680. . . . 1950.   **21.48**

Mainly from council registers.

V. Extracts . . . Edinburgh. 1681 to 1689. Edited by Marguerite   **21.49**
Wood and Helen Armet. 1954.

Mainly from council registers.

W. Extracts . . . Edinburgh. 1689 to 1701. Edited by Helen   **21.50**
Armet. 1962.

Mainly from council registers.

X. Extracts . . . Edinburgh. 1701 to 1718. . . . 1967.   **21.51**
Mainly from council registers.

WORKS PUBLISHED BY THE CONVENTION OF THE ROYAL BURGHS OF SCOTLAND, UNIFORM WITH BUT NOT PART OF THE SOCIETY'S SERIES*

a. Records of the Convention of the Royal Burghs of Scotland,   **21.52**
1295–1597. With extracts from other records relating to the affairs of the burghs of Scotland, 1345–1614. Edited by Sir James D. Marwick. 1870.
The 'other records' are dated 1347–1594.

b. Records of the Convention . . . , 1597–1614. With extracts   **21.53**
. . . , 1345–1614. . . . 1870.
Also inventory of writs concerning the privileges of the Scots in France, 1510–1635, compiled in 1638.

c. Extracts from the records of the Convention of the Royal   **21.54**
Burghs of Scotland, 1615–1676. Edited by Sir James D. Marwick. 1878.
1615–31, 1649–76.

d. Extracts . . . Convention . . . , 1677–1711. . . . 1880.   **21.55**
Includes sett of the burgh of Inverness, 1676; and 'Register containeing the state . . . of every burgh . . . 1692' (also printed in **21.13**). Also abstract of the acts of the Convention, 1631–49.

e. Extracts . . . Convention . . . , 1711–38 . . . 1885.   **21.56**

f. Index to Extracts from the records of the Convention of the   **21.57**
Royal Burghs of Scotland, with a glossary of peculiar words. 1295–1738. Edited by Sir James D. Marwick. 1890.

g. Extracts from the records of the Convention of the Royal   **21.58**
Burghs of Scotland, 1738–59. Edited by Thomas Hunter. 1915.

h. Extracts . . . Convention . . . , 1759–79. . . . 1918.   **21.59**

---

* See note on p. 86 above.

22.   SCOTTISH CLERGY SOCIETY

Place of publication: Edinburgh.

1. A sermon preached to the clergy of Aberdeen, April 12th, 1692. With introduction and notes. Edited by James T. F. Farquhar. 1901.

> Attributed to James Gordon, minister of Banchory-Devenick.

22.1

2. A catechism dealing chiefly with the Holy Eucharist. By Robert Forbes, A.M., afterwards Bishop of Ross and Caithness. Together with a prayer at the mixture of the chalice. Edited from the original mss. by John Dowden. 1904.

> 1738. Also extracts from a 1737 sermon by Forbes. The cover reads *An eighteenth century catechism.*

22.2

3. Sidelights on the church in revolution times. Aberdeen movement, 1688–1695. [Edited by W. W. Hawdon and George Sutherland.] 1907.

> Transcripts and extracts from papers, 1682–90, mainly relating to attempts to retain episcopalian ministers within the established church, 1689–90.

22.3

4. Records of the church in Kirriemuir. From A.D. 1560. Edited with introduction and notes by John A. Philip. 1909.

> Extracts, 1560–1750, from a ms. history by George Ogilvie, minister of Kirriemuir, d. 1771, with a few extracts from other sources up to the early 19th century.

22.4

23.   SCOTTISH GAELIC TEXTS SOCIETY*

Place of publication: Edinburgh.

1. Scottish verse from the Book of the Dean of Lismore. Edited by William J. Watson. 1937.   **23.1**
> Gaelic, with English translation. From an early 16th century ms.

2. The songs of John MacCodrum, bard to Sir James MacDonald of Sleat. Edited by William Matheson. 1938.   **23.2**
> Gaelic, with English translation. MacCodrum lived 1693–1779.

3. Heroic poetry from the Book of the Dean of Lismore. Edited by Neil Ross. 1939.   **23.3**
> Gaelic, with English translation. From an early 16th century ms.

4. Orain Dhonnchaidh Bhàin. The songs of Duncan Ban Macintyre. Edited by Angus Macleod. 1952.   **23.4**
> Gaelic, with English translation. Macintyre lived 1724–1812.

5. Prose writings of Donald MacKinnon, 1839–1914. Edited by Lachlan MacKinnon. 1956.   **23.5**
> Gaelic.

6. Prose writings of Donald Lamont, 1874–1958. Edited by Thomas M. Murchison. 1960.   **23.6**
> Gaelic.

7. Adtimchiol an chreidimh. The Gaelic version of John Calvin's Catechismus ecclesiae Genevensis. A facsimile reprint, including the prefixed poems and the shorter catechism of 1659, with notes and glossary, and an introduction. Edited by R. L. Thomson. 1962.   **23.7**
> Gaelic. From Edinburgh *c.* 1630 edition.

---

* 'School' editions of **23.**1, 2, 5, 8 were also published, giving full texts but omitting most of the critical apparatus.

8. Orain Iain Luim. Songs of John MacDonald, bard of   23.8
Keppoch. Edited by Annie M. Mackenzie. 1964.

Gaelic, with English translation. 17th century.

9. Orain agus luinneagan Gàidhlig le Màiri nighean Alasdair   23.9
Ruaidh. Gaelic songs of Mary MacLeod. Edited by J.
Carmichael Watson. 1965.

Gaelic, with English translation. 17th century. From 1934 edition.

10. Sporan Dhòmhnaill. Gaelic poems and songs by the late   23.10
Donald MacIntyre, the Paisley bard. Compiled and edited by
Somerled MacMillan. 1968.

Gaelic. MacIntyre d. 1964.

11. Foirm na n-urrnuidheadh. John Carswell's Gaelic transla-   23.11
tion of the Book of Common Order. Edited by R. L. Thomson,
in part from materials collected by the late Angus Matheson.
1970.

Gaelic, with partial English translation. From the first edition, Edinburgh
1567.

12. An Clàrsair Dall. Orain Ruaidhri mhic Mhuirich agus a   23.12
chuid ciùil. The Blind Harper. The songs of Roderick Morison,
and his music. Edited by William Matheson. 1970.

Gaelic, with English translation. Late 17th–early 18th centuries.

13. Bàrdachd Shìlis na Ceapaich. Poems and songs by Sileas   23.13
MacDonald, c. 1660–c. 1729. Edited by Colm O Baoill. 1972.

Gaelic, with English translation. Ascription to Sileas (Julia) MacDonald not
certain.

14. Eachann Bacach agus bàird eile de Chloinn Ghill-Eathain.   23.14
Eachann Bacach and other Maclean poets. Edited by Colm O
Baoill. 1979.

Gaelic, with English translation. Mid-17th–mid-18th centuries. Eachann
Bacach (Lame Hector) Maclean lived early-mid 18th century.

15. Orain Ghàidhealach mu Bhliadhna Theàrlaich. Highland   23.15
songs of the Forty-Five. Edited by John L. Campbell. 1984.

Gaelic, with English translations. A reprint, with corrections and additions,
of the edition originally published in 1933. The English title is unchanged,
but the Gaelic title of the 1933 edition was Duain Ghàidhealach mu Bhliadhna
Theàrlaich.

24.   SCOTTISH HISTORY SOCIETY, FIRST SERIES

Place of publication: Edinburgh.

1. Tours in Scotland, 1747, 1750, 1760, by Richard Pococke, Bishop of Meath. From the original ms. and drawings in the British Museum. Edited with a biographical sketch of the author by D. William Kemp. 1887.

24.1

> Letters to his mother and sister, dealing almost entirely with topographical and antiquarian matters. The great majority of the letters date from 1760.

2. The diary and general expenditure book of William Cunningham of Craigends, commissioner to the Convention of Estates and member of Parliament for Renfrewshire, kept chiefly from 1673 to 1680. Edited from the original manuscript by James Dodds. 1887.

24.2

> Abridged transcript, 1673–1715. Largely financial. Also rental, *c.* 1690s, and letter to (and claim for Cunningham's expenses from) the freeholders of Renfrewshire, 1696.

3. The Grameid. An heroic poem descriptive of the campaign of Viscount Dundee in 1689, and other pieces. By James Philip of Almerieclose, 1691. Edited from the original manuscript with translation, introduction, and notes by Alexander D. Murdoch. 1888.

24.3

> Latin, with English translation. The other poems (Latin) are 1688 and undated. Also Latin epitaph on William Aikman, *c.* 1707.

4. Register of the minister, elders and deacons of the Christian congregation of St Andrews. Comprising the proceedings of the kirk session and of the court of the superintendent of Fife, Fothrik and Strathearn, 1559–1600. Pt. 1: 1559–1582. Transcribed and edited from the original manuscript with preface and notes by D. Hay Fleming. 1889.

24.4

> Slightly abridged transcript, with occasional 'grosser details . . . omitted, compressed, or modified' (rather pointlessly, as most of these passages appear in full in **15.59**). See **24.7**.

5. The diary of the Reverend John Mill, minister of the parishes of Dunrossness, Sandwick and Cunningsburgh in Shetland,

24.5

1740–1803. With selections from local records and original documents relating to the district. Edited with introduction and notes by Gilbert Goudie. 1889.

> Mill began writing his 'diary' in *c*. 1770, prefacing it with recollections of his career since 1740. The abstracts and extracts from local records etc., 1571–1888, include extracts from Dunrossness kirk session minutes, 1764–1805.

6. Narrative of Mr James Nimmo, written for his own satis-   24.6
faction, to keep in some remembrance the Lord's way, dealing, and kindness towards him, 1654–1709. Edited from the original manuscript with introduction and notes by W. G. Scott-Moncrieff. 1889.

> Autobiography and theological reflections of a covenanter, 1654–*c*. 1705.

7. Register of the minister, elders and deacons of the Christian   24.7
congregation of St Andrews. . . . Pt. 2: 1582–1600. . . . 1890.

> Slightly abridged transcript.

8. A list of persons concerned in the rebellion, transmitted to   24.8
the commissioners of excise by the several supervisors in Scotland, in obedience to a general letter of the 7th May 1746, and a supplementary list with evidences to prove the same. With a preface by the Earl of Rosebery, and annotations by Walter Macleod. 1890.

9. The book of record. A diary written by Patrick first Earl of   24.9
Strathmore, and other documents relating to Glamis Castle, 1684–1689. Edited from the original mss. at Glamis with introduction and notes by A. H. Millar. 1890.

> The 'book', 1684–5, 1688–9, is mainly concerned with finance and estate administration, and includes material relating to years before 1684. The other docs. comprise a contract between the earl and Jacob de Wet for paintings to be done at Glamis, 1688, de Wet's account for the paintings, and an estimate for repair of the organ at Glamis.

10. A history of Greater Britain, as well England as Scotland,   24.10
compiled from the ancient authorities by John Major, by name indeed a Scot, but by profession a theologian, 1521. Translated from the original Latin and edited with notes by Archibald Constable. To which is prefixed a life of the author by Aeneas J. G. Mackay. 1892.

> Up to *c*. 1515. From Paris 1521 and Edinburgh 1540 editions. Major (or Mair) is primarily concerned with Scottish history and Anglo-Scots relations. Also bibliographies of the works of Major and his disciples, and transcripts of the Latin prefaces of Major's works, 1508–30, edited by Thomas G. Law.

11. The records of the commissioners of the General Assemblies   24.11
of the Church of Scotland [vol. i:] holden in Edinburgh in the
years 1646 and 1647. Edited from the original manuscript by
Alexander F. Mitchell and James Christie, with an introduction
by the former. 1892.

> Transcripts of the registers of the commissioners, 18 June 1646–18 July
> 1648. Also docs. on Anglo-Scots relations, 1644–7. For vols. ii and iii see
> 24.25, 58.

12. The court book of the barony of Urie in Kincardineshire,   24.12
1604–1747. Edited from the original manuscript with notes and
introduction by Douglas Barron. 1892.

> 1604–39, 1667–1747. Also rental, c. 1604.

13. Memoirs of the life of Sir John Clerk of Penicuik, baronet,   24.13
baron of the Exchequer. Extracted by himself from his own
journals, 1676–1755. Edited from the manuscript in Penicuik
House, with an introduction and notes, by John M. Gray. 1892.

> Clerk (d. 1755) traces his family back to c. 1568, and his journal ends 1754.
> Also list of his improvements on his estates, 1714–23. Also issued as 17.13.

14. Journal of the Hon. John Erskine of Carnock, 1683–1687.   24.14
Edited from the original manuscript with introduction and
notes, by Walter Macleod. 1893.

> Erskine took part in Argyll's rebellion in 1685, and was in exile in Holland
> both before and after it. Also indictment of Henry, Lord Cardross, 1675;
> notes by Erskine, 1682–4; fragment of his journal, 1701; accounts of
> expenses of his funeral, 1743; and papers relating to the Darien colony, 1700.

15. Miscellany of the Scottish History Society. Vol. i. . . . 1893.   24.15

> The library of James VI. 1573–1583. From a manuscript in the hand of Peter
> Young, his tutor. Edited, with introduction and notes, by George F.
> Warner. [Catalogue or inventory. Includes extract from a 1569 inventory,
> and apophthegms or sayings of James, c. 1575–c. 1582 (the latter Latin,
> French and English).]
> Documents illustrating Catholic policy in the reign of James VI. I. Summary
> of memorials presented to the King of Spain, by John Ogilvy of Poury and
> Dr John Cecil. 1596. II. Apology and defence of the king of Scotland, by
> Father William Creighton, S.J. 1598. Edited, with introduction and notes,
> by Thomas G. Law. [First item Spanish, with English translation. Also
> memoranda or notes of additions and alterations by Creighton for insertion
> in the 'Apology'.]
> Twenty-four letters of Sir Thomas Hope, bart., of Craighall, lord advocate of
> Scotland, 1626–1646. 1627–1646. Edited from the original manuscripts,
> with introduction and notes, by Robert Paul.
> Civil war papers. I. Correspondence of Sir John Cochran and others with
> James, Duke of Courland, 1643–1650. II. Montrose in Sweden, 1649–
> 1650. III. Intelligence-letter from London, 1649. IV. Montrose's flight

from Carbisdale, 1650. Edited, with introduction and notes, by H. F. Morland Simpson. [All the items relate to Montrose. The extracts from letters etc. in I are French and Latin, with English translations, and English. II consists of extracts from letters (Dutch, with English translations). IV is an account based on family tradition written by George Marsh in 1792.]

Thirty-four letters written to James Sharp, Archbishop of St Andrews, by the Duke and Duchess of Lauderdale and by Charles Maitland, Lord Hatton, 1660–1677. Edited from the originals in the episcopal chest, Edinburgh, with introduction and notes, by John Dowden.

The diary of the Rev. George Turnbull, minister of Alloa and Tyninghame, 1657–1704. Edited, from the original manuscript, with introduction and notes, by Robert Paul.

Masterton papers, 1660–1719. . . . Edited, with pedigree, introduction and notes, by Victor A. N. Paton. [Notes of events, 1660–1719, advice to his heirs, 1699, instructions to his wife, 1699 and 1702, all by Francis Masterton; notes on his family by Charles Masterton, 1712–13; and 'Lawes for regulating the Societie of Husbandmen within the shyre of Clackmannane, 1699'.]

Accompt of expenses in Edinburgh by Alexander Rose, son of the laird of Kilravock, 1715. Edited, from the original document, with introduction, by A. H. Millar.

Papers about the rebellions of 1715 and 1745. I. A journall of severall occurences in 1715, by Peter Clarke. II. Eight letters by William Nicolson, D.D., Bishop of Carlisle, to the Archbishop of York, 1716. III. Leaves from the diary of John Campbell, an Edinburgh banker in 1745. Edited, from the original manuscripts, with introduction and notes, by Henry Paton.

16. The account book of Sir John Foulis of Ravelston, 1671– 1707. Edited from the original manuscript, with introduction and glossary, by A. W. Cornelius Hallen. 1894. **24.16**

> Transcripts, 1671–3, 1679–81. 1705–7, and extracts, 1689–1705. Also notes on their families by George Bannatyne, 1512–1606 (for another transcript of which see **6**.38), Sir John Foulis, William Foulis of Woodhall, and others, 1600–1825.

17. Letters and papers illustrating the relations between Charles the Second and Scotland in 1650. Edited, with notes and introduction, by Samuel R. Gardiner. 1894. **24.17**

> Transcripts and extracts, 1649–51. Also account of the trial of Neil McLeod of Assynt before the Court of Justiciary, 1674.

18. Scotland and the Commonwealth. Letters and papers relating to the military government of Scotland, from August 1651 to December 1653. Edited, with introduction and notes, by Charles H. Firth. 1895. **24.18**

19. The Jacobite attempt of 1719. Letters of James Butler, second Duke of Ormond, relating to Cardinal Alberoni's project **24.19**

for the invasion of Great Britain on behalf of the Stuarts, and to
the landing of a Spanish expedition in Scotland. Edited, with an
introduction, notes and an appendix of original documents, by
William K. Dickson. 1895.

> French and Italian, with English translations or abstracts, and English.
> 1718–19.

20. The lyon in mourning, or a collection of speeches, letters,   **24.20**
journals, etc. relative to the affairs of Prince Charles Edward
Stuart. By the Rev. Robert Forbes, A.M., Bishop of Ross and
Caithness, 1746–1775. Edited from his manuscript, with a
preface, by Henry Paton. Vol. i. 1895.

> 1745–8. The collection was compiled 1746–75, and includes much informa-
> tion collected orally from participants in the '45 rising.

21. The lyon in mourning. . . . Vol. ii. 1895.   **24.21**

> 1745–50.

22. The lyon in mourning. . . . Vol. iii. 1896.   **24.22**

> 1745–75. Mainly Forbes' correspondence with other Jacobites.

23. Itinerary of Prince Charles Edward Stuart from his landing   **24.23**
in Scotland, July 1745, to his departure in September 1746.
Compiled from The lyon in mourning, supplemented and
corrected from other contemporary sources by Walter B.
Blaikie. With a map. 1897.

> Also Donald MacDonnell of Lochgarry's narrative of the rising, 1745–6,
> written (c. 1747) for Alexander MacDonnell of Glengarry.

24. Records of the presbyteries of Inverness and Dingwall,   **24.24**
1643–1688. Edited, with an introduction, from the original
manuscript, by William Mackay. 1896.

> Abridged transcripts and abstracts. Inverness, 1643, 1670–88; Dingwall,
> 1649–87.

25. The records of the commissioners of the General Assemblies   **24.25**
of the Church of Scotland [vol. ii:] holden in Edinburgh the
years 1648 and 1649. Edited from the original manuscript by
Alexander F. Mitchell and James Christie. 1896.

> 11 Aug. 1648–13 July 1650. Also declarations by Montrose, the General
> Assembly and Charles II, 1649–50. For vols. i and iii see **24.11, 58**.

26. Diary of Sir Archibald Johnston, Lord Wariston, 1639. The   **24.26**
preservation of the honours of Scotland, 1651–2. . . . 1896.

> Fragment of the diary of Sir Archibald Johnston, Lord Wariston, 1639.
> Edited by George M. Paul. [Includes some notes of 1640.]

Papers relative to the preservation of the honours of Scotland, in Dunnottar Castle, 1651–1652. Edited by Charles R. A. Howden. [1652–62 and *c.* 1702. Relate to controversy as to credit for preserving the regalia.]

The Earl of Mar's legacies to Scotland, and to his son, Lord Erskine, 1722–1727. Edited by the Hon. Stuart Erskine. [Reflections and suggestions on the past and future of Scotland and Ireland. Includes letters of James Stuart, the Old Pretender, to Mar, 1722–3.]

Letters written by Mrs Grant of Laggan concerning Highland affairs and persons connected with the Stuart cause in the eighteenth century. Edited by J. R. N. Macphail. [Letters of Anne Grant to Henry Steuart of Allanton, 1808.]

27. Memorials of John Murray of Broughton, sometime secretary to Prince Charles Edward, 1740–1747. Edited, with an introduction, notes and an appendix of original documents, by Robert F. Bell. 1898.   24.27

Memorials *c.* 1737–48, written between *c.* 1757 and Murray's death in 1777; and letters and papers, 1740–9 (French and English).

28. The compt buik of David Wedderburne, merchant of Dundee, 1587–1630. Together with the shipping lists of Dundee, 1580–1618. Edited from the original manuscripts, with introduction and notes, by A. H. Millar. 1898.   24.28

The compt book includes lists of charters, genealogical notes and miscellaneous memoranda, as well as financial entries. Shipping lists, 1580–9, 1612–19.

29. The diplomatic correspondence of Jean de Montereul and the brothers De Bellièvre, French ambassadors in England and Scotland, 1645–48. Edited, with an English translation, introduction and notes, by J. G. Fotheringham. Vol. i. 1898.   24.29

1645–7.

30. The diplomatic correspondence. . . . Vol. ii. 1899.   24.30

1647–8. Also related docs., 1643–8.

31. Scotland and the Protectorate. Letters and papers relating to the military government of Scotland from January 1654 to June 1659. Edited, with introduction and notes, by Charles H. Firth. 1899.   24.31

1651–9.

32. Papers illustrating the history of the Scots Brigade in the service of the United Netherlands, 1572–1782. Extracted by permission from the government archives at The Hague, and edited by James Ferguson. Vol. i: 1572–1697. 1899.   24.32

French; and English translations from Dutch. Transcripts and extracts. 1573–1690. Spine reads *Scots Brigade in Holland.*

33. Genealogical collections concerning families in Scotland, made by Walter Macfarlane, 1750–1751. Edited from the original manuscripts in the Advocates' Library, by James T. Clark. Vol. i. 1900.   **24.33**

Partly Latin, with English translation. Transcripts of genealogies compiled in the 17th and 18th centuries.

34. Genealogical collections. . . . Vol. ii. 1900.   **24.34**

Transcripts of genealogies compiled in the 16th–18th centuries.

35. Papers illustrating the history of the Scots Brigade. . . . Vol. ii: 1698–1782. 1899.   **24.35**

Transcripts and extracts, 1697–1797, 1812. For vol. iii see **24.38**.

36. Journals of Sir John Lauder, Lord Fountainhall, with his observations on public affairs and other memoranda, 1665–1676. Edited, with introduction and notes, by Donald Crawford. 1900.   **24.36**

Transcripts, some abridged. Journal of a tour in France, with notes of expenditure, 1665–7 (some French and Latin); notes of journeys in England and Scotland, 1667–72; chronicle of events connected with the Court of Session, 1668–76; observations on public affairs, 1669–70. Also accounts, 1670–5 (extracts); catalogue of books bought, 1667–79; and letter to his son, 1691.

37. Papal negotiations with Mary Queen of Scots during her reign in Scotland 1561–1567. Edited, from the original documents in the Vatican Archives and elsewhere, by John H. Pollen. 1901.   **24.37**

Latin, French, Italian and Spanish, mainly with English translations or abstracts. Transcripts (sometimes abbreviated) and extracts, 1542–69.

38. Papers illustrating the history of the Scots Brigade in the service of the United Netherlands, 1572–1782. Edited by James Ferguson. Vol. iii: I. The Rotterdam papers, 1709–82; II. The remembrance: a metrical account of the war in Flanders, 1701–12. By John Scot, soldier. 1901.   **24.38**

The papers consist of registers of marriages and baptisms, communion rolls, and extracts from accounts, 1708–89, all extracted from regimental records. Scot's poem covers 1701–11. For vols. i and ii see **24.32, 35**.

39. The diary of Andrew Hay of Craignethan, 1659–1660. Edited, with introduction and notes, by Alexander G. Reid. 1901.   **24.39**

Hay supported the extreme 'Protester' faction in the kirk.

40. The Cromwellian Union. Papers relating to the negotiations for an incorporating union between England and Scotland,   **24.40**

1651–1652. With an appendix of papers relating to the negotiations in 1670. Edited, with introduction and notes, by C. Sanford Terry. 1902.

> 1651–2, 1669–70.

41. The loyall dissuasive and other papers concerning the affairs of Clan Chattan: by Sir Aeneas Macpherson, knight of Invereshie, 1691–1705. Edited with notes and introduction from the originals at Cluny Castle, by Alexander D. Murdoch. 1902. **24.41**

> Much of the material relates to events in the Highlands before and after the 1688–9 Revolution. Includes a history of the Clan Chattan (upholding the Macphersons against the Macintoshes), and a denunciation of a genealogy of the Farquharsons. Also readers' comments on *The loyall dissuasive*, and an account of Sir Aeneas' death in 1705.

42. Chartulary of the abbey of Lindores, 1195–1479. Edited from the original manuscript at Caprington Castle, Kilmarnock, with translation and abstracts of the charters, illustrative notes, and appendices, by John Dowden. 1903. **24.42**

> Latin. *c.* 1180–1479. For another cartulary see **1.22**.

43. A letter from Mary Queen of Scots to the Duke of Guise, January 1562. Reproduced in facsimile from the original manuscript in the possession of the late John Scott, of Halkshill. Edited, with translation, historical introduction and appendix of original documents, by John H. Pollen. 1904. **24.43**

> French, with English translation. Also William Maitland of Lethington's account of negotiations with Queen Elizabeth, 1561; and other docs., 1561–2 (some French and Italian, with English translations).

44. Miscellany of the Scottish History Society. Vol. ii. . . . 1904. **24.44**

> The Scottish king's household and other fragments, from a fourteenth century manuscript in the Library of Corpus Christi College, Cambridge. Edited by Mary Bateson. [French, with English translation.]
> The Scottish nation in the University of Orléans, 1336–1538. Edited by John Kirkpatrick. [Latin, with English translation. Extracts from the university's 'Book of the Scottish nation'.]
> Muster-roll of the French garrison at Dunbar, 1553. Edited by Robert S. Rait. [French, with English translation.]
> The antiquity of the Christian religion among the Scots. From the original Latin of George Thomson, Scot, 1594. Translated and edited by Henry D. G. Law. [Translated from first edition, Rome and Douai 1594. An appeal to Scottish Catholics to support the Scots College at Douai.]
> The apology for William Maitland of Lethington, 1610. Edited by Andrew Lang. [Written by James Maitland to defend his father (who d. 1573) from attacks by historians, but unfinished. The ms. is dated 1616. Also extracts

from miscellaneous docs. concerning James Maitland and attempts to recover the forfeited Lethington estates, 1584–1625.]

Some letters and correspondence of George Graeme, Bishop of Dunblane and of Orkney, 1602–1638. Edited by L. G. Graeme. [Letters and miscellaneous docs., 1602–42.]

A Scottish journie, being an account in verse of a tour from Edinburgh to Glasgow in 1641. By P.J. Edited by Charles H. Firth.

Narratives illustrating the Duke of Hamilton's expedition to England in 1648. I. The relation of Mr Thomas Reade. II. The relation of Sir Philip Musgrave. Edited by Charles H. Firth. [Reade was secretary to English commissioners in Scotland; Musgrave was an English royalist.]

Certain papers of Robert Burnet, afterwards Lord Crimond, Gilbert Burnet, afterwards Bishop of Salisbury, and Robert Leighton, sometime Archbishop of Glasgow. Edited by H. C. Foxcroft. [Robert Burnet's reasons for his refusal to sign the Solemn League and Covenant, late 1640s; Gilbert Burnet's memorial of grievances and abuses of the Church of Scotland, late 1660s; and letters of Leighton to Gilbert Burnet, 1671, c. 1680–4.]

Letters and documents relating to Robert Erskine, physician to Peter the Great, Czar of Russia, 1677–1720. Edited by Robert Paul. [Some Latin and French, with English translations. 1692–1720.]

The will of Charlotte Stuart, Duchess of Albany. Edited by A. Francis Steuart. [Italian, with English translation. 1789.]

45. Letters of John Cockburn of Ormistoun to his gardener, 1727–1744. Edited, with introduction and notes, by James Colville. 1904.   24.45

46. The records of a Scottish cloth manufactory at New Mills, Haddingtonshire, 1681–1703. Edited from the original manuscripts, with introduction and notes, by W. R. Scott. 1905.   24.46

Minute book of the managers, 1681–91 (transcript) and 1701–3 (abridged transcript); and miscellaneous docs., 1681.

47. Chronicles of the Frasers. The Wardlaw manuscript, entitled 'Polichronicon seu policratica temporum, or, the true genealogy of the Frasers', 916–1674. By Master James Fraser, minister of the parish of Wardlaw (now Kirkhill), Inverness. Edited from the original manuscript, with notes and introduction, by William Mackay. 1905.   24.47

English. Abridged transcript omitting most material on English and foreign affairs. Includes much regional history for the 17th century. Begun 1666, completed after 1699.

48. The records of the proceedings of the Justiciary Court, Edinburgh, 1661–1678. Edited, with introduction and notes, from a ms. in the possession of John W. Weston, by W. G. Scott-Moncrieff, and with additional notes by the owner of the manuscript. Vol. i: 1661–1669. 1905.   24.48

49. The records of the proceedings of the Justiciary Court. . . .   24.49
Vol. ii: 1669–1678. 1905.

> 1669–74, with an account from another ms. of the trial (1678) of James
> Mitchell for attempting to murder the Archbishop of St Andrews.

50. Records of the baron court of Stitchill, 1655–1807.   24.50
Transcribed by George Gunn, and edited by Clement B. Gunn.
1905.

51. Geographical collections relating to Scotland made by   24.51
Walter Macfarlane. Edited from Macfarlane's transcript in the
Advocates' Library by Sir Arthur Mitchell. Vol. i. 1906.

> Topographical descriptions of many parishes and districts, 18th century.
> Macfarlane d. 1767.

52. Geographical collections . . . Vol. ii. 1907.   24.52

> Latin, with English translations, and English. Topographical descriptions,
> largely 16th and 17th centuries, including descriptions by Timothy Pont,
> Robert Gordon of Straloch, James Gordon, Sir John Scot of Scotstarvet and
> David Buchanan. Also includes Robert Gordon's discourse 'Anent the
> government of Scotland as it wes befor the late troubles' (i.e., before 1637).

53. Geographical collections . . . Edited. . . . by Sir Arthur   24.53
Mitchell and James T. Clark. Vol. iii. 1908.

> Antiquarian, historical and miscellaneous papers, as well as topographical
> descriptions. Mainly 16th and 17th centuries.

54. Statutes of the Scottish Church, 1225–1559. Being a   24.54
translation of Concilia Scotiae: Ecclesiae Scoticanae statuta tam
provincialia quam synodalia quae supersunt. With introduction
and notes by David Patrick. 1907.

> A translation of the entire text (statutes and miscellaneous related docs., c.
> 700–1563) of 6.116, with a few additional late 16th century docs.

55. Ochtertyre house booke of accomps, 1737–1739. Edited   24.55
with introduction and a glossary by James Colville. 1907.

> Household of William Murray of Ochtertyre. Also extract from inventory of
> furniture belonging to Sir Patrick Murray of Ochtertyre, 1763.

56. Charters, bulls and other documents relating to the abbey of   24.56
Inchaffray, chiefly from the originals in the charter chest of the
Earl of Kinnoull. Edited by William A. Lindsay, John Dowden
and J. Maitland Thomson. With map and facsimiles. 1908.

> Latin, with English abstracts, c. 1170s–c. 1609. See also 6.88.

57. A selection of Scottish Forfeited Estate papers, 1715; 1745.   **24.57**
Edited from the original documents, with introduction and
appendices, by A. H. Millar. 1909.

> Transcripts, extracts, abstracts and lists of docs., *c.* 1716–1806, but mainly
> 1746–1770s. Also abstracts of relevant acts of Parliament.

58. The records of the commissions of the General Assemblies of   **24.58**
the Church of Scotland [vol. iii:] holden in Edinburgh in 1650,
in St Andrews and Dundee in 1651, and in Edinburgh in 1652.
Edited from the original manuscript by James Christie. With an
introduction by the Hon. Lord Guthrie [Charles J. Guthrie.]
1909.

> 16 July 1650–30 May 1653. Also miscellaneous docs., 1650. For vols. i and ii
> see **24.11, 25.**

59. Papers relating to the Scots in Poland, 1576–1793. Edited   **24.59**
with an introduction by A. Francis Steuart. 1915.

> Some Latin and French, with English translations. 1576–1795.

60. De unione regnorum Britanniae tractatus. By Sir Thomas   **24.60**
Craig. Edited from the manuscript in the Advocates' Library,
with a translation and notes, by C. Sanford Terry. 1909.

> Written *c.* 1605.

61. Diary of Sir Archibald Johnston of Wariston, 1632–1639.   **24.61**
Edited from the original manuscript, with notes and introduction, by George M. Paul. 1911.

> 1632–4, 1637–9.

25. SCOTTISH HISTORY SOCIETY, SECOND SERIES*

Place of publication: Edinburgh.

1 (62). The household book of Lady Grisell Baillie, 1692–1733. 25.1
Edited, with notes and introduction, by Robert Scott-Moncrieff.
1911.

> Extracts. Also biographical notes on Robert Baillie of Jerviswood, who was
> executed in 1684; directions by Lady Baillie to servants, 1743; bills of fare,
> 1715–56; accounts of meat and drink, Mellerstain House, 1748–9; expenses
> of a visit to Bath and Bristol, 1729, and of a foreign tour, 1731–3; and
> memoranda (mainly advice for other travellers) of foreign tours, c. 1733–40.

2 (63). Origins of the 'Forty-Five, and other papers relating to 25.2
that rising. Edited by Walter B. Blaikie. 1916.

> 1742–9. Mainly narratives concerning the progress of the rising rather than
> its origins. Also a memorial of Henry, Cardinal of York, to the pope, 1766
> (Italian, with English translation.)

3 (64). Seafield correspondence from 1685 to 1708. Edited, with 25.3
introduction and annotations, by James Grant. 1912.

> Transcripts, with extracts from a few letters of 1651–83. Correspondence of
> James Ogilvy, 4th Earl of Findlater and 1st Earl of Seafield.

4 (65). Rentale Sancti Andree, being the chamberlain and 25.4
granitar accounts of the archbishopric in the time of Cardinal
Betoun, 1538–1546. Translated and edited by Robert K.
Hannay. 1913.

> Latin transcripts, 1538–9, with abbreviated English translations, 1538–46.

5 (66). Highland papers. Vol. i. Edited by J. R. N. Macphail. 25.5
1914.

> History of the Macdonalds. [Covers c. 1110–c. 1500. Written mid-late 17th
> century and attributed to Hugh Macdonald. Also illustrative docs.,
> 1337–1596 (Latin and English).]
> Macnaughtan of that Ilk. [Covers up to early 17th century. Includes charter
> of 1267 (Latin). Also roll of soldiers shipped from Lochkilkerran
> (Campbeltown Loch) by Alexander MacNaughtan, 1627.]

---

*The Society's numbering is followed, with a continuation of the cumulative
numbering adopted by Terry and Matheson appearing in brackets.

A succinct account of the family of Calder. [Covers up to late 18th century. Attributed to Lachlan Shaw, d. 1777.]

Papers relating to the murder of the laird of Calder. [Miscellaneous docs., 1594–6. John Campbell of Calder was shot in 1592.]

Genealogy of the Macras. [Covers up to mid-18th century. Attributed to Rev. John MacRa, d. 1704, with additions by Farquhar MacRa of Inverinate, d. 1789.]

Papers relating to the Macleans of Duart, 1670–1680. [Docs., 1631–81 and c. 1774, produced in court case of 1774 when Sir Allan Maclean sought to recover the Duart estates from the Campbells.]

6 (67). Selections from the records of the regality of Melrose, 1605–1661. Edited from the original volumes in the Register House, Edinburgh, and in the hands of Mr James Curle, by Charles S. Romanes. Vol. i. 1914.

25.6

Register of the regality court, 1605–9 (transcript) and 1657–61 (abstract); and abstract of the court's register of deeds 1641–51.

7 (68). Records of the earldom of Orkney, 1299–1614. Edited with introduction and notes by J. Storer Clouston. 1914.

25.7

English, some translated from Latin and Norwegian. Also extracts from the Orkneyinga Saga, c. 1000–1159.

8 (69). Selections from the records of the regality of Melrose. . . . Vol. ii: 1662–1676. 1915.

25.8

Abridged transcript and abstracts of the register of the regality court.

9 (70). The letter-book of Bailie John Steuart of Inverness, 1715–1752. Edited by William Mackay. 1915.

25.9

Abridged transcripts of 'selections' from letter-books, 1715–45, 1748–52.

10 (71). Rentale Dunkeldense, being accounts of the bishopric (A.D. 1505–1517), with Myln's 'Lives of the bishops' (A.D. 1483–1517). Translated and edited by Robert K. Hannay. And a note on the cathedral church by F. C. Eeles. 1915.

25.10

Abridged English translation of the accounts, and full translation of the last two-thirds of Alexander Myln's 'Lives'. For Latin texts of Myln and of a few of the accounts see 6.1. Also account of sums disbursed for the bishop by Mr James Crichton, 1558–9, and rentals from the books of assumption, 1560s.

11 (72). Letters relating to Scotland in the reign of Queen Anne. By James Ogilvy, first Earl of Seafield, and others. Edited by P. Hume Brown. 1915.

25.11

1702–8. All Seafield's letters, and most of the others, are addressed to Lord Godolphin. Includes paper by Sir George Mackenzie, Lord Tarbat, addressed to Anne on 'The first causes of Scotland's divisions', 1703; and papers on Jacobite conspiracies delivered to the Duke of Argyll, 1705. Spine reads *Lord Seafield's letters*.

12 (73). Highland papers. Vol. ii. Edited by J. R. N. Macphail.   25.12
1916.

The genealogie of the surname of M'Kenzie since ther coming into Scotland.
[By John M'Kenzie ot Applecross, 1667.]
Ane accompt of the genealogie of the Campbells. [Covers up to 1776.]
Writs relating chiefly to the lands of Glassarie and their early possessors.
[Latin, with English abstracts, and English. 1240–1672.]
Documents relating to the massacre at Dunavertie. [List of MacDougalls and
others killed, compiled c. 1661, and certificate by Sir James Turner in
favour of Colein M'Eacharne, 1662. The massacre took place in 1647.]
The ewill trowbles of the Lewes, and how the Macleoid of the Lewes was
with his whol trybe destroyed and put from the possession of the Lewes.
[Narrative covering 16th century to 1626 from a 17th century ms. Also
miscellaneous related docs., 1566–76 (Latin and English).]
Papers relating to the estates of the Chisholm and the Earl of Seaforth
forfeited in 1716. [Depositions before baron courts as to the rentals of the
former estates of Roderick Chisholm of Strathglass, 1721, and of Seaforth,
c. 1726; and rentals compiled from the depositions.]

13 (74). Selections from the records of the regality of Melrose,   25.13
and from the manuscripts of the Earl of Haddington. Edited
from the original volumes in the Register House, Edinburgh,
and in the possession of Mr James Curle, the Earl of Haddington
and others, by Charles S. Romanes. Vol. iii: 1547–1706. 1917.

Transcripts (some Latin with English translation or abstract), abstracts and
calendars of miscellaneous docs., including register of the regality court,
1682–4; rolls of the head courts, 1682–4; register of hornings and inhibitions,
1662–1706; and rentals, c. 1556 and c. 1564. Also inventory of Cairncross
charters, 1528–1668, and the charter of the weavers' incorporation of
Melrose, 1752.

14 (75). A contribution to the bibliography of Scottish   25.14
topography. By Sir Arthur Mitchell and C. G. Cash. Vol. i.
1917.

Arranged by counties and regions.

15 (76). A contribution to the bibliography of Scottish   25.15
topography. . . . Vol. ii. 1917.

Arranged by topics. An additional vol. in Aberdeen University Library
contains printed proofs arranged by topic with a ms. title page reading 'This
volume contains material collected for, but not used in Bibliography of
Scottish Topography. Scottish History Society 1917'.

16 (77). Papers relating to the army of the Solemn League and   25.16
Covenant, 1643–1647. Edited with an introduction by Charles S.
Terry. Vol. i. 1917.

The Scottish *Articles and ordinances of warre* from the London 1644 edition;
account of arms and ammunition for the expedition to England, 1644–7;

account of Sir Adam Hepburn of Humbie of money belonging to the Scottish army in England, 1644–5.

17 (78). Papers relating to the army of the Solemn League and Covenant. . . . Vol. ii. 1917.

25.17

Account of William Livingstone of money and victuals received for the use of the Earl of Callander's army, 1644–5; accounts of Sir Adam Hepburn of Humbie of money belonging to the Scottish armies in Scotland and England, 1645–6.

18 (79). Diary of Sir Archibald Johnston of Wariston. Vol. ii: 1650–4. Edited from the original manuscript, with notes and introduction by D. Hay Fleming. 1919.

25.18

Abridged transcript.

19 (80). Miscellany of the Scottish History Society. Vol. iii. 1919.

25.19

Dundee court-martial records, 1651. Edited by Godfrey Davies. [Extracts. Trials of English Cromwellian soldiers for looting, etc.]

The Bishop of Galloway's correspondence, 1679–1685. Edited by William Douglas. [1679–c. 1685. Bishop James Aitken.]

The diary of Sir James Hope, 1646–1654. Edited by Sir J. Balfour Paul. [Hope of Hopetoun. Partly concerned with his lead mining and other industrial interests.]

Instructions for the trial of Patrick Graham, 1476. Edited by Robert K. Hannay. [Latin, with English abstract. Instructions by Pope Sixtus IV for trial of the first Archbishop of St Andrews on charges of simony, blasphemy, etc.]

The Scottish contributions to the distressed church of France, 1622. Edited by D. Hay Fleming. [Receipt (French and English) for the contribution of the shire of Haddington; and extracts (including receipt) from the minutes of the kirk session of St Cuthbert's, Edinburgh.]

The Forbes baron court book, 1659–1678. Edited by J. Maitland Thomson. [Slightly abridged transcript. Also related docs., 1624, 1654.]

20 (81). Highland papers. Vol. iii. Edited by J. R. N. Macphail. 1920.

25.20

Papers relating to witchcraft, 1662–1677. [Relating to cases in Bute, 1662, to the alleged bewitching of Robert Douglas of Auchintulloch, 1665–7, and to sorcery in Appin, 1677.]

Memorial for Ffasfern. [Narrative by John Cameron of Ffasfern, 1753, denying charges made against him.]

Particular condescendance of some grievances. [Complaints by the commissioners of the General Assembly about the increase in popery and the insolence of priests and Jesuits, c. 1703, and about the insults and intrusions of episcopalians, c. 1714.]

Papers relating to Kintyre. [1596–1606. Includes list of tenants, 1596.]

Extracts from the collection of state papers in the Advocates' Library known as the Denmylne mss. [1607–25. Mainly relating to the 1614–15 rebellion by the MacDonalds of Islay.]

26. SCOTTISH HISTORY SOCIETY, THIRD SERIES*

Place of publication: Edinburgh.

1 (82). Register of the consultations of the ministers of
Edinburgh and some other brethren of the ministry. Vol. i:
1652–1657. Edited by William Stephen. 1921.

26.1

> Transcript. Negotiations on divisions in the kirk between the Protester and
> Resolutioner factions, and on relations with the Cromwellian regime. For
> vol. ii see **26.16**.

2 (83). Diary of George Ridpath, minister of Stitchel, 1755–
1761. Edited with notes and introduction by Sir James Balfour
Paul. 1922.

26.2

> Abridged transcript.

3 (84). Mary Queen of Scots and the Babington Plot. Edited,
from the original documents in the Public Record Office, the
Yelverton Mss., and elsewhere, by John H. Pollen. 1922.

26.3

> Mainly English, 1583–1611.

4 (85). Foreign correspondence with Marie de Lorraine, Queen
of Scotland. From the originals in the Balcarres papers. [Vol. i:]
1537–1548. Edited by Marguerite Wood. 1923.

26.4

> Mainly French, with English abstracts, but some English abstracts only. For
> vol. ii see **26.7**. Spine reads *Balcarres papers 1537–1548*.

5 (86). Papers from the collection of Sir William Fraser. Edited
by J. R. N. Macphail. 1924.

26.5

> Papers relating to Simon, Lord Lovat. [Account of trial of Thomas Fraser of
>   Beaufort, Captain Simon Fraser, etc., 1698, and related docs., 1697–8.]
> Papers relating to the Mearns. [Latin and English 15th to 19th centuries.
>   Includes valuations of Kincardineshire, 1657, 1669.]
> Writs relating to fishings in the Ythan. [Latin and English. 1534–67.]
> Royal proclamations. [1707–14.]
> Miscellaneous papers. [Latin and English. 1282, 1457, 1536–1837.]

---

*The Society's numbering is followed, with the cumulative numbering adopted by
Terry and Matheson appearing in brackets.

6 (87). Papers relating to the ships and voyages of the Company
of Scotland trading to Africa and the Indies, 1696–1707. Edited
by George P. Insh. 1924.   **26.6**

Spine reads *Darien shipping papers*.

7 (88). Foreign correspondence with Marie de Lorraine, Queen
of Scotland. From the originals in the Balcarres papers. [Vol. ii:]
1548–1557. Edited by Marguerite Wood. 1925.   **26.7**

Mainly French, with English abstracts, but some English abstracts only.
Includes some undated letters. Also Scots letters, 1549–59. Spine reads
Balcarres papers 1548–1557. For vol. i see **26.4**.

8 (89). Early records of the university of St Andrews. The
graduation roll, 1413–1579, and the matriculation roll, 1473–
1579. Transcribed and edited by James M. Anderson. 1926.   **26.8**

Latin. Also extracts (English) from the accounts of the Thirds of Benefices,
1568–79.

9 (90). Miscellany of the Scottish History Society. Vol. iv. 1926.   **26.9**

Commentary on the expedition to Scotland made by Charles Edward Stuart,
Prince of Wales, by Padre Giulio Cesare Cordara. Edited by Sir Bruce
Seton. [1745–6. Written 1751.]
The manuscript history of Craignish, by Alexander Campbell. Edited by
Herbert Campbell. [Written *c.* 1720.]
Miscellaneous charters, 1165–1300. From transcripts in the collection of the
late Sir William Fraser. Edited by William Angus. [Latin, with English
abstracts.]

10 (91). The Scottish correspondence of Mary of Lorraine,
including some three hundred letters from 20th February 1542–
3 to 15th May 1560. Edited by Annie I. Cameron. 1927.   **26.10**

Also letters *c.* 1571, 1578.

11 (92). The journal of Thomas Cuningham of Campvere,
1640–1654. With his thrissels-banner and explication thereof.
Edited by Elinor J. Courthope. 1928.   **26.11**

Cuningham was conservator at the Scottish staple port of Campvere.

12 (93). The sheriff court book of Fife, 1515–1522. Transcribed
and edited, with an introduction, notes, and appendices, by W.
Croft Dickinson. 1928.   **26.12**

Also Fife tax roll, 1517; 'The maner to hauld courtis', mid-16th century; and
the perquisites of the 'mair of fee' of Aberdeenshire, 1589. The introduction
analyses the history of sheriffs and sheriff courts in general.

13 (94). The prisoners of the '45. Edited from the state papers
by Sir Bruce G. Seton and Jean G. Arnot. Vol. i. 1928.   **26.13**

Miscellaneous docs., 1745–7.

14 (95). The prisoners of the '45. . . . Vol. ii. 1929.   **26.14**
Alphabetical list, A–L.

15 (96). The prisoners of the '45. . . . Vol. iii. 1929.   **26.15**
Alphabetical list, M–Z.

16 (97). Register of the consultations of the ministers of   **26.16**
Edinburgh. . . . Vol. ii: 1657–60. . . . 1930.
Abbreviated transcripts and abstracts. For vol. i see **26.1**.

17 (98). The minutes of the justices of the peace for Lanark-   **26.17**
shire, 1707–1723. Transcribed and edited by Charles A.
Malcolm. 1931.

18 (99). The Warrender papers. Edited by Annie I. Cameron   **26.18**
with an introduction by Robert S. Rait. Vol. i. 1931.
Mainly English, with some French and Latin. Transcripts or calendars of
letters and papers, mainly on public affairs, 1301, 1458, 1525–87.

19 (100). The Warrender papers. . . . Vol. ii. 1932.   **26.19**
As vol. i., 1587–1603.

20 (101). Flodden papers. Diplomatic correspondence between   **26.20**
the courts of France and Scotland, 1507–1517. Edited by
Marguerite Wood. 1933.
French, with English abstracts. Also 'Opinions' of the French clergy, 1510,
and draft treaty, 1512 (both Latin).

21 (102). Miscellany of the Scottish History Society. Vol. v.   **26.21**
1933.
Miscellaneous charters, 1315–1401, from transcripts in the collection of the
late Sir William Fraser. Edited by William Angus. [Latin, with English
abstracts.]
Bagimond's Roll for the archdeaconry of Teviotdale, from a thirteenth
century transcript in the Vatican Archives. Edited by Annie I. Cameron.
[Latin. Valuation of benefices made in the 1270s. See also **26.33** and **27.2**.]
Letters from John, Earl of Lauderdale, and others, to Sir John Gilmour,
president of Session. Edited by Henry M. Paton. [1651–68.]
Letters to John Mackenzie of Delvine from the Rev. Alexander Monro, 1690
to 1698. Edited by William K. Dickson.
Jacobite papers at Avignon. Edited by Henrietta Tayler. [French. 1716–49.]
Marchmont correspondence relating to the '45. Edited by G. F. C. Hepburne
Scott. [Letters to Hugh, 3rd Earl of Marchmont, 1745–6.]
Two fragments of autobiography, by George Keith, 10th Earl Marischal of
Scotland. Edited by J. Y. T. Greig. [French. 1740s.]

22 (103). Highland papers. Vol. iv. Edited by J. R. N.   **26.22**
Macphail. With a biographical introduction by William K.
Dickson. 1934.

Writs of and relating to the Campbells of Strachur. [Latin and English. Transcripts and summaries, 1334–1632.]
The Campbells of Auchinbreck. [Written 1740s.]
An account of the name of McLea. [Written 1743.].
The end of the active resistance to William of Orange in Scotland. [1690. Extracts from the *Account* printed in full in **26.46–7**.]
The Appin murder. [A letter describing the murder of Colin Campbell of Glenure, 1752, and some undated notes on the subsequent trial of James Stewart.]
Vatican transcripts. [Latin, with English abstracts. 1359–1499.]
Miscellaneous. [Latin and English. Charters etc., 1296–1716.]

23 (104). Calendar of Scottish supplications to Rome. [Vol. i:] 1418–1422. Edited by E. R. Lindsay and Annie I. Cameron. 1934. **26.23**

For vols. ii-iv see **26.48**, **27.7**.

24 (105). Early letters of Robert Wodrow, 1698–1709. Edited from the manuscript in Edinburgh University Library, with notes and extracts from the answers to these letters in the National Library of Scotland, by L. W. Sharp. 1937. **26.24**

For later letters by Wodrow see **43.5**.

25 (106). Warrender letters. Correspondence of Sir George Warrender, bt., lord provost of Edinburgh, and a member of Parliament for the city, with relative papers. 1715. Transcribed by Marguerite Wood. Edited with an introduction and notes by William K. Dickson. 1935. **26.25**

Mainly relating to the '15 rising.

26 (107). Commentary on the rule of St Augustine by Robertus Richardinus. Edited by G. G. Coulton. 1935. **26.26**

Latin, with English abstract. From Paris 1530 edition.

27 (108). Survey of Lochtayside, 1769. Edited with an introduction by Margaret M. McArthur. 1936. **26.27**

Surveys by John Farquharson and John McArthur.

28 (109). Ayr burgh accounts, 1534–1624. Transcribed and edited with an introduction by George S. Pryde. 1937. **26.28**

Abstracts, with transcripts for sample years.

29 (110). The court book of the barony of Carnwath, 1523–1542. Edited with an introduction by W. Croft Dickinson. 1937. **26.29**

The introduction analyses the history of baron courts in general. Appended to the volume is 'Scottish History Society. Fifty years, 1886–1936. By W. K. Dickson', which had been issued separately in 1936.

30 (111). A Scottish chronicle known as the chronicle of Holyrood. Edited by Marjorie O. Anderson. 1938. 26.30

Latin, with English translation after 1065–6. 13th century ms. up to 1189, with 14th or 15th century additions (including entries relating to Scots affairs, 1286–1318, 1355–6). For another edition see **6.23**.

31 (112). The Jacobite court at Rome in 1719. From original documents at Fettercairn House and at Windsor Castle. Edited by Henrietta Tayler. 1938. 26.31

Narrative by Alexander, Lord Pitsligo, 1719–20, and miscellaneous letters, 1719–27, 1751.

32 (113). Charters of the abbey of Inchcolm. Edited by D. E. Easson and Angus Macdonald. 1938. 26.32

Mainly Latin, with English abstracts, *c.* 1162–1569; and English abstracts only, 1555–1602. Also rentals, 1573–1605; and abstracts of royal letters, 1532.

33 (114). Miscellany of the Scottish History Society. Vol. vi. 1939. 26.33

Bagimond's Roll: statement of the tenths of the kingdom of Scotland. Edited by Annie I. Dunlop. [Latin. Valuation of benefices made in the 1270s. See also **26.21** and **27.2**.]
Foundation-charter of the collegiate church of Dunbar, A.D. 1342. Edited by D. E. Easson. [Latin, with English abstract.]
Letters from John, second Earl of Lauderdale, to John, second Earl of Tweeddale and others. Edited by Henry M. Paton. [1659–72.]
Memories of Ayrshire about 1780. By John Mitchell. Edited by William K. Dickson. [Relating largely to parish of Beith.]

34 (115). Diary of Sir Archibald Johnston of Wariston. Vol. iii: 1655–1660. Edited from the original manuscript, with notes and introduction by James D. Ogilvie. 1940. 26.34

Abridged transcript.

35 (116). Miscellany of the Scottish History Society. Vol. vii. 1941. 26.35

The diary of Sir William Drummond of Hawthornden, 1657–1659. Edited by Henry W. Meikle.
The exiled Stewarts in Italy, 1717–1807. Edited by Helen C. Stewart. [Mainly Italian and French, with English translations. Miscellaneous docs.]
The Locharkaig treasure. Edited by Marion F. Hamilton. [Miscellaneous docs., 1750–4, concerning gold buried by Jacobites in 1746.]

36 (117). Two missions of Jacques de la Brosse. An account of the affairs of Scotland in the year 1543, and the journal of the siege of Leith, 1560. Edited by Gladys Dickinson. 1942. 26.36

French, with English translations.

37 (118). Minutes of the synod of Argyll. [Vol. i:] 1639–1651. 26.37
Edited by Duncan C. Mactavish. 1943.

Also decreets of plantation, 1650–1.

38 (119). Minutes of the synod of Argyll. [Vol. ii:] 1652– 26.38
1661. . . . 1944.

39 (120). Selections from the Monymusk papers (1713–1755). 26.39
Transcribed and edited by Henry Hamilton. 1945.

Estate papers.

40 (121). Charters of the abbey of Coupar Angus. Vol. i: 26.40
1166–1376. Transcribed and edited by D. E. Easson. 1947.

Latin, with English abstracts.

41 (122). Charters of the abbey of Coupar Angus. Vol. ii: 26.41
1389–1608. . . . 1947.

Latin, with English abstracts, 1389–1608; and English abstracts only,
1552–1608.

42 (123). Accounts of the collectors of Thirds of Benefices, 26.42
1561–1572. Edited by Gordon Donaldson. 1949.

Transcripts and abstracts. Includes lists of ministers and readers and their
stipends.

43 (124). Miscellany of the Scottish History Society. Vol. viii. 26.43
1951.

Miscellaneous monastic charters. Edited by D. E. Easson. [Latin, with
English abstracts. Scone, Balmerino and Inchcolm, 1230–1532.]
A letter of James III to the Duke of Burgundy. Edited by C. A. J.
Armstrong. [Latin, with English abstract. c. 1471.]
The English army at Flodden. Edited by J. D. Mackie. [Financial papers,
1514.]
Lord Chancellor Glamis and Theodore Beza. By Gordon Donaldson. [Letter
of Glamis to Beza (Latin, with English translation), with Beza's answer
(English). c. 1576.]
Documents relating to Prince Charles Edward's grandson. Edited by
Henrietta Tayler. [French and English. 1817. Charles Edward Stuart,
Count Roehenstart.]
Papers relating to a Renfrewshire farm, 1822–30. Edited by George S. Pryde.
[Castlewalls, parish of Lochwinnoch.]

44 (125). Scottish population statistics, including Webster's 26.44
analysis of population, 1755. Edited by James G. Kyd. 1952.

Including summaries of censuses by county, 1801–1951.

45 (126). The letters of James the Fourth, 1505–1513. Calendared by Robert K. Hannay. Edited with a biographical memoir and an introduction by R. L. Mackie assisted by Anne Spilman. 1953.   **26.45**

Calendar. The memoir is of Hannay.

46 (127). An account of the proceedings of the Estates in Scotland, 1689–90. Edited by E. W. M. Balfour-Melville. Vol. i. 1954.   **26.46**

Reprint of a London periodical. Convention of Estates and Parliament.

47 (128). An account of the proceedings of the Estates in Scotland, 1689–90. . . . Vol. ii. 1955.   **26.47**

Also an account of William of Orange's acceptance of the government of Scotland, January 1689, from a London pamphlet.

48 (129). Calendar of Scottish supplications to Rome. [Vol. ii:] 1423–1428. Edited by Annie I. Dunlop. 1956.   **26.48**

Addenda to this volume appear in **27.7**. For vols. i, iii, iv see **26.23, 27.7**.

49 (130). Early records of the burgh of Aberdeen, 1317, 1398–1407. Edited by W. Croft Dickinson. 1957.   **26.49**

Latin. Transcripts, 1317, 1398–1400, and extracts, 1401–7.

50 (131). Miscellany of the Scottish History Society. Vol. ix. 1958.   **26.50**

Papers relating to the captivity and release of David II. Edited by E. W. M. Balfour-Melville. [Two Latin docs., one with English abstract. 1355–7, 1364.]

Accounts of Sir Duncan Forestar of Skipinch, comptroller, 1495–1499. Edited by Peter Gouldesbrough. [Latin.]

Report by de la Brosse and D'Oysel on conditions in Scotland, 1559–1560. Edited by G. Dickinson. [French. By Jacques de la Brosse and Henri Cleutin D'Oysel.]

The diary of Sir James Hope, 1646. Edited by P. Marshall. [Hope of Hopetoun. Concerns mainly a visit to the Netherlands and Hope's lead mining and other industrial interests.]

An account of proceedings from Prince Charles' landing to Prestonpans. Edited by Donald Nicholas. [1745. Written *post* 1770, probably by a member of the Clanranald.]

51 (132). Wigtownshire charters. Edited by R. C. Reid. 1960.   **26.51**

Transcripts (Latin) and abstracts. *c.* 1190, early 14th century–1585, 1661.

52 (133). John Home's survey of Assynt. Edited by R. J. Adam. 1960.   **26.52**

1774–5. Also rentals and lists of inhabitants, 1759–75, factors' accounts, 1764–73, and Home's accounts, 1774–5.

53 (134). The court book of the burgh of Kirkintilloch, 1658–   **26**.53
1694. Edited by George S. Pryde. 1963.

The introduction analyses the history of burghs of barony in general.

54 (135). Acta facultatis artium Universitatis Sanctiandree,   **26**.54
1413–1588. Edited by Annie I. Dunlop. Vol. i. 1964.

1413–53. Also English synopsis covering both vols.

55 (136). Acta facultatis artium Universitatis Sanctiandree,   **26**.55
1413–1588. . . . Vol. ii. 1964.

1453–1588. English synopsis in vol. i. The pagination of the two vols. is
continuous, and they were also issued (as a single vol.) as **19**.7.

27. SCOTTISH HISTORY SOCIETY, FOURTH SERIES*

Place of publication: Edinburgh.

1 (137). Argyll estate instructions. Mull, Morvern, Tiree. 1771–1805. Edited by Eric R. Cregeen. 1964.   27.1

Instructions of the 5th Duke of Argyll to his chamberlains.

2 (138). Miscellany of the Scottish History Society. Vol. x. 1965   27.2

E. W. M. Balfour-Melville (1887–1963). A memoir by D. B. Horn.
Bagimond's Roll for the diocese of Moray. Edited by Charles Burns. [Latin. Valuation of benefices made in the 1270s. See also **26.21, 33.**]
Accounts of the king's pursemaster, 1539–1540. Edited by Athol L. Murray.
Papers of a Dundee shipping dispute, 1600–1604. Edited by W. A. McNeill. [Letters and other papers by John Wallwood concerning a dispute with William Lindsay.]
A Scottish liturgy of the reign of James VI. Edited by Gordon Donaldson. [Draft liturgy of 1616 or 1617.]
Lists of schoolmasters teaching Latin, 1690. Edited by Donald J. Withrington. [Lists cover only certain shires and burghs in central and eastern Scotland. Also instructions to the commissioners for visiting universities and schools.]
Letters of Andrew Fletcher of Saltoun and his family, 1715–1716. Edited by Irene J. Murray.
Sir John Clerk's observations on the present circumstances of Scotland, 1730. Edited by T. C. Smout.
A Renfrewshire election account, 1832. Edited by William Ferguson. [Account of Andrew Paterson, solicitor, when acting as agent for Robert Cunninghame Bontine of Ardoch.]

3 (139). Letters of John Ramsay of Ochtertyre, 1799–1812. Edited by Barbara L. H. Horn. 1966.   27.3

Abridged transcripts of letters to Elizabeth Dundas (née Graham).

4 (140). The court books of Orkney and Shetland, 1614–1615. Edited by Robert S. Barclay. 1967.   27.4

Records of the sheriff courts of Orkney, 1614–15, and Shetland, 1615. Appended to the volume is 'Scottish History Society, 1886–1966. A commemorative record', which was also issued separately.

---

*The Society's numbering is followed, with a continuation of the cumulative numbering adopted by Terry and Matheson appearing in brackets.

5 (141). The minutes of Edinburgh Trades Council, 1859–1873.   **27.5**
Edited by Ian MacDougall. 1968.

Abridged transcript.

6 (142). The Dundee textile industry, 1790–1885. From the   **27.6**
papers of Peter Carmichael of Arthurstone. Edited by Enid
Gauldie. 1969.

Abridged transcript of Carmichael's autobiography, 1790–1842, and of
Alexander Monfries' Memoir of Carmichael, 1842–85. Both works contain
extracts from Carmichael's letters.

7 (143). Calendar of Scottish supplications to Rome. [Vol. iii:]   **27.7**
1428–1432. Edited by Annie I. Dunlop and Ian B. Cowan. 1970.

Includes addenda 1423–4 to vol. ii (**26.48**). Continued in *Calendar of Scottish
supplications to Rome. Vol. iv: 1433–1447.* Edited by Annie I. Dunlop and
David MacLauchlan. 1983. For vol. i see **26.23**.

8 (144). Papers on Sutherland estate management, 1802–1816.   **27.8**
Edited by R. J. Adam. Vol. i. 1972.

Miscellaneous docs.

9 (145). Papers on Sutherland estate management, 1802–1816.   **27.9**
Vol. ii. . . . 1972.

Letters.

10 (146). William Melrose in China, 1845–1855. The letters of a   **27.10**
Scottish tea merchant. Edited by Hoh-cheung Mui and Lorna
H. Mui. 1973.

Also accounts, lists of ships, etc.

11 (147). Papers on Scottish electoral politics, 1832–1854.   **27.11**
Edited by J. I. Brash. 1974.

Abridged transcripts of letters and other papers relating to Conservative
organisation and activities in the Midlothian constituency. Also Donald
Horne's election surveys, 1834–40.

12 (148). Calendar of papal letters to Scotland of Clement VII of   **27.12**
Avignon, 1378–1394. Edited by Charles Burns. 1976.

Includes a memoir of Annie I. Dunlop by Ian B. Cowan.

13 (149). Calendar of papal letters to Scotland of Benedict XIII   **27.13**
of Avignon, 1394–1419. Edited by Francis McGurk. 1976.

14 (150). Scottish industrial history. A miscellany. 1978.   **27.14**

Introductory essay. By R. H. Campbell.
Journal of Henry Kalmeter's travels in Scotland, 1719–1720. Edited by T. C.
   Smout. [Partly in original English, partly translated from the Swedish

original. Kalmeter was 'the first and possibly the most interesting of the industrial spies who came to Scotland from Sweden' in the 18th century.]

Journal of Henry Brown, woollen manufacturer, Galashiels, 1828–1829. Edited by C. Gulvin.

The North British Railway inquiry of 1866. Edited by W. Vamplew. [Shareholders' inquiry into fabricated accounts.]

The beginning and the end of the Lewis chemical works, 1857–1874, by D. Morison. Edited by T. I. Rae. [Written 1895 by the production foreman.]

15 (151). Papers on Peter May, land surveyor, 1749–1793. Edited by Ian H. Adams. 1979.   27.15

May was employed as surveyor by the Annexed Estate Commissioners and other clients, and as factor by the Earls of Findlater and Bute.

16 (152). Autobiography of John McAdam (1806–1883) with selected letters. Edited by Janet Fyfe. 1980.   27.16

Autobiography, 1806–80; letters, 1833–79. A radical and Chartist, McAdam corresponded with many European and British reformers and nationalists, including Mazzini, Garibaldi and Kossuth.

17 (153). Stirling presbytery records, 1581–1587. Edited by James Kirk. 1981.   27.17

Presbytery minutes.

18 (154). The government of Scotland under the covenanters, 1637–1651. Edited by David Stevenson. 1982.   27.18

Calendars of the registers of the committee of estates, Oct.–Nov. 1645 and May 1648; of the committee for dispatches, Jan.–Mar. and May–Aug. 1649; and of the committee for managing the affairs of the army, Apr.–May 1651. The introduction analyses the structure of government under the covenanters.

19 (155). The knights of St John of Jerusalem in Scotland. Edited by Ian B. Cowan, P. H. R. Mackay and Alan Macquarrie. 1983.   27.19

Rental of the lordship and preceptory of Torphichen, 1539–40, with interpolations added up to 1565; miscellaneous docs. relating to the knights, 1215–1567 (mainly Latin, with English abstracts); and calendar of material relating to Scotland in the archives of the knights in the National Library of Malta, 1338–1569.

20 (156). A Scottish firm in Virginia, 1767–1777. W. Cuninghame and Co. Edited by Thomas M. Devine. 1984.   27.20

Transcripts, from letter books, of the letters of James Robinson, the 'superintending factor' (normally based in Falmouth, Virginia) of a tobacco trading firm. The letters are addressed to the factors of the firm in Virginia, 1767–73, and to the firm's headquarters in Glasgow, 1772–7.

21 (157). The Jacobean Union. Six tracts of 1604. Edited by   27.21
Bruce R. Galloway and Brian P. Levack. 1985.

Of the union of Britayne. By Robert Pont. [A contemporary English
translation of the Latin edition, Edinburgh and London 1604. Pont was
minister of St Cuthbert's, Edinburgh.]

A treatise about the union of England and Scotland. [Printed from an
incomplete ms. written by an unknown Scot.]

A treatise of the happie and blissed unioun. By John Russell. [Printed from
the original ms., with variations contained in a revised version noted.
Russell was a Scot, probably a lawyer.]

A brief consideracion of the unyon of twoe kingedomes. By John Doddridge.
[From the only complete ms., and other mss. of sections of the tract.
Doddridge was appointed solicitor general of England in 1604.]

Of the union. By Sir Henry Spelman. [From a ms. in the author's hand.
Spelman was an English lawyer and antiquary.]

Historicall collections. By Sir Henry Savile. [From a contemporary ms.
Savile was an English classical scholar.]

28.   SCOTTISH LOCAL HISTORY GROUP

Place of publication: Glasgow

SCOTTISH LOCAL HISTORY TEXTS

1. Shipping in Dumfries and Galloway in 1820. Edited and with notes by Innes F. Macleod. 1973.

    Entries relating to ships registered at Dumfries, Kirkcudbright, Portpatrick, Stranraer and Wigtown extracted from *A list of the shipping registered in the different ports of Scotland*, Glasgow 1821. Also a list of ships arrived at and cleared from Dumfries, Kirkcudbright and Annan, from the *Dumfries Weekly Journal*, 8 Oct. 1822.

    28.1

2. The Upper Ward of Lanarkshire (1837). By David Wilson. Edited by Innes F. Macleod. 1984.

    'On the present state of the Upper Ward . . .' from *Prize Essays and Transactions of the Highland and Agricultural Society of Scotland*, New Series, vol. v (1837).

    28.2

3. Statistics of Selkirkshire (1832). By James Hogg. Edited by Innes F. Macleod. 1984.

    From *Prize Essays* . . ., New Series, vol. iii (1832).

    28.3

OLD GALLOWAY PAPERS

1. Old Kirkcudbright. Descriptions, engravings, maps, photographs, and walks. Edited and with notes by Innes F. Macleod. 1973.

    Includes extracts from descriptions, 1684–1866.

    28.4

2. A Galloway entertainment: folklore, amusements, songs and poems. Edited and with notes by Innes F. Macleod. 1973.

    28.5

3. Poems chiefly in the Scottish dialect (1796). By John Lauderdale of Kirkinner. Edited by Innes F. Macleod. 1984.

    Selections from *A collection of poems chiefly* . . ., Edinburgh 1796. Lauderdale (born *c*. 1740) left County Antrim and settled in Kirkinner parish in the late 18th century.

    28.6

4. Reminiscences of Wigtonshire (1872). By Samuel Robinson.   **28.7**
Edited by Innes F. Macleod. 1984.

   Abridged and re-arranged from *Reminiscences of Wigtonshire about the close of*
   the last century, with contrasts, and appendices of odds and ends in rhyme,
   Hamilton 1872. Robinson, a stonemason, lived 1786–1875.

29. SCOTTISH RECORD SOCIETY, OLD SERIES*

Place of publication: Edinburgh.

1. The commissariot record of Edinburgh. Register of testa- **29.1**
ments. Pt. 1: volumes 1 to 35—1514–1600. Edited by Francis J.
Grant. 1897. (No part no.).

> Index to testaments confirmed 1567–1800, with a few entries from other
> sources 1514–32, 1564–5. Published by the British Record Society, Scottish
> Section, as vol. xvi of the Index Library.

2. The commissariot record of Edinburgh. Register of testa- **29.2**
ments. Pt. 2: volumes 35 to 81—1601–1700. Edited by Francis
J. Grant. 1898. (Pts. 1, 2, 4).

> Index to testaments confirmed 1601–7, 1608–29, 1630–1700, with gaps filled
> from a minute book.

3. The commissariot record of Edinburgh. Register of testa- **29.3**
ments. Pt. 3: volumes 81 to 131—1701–1800. Edited by Francis
J. Grant. 1899. (Pts. 5–7).

> Index.

4. The commissariot record of Inverness. Register of testaments, **29.4**
1630–1800. Edited by Francis J. Grant. 1897. (No pt. no.).

> Index to testaments confirmed 1630–4, 1666–70, 1676–81, 1713–1800.
> Published by the British Record Society, Scottish Section, as part of vol. xx
> of the Index Library.

5. The commissariot record of Hamilton and Campsie. Register **29.5**
of testaments 1564–1800. Edited by Francis J. Grant. 1898.
(Pt. 3).

> Index to testaments confirmed 1564–75, 1591–1641, 1651–81, 1711–45,
> 1760–1800 with some gaps filled from original testaments. Also published by
> the British Record Society, Scottish Section, as part of vol. xx of the Index
> Library.

---

* The numbering is that adopted by the Society, but most of **29.**1–83 were originally
issued in parts. Sometimes one of these parts corresponds with a vol., sometimes several
parts together make up a vol., and sometimes a single part contains several vols. The
original part numbers are given in brackets at the end of the title entries.

6. The commissariot record of Aberdeen. Register of testaments, 1715–1800. Edited by John Macleod. 1899. (Pt. 8).   **29.6**

> Index to original testaments, as there is no register.

7. The commissariot record of Glasgow. Register of testaments, 1547–1800. Edited by Francis J. Grant. 1901. (Pts. 9–13).   **29.7**

> Index to testaments confirmed 1547–55, 1563–5, 1602–92, 1694–1701, 1706–8, 1717–1800.

8. The commissariot record of St Andrews. Register of testaments, 1549–1800. Edited by Francis J. Grant. 1902. (Pts. 14–17).   **29.8**

> Index to testaments confirmed 1549–51, 1583–1600, 1605–7, 1613–21, 1624–9. 1634–41, 1648–57, 1661–2, 1672–6, 1681–1724, 1744–60, 1769–1800, with index 1724–44 and 1769–1800 from a minute book.

9. The commissariot record of Argyle. Register of testaments, 1674–1800. Edited by Francis J. Grant. 1902. (Pt. 18).   **29.9**

> Index to testaments confirmed 1674–8, 1684–95, 1705–1800.
> See also **29.33** for 1693–1702.

10. The commissariot record of Caithness. Register of Testaments, 1661–1664. Edited by Francis J. Grant. 1902. (Pt. 18).   **29.10**

> Index to testaments confirmed 1661–4.

11. The commissariot record of the Isles. Register of testaments, 1661–1800. Edited by Francis J. Grant. 1902. (Pt. 18).   **29.11**

> Index to testaments confirmed 1661–75, 1705–1800.

12. The commissariot record of Peebles. Register of testaments, 1681–1699. Edited by Francis J. Grant. 1902. (Pt. 18).   **29.12**

> Index to testaments confirmed 1681–99.

13. The commissariot record of Brechin. Register of testaments, 1576–1800. Edited by Francis J. Grant. 1902. (Pt. 19).   **29.13**

> Index to testaments confirmed 1576–1602, 1609–14, 1621–42, 1656–65, 1677–1742, 1750–77, with some gaps filled from original testaments.

14. The commissariot record of Dumfries. Register of testaments, 1624–1800. Edited by Francis J. Grant. 1902. (Pt. 20).   **29.14**

> Index to testaments confirmed 1624–31, 1637–43, 1656–9, 1661–2, 1673–93, 1716–1800, with index 1693–1716 from a minute book.

15. The commissariot record of Dunblane. Register of testaments, 1539–1800. Edited by Francis J. Grant. 1903. (Pt. 21).   **29.15**

> Index to testaments confirmed 1539–47, 1553–8, 1598–1612, 1615–24, 1629–33, 1635–7, 1661–3, 1666–89, 1694–1800.

16. The commissariot record of Dunkeld. Register of testa-   **29.16**
ments, 1682–1800. Edited by Francis J. Grant. 1903. (Pt. 22).

Index to testaments confirmed 1687–96, 1712–76, with some gaps filled from
original testaments.

17. The commissariot record of Kirkcudbright. Executry   **29.17**
papers, 1663–1800. Edited by Francis J. Grant. 1903. (Pt. 22).

Index. Also a list of deaths and burials for the parish of Borg *c.* 1682–4.

18. The commissariot record of Lauder. Register of testaments,   **29.18**
1561–1800. Edited by Francis J. Grant. 1903. (Pt. 23).

Index to testaments confirmed 1561–6, 1627–34 (incomplete), 1634–41,
1650–65, 1667–82, with some gaps filled from other sources.

19. The commissariot record of Lanark. Register of testaments,   **29.19**
1595–1800. Edited by Francis J. Grant. 1903. (Pt. 24).

Index to testaments confirmed 1595–1602, 1620–36, 1638–9, 1643–4, 1650–
8, 1661–71, 1673–1800.

20. The commissariot record of Moray. Register of testaments,   **29.20**
1684–1800. Edited by Francis J. Grant. 1904. (Pt. 25).

Index to testaments confirmed 1684–1744, 1746–69, 1771–1800.

21. The commissariot record of Orkney and Shetland. Register   **29.21**
of testaments. Pt. 1: Orkney, 1611–1684. Pt. 2: Shetland,
1611–1649. Edited by Francis J. Grant. 1904. (Pt. 25).

Indices to testaments confirmed 1611–15, 1618–62, 1663–71, 1679–84, with
no Shetland entries after 1649. For Orkney see also **30.6**.

22. The commissariot record of Stirling. Register of testaments,   **29.22**
1607–1800. Edited by Francis J. Grant. 1904. (Pts. 26–7).

Index to testaments confirmed 1607–28, 1630–1728, with entries up to 1800
from original testaments.

23. The commissariot record of Wigtown, testaments, 1700–   **29.23**
1800. Edited by Francis J. Grant. 1904. (Pt. 28).

Index to original testaments, as there is no register.

24. Miscellaneous executry papers preserved in H.M. Register   **29.24**
House. 1481–1740. Edited by Francis J. Grant. 1904. (Pt. 28).

Index.

25. Register of burials in the chapel royal or abbey of   **29.25**
Holyroodhouse, 1706–1900. [Edited by Francis J. Grant.] 1900.
(Pt. 12).

Reprinted from *The Scottish Antiquary*, vol. xv. Last entry 1895.

26. Register of interments in the Greyfriars burying-ground,   **29.26**
Edinburgh, 1658–1700. Edited by Henry Paton. 1902. (No pt.
no.).
   Index of interments 1658–77, 1683–1700.

27. The register of marriages for the parish of Edinburgh,   **29.27**
1595–1700. Edited by Henry Paton. 1905. (Pts. 29–34).
   Index.

28. The register of apprentices of the city of Edinburgh,   **29.28**
1583–1666. Edited by Francis J. Grant. 1906. (Pt. 35).
   Index.

29. Protocol book of Gavin Ros, N.P., 1512–1532. Edited by   **29.29**
John Anderson and Francis J. Grant. 1908. (Pts. 36–9).
   Calendar. Mainly relating to Ayr, Ayrshire and Lanarkshire.

30. Register of baptisms, chapels at Bairnie and Tillydesk,   **29.30**
1763–1801, and index. Edited by John Macgregor. 1908. (Pt.
39).
   Episcopalian chapels. Bairnie 1763–75; Tillydesk 1775–83, with a few entries
   1788–1801.

31. Index to genealogies, birthbriefs, and funeral escutcheons   **29.31**
recorded in the Lyon Office. By Francis J. Grant. 1908. (Pt. 40).
   17th to 19th centuries.

32. Index to the register of burials in the churchyard of   **29.32**
Restalrig. 1728–1854. Edited by Francis J. Grant. 1908. (Pt.
41).

33. The commissariot of Argyll. Register of inventories, 1693–   **29.33**
1702. Edited by Francis J. Grant. 1909. (Pt. 44).
   Index. See also **29.9**.

34. The commissariot of Edinburgh. Consistorial processes and   **29.34**
decreets, 1658–1800. Edited by Francis J. Grant. 1909. (Pt. 47).
   Chronological list, with index.

35. The register of marriages for the parish of Edinburgh,   **29.35**
1701–1750. Edited by Henry Paton. 1908. (Pts. 42–3, 45–6, 48).
   Index.

36. Charter chest of the earldom of Wigtown, 1214–1681;   **29.36**
charter chest of the earldom of Dundonald, 1219–1672. Edited
by Francis J. Grant. 1910. (Pt. 49).
   Transcripts of inventories compiled in 1681 and *c.* 1672 respectively.
   Separate paginations.

37. Protocol book of Sir Alexander Gaw, 1540–1558. Edited by
John Anderson and William Angus. 1910. (Pt. 50).   **29.37**

Calendar. Mainly relating to Fife and Perthshire, especially Abernethy.

38. Parish register of Durness, 1764–1814. Edited by Hew
Morrison. 1911. (Pt. 53).   **29.38**

Baptisms 1764–1814; and marriages 1765–1814.

39. Protocol book of Sir William Corbet, 1529–1555. Edited by
John Anderson and William Angus. 1911. (Pt. 52).   **29.39**

Calendar. Mainly relating to Berwickshire and Roxburghshire, especially the
parishes of Linton and Merton.

40. Register of baptisms, proclamations, marriages and mort-
cloth dues contained in kirk-session records of the parish of
Torphichen, 1673–1714. Edited by John Macleod. 1911.
(Pt. 52).   **29.40**

Index. Proclamations 1673–1714; mortcloth dues 1673–1704; baptisms
1675–9, 1687–91.

41. Index to the register of marriages and baptisms in the parish
of Kilbarchan, 1649–1772. Edited by Francis J. Grant. 1912.
(Pt. 58).   **29.41**

Index. Marriages 1649–51, 1652–62, 1672–83, 1689–94; proclamations of
marriages 1740–72; baptisms 1651–62, 1672–83, 1688–1711, 1740–69.

42. Inventory of documents relating to the Scrymgeour family
estates, 1611. Edited by J. Maitland Thomson. 1912. (Pts.
57–8).   **29.42**

Calendar. Late 13th century–1611, with additions to 1636.

43. Protocol book of Mr Gilbert Grote, 1552–1573. Edited by
William Angus. 1914. (Pt. 63).   **29.43**

Calendar. Mainly relating to Edinburgh.

44. Parish registers of Dunfermline, 1561–1700. Edited by
Henry Paton. 1911. (Pts. 52, 54, 66, 70–1, 128–9, 132, 134).   **29.44**

Transcripts and calendar. Baptisms and marriages, 1561–91, 1598–1685
(incomplete).

45. Melrose parish registers of baptisms, marriages, proclamations of marriages, session minutes (1723–1741) and mortuary
rolls, 1642–1820. Edited by Charles S. Romanes. 1913. (Pts.
50–1, 54–6, 59, 62, 70).   **29.45**

The arrangement of the contents is very confusing, as follows: baptisms,
1642–86, 1690–1723; baptisms, marriages and discipline, 1723–1819
(including kirk session minutes, 1723–41); proclamations for marriages,

1624; marriages, 1645–66; testimonials, 1652–66; marriages, 1690–1723, 1739–1820; mortuary roll (deaths or burials), 1760, 1763–81; use of mortcloth, 1669–1702; baptisms, 1650s; marriages, 1695–1703; deaths, 1781–1819.

46. Parish of Holyroodhouse or Canongate. Register of marriages, 1564–1800. Edited by Francis J. Grant. 1915. (Pts. 54–5, 60–1, 64–5, 68).   **29.46**

Index. 1564–7, 1600–31, 1645–75, 1685–1800. Marriages 1600–31 are indexed in an appendix, having been overlooked when the main index was compiled.

47. Monumental inscriptions in St Cuthbert's churchyard, Edinburgh. (Older portion). Compiled by John Smith. Edited by Sir James Balfour Paul. 1915. (Pt. 69).   **29.47**

48. Parish registers of Canisbay (Caithness), 1652–1666. Edited by Donald Beaton. 1914. (Pt. 67).   **29.48**

Baptisms 1652–66; marriage contracts 1652–61, 1663–6; and marriages 1653–60.

49. Register of births and marriages for the episcopal congregation at St Andrews, 1722–1787. Edited by Edward G. A. Winter. 1916. (Pt. 73).   **29.49**

Mainly births and baptisms. Also a list of subscriptions to the episcopal church at St Andrews, 1747–72.

50. Parish lists of Wigtownshire and Minnigaff, 1684. Edited by William Scot. 1916. (Pt. 72).   **29.50**

Lists of all persons aged over twelve, indicating those who were religious dissidents.

51. Monumental inscriptions in St Cuthbert's churchyard, Edinburgh. (Newer portion). Compiled by John Smith. Edited by Sir James Balfour Paul. 1919. (Pt. 82).   **29.51**

52. Protocol books of Dominus Thomas Johnsoun, 1528–1578. Edited by James Beveridge. 1920. (Pts. 76, 78, 83, 87).   **29.52**

Calendar. Mainly relating to Linlithgow.

53. Register of marriages of the city of Edinburgh, 1751–1800. Edited by Francis J. Grant. 1922. (Pts. 79–81, 84–6, 88–92).   **29.53**

Index.

54. An inventory of Lamont papers (1231–1897). Collected, edited and presented . . . by Sir Norman Lamont of Knockdow. 1914. (No part no.).   **29.54**

Calendar, with some transcripts (Latin, with English abstracts). *Further additions (1442–1859) and corrections to an inventory of Lamont papers*, with an index, was issued in 1918 (pagination continuous).

55. Calendar of writs preserved at Yester House, 1166–1625. Compiled by Charles C. H. Harvey and John Macleod. 1930. (Pts. 74–5, 77, 106, 113).   29.55
Includes transcripts of the earlier writs (Latin, with English translations). Hays of Yester.

56. The burgesses and guild brethren of Glasgow, 1573–1750. Edited by James R. Anderson. 1925. (Pts. 93–8).   29.56
Chronological list, with indexes.

57. Protocol books of James Foulis, 1546–1553, and Nicol Thounis, 1559–1564. Edited by James Beveridge and James Russell. 1927. (Pts. 100, 105).   29.57
Calendars. Separate paginations. Mainly relating to Linlithgow.

58. Some family papers of the Hunters of Hunterston. Edited by M. S. Shaw. 1925. (Pt. 99).   29.58
Latin, with English translations, and English. Transcripts and calendars, 1296–1912.

59. Roll of Edinburgh burgesses and guild-brethren, 1406–1700. Edited by Charles B. B. Watson. 1929. (Pts. 101–4, 108–9).   29.59
Index.

60. Register of Edinburgh apprentices, 1666–1700. Edited by Charles B. B. Watson. 1929. (Pt. 110).   29.60
Index.

61. Register of Edinburgh apprentices, 1701–1755. Edited by Charles B. B. Watson. 1929. (Pt. 111).   29.61
Index.

62. Roll of Edinburgh burgesses and guild-brethren, 1701–1760. Edited by Charles B. B. Watson. 1930. (Pts. 112, 114–15).   29.62
Index. For some additions, 1740–60, see 29.68.

63. Protocol book of Sir John Cristisone, 1518–1551. Edited by R. H. Lindsay. 1930. (Pts. 107, 113).   29.63
Calendar. Mainly relating to Aberdeen, south Aberdeenshire (especially Monymusk), and north Kincardineshire.

64. Protocol book of John Foular, 9th March 1500–1 to 18th   **29.64**
September 1503. Transcribed and summarised by Walter
Macleod, with introduction and index by Marguerite Wood.
1930. (No part no.).

> Mainly Latin, with English translations, 1496, 1501–3. Mainly relating to
> Edinburgh. See also **29.72, 75, 30.10.**

65. Protocol book of Sir Robert Rollock, 1534–1552. Edited by   **29.65**
William Angus. 1931. (Pt. 118).

> Calendar. Mainly relating to Perth and Perthshire.

66. The burgesses and guild-brethren of Glasgow, 1751–1846.   **29.66**
Edited by James R. Anderson. 1935. (Pts. 116–17, 119–21, 123,
127).

> Chronological list, with indexes.

67. Inventory of Pitfirrane writs, 1230–1794. Edited by William   **29.67**
Angus. 1932. (Pt. 122).

> Compiled in 1834. Halkets of Pitfirrane.

68. Roll of Edinburgh burgesses and guild-brethren, 1761–   **29.68**
1841. Edited by Charles B. B. Watson. 1933. (Pts. 124–5).

> Index. Includes additional burgesses for 1740–60 (see **29.62**).

69. Services of heirs, Roxburghshire, 1636–1847. Edited by   **29.69**
John Macleod. 1934. (Pt. 126).

> Chronological list compiled in 1875.

70. The Binns papers, 1320–1864. Edited by Sir James Dalyell   **29.70**
of Binns and James Beveridge. 1938. (Pts. 130–1, 135).

> Calendar. Dalyells of the Binns.

71. Calendar of writs of Munro of Foulis, 1299–1823. Edited by   **29.71**
C. T. McInnes. 1940. (Pts. 136–7).

72. Protocol book of John Foular, 1503–1513. Volume i   **29.72**
(continued). [Edited by Marguerite Wood.] 1941. (Pts. 138–9,
141).

> Calendar. 'Volume i' refers to the original ms. Mainly relating to Edinburgh.
> See also **29.64, 75, 30.10.**

73. Roll of Dumbarton burgesses and guild-brethren, 1600–   **29.73**
1846, with a continuation thereof to the present day. Compiled
from the town council records and other sources by Fergus
Roberts. 1937. (Pt. 133).

> Index.

74. Protocol book of James Young, 1485–1515. Edited by   **29.74**
Gordon Donaldson. With an introduction by Henry M. Paton.
1952. (Pts. 140, 142–3, 146, 151, 154, 157, 160).

> Calendar. Mainly relating to Canongate and Edinburgh.

75. Protocol book of John Foular, 1514–1528. Volumes ii and   **29.75**
iii. Edited by Marguerite Wood. 1953. (Pts. 144, 147, 149–50,
161).

> Calendar. 'Volumes ii and iii' refers to the original mss. Mainly relating to
> Edinburgh. See also **29.64, 72, 30.10**.

76. The Faculty of Advocates in Scotland, 1532–1943, with   **29.76**
geneaological notes. Edited by Sir Francis J. Grant. 1944. (Pt.
145).

> List of members of the faculty, with a list of pre-1532 advocates.

77. Court of the Lord Lyon. List of his majesty's officers of   **29.77**
arms and other officials, with geneaological notes, 1318–1945.
Edited by Sir Francis J. Grant. 1945. (Pt. 148).

78. Register of marriages of the parish of Unst, Shetland,   **29.78**
1797–1863. Edited by Sir Francis J. Grant. 1947. (Pt. 152).

> Index. 1797–1802, 1811–63.

79. Inventory of the principal progress-writs of the barony of   **29.79**
Innes, 1225–1767. Edited by Sir Thomas Innes of Learney.
1948. (Pt. 153).

> Compiled in 1767.

80. Marriages at Gretna Hall, 1829–Ap. 30, 1855. Edited by   **29.80**
E. W. J. M'Connel. 1949. (Pt. 155).

> Index.

81. Registers of the episcopal congregation in Leith, 1733–1775.   **29.81**
Edited by Angus Macintyre. 1949. (Pt. 156).

> Baptisms 1733–75; marriages 1738–75; and confirmations 1736–69.

82. Edinburgh poll tax returns for 1694. Edited by Marguerite   **29.82**
Wood. 1951. (Pt. 158).

> Index. Old Kirk and Tolbooth parishes only.

83. Register of the burgesses of the burgh of the Canongate from   **29.83**
27th June 1622 to 25th September 1733. Edited by Helen
Armet. 1951. (Pt. 159).

> Index.

84. The court book of Shetland, 1602–1604. Edited with introduction, glossary and index, by Gordon Donaldson. 1954.   29.84
   Sheriff and justice court.

85. Book of records of the ancient privileges of the Canongate. Edited by Marguerite Wood. 1955.   29.85
   Calendar. 1439–1658. Rentals, tax rolls, seals of cause to incorporations, etc.

86. Protocol book of Mark Carruthers, 1531–1561. Edited by R. C. Reid. 1956.   29.86
   Calendar. Mainly relating to Dumfries and Dumfriesshire.

87. Court minutes of Balgair, 1706–1736. Edited by Jean Dunlop. 1957.   29.87
   Balgair was not a barony, so the court was that of the lands of Balgair (which were held by the Galbraiths).

88. The Lag charters, 1400–1720. Sir Philip J. Hamilton-Grierson's calendar. Edited by Athol L. Murray. 1958.   29.88
   Calendar of Grierson of Lag charters, compiled c. 1913.

89. The burgh court book of Selkirk, 1503–1545. Edited by John Imrie, Thomas I. Rae and W. D. Ritchie. 2 pts. 1960–9.   29.89
   Transcripts and calendars. The third and final part has not been published.
   1: 1503–31.
   2: 1531–41.

90. The buik of the kirk of the Canagait, 1564–1567. Edited by Alma B. Calderwood. 1961.   29.90
   Kirk session minutes, and registers of baptisms, marriages, proclamations of banns, and communicants.

91. Inhabitants of the Argyll estate, 1779. Edited by Eric R. Cregeen. 1963.   29.91

92. Register of Edinburgh apprentices, 1756–1800. Edited by Marguerite Wood. 1963.   29.92
   Index.

93. The parishes of medieval Scotland. By Ian B. Cowan. 1967.   29.93

94. Records of the Church of Scotland preserved in the Scottish Record Office and General Register Office, Register House, Edinburgh. 1967.   29.94
   Also issued as appendix to *Records of the Scottish Church History Society*, vol. xvi.

95. Calendar of irregular marriages in the South Leith kirk session records, 1697–1818. Edited by James S. Marshall. 1968.   29.95

30. SCOTTISH RECORD SOCIETY, NEW SERIES

Place of publication: Edinburgh.

1. Fasti Ecclesiae Scoticanae medii aevi ad annum 1638. Second draft. By Donald E. R. Watt. 1969.   **30.1**

Lists of principal officials of dioceses, cathedrals and collegiate churches.

2. Directory of former Scottish commonties. Edited by Ian H. Adams. 1971.   **30.2**

3. Scottish parish clergy at the Reformation, 1540–1574. By Charles H. Haws. 1972.   **30.3**

List of parishes showing clergy who served in them or drew their revenues; and list of those who served in the post-Reformation church as super-intendents, ministers, exhorters and readers, indicating their antecedents.

4. Annan parish censuses, 1801–21. Edited by George Gilchrist. 1975.   **30.4**

1801, 1811 and 1821, with tax roll, 1798.

5. A directory of landownership in Scotland c. 1770. Edited by Loretta R. Timperley. 1976.   **30.5**

Compiled mainly from valuation rolls.

6. Orkney testaments and inventories, 1573–1615. Edited by Robert S. Barclay. 1977.   **30.6**

Calendar, with selected transcripts, of all testaments relating to deaths 1573–1615 which were registered 1612–32.

7. Painters in Scotland, 1301–1700. A biographical dictionary. Compiled and edited by Michael R. Apted and Susan Hannabuss. 1978.   **30.7**

8. The Urquhart censuses of Portpatrick, 1832–53. Edited by N. L. Tranter. 1980.   **30.8**

1832, 1844, 1846, 1852, 1853. Compiled by the Rev. Andrew Urquhart.

9. West Lothian hearth tax, 1691, with county abstracts for Scotland. Edited by Duncan Adamson. 1981.   **30.9**

An index (separate, but pagination continuous) compiled by Iain Scott and Hector Crawford was also issued.

10. Protocol book of John Foular, 1528–1534. Edited by John   **30**.10
Durkan. 1985.

Mainly relating to Edinburgh. See also **29**.64, 72, 75.

11. Visitation of the diocese of Dunblane and other churches,   **30**.11
1586–1589. Edited by James Kirk. 1984.

Visitation of 25 parishes (only 15 of which were within the pre-Reformation
diocese of Dunblane) by James Anderson, minister of Stirling. Also James
VI's commissions to Anderson to act as commissioner of Dunblane, and to
David Lindsay to act as commissioner for Lothian, 1586.

31. SCOTTISH TEXT SOCIETY, OLD SERIES*

Place of publication: Edinburgh.

1. The kingis quair: together with A ballad of good counsel: by   **31.1**
King James I of Scotland. Edited by Walter W. Skeat. 1884.
(Pt. 1).
> Verse. For a revised edition see **32.1**

2. The poems of William Dunbar. Edited by John Small. 3 vols.   **31.2**
1893.
> i : Introduction. By A. J. G. Mackay. With prefatory note. (Pt. 16). [Also
> extracts from records relating to Dunbar, 1477–1513.]
> ii : Poems. (Pts. 2, 4).
> iii: Notes and glossary by Walter Gregor. And an appendix on the
> intercourse between Scotland and Denmark, by A. J. G. Mackay. (Pts. 21,
> 29).

3. Ane treatise callit The court of Venus, deuidit into four   **31.3**
buikis. Newlie compylit be Iohne Rolland in Dalkeith, 1575.
Edited by Walter Gregor. 1884. (Pt. 3).
> Verse.

5. The historie of Scotland wrytten first in Latin by the most   **31.4**
reuerend and worthy Jhone Leslie, Bishop of Rosse, and
translated in Scottish by Father James Dalrymple, religious in
the Scottis Cloister of Regensburg, the zeare of God, 1596.
Edited by E. G. Cody. 2 vols. 1888–95. (Pts. 5, 14; pts. 19, 34).
> 330 B.C.–1561. Translated from the first edition, Rome 1578. For a
> vernacular version (1437–1561) completed in 1570 see **6.41**.

---

* Many volumes in the first series were originally issued in several parts, and Terry,
Catalogue, listed them under the earliest part number included in a vol. (or, in the case of
works running to more than one vol., under the earliest part number included in the
vols.). This means that there are gaps in the numerical sequence in which the vols. are
listed. The original part numbers are given in brackets at the end of title entries.

6. The actis and deidis of the illustere and vailzeand campioun   31.5
Schir William Wallace, knicht of Ellerslie. By Henry the
Minstrel, commonly known as Blind Harry. Edited by James
Moir. 1889. (Pts. 6, 7, 17).

> Verse. From a ms. of 1488, collated with the Edinburgh 1570 edition. For
> other editions see **33.13** and **34.4, 5.**

8. Sir Tristrem. Edited by George P. McNeill. 1886. (Pt. 8).   31.6

> Verse. A Scottish romance from the Auchinleck ms., early 14th century.

9. The poems of Alexander Montgomerie. Edited by James   31.7
Cranstoun. 1887. (Pts. 9–11).

> Montgomerie d. 1598. See **31.26** for a supplementary vol.

12. The richt vay to the kingdom of heuine. By John Gau.   31.8
Edited, with introduction and notes, by Arthur F. Mitchell. The
glossarial index by T. G. Law. 1888. (Pt. 12).

> From the Malmo 1533 edition. For another edition see **6.22.**

13. Legends of the saints in the Scottish dialect of the fourteenth   31.9
century. Edited from the unique manuscript in the University
Library, Cambridge. With introduction, notes, and glossarial
index, by W. M. Metcalfe. 3 vols. 1896.

> Verse.
> i : Introduction and text. (Pts. 13, 18).
> ii : Completion of text. (Pts. 23, 25).
> iii: Notes and indices. (Pts. 35, 37).

15. Certain tractates. Together with the book of four score three   31.10
questions and a translation of Vincentius Lirinensis. By Ninian
Winzet. Edited, with introduction, notes, and glossarial index,
by J. King Hewison. 2 vols. 1888–90.

> i: (Pt. 15). ['Certane tractatis', 'The last blast of the trompet' and 'The buke
> of four scoir thre questions', from the editions detailed under **15.34,** which
> also prints these works. Also docs. relating to Winzet etc., late 16th
> century (Latin and English).]
> ii: (Pt. 22). [The translation of Vincentius. This is also printed in **15.34,**
> which see for details. Also docs. relating to Winzet etc., late 16th century
> (Latin, German and English).]

20. Satirical poems of the time of the Reformation. Edited by   31.11
James Cranstoun. 2 vols. 1891–3.

> i : (Pts. 20, 24). [Texts. 1565–84.]
> ii: (Pts. 28, 30). [Notes and glossary. Also two poems by Thomas
> Churchyard, on the siege of Edinburgh Castle (from the 1575 and 1578
> editions) and on the career and execution of the Earl of Morton (from the
> 1593 edition).]

26. Vernacular writings of George Buchanan. Edited by P. Hume Brown. 1892 (Pt. 26).   **31.12**

> 1560s and 1570s.

27. Scottish alliterative poems in riming stanzas. Edited, with introduction, appendix, notes and glossary, by F. J. Armours. 1897. (Pts. 27, 38).   **31.13**

> From 14th–16th century mss. and printed editions. Contains 'The knightly tale of Golagros and Gawane', Sir Richard Hollands' 'The buke of the howlat' (for other editions see **6.**3 and **16.**6), 'Rauf Coilzear', 'The awntyr off Arthure' and 'The pistill of Susan'. 'The awntyr' is now regarded as English rather than Scots. 'The knightly tale' and 'Rauf' are sometimes attributed to Hary, the author of 'The Wallace'.

31. The Bruce. Or the book of the most excellent and noble prince Robert de Broyss, King of Scots. Compiled by Master John Barbour, Archdeacon of Aberdeen, A.D. 1375. Edited from Ms. G. 23 in the library of St John's College Cambridge, written A.D. 1487; collated with the ms. in the Advocates' Library at Edinburgh, written A.D. 1489 and with Hart's edition, printed A.D. 1616. With a preface, notes, and glossarial index by Walter W. Skeat. 2 vols. 1894.   **31.14**

> Verse. For other editions see **34.**12, 13, **36.**28.
> i : Containing the preface and books I to XIII. (Pts. 31, 33).
> ii: Containing books XIV to XX, notes, and glossary. (Pt. 32).

36. The poems of Alexander Scott. Edited by James Cranstoun. 1896. (Pt. 36).   **31.15**

> Mid-16th century. From the Bannatyne ms., 1568.

39. A compendious book of godly and spiritual songs, commonly known as 'The gude and godlie ballatis'. Reprinted from the edition of 1567. Edited, with introduction and notes, by Arthur F. Mitchell. 1897. (Pt. 39).   **31.16**

40. The works of Sir William Mure of Rowallan. Edited, with introduction, notes, and glossary, by William Tough. 2 vols. 1898. (Pts. 40, 41).   **31.17**

> Mainly verse. Mure lived 1594–1657. Vol. ii includes 'The Historie and descent of the house of Rowallane' (prose).

42. The historie and cronicles of Scotland from the slauchter of King James the First to the ane thousande fyve hundreith thrie scoir fyftein zeir. Written and collected by Robert Lindesay of Pitscottie. Being a continuation of the translation of the chronicles written by Hector Boece and translated by John Bellenden. . . . Edited by A. J. G. Mackay. 3 vols. 1899–1911.   **31.18**

i : (Pt. 42). [1437–1542. Up to 1460 Pitscottie's work is a translation of Hector Boece. For Bellenden's translation see 33.10.]
ii : (Pt. 43). [1542–76.]
iii: Glossary and index. (Pt. 60). [Matheson, *Catalogue*, lists this vol. as 60.]

44. Gilbert of the Haye's prose manuscript (A.D. 1456). Edited, with introduction, by J. H. Stevenson. 2 vols. 1901–14. **31.19**

Translations of French originals. Also partly printed in 1.27, which see for details.
i : The buke of the law of armys, or buke of bataillis. (Pt. 44).
ii: The buke of knychthede and The buke of the governaunce of princis. (Pt. 62). [Matheson, *Catalogue*, lists this vol. as 62.]

45. Catholic tractates of the sixteenth century, 1573–1600. Tyrie's Refutation, 1573 Hay's Demandes, 1580. Hamilton's Catholik traictise, 1581. Burne's Disputation, 1581. Canisius' Catechism, 1588. Hamilton's Facile traictise, 1600. Ane schort Catholik confession, ms. Selections edited, with introduction and glossary, by Thomas G. Law. 1901. (Pt. 45). **31.20**

The tracts by James Tyrie, John Hay, John Hamilton, Nicol Burne and (translating Pierre Canisius) Adam King are all from printed editions. Also Patrick Anderson's *The ground of the Catholike and Roman religion* and Alexander Baillie's *A true information*, from the 1623 and 1628 editions.

46. The New Testament in Scots. Being Purvey's revision of Wycliffe's version turned into Scots by Murdoch Nisbet, *c.* 1520. Edited from the unique ms. in the possession of Lord Amherst of Hackney by Thomas G. Law. 3 vols. 1901–5. (Pts. 46, 49, 52). **31.21**

47. Livy's history of Rome. The first five books, translated into Scots by John Bellenden, 1533. Edited, with introduction, notes, and glossary, by William A. Craigie. 2 vols. 1901–3. (Pts. 47, 51). **31.22**

48. The poems of Alexander Hume (?1557–1609). Edited from the text of Waldegrave (1599), with notes, appendices, and glossary, by Alexander Lawson. 1902. (Pt. 48). **31.23**

Mainly religious. Also several prose religious tracts including 'Ane afold admonitioun', for details of which see the edition of some of Hume's works at 6.44. The 'Admonitioun' is also printed in 43.11.

50. The original chronicle of Andrew of Wyntoun. Printed on parallel pages from the Cottonian and Wemyss mss., with the variants of the other texts. Edited, with introduction, notes, and glossary, by F. J. Amours. 6 vols. 1903–14. **31.24**

Verse. Wyntoun began writing his chronicle in the 1390s. Beginning as a general history, it concentrates on Scotland from book IV onwards. After 1286 the work's character changes markedly; the earlier attention to ecclesiastical history disappears and the chronicle concentrates on narrating the wars with England up to 1408.

i : Introduction, notes, glossary and index. (Pt. 63). [Matheson, *Catalogue*, lists this vol. as 63.]
ii : (Texts: books I–III). (Pt. 50).
iii: Texts: books IV, V (Ch. I–XII). (Pt. 53).
iv: Texts: books V (Ch. XIII, XIV), VI, VII (Ch. I–VII). (Pt. 54).
v : Texts: books VII (Ch. VIII–X), VIII (Ch. I–XXIV). (Pt. 56).
vi: Texts: books VIII (Ch. XXV–XL) and IX. (Pt. 57).

55. The poems of Robert Henryson. Edited by G. Gregory Smith. 3 vols. 1906–14. **31.25**

Henryson d. *c.* 1506.
i : Introduction, appendix, notes, index of words and glossary, general index. (Pt. 64). [Matheson, *Catalogue*, lists this vol. as 64.]
ii : (Text—vol. i). (Pt. 55).
iii: (Text—vol. ii). (Pt. 58).

59. Poems of Alexander Montgomerie, and other pieces from Laing ms. no. 447. Supplementary volume. Edited, with introduction, appendices, notes, and glossary, by George Stevenson. 1910. (Pt. 59). **31.26**

Supplements **31.7**. Also extracts from docs. relating to Montgomerie, 1583–97.

61. A bibliography of Middle Scots poets. With an introduction on the history of their reputations. By William Geddie. 1912. (Pt. 61). **31.27**

65. Pieces from the Makculloch and the Gray mss., together with the Chepman and Myllar prints. Edited by George Stevenson. 1918. (Pt. 65). **31.28**

Verse interpolations written in late 15th and early 16th centuries in earlier mss., and poems printed Edinburgh 1508.

32.   SCOTTISH TEXT SOCIETY, NEW SERIES

Place of publication: Edinburgh.

1. The kingis quair: together with A ballad of good counsel: by King James I of Scotland. Edited by Walter W. Skeat. Second and revised edition. 1911.

32.1

Verse. See **31.1** for the first edition; and **18.2** for another edition.

2. Lancelot of the Laik, from Cambridge University Library Ms. Edited by Margaret M. Gray. 1912.

32.2

Verse romance. Also printed as **15.49**.

3. The poetical works of William Drummond of Hawthornden, with 'A cypresse grove'. Edited by L. E. Kastner. Vol. i. 1913.

32.3

For other editions see **3.6** and **15.18**.

4. The poetical works of William Drummond of Hawthornden. . . . Vol. ii. 1913.

32.4

Includes the prose 'A cypresse grove'.

5. Poems of John Stewart of Baldynneis, from the ms. in the Advocates' Library, Edinburgh. Edited by Thomas Crockett. Vol. ii: (Text). 1913.

32.5

From a ms. of *c*. 1586. Vol. i was never published.

6. The works of William Fowler, secretary to Queen Anne, wife of James VI. Edited, with introduction, appendix, notes, and glossary, by Henry W. Meikle. Vol. i: (Verse). 1914.

32.6

Fowler d. 1612. For vols. ii and iii see **33.7, 14**.

7. The Maitland folio manuscript. Containing poems by Sir Richard Maitland, Dunbar, Douglas, Henryson and others. Edited by William A. Craigie. Vol. i. 1919.

32.7

Maitland d. 1586; William Dunbar d. *c*. 1530; Gavin Douglas d. 1522; Robert Henryson d. *c*. 1506. For vol. ii see **32.20**.

8. The thre prestis of Peblis how thai tald thar talis. Edited from the Asloan and Charteris texts by T. D. Robb. 1920.

32.8

Verse. From an early 16th century ms. and the 1603 edition.

9. The Maitland quarto manuscript. Containing poems by Sir Richard Maitland, Arbuthnot and others. Edited by William A. Craigie. 1920.

32.9

Maitland d. 1586; Alexander Arbuthnot d. 1583.

10. Habakkuk Bisset's Rolment of courtis. Edited by Sir Philip J. Hamilton-Grierson. Vol. i. 1920.

32.10

Completed by 1626. Historical narrative and analysis mainly concerned with Scots law, legal procedures, courts and pre-Reformation religious organization. Book I. For Vols. ii and iii, see **32.13, 18**.

11. The poetical works of Sir William Alexander, Earl of Stirling. Edited by L. E. Kastner and H. B. Charlton. Vol. i: the dramatic works. With an introductory essay on the growth of the Senecan tradition in Renaissance tragedy. 1921.

32.11

Alexander lived 1567?–1640. For vol. ii, see **32.24**.

12. The buik of Alexander or the buik of the most noble and valiant conquerour Alexander the Grit. Edited, in four volumes, from the unique printed copy in the possession of the Earl of Dalhousie, with introductions, notes, and glossary, together with the French originals (Li fuerres de gadres and Les voeux du paon), collated with numerous mss., by R. L. Graeme Ritchie. Vol. ii: containing part 2 of The buik of Alexander . . ., and part 1 of Les voeux du paon, now edited for the first time. . . . 1921.

32.12

Verse romance. From the first edition, Edinburgh *c.* 1580. By John Barbour, d. 1395. The pagination of the four vols. is continuous. For vols. i, iii and iv see **32.17, 21, 25**. See **6.49** for another edition.

13. Habakkuk Bisset's Rolment. . . . Vol. ii. 1922.

32.13

Books II–VI. For vols. i and iii see **32.10, 18**.

14. The Asloan manuscript. A miscellany in prose and verse, written by John Asloan in the reign of James the Fifth. Edited by William A. Craigie. Vol. i. 1923.

32.14

A treatise on penance and confession by 'Master Jhon Irland'; a metrical version of an account of the game of chess by Jacobus de Cessolis; a universal geography, partly from Ralph Higden's 'Polychronicon'; the 'Porteous of nobleness', probably transcribed from the Edinburgh 1508 edition (which was in turn translated from Alain Chartier, 'Le breviaire des nobles'); two treatises on the origin of the Scots (another version of one of which is also printed in **6.22**); 'A short memorial of the Scottish chronicles for addition' with entries for 1420–60 (sometimes known as the Auchinleck chronicle); a chronicle (of no independent value) to 1513; The spectacle of love, translated by G. Myll (also printed in **6.21**); and a treatise on the six days of creation and the six ages of the world. For vol. ii see **32.16**.

15. Fergusson's Scottish proverbs, from the original print of 1641, together with a larger manuscript collection of about the same period hitherto unpublished. Edited by Erskine Beveridge. 1924.

32.15

Collected by David Fergusson, minister of Dunfermline, d. 1598.

16. The Asloan Manuscript. . . . Vol. ii. 1925.

32.16

Verse.

17. The buik of Alexander or the buik of the most noble and valiant conquerour Alexander the Grit. By John Barbour, Archdeacon of Aberdeen. Edited . . . by R. L. Graeme Ritchie. Vol. i: Containing part 1 of The buik of Alexander . . ., and Li fuerres gadres. . . . 1925.

32.17

Verse romance. For vols. ii–iv see 32.12, 21, 25.

18. Habakkuk Bisset's Rolment . . . Vol. iii. 1926.

32.18

Introduction, notes to vols. i–ii (32.10, 13), and glossary.

19. The meroure of wyssdome. Composed for the use of James IV, King of Scots, A.D. 1490. By Johannes de Irlandia, professor of theology in the university of Paris. Edited by Charles Macpherson. Vol. i. 1926.

32.19

Books I–II. Some verse (Latin). For vol. ii see 34.2.

20. The Maitland folio manuscript. . . . Vol. ii. 1927.

32.20

Introduction, notes, vocabulary, and index. For vol. i see 32.7.

21. The buik of Alexander. . . . Vol. iii: Containing part 3 of The buik of Alexander . . . and part 2(1) of Les voeux du paon, now edited for the first time. . . . 1927.

32.21

For vols. i, ii and iv see 32.17, 12, 25.

22. The Bannatyne manuscript. Writtin in tyme of pest, 1568. By George Bannatyne. Edited by W. Tod Ritchie. Vol. ii. 1928.

32.22

Verse. The ms. is dated 1568. For vols. i, iii and iv see 33.5, 32.23, 26. See 11.1 for another edition.

23. The Bannatyne manuscript. . . . Vol. iii. 1928.

32.23

24. The poetical works of Sir William Alexander. . . . Vol. ii: The non-dramatic works. 1929.

32.24

For vol. i see 32.11.

25. The buik of Alexander. . . . Vol. iv: Containing part 4 of   **32.25**
The buik of Alexander . . ., and part 2(2) of Les voeux du paon,
now edited for the first time. . . . 1929.

   For vols. i–iii see **32**.17, 12, 21.

26. The Bannatyne manuscript. . . . Vol. iv. 1930.   **32.26**

33. SCOTTISH TEXT SOCIETY, THIRD SERIES

Place of publication: Edinburgh.

1. The works of Sir David Lindsay of the Mount, 1490–1555. Edited by Douglas Hamer. Vol. i: Text of the poems. 1931.   **33.1**

Also Henry Charteris' preface to the Edinburgh 1568 edition of Lindsay's works. For vols. ii–iv see **33.2, 6, 8**.

2. The works of Sir David Lindsay. . . . Vol. ii: Ane satyre of the thrie estaitis. 1931.   **33.2**

Prose account of the 1540 performance, by Sir William Eure; the Bannatyne ms. version, 1568; and the Edinburgh 1602 edition.

3. The seuin seages. Translatit out of prois in Scottis meter be Iohne Rolland in Dalkeith. . . . Edited, with introduction, notes, and glossary, by George F. Black. 1932.   **33.3**

Verse. From the Edinburgh 1578 edition. For another edition see **6.60**.

4. Miscellany volume. 1933.   **33.4**

The Scottish Text Society. 1882–1932. By Walter B. Menzies. [A history.]
The sea law of Scotland. Edited by T. Callander Wade. [By William Welwood. English and Scots versions, from the Edinburgh 1590 editions.]
Philotus. Edited by A. J. Mill. [Play (verse). From the Edinburgh 1603 edition. Also printed as **6.53**.]
The joy of tears (Sir William Mure). [Edited by C. Davis. Verse. From the 1635 edition.]
Robert Wedderburn, notary and poet. By Walter B. Menzies. [Biographical. Wedderburn lived 1546–1611.]
The quare of jelusy. Edited by J. T. T. Brown. [Verse. Doubtfully attributed to James Auchinleck. Late 15th century? Also printed in **6.21** and **19.2**.]

5. The Bannatyne manuscript. . . . Vol. i. 1934.   **33.5**

Introduction, text of a duplicate of part of the ms., and indices. Also docs. relating to Bannatyne and his family; and an abbreviated version of **6.38**. For vols. ii–iv see **32.22, 23, 26**.

6. The works of Sir David Lindsay. . . . Vol. iii: Notes to the poems. 1934.   **33.6**

For vols. i, ii and iv see **33.1, 2, 8**.

7. The works of William Fowler. . . . Vol. ii: (Prose). 1936.   **33.7**

Includes 'An answer to . . . an apostat named M. Io. Hammiltoun' from the Edinburgh 1581 edition; Fowler's translation of Machiavelli, 'The prince'; and an account of the baptism of Prince Henry, from the Edinburgh 1594 edition. For vols. i and iii see **32.6** and **33.14**.

8. The works of Sir David Lindsay. . . . Vol. iv: Introduction, bibliography, notes to Ane satyre, appendices and indexes, glossary. 1936.   **33.8**

For vols. i–iii see **33.**1, 2, 6.

9. The Scottish works of Alexander Ross, M.A., schoolmaster at Lochlee. Consisting of Helenore, or the fortunate shepherdess; songs; The fortunate shepherd, or the orphan. Edited, with notes, glossary and life, by Margaret Wattie. 1938.   **33.9**

From the Aberdeen 1768 edition and mss. Ross lived 1699–1784.

10. The chronicles of Scotland, compiled by Hector Boece. Translated into Scots by John Bellenden, 1531. Edited, in continuation of the work of the late Walter Seton, by R. W. Chambers and Edith C. Batho. Vol. i. 1938.   **33.10**

Ends in 1437. Boece's work (Latin) was first published Paris 1527. Bellenden's translation was published Edinburgh *c.* 1540, but this edition is based on a ms. copy presented to James V. For vol. ii see **33.16**.

10A. Ten facsimiles from the manuscript of Bellenden's translation of The chronicles of Scotland by Hector Boece formerly in the possession of King James V and now belonging to J. Pierpont Morgan, by whom they are presented to members of the Scottish Text Society.   **33.11**

11. Ratis raving and other early Scots poems on morals. Edited, with an appendix of other pieces from Cambridge University Library ms. Kk. 1. 5, no. 6, by R. Girvan. 1939.   **33.12**

From a late 15th century ms. The 'other pieces' are similar, but some are prose.

12. The actis and deidis of Schir William Wallace, 1570. With introduction by Sir William A. Craigie. 1940.   **33.13**

Verse. Facsimile of the 1570 edition. Also facsimile of the beginning of the 1594 edition; and text of the fragments of the *c.* 1508 edition. For other editions of Blind Harry's Wallace see **31.5** and **34.4, 5**.

13. The works of William Fowler. . . . Edited by Henry W. Meikle, James Craigie and John Purves. Vol. iii: (introduction, notes, glossary, and index). 1940.   **33.14**

For vols. i and ii see **32.6** and **33.7**.

14. Thomas Hudson's Historie of Judith. Edited by James
Craigie. With introduction, notes, appendices, and glossary.
1941.

    Verse. Translation of a French original. From the Edinburgh 1584 edition.

33.15

15. The chronicles of Scotland, compiled by Hector Boece. . . .
Edited by Edith C. Batho and H. Winifred Husbands, with the
co-operation of R. W. Chambers and the late Walter Seton. Vol.
ii. 1941.

    Also a biography of John Bellenden by E. A. Sheppard. For vol. i see **33.10**.

33.16

16. The Basilicon doron of King James VI. With an introduction, notes, appendices, and glossary. Edited by James
Craigie. Vol. i: (Text). 1944.

    From the ms. draft and the Edinburgh 1599 and 1603 editions. For vol. ii see
33.19.

33.17

17. The Mar Lodge translation of The history of Scotland. By
Hector Boece. Edited by George Watson. Vol. i. 1946.

    Translated shortly after publication of Boece's work, Paris 1527, with gaps in
the ms. filled from the Edinburgh c. 1540 edition of John Bellenden's
translation. No more published.

33.18

18. The Basilicon doron of King James VI. . . . Vol. ii:
(Introduction etc.). 1950.

    For vol. i see **33.17**.

33.19

19. The works of Allan Ramsay. Edited by Burns Martin and
John W. Oliver. Vol. i: (Poems: 1721). [1951.]

    Ramsay lived 1686–1758. For vols. ii-vi see **33.21, 30, 34.6–8**.

33.20

20. The works of Allan Ramsay. . . . Vol. ii: (Poems: 1728).
1953.

33.21

21. The poems of Robert Fergusson. Edited by Matthew P.
McDiarmid. Vol. i: (Introduction). 1954.

    Fergusson lived 1750–74. Also docs. relating to Fergusson and his family,
1747–75.

33.22

22. The poems of James VI of Scotland. Edited by James
Craigie. Vol. i: (The essayes of a prentise and Poeticall exercises
at vacant houres). 1955.

    From the 1584 and 1591 editions. The 'Essayes' include a prose treatise on
Scots poetry. For vol. ii see **33.27**.

33.23

23. Devotional pieces in verse and prose. From ms. Arundel 285
and ms. Harleian 6919. Edited by J. A. W. Bennett. 1955.

    The ms. is mid-16th century.

33.24

24. The poems of Robert Fergusson. . . . Vol. ii: Text, appendices, notes, glossary, and indices. 1956.   **33.25**

25. Virgil's Aeneid. Translated into Scottish verse by Gavin Douglas, Bishop of Dunkeld. Edited with an introduction, notes, and glossary by David F. C. Coldwell. Vol. ii: (Text). 1957.   **33.26**

> Translation made 1512–13. For vols. i, iii and iv see **33.31**, 28, 29. For another edition see **6.67**.

26. The poems of James VI of Scotland. . . . Vol. ii: (Unpublished and uncollected poems, glossary, and index). 1958.   **33.27**

> Includes James' translation of the Psalms. For vol. i see **33.23**.

27. Virgil's Aeneid. . . . Edited with notes and glossary by David F. C. Coldwell. Vol. iii: (Text). 1959.   **33.28**

28. Virgil's Aeneid. . . . Vol. iv: (Text). 1960.   **33.29**

29. The works of Allan Ramsay. . . . Edited by Alexander M. Kinghorn and Alexander Law. Vol. iii: (Poems: miscellaneous and uncollected). 1961.   **33.30**

30. Virgil's Aeneid. . . . Vol. i: (Introduction, notes to the text, glossary and proper names). 1964.   **33.31**

34. SCOTTISH TEXT SOCIETY, FOURTH SERIES

Place of publication: Edinburgh.

1. The English and Latin poems of Sir Robert Ayton. Edited by Charles B. Gullans. 1963.
    34.1
    Ayton lived 1569?–1638. Also letters by Ayton, 1615–31; and genealogy of the Aytons of Fife by Sir James Balfour, mid-17th century. For other editions of the poems see **6**.20 and **11**.38.

2. The meroure of wysdome. . . . Edited by F. Quinn. Vol. ii. 1965.
    34.2
    Books III–V. Also chapter headings of the unpublished books VI–VII. For vol. i see **32**.19.

3. The shorter poems of Gavin Douglas. Edited by Priscilla J. Bawcutt. 1967.
    34.3
    Douglas lived 1474?–1522.

4. Hary's Wallace. (Vita nobilissimi defensoris Scotie Wilelmi Wallace militis). Edited by Matthew P. McDiarmid. Vol. i. 1968.
    34.4
    Books I–IX. For earlier editions see **31**.5 and **33**.13.

5. Hary's Wallace. . . . Vol. ii. 1969.
    34.5
    Books X–XII.

6. The works of Allan Ramsay. . . . Vol. iv: (A biographical and critical introduction to the Works of Allan Ramsay: letters: prose: poems not hitherto collected: poems attributed to Ramsay: poems about Ramsay). 1970.
    34.6
    For vols. i–iii see **33**.20, 21, 30.

7. The works of Allan Ramsay. . . . Vol. v: (Journal of the Easy Club: A collection of Scots proverbs: the early drafts of The gentle shepherd). 1972.
    34.7
    Journal 1712–15; proverbs 1737.

8. The works of Allan Ramsay. . . . Vol. vi: (Editors' intro-duction: notes to volumes i–v: glossary of Scots words in
    34.8

volumes iii and iv: biographical index: index of first lines: general index). 1974.

9. Andrew Crawfurd's collection of ballads and songs. Edited by E. B. Lyle. Vol. i. 1975.   **34.9**

> Crawfurd lived 1786–1854. Vol. ii not yet published.

10. James Watson's Choice collection of comic and serious Scots poems. Edited by Harriet H. Wood. Vol. i. 1977.   **34.10**

> Facsimile of the 1869 edition, which was a reprint of the first edition of 1706–11.

11. The complaynt of Scotland (*c*. 1550). By Mr Robert Wedderburn. Introduction by Alasdair M. Stewart. 1979.   **34.11**

12. Barbour's Bruce. Edited by Matthew P. McDiarmid and James A. C. Stevenson. Vol. ii. 1980.   **34.12**

> Verse. Books I–X. Vol. i not yet published. For other editions see **31.14**, **36.28**.

13. Barbour's Bruce. . . . Vol. iii. 1981.   **34.13**

> Books XI–XX.

14. Minor prose works of King James VI and I. Daemonologie, The trve lawe of free monarchies, A counterblaste to tobacco, A declaration of sports. Edited by James Craigie and prepared for the press by Alexander Law. 1982.   **34.14**

> From the first editions, Edinburgh 1597 and 1598, and London 1604 and 1618, respectively. Also fragments of a draft of Daemonologie in James's own hand; James' speech to the jury at a witchcraft trial, 1591; the Declaration as originally issued in 1617 in Lancashire; and passages added to the Declaration when it was reissued in 1633.

35. SOCIETY OF ANTIQUARIES OF SCOTLAND*

Place of publication: Edinburgh.

8. Records of the priory of the Isle of May. Edited by John   **35.1**
Stuart. 1868.

> Mainly Latin. Charters etc., mid-12th century–1552. Also extracts from treasurers' accounts, 1490–1504.

9. Records of the monastery of Kinloss, with illustrative   **35.2**
documents. Edited by John Stuart. 1872.

> Mainly Latin. Contains the chronicle of John Smyth (d. 1557); lives of Abbots Thomas Crystall (d. 1535) and Robert Reid (d. 1558) by John Ferrerius; discourses by Adam Elder, 1558; charters of the priory of Beauly (abstracts), 1571–80; Kinloss charters, 1175–1565; and a rental from the books of assumptions of Thirds, 1574.

---

*Only publications relevant to this volume are listed.

36. SPALDING CLUB

Place of publication: Aberdeen, unless otherwise stated.

1. History of Scots affairs, from MDCXXXVII to MDCXLI.   **36.1**
By James Gordon, parson of Rothiemay. Edited by Joseph
Robertson and George Grub. Vol. i. 1841.

> 1637–8. Also James Man's introduction to his projected *Memoirs of Scotish
> affairs from 1624 to 1651*, from the first edition, 1741; extracts from minutes
> of Rothiemay kirk session, 1604–86; and other docs. relating to Gordon,
> 1653–62.

2. History of Scots affairs. . . . By James Gordon. Vol. ii. 1841.   **36.2**
> 1638–9.

3. The miscellany of the Spalding Club. Edited by John Stuart.   **36.3**
Vol. i. 1841.

> The Straloch papers. [Latin and English. 1585–1665. Mainly correspon-
> dence of Robert Gordon of Straloch.]
> Necrologia coenobii Sancti Francisci apud Abredonenses. [Obits, 15th and
> 16th centuries.]
> Trials for witchcraft. MDXCVI–MDXCVII. [1596–8. Aberdeen.]
> Letters from Professor [Thomas] Blackwell, and others, to John Ross of
> Arnage, provost of Aberdeen. MDCCXI–MDCCXII. [On toleration and
> lay patronage.]
> Diary of the Reverend William Mitchell, minister at Edinburgh. MDCCXVII.
> Nepenthes, or the vertves of tabacco, by William Barclay, A.M. and M.D.
> [From first edition, Edinburgh 1614.]
> March of the Highland army, in the years 1745–46. By Captain James Stuart,
> of Lord Ogilvie's regiment. MDCCXLV–XLVI. [Orders to the army of
> Prince Charles Edward, and notes on its route.]
> Extracts from the diary of the Reverend John Bisset, minister at Aberdeen.
> MDCCXLV–XLVI. [On the 'Forty-Five.]
> Letters from Lord Lewis Gordon, and others, to the laird of Stonywood.
> MDCCXLV–XLVI. [James Moir of Stonywood. Not all the letters are
> addressed to him. On the 'Forty-Five.]

4. History of Scots affairs. . . . By James Gordon. Vol. iii. 1841.   **36.4**
> 1639–40. Also docs. on the 1640 general assembly.

5. Abredoniae vtrivsque descriptio. A description of both touns   **36.5**
of Aberdeen. By James Gordon, parson of Rothemay. With a

selection of the charters of the burgh. Edited by Cosmo Innes. Edinburgh. 1842.

> Description, mid-17th century (English translation from Latin; for a better translation see **37**.37); charters, late 12th century–1613 (partly Latin).

6. The miscellany of the Spalding Club. Edited by John Stuart. **36.6**
Vol. ii. 1842.

> Letters from Simon Lord Lovat to his kinsman in Aberdeenshire. MDCCXL–XLV. [To Charles Fraser of Inverallochy.]
>
> The chronicle of Aberdeen. MCCCCXCI–MDXCV. [Late 16th century notes inserted in Aberdeen registers of baptisms, marriages and deaths by Walter Cullen. Includes some verse.]
>
> Act for delyverie of dead bodies to the colledge of Aberdene. MDCXXXVI. [By the privy council.]
>
> Decreet of spulzie. John Ogilvy of Stratherne, and Mr James Ogilvy, commendator of Dryburgh Abbey, his tutor, against Lauchlane Macintosh, and others. MDLXXI. [1517, not 1571.]
>
> The kingis lettres, commandan the Erle of Murray, leivtenent, to pass vpoun the Clanhattan and Bagenacht, for to destroy thame alvtherlie. MDLXXXIII. [1528, not 1583. Letters of fire and sword.]
>
> A brieff account of the watch undertaken by Cluny Macpherson. MDCCXLIV. [Ewen Macpherson of Cluny.]
>
> Papers from the charter chest at Monymusk. MDXC–MDCCXX.
>
> The Arbuthnot papers. MCCCCLXXXVII–MDCLXXXI. [Latin and English.]
>
> Extracts from the register of the regality court of Spynie. MDXCII–MDCI.
>
> Extracts from the manuscript collections of the Rev. Robert Wodrow. MDCV–MDCXCVII. [Letters on the church history of the North East.]
>
> Papers from the charter chest at Pittodrie. MDXXIV–MDCXXVIII. [Latin and English. Mainly relating to Sir Thomas Erskine, secretary to James V.]
>
> The Errol papers. [Latin and English. Docs. on the jurisdiction of the constable, 1314–1727; bands of manrent, friendship and alliance, 1466–1612; letters, late 16th–early 18th centuries; charters etc., late 12th century–1633.]
>
> Papers by Thomas Innes, principal of the Scots College at Paris, and documents connected with his family. [1683–1787.]
>
> The order of combats for lyfe in Scotland. [Undated, from early 18th century ms. copy.]
>
> Memoir of John, second Earl of Perth. [Autobiography, 1657.]
>
> Bulla Urbani IV priori et fratribus monasterii vallis S. Andree de Pluskardyn concessa. A.D. MCCLXIII.

7. Extracts from the presbytery book of Strathbogie. A.D. **36.7**
MDCXXXI–MDCLIV. Edited by John Stuart. 1843.

8. A fragment of a memoir of Field-Marshal James Keith, **36.8**
written by himself, 1714–1734. Presented by Thomas Constable. Edinburgh. 1843.

9. Collections for a history of the shires of Aberdeen and Banff.   **36.9**
Edited by Joseph Robertson. 1843.

[An index to this vol. is included in **36.37**.]
Praefecturarum Aberdonensis et Banfiensis in Scotia ultra-montana nova
    descriptio, auctore Roberto Gordonio. [From vol. vi of Joannis Blaeu,
    Atlas major, Amsterdam 1662.]
Description of Aberdeenshire. [By Sir Samuel Forbes of Foveran, 1716–17.]
A view of the diocese of Aberdeen. [By Alexander Keith, 1732. The editor of
    the vol. has inserted many illustrative docs. (mainly Latin), 12th–18th
    centuries, into Keith's work.]

10. A short abridgement of Britane's distemper, from the yeare   **36.10**
of God MDCXXXIX to MDCXLIX. By Patrick Gordon of
Ruthven. Edited by John Dunn. 1844.

Narrative of events, mainly concerned with the risings of Huntly and
Montrose against the covenanters.

11. A breiffe narration of the services done to three noble   **36.11**
ladyes, by Gilbert Blakhal, priest of the Scots mission in France,
in the Low Countries, and in Scotland, MDCXXXI–MDCXLIX.
Edited by John Stuart. 1844.

The noble ladies were the sisters Lady Isabel Hay and Sophia Hay (Lady
Aboyne), and the latter's daughter Henrietta (known as Madame de
Gordon). Also extracts from 1704 list of Catholics in Aberdeenshire.

12. Extracts from the council register of the burgh of Aberdeen.   **36.12**
Edited by John Stuart. [Vol. i:] 1398–1570. 1844.

Some Latin. For vol. ii see **36.19**.

13. Registrum episcopatus Aberdonensis. Ecclesie cathedralis   **36.13**
Aberdonensis regesta que extant in unum collecta. Edited by
Cosmo Innes. Vol. i. Edinburgh. 1845.

1062–1559. Also issued (with **36.14**) as **15.65**.

14. Registrum episcopatus Aberdonensis. . . . Vol. ii. Edin-   **36.14**
burgh. 1845.

c. 1180–1566.

15. Selections from the records of the kirk session, presbytery,   **36.15**
and synod of Aberdeen. Edited by John Stuart. 1846.

Kirk session, 1562–78, 1602–40, 1651–9; presbytery, 1598–1610; synod,
1651–81. Also extracts from Thomas Morer's *A short account of Scotland*,
1689, from the London 1715 edition. Spine reads *Selections from ecclesiastical
records of Aberdeen*.

16. The miscellany of the Spalding Club. Edited by John Stuart. **36.16**
Vol. iii. 1846.

Letters of Lord Grange. [1731–41. James Erskine of Grange.]
The book of the annual rentaris and wedsettaris within the schirrefdome of
   Abirdein. 1633.
Minutes of the committee for loan monies and taxations of the shire of
   Aberdeen. 1643.
Summons against the magistrates of Aberdeen. 1591. [To appear before the
   privy council.]
Process against the Egyptians, at Banff. 1700. [1700–1, before the sheriff
   court. Against James Macpherson, supposed author of 'Macpherson's
   rant', and others.]
List of goods plundered from tenants in Cromar. 1644–47.
Protestation by Sir Alexander Irvine of Drum against the presbytery of
   Aberdeen. 1652.
The Gordon letters. [1568–1742 and some undated. Include many royal
   letters.]
Inquisitio facta apud Keandrochit de privilegiis reliquiae Sancti Fillani.
   Aprilis 22, 1428. [Staff of St Fillan.]
Articles of agreement between the Earl of Huntly and the Regent Murray,
   1569.

17. Illustrations of the topography and antiquities of the shires **36.17**
of Aberdeen and Banff. Edited by Joseph Robertson. Vol. ii.
1847.

Latin and English. 12th–18th centuries. Charters and miscellaneous docs. on
parishes in presbyteries of Kincardine, Fordyce, Strathbogie, Aberlour,
Abernethy, Turriff and Deer. For vols. i, iii and iv see **36.37, 29, 32.**

18. A genealogical deduction of the family of Rose of Kilravock. **36.18**
With illustrative documents from the family papers, and notes.
Edited by Cosmo Innes. Edinburgh. 1848.

Deduction written in 1683–4 by Hew Rose, minister of Nairn (including
Latin transcripts of some docs.); with a continuation written in 1753 by
Lachlan Shaw. Illustrative docs., Latin and English, 1294–1815.

19. Extracts from the council register of the burgh of Aberdeen. **36.19**
Edited by John Stuart. Vol. ii: 1570–1625. 1848.

Continued in **21.8.**

20. The miscellany of the Spalding Club. Edited by John Stuart. **36.20**
Vol. iv. 1849.

Papers from the charter chest at Dun. MCCCCLI–MDCCXIII. [Latin and
English. Also (in appendix to preface) obits of lairds and ladies of Dun,
compiled 16th–18th centuries; and two genealogical accounts of the
Erskines of Dun, 18th century.]
Papers from the charter chest of the Earl of Airlie, at Cortachy Castle.
MCCCCXX–MDLX. [Latin and English.]

Papers from the charter chest of the Duke of Richmond, at Gordon Castle. [Latin and English. Miscellaneous docs., 1338–1769; bands of manrent, friendship and alliance, 1444–1670.]

The rentaill of the lordschipe of Huntlye, alias Strauthbogye, maid be the richt noble and michtie George, Marquis of Huntly, Erll of Engzie, Lord Gordone and Badzenoche, etc. for his lordschipis landis followinge, conform to the sett maid at Witsonday, ane thousand and sax hundrethe yeirs. [Also (in appendix to preface) notes on servants' wages at Warthill, 1720–44.]

Two letters of 1746. [On the 'Forty-Five rising.]

Instrumentum super aucis Sancti Cuthberti. 1489. [On St Cuthbert's ducks on Farne Island.]

21. Memorialls of the trubles in Scotland and in England. A.D. 1624–A.D. 1645. By John Spalding. Edited by John Stuart. Vol. i. 1850.

36.21

1624–40. Mainly concerned with the civil wars in the North East. Also docs. on burning of the tower of Frendraught, 1630; relating to Bishops Adam Bannatyne and William Forbes; on Gilderoy and other broken men, 1630s; and extracts from the diary of Dr John Forbes, 1640. For another (inferior) edition see **6.28**.

22. Letters, illustrative of public affairs in Scotland, addressed by contemporary statesmen to George, Earl of Aberdeen, lord high chancellor of Scotland. MDCLXXXI–MDCLXXXIV. Edited by John Dunn. 1851.

36.22

Also docs. relating to the earl, 1661–82.

23. Memorialls of the trubles. . . . By John Spalding. . . . Vol. ii. 1851.

36.23

1641–5. Also letters of Andrew Cant and George Gillespie, 1640–1; docs. relating to losses of the burgh of Aberdeen, 1639–46; and extracts from diaries of Dr John Forbes, 1642–6, and Alexander Jaffray, 1644.

24. The miscellany of the Spalding Club. Edited by John Stuart. Vol. v. 1852.

36.24

Extracts from the registers of the burgh of Aberdeen. [Latin and English. 1317, 1399–1407, 1441–1508.]

Extracts from the accounts of the burgh of Aberdeen. [Latin and English. 1398, 1433–8, 1453, 1548–51, 1559–66, 1577–8, 1581–1657.]

Letters to Dr James Fraser. MDCLXXIX–MDCLXXXIX.

Documents from the charter chest of the Earl of Airlie. 1578–1682.

Decreet of the synod of Perth, in the case between William, Bishop of St Andrews, and Duncan de Aberbuthenoth. A.D. MCCVI. [Latin.]

Extracts from the court books of the baronies of Skene, Leys, and Whitehaugh. 1613–1687. [Skene, 1613–33; Leys, 1621–1709; and Whitehaugh, 1686–7.]

Miscellaneous charters and contracts from copies at Panmure House, made from the original documents. [Latin and English, c. 1152–1547.]

Birth brieves from the registers of the burgh of Aberdeen. 1637–1705. [See also **38**.10.]

Missives to the provost, baillies, and council, of the burgh of Aberdeen. 1594–1688. [1594–1690.]

Documents relating to Orkney and Shetland. 1438–1563.

Statuta et leges ludi literatii grammaticorum Aberdonensium. 1553.

25. The civil and ecclesiastical history of Scotland; by Thomas Innes. A.D. LXXX–DCCCXVIII. Edited by George Grub. 1853.   **36**.25

Innes d. 1744.

26. Fasti Aberdonenses. Selections from the records of the University and King's College of Aberdeen, 1494–1854. Edited by Cosmo Innes. 1854.   **36**.26

27. Sculptured stones of Scotland. Edited by John Stuart. [Vol. i.] 1856.   **36**.27

For vol. ii see **36**.35.

28. The Brus. From a collation of the Cambridge and Edinburgh manuscripts. Edited by Cosmo Innes. 1856.   **36**.28

Verse. By John Barbour, d. 1395. From late 15th century mss. For other editions see **31**.14, **34**.12, 13.

29. Illustrations of the topography and antiquities of the shires of Aberdeen and Banff. [Edited by Joseph Robertson.] Vol. iii. 1857.   **36**.29

Latin and English. 12th–18th centuries. Charters and miscellaneous docs. on parishes in presbyteries of Ellon, Aberdeen, Garioch and Turriff. For vols. i, ii and iv see **36**.37, 17, 32.

30. The book of the thanes of Cawdor. A series of papers selected from the charter room at Cawdor, 1236–1742. Edited by Cosmo Innes. Edinburgh. 1859.   **36**.30

Latin and English.

31. Passages from the diary of General Patrick Gordon of Auchleuchries. A.D. 1635–A.D. 1699. Edited by Joseph Robertson. 1859.   **36**.31

An autobiography rather than diary. Mainly relating to his service in Russia. Also charters etc., Latin and English, 1370–1730.

32. Illustrations of the topography and antiquities of the shires of Aberdeen and Banff. [Edited by Joseph Robertson.] Vol. iv. 1862.   **36**.32

Latin and English. Late 11th–18th centuries. Charters and miscellaneous docs. on parishes in presbyteries of Deer and Alford. For vols. i–iii see **36**.37, 17, 29.

33. The diary of Alexander Brodie of Brodie, MDCLII–MDCLXXX, and of his son, James Brodie of Brodie, MDCLXXX–MDCLXXXV. Consisting of extracts from the existing manuscripts, and a republication of the volume printed at Edinburgh in the year 1740. Edited by David Laing. 1863.   **36.33**

Also letters etc., 1645–50.

34. Ane account of the familie of Innes, compiled by Duncan Forbes of Culloden, 1698. With an appendix of charters and notes. Edited by Cosmo Innes. 1864.   **36.34**

Charters, letters etc. Latin and English. Mid-12th–18th centuries.

35. Sculptured stones of Scotland. Edited by John Stuart. Vol. ii. Edinburgh. 1867.   **36.35**

For vol. i see **36.27**.

36. The book of Deer. Edited by John Stuart. Edinburgh. 1869.   **36.36**

Latin. 9th century gospel book containing 11th and 12th century Gaelic notes.

37. Illustrations of the topography and antiquities of the shires of Aberdeen and Banff. Edited by George Grub. Vol. i. 1869.   **36.37**

Preface and index to **36.9, 17, 29, 32**.

38. Notices of the Spalding Club. With the annual reports, lists of members and works printed for the Club, 1839–71. Edited by John Stuart. Edinburgh. 1871.   **36.38**

WORKS UNIFORM WITH BUT NOT PART OF THE CLUB'S SERIES

A. List of pollable persons within the shire of Aberdeen. 1696. Edited by John Stuart. 2 vols. 1844.   **36.39**

Lists compiled in September 1695.
i : [Presbyteries of Kincardine, Garioch, Alford and Deer.]
ii: [Presbyteries of Deer, Ellon, Turriff, Strathbogie and Aberdeen.]

B. Essays, chiefly on Scottish antiquities. By the late John Stuart, esquire, of Inchbreck, professor of Greek in the Marischal College and University of Aberdeen. With a brief sketch of the author's life. Edited by Alexander Stuart of Inchbreck. 1846.   **36.40**

John Stuart d. 1827.

C. Breviarium Aberdonense. Edited by William Blew. 2 parts. London. 1854.   **36**.41

Also issued as **6**.99, which see for details, and **15**.72.

D. Diary of Alexander Jaffray, provost of Aberdeen, one of the Scottish commissioners to King Charles II, and a member of Cromwell's Parliament: to which are added particulars of his subsequent life, given in connexion with memoirs of the rise, progress, and persecutions of the people called Quakers in the north of Scotland; among whom he became one of the earliest members. By John Barclay. 3rd edition. 1856.   **36**.42

'Diary' (an autobiography), 1614–61; memoirs, 1653–early 18th century. First edition London 1833.

E. Deeds of foundation of bursaries at the University and King's College, Aberdeen. Printed by order of the Senatus Academicus. 1857.   **36**.43

Latin and English. 1623–1853.

F. Memoranda relating to the family of Forbes of Waterton, from a ms. of the deceased John Forbes, (b. 1754, who was served heir to the last Thomas Forbes of Waterton in 1775), and is now printed solely for the use of members of the family. 1857.   **36**.44

Includes extracts from docs., 1573–1753, and brief abstracts, 1396–1775.

37. NEW SPALDING CLUB*

Place of publication: Aberdeen.

1. Memorials of the family of Skene of Skene, from the family papers, with other illustrative documents. Edited by William F. Skene. 1887.
37.1

> Includes foreign letters to Sir John Skene, 1586–98 (Latin); verses addressed to Sir John on publication of *Regiam majestatem*, 1609 (Latin); letters relating to Sir John, 1613–14; papers relating to the Skenes of Belhelvie, 1587–1602; and miscellaneous docs., 1619, 1630, 1684, 1724.

2. Cartularium ecclesiae Sancti Nicholai Aberdonensis. Recognovit Jacobus Cooper. Vol. i. 1888.
37.2

> Mainly charters and rentals, 14th–late 16th centuries, but includes extracts from Fordun's Chronicle, and Edward III's renunciation of superiority over Scotland, 1329. From a 15th-16th century cartulary. For English translations and abstracts see vol. ii (**37.7**).

3. Lacunar basilicae Sancti Macarii Aberdonensis. The heraldic ceiling of the cathedral church of St Machar, Old Aberdeen. Described in historical and armorial detail by William D. Geddes and Peter Duguid. 1888.
37.3

> The ceiling dates from the early 16th century.

4. Fasti Academiae Mariscallanae Aberdonensis. Selections from the records of the Marischal College and University, MDXCIII–MDCCCLX. Edited by Peter J. Anderson. Vol. i: Endowments. 1889.
37.4

> Partly Latin, with English translations or abstracts. 1592–1860. For vols. ii and iii see **37.19, 20**.

---

*Many vols. in the series Aberdeen University Studies (AUS) were issued 'in conjunction with' the New Spalding Club, and some of these appeared in both series. These latter vols. are listed below (**35.21–43**). For other relevant vols. in the AUS series, see **2.1–10** above. A number of New Spalding Club vols. are divided into sections, and have separate sectional paginations as well as the continuous vol. paginations. The sections sometimes occur bound separately, as if forming completed vols.

5. Selections from Wodrow's biographical collections. Divines of the North-East of Scotland. Edited by Robert Lippe. 1890.   **37.5**

Late 16th and early 17th century divines. Robert Wodrow d. 1734. Also a list of all Wodrow's biographical collections.

6. The miscellany of the New Spalding Club. Vol. i. 1890.   **37.6**

Register of burgesses of guild and trade of the burgh of Aberdeen, 1399–1631. Edited by Alexander M. Munro.
Inventories of ecclesiastical records of North-Eastern Scotland. Edited by Peter J. Anderson.

7. Cartularium ecclesiae Sancti Nicholai. . . . Vol. ii. 1892.   **37.7**

English translations and abstracts of contents of vol. i (**37.2**). Also miscellaneous docs., 1294–1630; and 'An accurate and minute description of the East Kirk, 1818', by James Logan.

8. The annals of Banff. Compiled by William Cramond. Vol. i. 1891.   **37.8**

Extracts (mainly after 1500) from 'all available sources' up to 1891.

9. Musa Latina Aberdonensis. Arthur Johnston. Vol. i: The Parerga of 1637. Edited by Sir William D. Geddes. 1892.   **37.9**

With English abstracts. From the second edition, Middelburg 1637, with variants from the first edition, Aberdeen 1632. Many of the poems relate to public affairs. For vols. ii and iii see **37.16, 38**.

10. The annals of Banff. . . . Vol. ii. 1893.   **37.10**

Extracts from sources relating to the church, school etc., mainly after 1500 (but including some charters from 1289 — partly Latin, with English translations), largely from synod, presbytery and kirk session minutes.

11. Officers and graduates of University and King's College, Aberdeen, MVD–MDCCCLX. Edited by Peter J. Anderson. 1893.   **37.11**

Also the Nova fundatio, late 16th century (Latin, with English abstract), and docs. relating to it, 1578–1638; and extracts relating to academic oaths, 1531–1887.

11A. Hand-list of bibliography of the shires of Aberdeen, Banff, and Kincardine. By A. W. Robertson. 1893.   **37.12**

12. Hectoris Boetii Murthlacensium et Aberdonensium episcoporum vitae. Edited and translated by James Moir. 1894.   **37.13**

From the first edition, Paris 1522. See **6.12** for another edition.

13. The records of Aboyne, MCCXXX–MDCLXXXI. Edited by Charles, XI Marquis of Huntly, Earl of Aboyne. 1894.   **37.14**

Partly Latin, with English abstracts. Charters and other docs., 1460–1676.

14. Historical papers relating to the Jacobite period, 1699–1750. **37.15**
Edited by James Allardyce. 1895.

> 1699–1747. Relate mainly to Jacobite activities in Highlands and North East. Also account of Lord Forbes' losses through depredations by Highlanders, 1689–90.

15. Musa Latina Aberdonensis. Arthur Johnston. Vol. ii: The **37.16**
Epigrammata and remaining secular poems. Edited by Sir
William D. Geddes. 1895.

> With English abstracts. 'Epigrammata' (on contemporary Scottish nobles and bishops) from a 1637 collection of poems, with additions from the Middelburg 1642 edition of Johnston's works. For vols. i and iii see **37.9, 38**.

16. Historical papers relating to the Jacobite period. . . . Vol. ii. **37.17**
1896.

> Miscellaneous docs., 1716–50. Includes depositions relating to trials of Jacobites, 1746; and reports from commanders of troops posted in the Highlands, 1749–50. Pagination continuous with vol. i.

17. Records of the meeting of the exercise of Alford, **37.18**
MDCLXII–MDCLXXXVIII. Edited by Thomas Bell. 1897.

> Abridged transcript. Presbytery minutes.

18. Fasti Academiae Mariscallanae. . . . Vol. ii: Officers, **37.19**
graduates, and alumni. 1898.

> For vol. i see **37.4**.

19. Fasti Academiae Mariscallanae. . . . Vol. iii: Index to **37.20**
Vol. ii. Compiled by James F. K. Johnstone. 1898.

> Also a charter by both Marischal College and King's College, 1656.

20. Records of Old Aberdeen, MCLVII–MDCCCXCI. Edited **37.21**
by Alexander M. Munro. Vol. i: 1899.

> Includes charters and acts of Parliament, 1157–1729 (partly Latin with English translations); extracts from burgh council minutes, 1602–1854, and from merchant and craft records, 1608–1798; lists of inhabitants, 1636, and of pollable persons, 1696; extracts from treasurer's accounts, 1660–1746; and valuation roll, 1796. Also issued as AUS. 2 dated 1900. For vol. ii see **37.37**.

21. Place names of West Aberdeenshire. By James Macdonald. **37.22**
Edited by Charles E. Troup. 1899.

> Also issued as AUS. 3.

22. The family of Burnett of Leys, with collateral branches. From **37.23**
the mss. of George Burnett. Edited by James Allardyce. 1901.

> Includes miscellaneous docs., 1247–1793 (partly Latin, with English abstracts). Also issued as AUS. 4. For genealogical trees intended for this vol. but omitted, see **37.53**.

23. The records of Invercauld, MDXLVII–MDCCCXXVIII.   37.24
Edited by John G. Michie. 1901.

Miscellaneous docs., mainly from the papers of the Farquharsons of
Invercauld. Also issued as AUS. 5.

24. The Albemarle papers, being the correspondence of William   37.25
Anne, second Earl of Albemarle, commander-in-chief in
Scotland, 1746–1747. With an appendix of letters from Andrew
Fletcher, lord justice-clerk to the Duke of Newcastle, 1746–
1748. Edited with introduction and notes by Charles S. Terry.
Vol. i. 1902.

Contains the Albemarle papers. Also issued as AUS. 7.

25. The Albemarle papers. . . . Vol. ii. 1902.   37.26

Contains only the introduction and Andrew Fletcher's letters. Pagination
continuous with vol. i. Also issued as AUS. 7.

26. The house of Gordon. Edited by John M. Bulloch. Vol. i.   37.27
1903.

Genealogical. Includes the Balbithan ms. (a 1730 transcript of an earlier
Gordon genealogy); and lists of Gordons from the records of services of heirs,
1545–1799, Aberdeen poll tax, 1696, universities, etc. Also issued as AUS. 8.
For vols. ii and iii see 37.34, 40.

27. The records of Elgin, 1234–1800. Compiled by William   37.28
Cramond. Vol. i. 1903.

Extracts from various records including exchequer rolls, 1365–1560; register
of the great seal, 1306–1649; burgh records, 1540–1803; and register of the
privy council, 1549–1630. Also issued as AUS. 9. For vol. ii see 37.36.

28. Records of the sheriff court of Aberdeenshire. Edited by   37.29
David Littlejohn. Vol. i: records prior to 1600. 1904.

Lists of contents, and extracts. Diet books, 1503–11, 1557–60, 1574–6,
1584, 1595–6; decree books, 1597–9. Also issued as AUS. 11. For vols. ii and
iii see 37.32, 33.

29. The Blackhalls of that Ilk and Barra, hereditary coroners   37.30
and foresters of the Garioch. By Alexander Morison. 1905.

Includes charters etc., 1503–1710 (mainly Latin, with English abstracts).
Also issued as AUS. 16.

30. Records of the Scots colleges at Douai, Rome, Madrid,   37.31
Valladolid and Ratisbon. Vol. i: registers of students. Edited by
Peter J. Anderson. 1906.

Latin. Douai, 1581–1772; Rome, 1602–1900; Madrid, 1632–1734;
Valladolid, 1769–c. 1900; Ratisbon, 1713–c. 1855. Also register of Ratisbon
monks, 1597–1742 and Ratisbon 'syllabus' of benefactors etc., 1681–1853.
Vol. ii was never published. Also issued as AUS. 17.

31. Records of the sheriff court of Aberdeenshire. . . . Vol. ii: records, 1598–1649. 1906.   37.32

Lists of contents, and extracts. Diet books, 1598–1622, 1629–34; minute books of judicial enactments, 1605–14, 1619–33, 1638–48; decree books, 1617–18, 1631–44. Also issued as AUS. 24.

32. Records of the sheriff court of Aberdeenshire. . . . Vol. iii: records, 1642–1660, with supplementary lists of officials, 1660–1907, and index to volumes i, ii, iii. 1907.   37.33

Lists of contents, and extracts. Decree books, 1642–9; minute books of judicial enactments, 1649–60; diet books, 1649–53, 1656–9. Also issued as AUS. 27.

33. The house of Gordon. . . . Vol. ii. 1907.   37.34

Includes histories and genealogies of the Gordons by John Ferrerius, 1545, Robert Gordon of Straloch, mid-17th century (both Latin), and Sir Robert Gordon of Gordonstoun and his son Robert, 1659; and ballads relating to the Gordons. Also issued as AUS. 30. For vols. i and iii see **37.27, 40.**

34. The miscellany of the New Spalding Club. Vol. ii. 1908.   37.35

[Also issued as AUS. 31.]
Summary of fiars prices in Aberdeenshire, 1603–19, with lists of jurors. Compiled by David Littlejohn.
Register of St Paul's Episcopal Chapel, Aberdeen, 1720–1793. Edited by Alexander E. Smith. [Register of baptisms. Also deed of foundation of St Paul's, 1722.]
Aberdeen burgess register, 1631–1700. Edited by Alexander M. Munro.

35. The records of Elgin. . . . Vol. ii. 1908.   37.36

Charters etc., 1296–1547 (Latin); extracts from kirk session minutes, 1584–1779, from presbytery minutes, 1636–1800, and from burgh council minutes, 1566–1800. Also issued as AUS. 35. For vol. i see **37.28.**

36. Records of Old Aberdeen, MCCCCXCVIII–MCMIII. . . . Vol. ii. 1909.   37.37

Extracts from kirk session minutes and accounts, 1621–1758, and from minutes of heritors relating to poor relief, 1751–2; James Gordon's description of the burgh, mid-17th century (Latin, with English translation. See **36.5** for another edition); James Logan's description of St Machar's Cathedral, *c.* 1825; and miscellaneous docs., late 12th century, 1498, 1532 (Latin, with English translations). Also issued as AUS. 42. For vol. i see **37.21.**

37. Musa Latina Aberdonensis. Vol. iii: poetae minores. Edited by William K. Leask. 1910.   37.38

With English abstracts. 16th–17th centuries. The poems contain many references to contemporaries. Also issued as AUS. 43. For vols. i and ii see **37.9, 16.**

38. Records of Inverness. Edited by William Mackay and   **37.39**
Herbert C. Boyd. Vol. i: burgh court books: 1556–86. 1911.

Extracts. Also issued as AUS. 45. For vol. ii see **37.44**.

39. Gordons under arms. A biographical muster roll of officers   **37.40**
named Gordon in the navies and armies of Britain, Europe,
America and in the Jacobite risings. By Constance O. Skelton
and John M. Bulloch. 1912.

Spine reads *The house of Gordon*. *Vol. iii* Also issued as AUS. 59. For vols. i
and ii see **37.27, 34**.

40. History of the Society of Advocates in Aberdeen. Edited by   **37.41**
John A. Henderson. 1912.

Includes list of members, 1549–1911; extracts from records of the society,
1685–1876; and charters, 1774–1862 (Latin, with English translations). Also
issued as AUS. 60. A *Supplemental history of the Society of Advocates in
Aberdeen, 1912–1938* was published in 1939.

41. Territorial soldiering in the North-East of Scotland during   **37.42**
1759–1814. By John M. Bulloch. 1914.

Includes muster rolls etc. Also issued as AUS. 68.

42. Records of the county of Banff, 1660–1760. One hundred   **37.43**
years of county government. Compiled by James Grant. With an
introduction by Alistair and Henrietta Tayler. 1922.

Partly Latin. Docs. relating to activities of sheriffs, barons and freeholders,
commissioners to Parliament, commissioners of supply, excise and poll tax,
and justices of the peace.
Also issued as AUS. 87.

43. Records of Inverness. Edited by William Mackay and   **37.44**
George S. Laing. Vol. ii: burgh court books: 1602–37; minutes
of town council: 1637–88. 1924.

Extracts from court books, 1602–33, and minutes, 1638–88. For vol. i see
37.39.

44. New Spalding Club. Rules and lists of members, 1887,   **37.45**
1890, 1894, 1898, 1903.

Not in Terry, *Catalogue*, but in official Club binding.

45. New Spalding Club. Reports. 2 vols., 1887–1916.   **37.46**

Not in Terry, *Catalogue*.
i : Nos. 1–21, 1887–1907.
ii: Nos. 22–30, 1908–16.

WORKS UNIFORM WITH BUT NOT PART OF THE CLUB'S SERIES

A. Descent of the family of Skene. [Compiled by Henry J. Trotter. 1888.]   37.47

Folding genealogical table.

B. The armorial ensigns of the royal burgh of Aberdeen, with some observations on the legend relating to the capture and demolition of the castle. By John Cruickshank. Edited by Peter J. Anderson. 1888.   37.48

Includes extracts (partly Latin) from relevant docs.

C. Charters and other writs illustrating the history of the royal burgh of Aberdeen, MCLXXI–MDCCCIV. Edited, with translations, by Peter J. Anderson. 1890.   37.49

Late 12th century–1885. Also inventories of records relating to the burgh.

D. Genealogical tree of the family of Burnett of Leys with the collateral branches. Prepared by W. Kendall Burnett. 1893.   37.50

Sometimes bound with 37.53 as a single volume.

E. The thanage of Fermartyn, including the district commonly called Formartine, its proprietors, with genealogical deductions; its parishes, ministers, churches, churchyards, antiquities, etc. By William Temple. 1894.   37.51

F. Memorials of the family of Forbes of Forbesfield, with notes on connected Morgans, Duncans and Fergusons. By Alexander Forbes. 1905.   37.52

Includes miscellaneous docs., 1633 (Latin), 1763–1859.

G. Report to the council of the New Spalding Club upon the Burnett mss. preserved in the Staats-Archiv at Hannover and the Marshal Keith letters in the Royal Library at Berlin. By Robert S. Rait. 1898.   37.53

Abstracts of letters of Thomas Burnett (mainly to Leibnitz and the Electress Sophia), 1705–13, and of letters mainly by Marshal James Keith, 1748–55 (though a misprint dates one letter 1775 instead of 1755). Some copies, in New Spalding Club binding with *Burnett Papers* on spine, are bound up with 'Genealogical trees of branches of the Burnett family' (which are paginated 347–59 and marked 'Appendix XLVI', having been intended for inclusion in 37.23 but omitted from that vol.) and with 37.50.

38.   THIRD SPALDING CLUB

Place of publication: Aberdeen.

1. Bibliographia Aberdonensis. Being an account of books
relating to or printed in the shires of Aberdeen, Banff,
Kincardine, or written by natives or residents or by officers,
graduates or alumni of the universities of Aberdeen. By James
F. K. Johnstone and Alexander W. Robertson. 2 vols. 1929–
30.

> i : 1472–1640.
> ii: 1641–1700.

38.1

2. The prehistoric antiquities of the Howe of Cromar. By Sir
Alexander Ogston of Glendavan. 1931.

38.2

3. The Jacobite cess roll for the county of Aberdeen in 1715.
From the ms. of John Forbes of Upper Boyndlie, now in the
possession of J. C. M. Ogilvie-Forbes of Boyndie. Edited with
introduction, notes and genealogical tables by Alistair and
Henrietta Tayler. 1932.

38.3

4. The valuation of the county of Aberdeen for the year 1667.
Printed from the original manuscript (now at Fettercairn House)
by permission of Lord Clinton. Edited with introduction, notes
and genealogical tables by Alistair and Henrietta Tayler. 1933.

> Changes in land ownership occurring in the 1672 roll are noted.

38.4

5. Mystics of the North-East. Including I. Letters of James
Keith, M.D., and others to Lord Deskford. II. Correspondence
between Dr George Garden and James Cunningham. Edited,
with introduction and notes, by G. D. Henderson. 1934.

> Letters to Lord Deskford, 1713–23, and Garden–Cunningham correspon-
> dence, 1709–10.

38.5

6. The miscellany of the Third Spalding Club. Vol. i. 1935.

> Court book of the barony of Fintray, 1711–1726. Edited by James
> Cruickshank. [Extracts.]
> Letters of George, tenth Earl Marischal. Edited by Alistair and Henrietta
> Tayler. [1715–72.]

38.6

Memorandum book of John Grant, carried to Edinburgh, 1771. Edited by G. D. Henderson. [Account of Grant's journey from Dundurcas (of which he was parish minister) to Edinburgh, and of his stay there.]

Alexander Jaffray's recollections of Kingswells, 1755–1800. Edited by G. M. Fraser. [Autobiographical notes, not confined to Kingswells.]

The medieval roof of the nave of St Machar's Cathedral. Information compiled by William Kelly.

An Elgin hotel bill of 1785.

Highways and bridges in Aberdeenshire in 1739. Edited by G. M. Fraser. [Estimate for repairs.]

7. **Drawings of Aberdeenshire castles. By James Giles. Edited by W. Douglas Simpson. 1936.**   **38.7**

1838–55.

8. **The house of Forbes. Edited by Alistair and Henrietta Tayler. 1937.**   **38.8**

Includes extracts from many docs.

9. **The book of Dunvegan. Being documents from the muniment room of the MacLeods of MacLeod at Dunvegan Castle, Isle of Skye. Edited by R. C. MacLeod of MacLeod. 2 vols. 1938–9.**   **38.9**

i : 1340–1700.
ii: 1700–1920.

10. **The miscellany of the Third Spalding Club. Vol. ii. 1940.**   **38.10**

The three Spalding Clubs: A century in retrospect. By W. Douglas Simpson.

Testimonial book of Aberdeen. Testimonialis grantit be ye ballies sen ye last day of Merche 1589. Edited by Louise B. Taylor. [Birth brieves etc., 1589–1603. See also 36.24.]

The raid on Glenkindie in 1698. Documents edited by John Macgregor. [Docs. 1698–1700. Judicial raid by commissioners of justiciary.]

George Skene's account of a journey to London in 1729. Edited by G. D. Henderson and A. T. McRobert.

Four needlework panels attributed to Mary Jamesone, in the west church of St. Nicholas, Aberdeen. By William Kelly. [Mid-17th century.]

Chamberlain's account, 1650, Dunnottar. (From Sir Patrick Keith Murray of Ochtertyre's papers: transcribed in 1910 by the late Dean Christie). [Account for 1650–1, dated 1656.]

Copy of a manuscript entitled 'A genealogie of the barons in the Mearns of late memory deschending lineally unto the year of God 1578'.

The music school of Old Machar. From the mss. of Professor C. Sanford Terry. Edited with an introduction by Harry M. Willsher. [Early 17th century–1891.]

Account for building a new road on Tyrebagger Hill, 1759–60. Edited by James Cruickshank. [Docs. 1759–75.]

A King's College [Aberdeen] dinner account of 1670. [Dated 1671.]

11. Logan's collections. Edited by James Cruickshank. 1941.   **38.11**

Descriptions and drawings of buildings in and around Aberdeen, *c.* 1818–20, by James Logan. Also 'Three fifteenth century effigies of canons in Aberdeen Cathedral', by Francis C. Eeles.

12. The book of Glenbuchat. Edited by W. Douglas Simpson. 1942.   **38.12**

Includes Latin, French and English docs., 1473–1868.

13. The inscriptions of Pictland. An essay on the sculptured and inscribed stones of the North-East and North of Scotland: with other writings and collections. By Francis C. Diack. Edited by William M. Alexander and John Macdonald. 1944.   **38.13**

14. Life and labour on an Aberdeenshire estate, 1735–1750. (Being selections from the Monymusk papers). Transcribed and edited by Henry Hamilton. 1946.   **38.14**

1735–57.

15. James Beattie's day-book. 1773–1798. Edited with an introduction and notes by Ralph S. Walker. 1948.   **38.15**

Accounts of personal and household expenditure. Also extracts from his memoranda, 1774–94.

16. James Gordon's diary. 1692–1710. Edited by G. D. Henderson and H. H. Porter. 1949.   **38.16**

17. Powis papers. 1507–1894. Edited with introduction by John G. Burnett. 1951.   **38.17**

Papers of Frasers and Leslies of Powis.

18. The place-names of Aberdeenshire. By William M. Alexander. 1952.   **38.18**

19. Charters and other records of the city and royal burgh of Kirkwall. With the treaty of 1468 between Denmark and Scotland. Edited by John Mooney. Noltland Castle. Written by W. Douglas Simpson. 1952.   **38.19**

Latin, with English translation, and English. 1468–1929.

20. George Strachan. Memorials of a wandering Scottish scholar of the seventeenth century. By G. L. Dellavida. 1956.   **38.20**

Account of a noted collector of Oriental manuscripts.

21. The miscellany of the Third Spalding Club. Vol. iii. 1960.   **38.21**

Professor James Garden's letters to John Aubrey, 1692–1695. Transcribed and edited by Cosmo A. Gordon.

An apology for the Aberdeen evictions. Transcribed and edited by M. K. and C. Ritchie. [*c.* 1718–19. A presbyterian defence of the depriving of episcopalian ministers of their parishes.]

The development of Castle Fraser. By W. Douglas Simpson.

22. The lordship of Strathavon. Tomintoul under the Gordons.   **38.22**
By Victor Gaffney. 1960.

Includes rentals, 1680–1809, and documents relating to the forest of Glenaven, 1750–1841.

39. SPOTTISWOODE SOCIETY

Place of publication: Edinburgh, unless otherwise stated.

1. History of the affairs of church and state in Scotland, from the beginning of the Reformation to the year 1568. By the Right Rev. Robert Keith, primus of the Scottish Episcopal Church. With biographical sketch, notes, and index, by the editor. Vols. i and ii edited by John P. Lawson; vol. iii edited by C. J. Lyon. 3 vols. 1844–50.

39.1

> Reprinted from the first edition, Edinburgh 1734, vol. i (no more published). Some French and Latin.
> i : [Church and state affairs, 1524–60; and miscellaneous docs., 1527–60.]
> ii : [State affairs, 1560–8.]
> iii: [Church affairs, 1560–8; and miscellaneous docs., 1559–78.]

2. The works of the Right Rev. John Sage, a bishop of the church in Scotland; with memoir and notes. 3 vols. 1844–6.

39.2

> Pagination continuous in vols. ii–iii.
> i : [*The fundamental charter of presbytery*. From the first edition, London 1695. Also a memoir of Sage.]
> ii : [*The principles of the Cyprianic age*. From the first edition, 1695.]
> iii: [*The principles of the Cyprianic age*.]

3. The Spottiswoode miscellany: a collection of original papers and tracts, illustrative chiefly of the civil and ecclesiastical history of Scotland. [Edited by James Maidment.] Vol. i. 1844.

39.3

> Genealogy of the family of Spottiswoode, from the ms. collection of Father Augustin Hay. [Richard Augustine Hay, 1661–1736.]
> Papers relative to the murder of Matthew Sinclair by John Spottiswoode of that Ilk, 1611. From the Balfour mss. in the Library of the Faculty of Advocates.
> Refutatio libelli de regimine Ecclesiae Scoticanae, 1620, by Archbishop Spottiswoode. [From the first edition, London 1620. An answer to a pamphlet by David Calderwood.]
> The sermon preached by the right reverend father in God the Archbishop of St Andrews to the General Assembly holden at Perth, the 25th of August 1618. [By Archbishop John Spottiswoode. From the *True narration* of the assembly by David Lindsay, Bishop of Brechin, London 1621.]
> The life of the right reverend father in God, James Spottiswoode, Lord Bishop of Clogher. [From the ms. of Father Richard Augustine Hay.]

Spottiswoode lived 1567–1645. Authorship uncertain, though the last part is by Hay.]

Poems by Sir Henry Spottiswoode. [Mainly concerned with the civil wars, *c.* 1639–47.]

Address of Sir Robert Spottiswoode, lord president of the College of Justice, to the members of the Faculty of Advocates, summer session 1633.

Two letters relative to the murder of Sir Robert Spottiswoode and other royalists, dated from St Andrews 20th January 1645–6. [The letters are from a London 1646 pamphlet; both are dated 26 January. Also Major Nathaniel Gordon's declaration, 20 January 1646.]

Captain John Spottiswoode's petition to the estates of Parliament before the pronouncing of his sentence, 28th May 1650.

Lochiel's interview with Sir Robert Spottiswoode on the night before his murder and his account of that tragedy. [From **1.24.**]

Speech of John Spottiswoode, esq., to the Berwickshire freeholders, 1702. [Reprinted from the first edition, 1703.]

The trimmer: or some necessary cautions concerning the union of the kingdoms of Scotland and England. [By John Spottiswoode. From the first edition, Edinburgh 1706.]

Account of the battle of Balrinnes, 3d of October 1594. From a ms. formerly belonging to the Rev. Robert Wodrow. [Battle of Glenlivet.]

Letter addressed to His Majesty King James VI by Johne Harisone, giving an account of his visit to Barbarie to liberate captives. 28th November 1618.

Eximii animi dotibus, et in dei vinea cultoris fidelis, Domini Gulielmi Forbesii, Edinburgeni Episcopi, vita. 1634. [Verse. By Andrew Stephens or Stephenson.]

Information anent his majestie's printers in Scotland. [By Robert and James Bryson, against Robert Young. 1641.]

Answers for James Anderson, his majesty's printer, and Agnes Campbell, his mother, to the petition of Robert Saunders, printer in Glasgow. [1681? Saunders' petition was addressed to Parliament.]

Account of the shire of Forfar, circa 1682, by John Ochterlony, esq. of Guynd.

Documents relative to the palace of Linlithgow, 1540–1648.

Narrative of the retreat of a portion of the allied forces from Madrid to Ciudad Rodrigo during the war of the succession in Spain, July 1706. By a corporal in Harvey's Dragoons.

Letters of Simon Lord Fraser of Lovat to George Crawford, esq. 1728–30.

Letter from an English traveller at Rome to his father, of the 6th of May 1721 O.S. [From the first edition, 1721. Describes meetings with James Stuart, the Old Pretender. Ascribed to William Godolphin, Marquis of Blandford. Also printed in **8.1.**]

Some account of the nature and constitution of the ancient Church of Scotland. [In the form of a letter by 'A.B.', written *c.* 1730–40.]

3A. The Spottiswoode miscellany. . . . Edited by James Maidment. Vol. ii. 1845. 39.4

Processus factus contra Templarios in Scotia, 1309.

Charter by Mary Queen of Scots, with consent of the three estates, in favour of James Sandilands, Lord St John, of the possessions of the Templars and Hospitallers, 24th January 1563. [Latin.]

Letter from Sir Robert Anstruther to Lord Chancellor Hay, relative to the ransom of Angus Morraye, detained as a slave in Barbary. [Written between 1622 and 1627.]

Trial of Isobel Young for witchcraft, February 4, 1629. [Abridged, in the late 17th century, by Sir Alexander Seton, Lord Pitmedden, from the Justiciary Court's books of adjournal.]

Trial of Agnes Finnie for witchcraft, Dec. 18, 1664. [Ditto.]

Notes of cases of witchcraft, sorcery, etc. 1629–1662. From the books of adjournal.

Diurnal of occurrences chiefly in Scotland, commencing 21st August 1652, and ending April 13, 1654. [Reprinted from *Mercurius Politicus*.]

The Kincardine papers, 1649–1679. [Partly French. Miscellaneous letters, by Elizabeth, Queen of Bohemia and her daugher, by Mary, princess of Orange, by James, Duke of York, 1676–9, and by the Earl of Kincardine, 1678.]

Extracts from the kirk-session register of Perth, 1577–1634.

Illustrative matter relative to Perth. [Notes on the preceding item.]

Warrant by Charles II in favour of Don Rostaino Cantelmi, Duke of Popoli and Prince of Petterano, to enable him to prove his descent from the ancient kings and queens of Scotland, 25th August 1681.

Ceremonial of the funeral of Field-Marshall Robert Douglas, Stockholm, June 1662. [Letter dated 14 June 1662.]

An account of the Lewis and some of the other Western Isles. From the collections of Macfarlane of that Ilk. [Descriptions of Lewis by John Morisone; of Tiree, Canna, Coll and Iona by John Fraser, and of most of the Hebrides (anonymous). All late 17th century.]

Papers relative to the submission of Angus MacDonald of Isla to His Majesty James VI, 1596.

Letter from John Coke, esq. of Holkham, to the lords of the Scottish Privy Council, 29th June 1626. [Concerning Scots levies to serve under Count Mansfeld.]

List of the Scotish officers under Gustavus Adolphus, King of Sweden. [From a pamphlet of 1714.]

Short account of the grievances of the episcopal clergy in Scotland. [From a pamphlet of *c.* 1711.]

Memoirs of John Duke of Melfort, being an account of the secret intrigues of the Chevalier de St George, particularly relating to the present times, MDCCXIV. [Reprinted from first edition, London 1714. Supposedly by Melfort but in reality a forgery.]

Account of the battle of Sheriffmuir, in a letter from a gentleman in Stirling to a friend in Edinburgh, 15th November 1715. [From a broadside.]

A true account of the proceedings at Perth, 1716, by the Master of Sinclair. [From the first edition, London 1716. The work is not by Sinclair.]

Memorial relative to the prisoners engaged in the rebellion, 1715. [Printed from a ms. and the first edition, 1716. By Sir David Dalrymple.]

Relics of the rebellion, 1745–6. [Miscellaneous letters and papers.]

Instances of popular credulity at the commencement of the eighteenth century. [Accounts from Ireland, France and Italy, *c.* 1700–15.]

4. The funeral sermons, orations, epitaphs, and other pieces on the death of the Right Rev. Patrick Forbes, Bishop of Aberdeen.   39.5

From the original edition of 1635. With biographical memoir
and notes by Charles F. Shand. 1845.

> Latin and English.

5. Considerationes modestae et pacificae controversiarum de   **39.6**
justificatione, purgatorio, invocatione sanctorum, Christo
mediatore, et eucharistia. Per Gulielmum Forbesium, S.T.D., et
episcopum Edinburgensem primum. Opus posthumum diu
desideratum. Editio quarta, una cum versione Anglica. [Edited
by George H. Forbes?] 2 vols. Oxford. 1850–6.

> Published as part of the Library of Anglo-Catholic Theology after it had been
> 'in part printed for the Spottiswoode Society'. Based on the first edition,
> London 1658, which was edited by Thomas Sydserf, Bishop of Galloway.
> i : De justificatione.
> ii: De purgatorio, invocatione sanctorum, Christo mediatore, et eucharistia.
> [Also the prefaces to the first two editions, and Sydserf's 'Vita authoris' (all
> Latin) and contents list for both vols.]

6. History of the Church of Scotland, beginning the year of our   **39.7**
Lord 203, and continued to the end of the reign of King
James VI. By the Right Rev. John Spottiswoode, Archbishop of
St Andrews, and lord chancellor of Scotland. With biographical
sketch and notes, by Michael Russell. [Edited by Mark Napier
and Michael Russell.] 3 vols. 1847–51.

> Also issued as **6.96**, which see for details.

40.   STAIR SOCIETY

Place of publication: Edinburgh.

1. An introductory survey of the sources and literature of Scots law. By various authors. With an introduction by Hugh P. Macmillan, Lord Macmillan. 1936.   **40.**1

Native sources.
    The statutory law. By William Watson, Lord Thankerton.
    Early records of Council and Session, 1466–1659. By Robert K. Hannay.
    Practicks, 1469–1700. By Hector McKechnie.
    The printed law reports, 1540–1935. By James S. Leadbetter.
    The institutional writers, 1600–1829. By A. C. Black.
    Regiam majestatem and the auld lawes. By Thomas M. Cooper.
    Privy Council records, 1545–1707. By W. K. Dickson.
    Financial and administrative records, 1264–1724. By J. A. Inglis.
    Burgh court records, 1319–1834. By David Robertson and Marguerite Wood.
    Sheriff and other local court records, 1385–1935. By C. A. Malcolm.
    The courts of the officials and the commissary courts, 1512–1830. By F. P. Walton.
    Presbyterian court records, 1560–1935. By Sir Francis J. Grant.
    Custom. By David Anderson, Lord St Vigeans.
Non-native sources.
    Roman law. By David B. Smith.
    Canon law. By David B. Smith.
    Feudal law. By John Girvan.
    The influence of English law. By E. J. MacGillivray.
    French and Dutch influences. By John C. Gardner.
    The influence of the law of Moses. By John C. Gardner.
    The law merchant. By Charles D. Murray, Lord Murray.
    The law of nature. By John L. Wark, Lord Wark.
Indirect sources.
    Charters, cartularies and deeds, 1094–1700. By William Angus.
    Vatican Archives, 1073–1560. By Annie I. Cameron.
    Brocards. By Robert Munro, Lord Alness.
    Notorial protocol books, 1469–1700. By William Angus. [Includes extracts from protocol books 1412–1566.]
    Style books. By E. M. Wedderburn and A. E. Lawrie.
    Scottish legal periodicals, 1829–1935. By James C. Brown.
Special subjects.
    Admiralty and maritime law. By A. R. G. McMillan.
    Celtic law. By John Cameron.

Constitutional law and history. By J. R. Philip.
Criminal law. By Stair A. Gillon.
Heraldic law. By Thomas Innes of Learney.
Judicial administration in session and justiciary. By Robert K. Hannay.
The law of nations. By William Wilson.
Peerage law. By Thomas Innes of Learney.
Jurisprudence and philosophy of law. By S. G. Kermack.
Udal law. By W. Jardine Dobie.
Allodial law. By W. Jardine Dobie.

1A. Index to an introductory survey of the sources and literature of Scots law. Compiled by James C. Brown. 1939.   **40.2**

2. Acta Curiae Admirallatus Scotiae, 6th Sept. 1557–11th March 1561–2. Edited by Thomas C. Wade. 1937.   **40.3**

> English, with headings in Latin. 1558, 1559, 1560–2. Also notarial protocols, 20 July 1556–25 Aug. 1557 (English and Latin. Mainly relating to Edinburgh), probably by John Mosman, clerk of the court, from the same ms.

3. Hope's Major practicks, 1608–1633. Edited by James A. Clyde. Vol. i. 1937.   **40.4**

> By Sir Thomas Hope of Craighall, c. 1580–1646. Completed c. 1633. Law and government, civil and ecclesiastical; personal rights; real rights; wills and succession.

4. Hope's Major practicks, 1608–1633. . . . Vol. ii. 1938.   **40.5**

> Courts and jurisdictions; actions and diligence; process and evidence; crimes; justices of the peace; jurisdiction of burghs; ship laws; and cockets.

5. Baron David Hume's lectures, 1786–1822. Edited and annotated by G. Campbell H. Paton. Vol. i. 1939.   **40.6**

> Part 1, rights arising from distinctions of persons. Lectures as delivered 1821–2, with appendices from lectures of 1796–7. For vols. ii–vi and supplement see **40.**14, 16, 18–21.

6. Lord Hermand's consistorial decisions, 1684–1777. Edited by F. P. Walton. With biographical sketch of Lord Hermand by James Fergusson. 1940.   **40.7**

> Probably compiled 1775–7. George Fergusson was one of the commissaries of Edinburgh, 1775–99, and took the title Lord Hermand on becoming a lord of session in 1799.

7. St Andrews formulare, 1514–1546. Text transcribed and edited by Gordon Donaldson and C. Macrae. Vol. i. 1942.   **40.8**

> Latin. Book of ecclesiastical styles or forms compiled after 1521 by Mr John Lauder, c. 1490–1551. Includes a few earlier documents, one as early as 1417.

8. Acta dominorum Concilii, 26 March 1501–27 January 1502– 3. Transcribed by J. A. Crawford. Edited with an introduction by James A. Clyde. 1943.   **40**.9

Mainly English. Abridged transcripts and abstracts.

9. St Andrews formulare, 1514–1546. Edited by Gordon Donaldson, with prefatory note by David B. Smith. Vol. ii. 1944.   **40**.10

Latin.

10. The register of brieves, as contained in the Ayr Ms., the Bute Ms., and Quoniam attachiamenta. Edited by Thomas M. Cooper, Lord Cooper. 1946. Thomas Thomson's Memorial on old extent. Edited by James D. Mackie. 1946.   **40**.11

The two works have separate title pages, but pagination is continuous. The brieves (styles or forms of process) are taken from 14th century mss. (Latin, with English abstracts); on the spine and half-title they are misleadingly dated '1286–1386'. The Memorial, completed in 1816, concerns a traditional land valuation.

11. Regiam majestatem and Quoniam attachiamenta, based on the text of Sir John Skene. Edited and translated with introduction and notes by Thomas M. Cooper, Lord Cooper. 1947.   **40**.12

Latin, with English translation. Skene's edition is Edinburgh 1609. Regiam majestatem is a legal compilation, probably early 14th century, based largely on the treatise ascribed to Ranulf de Glanvill. Quoniam attachiamenta is a 14th century manual on court procedure.

12. The justiciary records of Argyll and the Isles, 1664–1705. Transcribed and edited, with an introduction, by John Cameron. Vol. i. 1949.   **40**.13

Slightly abridged transcript of the books of adjournal. For vol. ii see **40**.27.

13. Baron David Hume's lectures, 1786–1822. . . . Vol. ii. 1949.   **40**.14

Part 2, law of obligations or personal claims (i). Lectures as delivered 1821–2, with appendices from lectures of 1796–7.

14. Selected cases from acta dominorum Concilii et Sessionis. From 27th May 1532, the inception of the court, to 5 July 1533. Edited by Ian H. Shearer. 1951.   **40**.15

Calendar.

15. Baron David Hume's lectures, 1786–1822. . . . Vol. iii. 1952.   **40**.16

Part 2, law of obligations or personal claims (ii). Part 3, real rights (i). Lectures as delivered 1821–2, with appendices from 1796–7 and other lectures.

16. Selected justiciary cases, 1624–1650. Edited and annotated   **40**.17
by Stair A. Gillon. Vol. i. 1953.

> 1624–39. Abridged transcript from the books of adjournal. For vols. ii and iii
> see **40**.29–30.

17. Baron David Hume's lectures, 1786–1822. . . . Vol. iv.   **40**.18
1955.

> Part 3, real rights (ii). Part 4, real rights 'according to feudal notions', and
> succession (i). Lectures as delivered 1821–2.

18. Baron David Hume's lectures, 1786–1822. . . . Vol. v.   **40**.19
1957.

> Part 4, real rights 'according to feudal notions', and succession (ii). Part 5,
> law of actions (i). Lectures as delivered 1821–2.

19. Baron David Hume's lectures, 1786–1822. . . . Vol. vi.   **40**.20
1958.

> Part 5, law of actions (ii); teinds and patronage. Lectures as delivered
> 1821–2.

19A. A supplement to Baron Hume's lectures. Edited and   **40**.21
annotated by the editor of the printed volumes. 1957.

> Typescript deposited in a few Scottish libraries. The title page is headed 'The
> Stair Society' but the volume is not included in the Society's official list of
> publications. Comprises mainly material included in Hume's lectures in
> earlier years but not in 1821–2.

20. An introduction to Scottish legal history. By various   **40**.22
authors. With an introduction by Wilfrid G. Normand, Lord
Normand. [Edited by G. Campbell H. Paton.] 1958.

> Part 1: The general development of Scots Law.
> > From David I to Bruce, 1124–1329. The Scoto-Norman law. By Thomas
> > M. Cooper, Lord Cooper of Culross.
> > The dark age, 1329–1532. By G. Campbell H. Paton.
> > The transition to the modern law, 1532–1660. By J. Irvine Smith.
> > The rise of modern Scots law, 1660–1707. By J. Irvine Smith.
> > The eighteenth century and later. By G. Campbell H. Paton.
>
> Part 2: The history of particular branches of Scots law and practice.
> A. The law of persons.
> > Husband and wife: pre-Reformation canon law of marriage of the officials'
> > courts. By James D. Scanlan.
> > Husband and wife: (a) post-Reformation canon law of marriage of the
> > commissaries' courts, and (b) modern common and statute law. By Ronald
> > D. Ireland.
> > Husband and wife: divorce, nullity of marriage and separation. By Ronald
> > D. Ireland.
> > Husband and wife: property rights and relationships. By G. Campbell H.
> > Paton.
> > Parent and child. By Alexander E. Anton.

Guardian and ward. By George A. Montgomery.
Master and servant. By Thomas B. Smith.
B. The law of property.
Heritable rights: the early feudal tenures. By Isabel A. Milne.
Heritable rights: from early times to the twentieth century. By H. H. Monteath.
Moveable rights. By A. J. Mackenzie Stuart.
Succession. By J. Irvine Smith.
Insolvency. By Andrew D. Gibb.
Diligence. By David Maxwell.
C. Other branches.
Contract and quasi-contract. By A. J. Mackenzie Stuart.
Delict and quasi-delict. By Hector McKechnie.
Criminal law. By J. Irvine Smith and Ian Macdonald.
Evidence. By David M. Walker.
D. The courts and procedure.
The central courts before 1532. By Archibald A. M. Duncan.
The central courts after 1532. By Thomas M. Cooper, Lord Cooper.
The sheriff court: before the sixteenth century. By Isabel A. Milne.
The sheriff court: sixteenth century and later. By C. A. Malcolm.
The church courts. By Gordon Donaldson.
The franchise courts. By Peter McIntyre.
The burgh courts and allied jurisdictions. By George S. Pryde.
Courts of special jurisdiction. By W. Croft Dickinson.
The High Court of Justiciary. By W. Croft Dickinson.
Civil procedure. By David Maxwell.
Criminal procedure. By J. Irvine Smith.
The Parliament House and its antecedents. By C. A. Malcolm.
Lists of lord chancellors, lord presidents and lord justice clerks from 1532.

21. The practicks of Sir James Balfour of Pittendreich.   40.23
Reproduced from the printed edition of 1754. Edited by Peter G.
B. McNeill. vol. i. 1962.

Facsimile of the Edinburgh 1754 edition. Probably compiled 1574–83, but
with a few additions up to *c*. 1610 (though Balfour d. 1583).

22. The practicks of Sir James Balfour of Pittendreich. . . .   40.24
Vol. ii. 1963.

Pagination continuous with vol. i.

23. The origins and development of the jury in Scotland. By Ian   40.25
D. Willock. 1966.

24. William Hay's lectures on marriage. Transcribed, translated   40.26
and edited by John C. Barry. 1967.

Latin, with English translation. Ms. dates from 1530s. Hay lived *c*.
1470–1542 and delivered the lectures at King's College, Aberdeen.

25. The justiciary records of Argyll and the Isles, 1664–1742.   **40**.27
Edited by John Imrie. Vol. ii. 1969.

> Abridged transcript of books of adjournal, 1705–11 and 1726–42, and of criminal processes 1711–22. Pagination continuous with vol. i (**40**.13).

26. Miscellany One. By various authors. With a preface by   **40**.28
James L. M. Clyde, Lord Clyde. 1971.

> George Neilson: the march laws. 1. George Neilson (1858–1923). A memoir by E. L. G. Stones. 2. The march laws. Edited by Thomas I. Rae.
> De composicione cartarum. Edited by James J. Robertson. [Latin, with English translation. Early 15th century treatise.]
> Not improven: Advocate and Leslie v. Brown and Johnston, 1582. Edited by Ian D. Grant. [John Leslie of Wardhouse *v* Thomas Brown and Gilbert Johnston of Standingstones. Docs. in a case of forgery, from Court of Session records.]
> Sir John Skene and the exchequer, 1594–1612. By Athol L. Murray. [Includes papers by Skene on exchequer and financial reform.]
> The English and the public records of Scotland, 1650–1660. By David Stevenson.
> Division of the commonty of Hassendean, 1761–1763. By Ian H. Adams.
> A royal debtor at Holyrood. By A. J. Mackenzie Stuart. [Docs. 1801–2 concerning Charles-Philippe, Comte d'Artois (later King Charles X of France).]
> The Paisley Union Bank robbery. By J. Bennett Miller. [1811.]

27. Selected justiciary cases, 1624–1650. Edited with an intro-   **40**.29
duction by J. Irvine Smith. Vol. ii. 1972.

> 1630–42. Pagination continuous with vol. i (**40**.17).

28. Selected justiciary cases, 1624–1650. . . . Vol. iii. 1974.   **40**.30

> 1643–50. Pagination continuous with vols. i and ii.

29. The minute book of the Faculty of Advocates. Edited by   **40**.31
John M. Pinkerton. Vol. i: 1661–1712. 1976.

> Minutes of the Edinburgh faculty. For vol. ii see **40**.34.

30. The records of the synod of Lothian and Tweeddale,   **40**.32
1589–96, 1640–49. Edited with an introduction by James Kirk.
1977.

> From original minute books, except 1640–3 from a rather later copy.

31. Perpetuities in Scots law. By Robert Burgess. 1979.   **40**.33

32. The minute book of the Faculty of Advocates. . . . Vol. ii: **40**.34
1713–1750. 1980.

33. Stair tercentenary studies. By various scholars. Edited by   **40.35**
David M. Walker. 1981.

Stair's public career. By Gordon M. Hutton.
The background of the Institutions. By David M. Walker.
Purposes and pattern of the Institutions. By Gordon M. Hutton and David
  M. Walker.
Sources and models. By William M. Gordon, James J. Robertson, A. J.
  Carty, John M. Halliday and W. David H. Sellar.
The content of the Institutions. By David M. Walker.
Stair's general concepts. By Peter G. Stein and D. Neil MacCormick.
Evaluation of the Institutions. By G. Campbell H. Paton, John W. G.
  Blackie, F. H. Lawson, Klaus Luig and David M. Walker.

34. The court of the official in pre-Reformation Scotland. Based   **40.36**
on the surviving records of the officials of St Andrews and
Edinburgh. By Simon Ollivant. 1982.

35. Miscellany two. By various authors. Edited by David Sellar.   **40.37**
1984.

Courtesy, battle, and the brieve of right, 1368—A story continued. By David
  Sellar. [Includes an account (Latin, with English translation) of a judicial
  duel between Sir Thomas Erskine and Sir James Douglas of Dalkeith,
  1368, taken from Fordun's Chronicle.]
Problems of sovereignty and law in Orkney and Shetland. By Gordon
  Donaldson. [Includes extracts from and abstracts of docs. relating to
  Danish attempts to redeem Orkney and Shetland, 1485–1749.]
The statutes of Ettrick Forest, 1499. By John M. Gilbert. [Transcript and
  commentary.]
Jurisdiction in heritage and the lords of Council and Session after 1532. By
  Hector L. MacQueen. [Includes extracts from Court of Session records
  relating to cases of Patrick Wemyss of Pettincreif v Arthus Forbes of
  Reres, 1543, and Sir James Caldwell v Sir John Mason, 1546.]
Discours particulier d'Escosse, 1559/60. Edited, with an introduction, by
  Peter G. B. McNeill. [French, with English translation. For details see the
  earlier edition at 6.6.]
A Gaelic contract of lease, c. 1603 x 1616. Edited, with introduction and
  commentary, by Ronald Black. [Gaelic, with English translation. Probably
  granted by Duncan MacDougall of Dunollie.]
The commissary court of Aberdeen in 1650. Edited by David Stevenson.
  [Transcript of regulations for the conduct of the court.]
The life and career of John Snell (c. 1629–1679). By Lionel Stones. [Includes
  transcripts of Snell's will, 1679, and of documents relating to his life,
  1661–79.]
The memorials in Haggart and H.M. Advocate v Hogg and Soutar, 1738.
  Edited, with introduction and commentary, by Bernard S. Jackson.
  [David Haggart of Cairnmuir v. James Hogg and Thomas Soutar of
  Russlo. From the records of the Justiciary Court.]
The electoral system in the Scottish counties before 1832. By William
  Ferguson.
'A man of no common stamp': Sir William Gibson Craig of Riccarton, clerk
  register of Scotland, 1862–1878. By Margaret D. Young.

36. Formulary of old Scots legal documents. Compiled by Peter **40.**38
Gouldesbrough. With a supplementary essay on early Scottish
conveyancing. By Gordon Donaldson. 1985.

> Partly Latin, with English translations. 11th–16th centuries (*Essay*) and
> 15th–19th centuries (*Formulary*). As the documents transcribed in the
> *Formulary* are published as typical examples of the various 'styles' or forms of
> documents, personal and place names have been omitted, but these are
> retained in the *Essay*.

41.   SUTHERLAND ASSOCIATION*

Place of publication: Edinburgh.

2. The tour of Dr Richard Pococke, Lord Bishop of Ossory,   **41**.1
through Sutherland and Caithness in 1760, with introduction
and notes by Daniel W. Kemp. 1888.

Extracts from Pococke's letters, which are fully transcribed in **24**.1.

---

* Only publications relevant to this volume are listed.

42. VIKING SOCIETY FOR NORTHERN RESEARCH, OLD LORE SERIES*

Place of publication: London.

1. Diplomatarium Orcadense et Hialtlandense. Fornbréfasafn Orkneyinga og Hjaltlendinga. Orkney and Shetland records. Collected and edited by Alfred W. Johnston and Amy Johnston. With introduction and index by Alfred W. Johnston. Vol. i. 1907–13.   **42.1**

> Half-title page adds 'Old-Lore Series, vol. vii'. Mainly Latin, with English translations. Transcripts and extracts of miscellaneous docs., 1056–1634.

2. Diplomatarium Orcadense et Hialtlandense. . . . Collected and edited by Alfred W. Johnston and Amy Johnston. Vol. ii: Orkney and Shetland sasines (Shetland sasines, 1623–1628). Edited by Henry Paton and Henry M. Paton, Vol. i. 1907–42.   **42.2**

> Half-title page adds 'Old-Lore Series, vol. xii'.

3. Diplomatarium Orcadense et Hialtlandense. . . . Vol. iii: Orkney and Shetland sasines (Orkney sasines 1617–1621). Edited by Henry Paton and Henry M. Paton. Vol. ii. 1908–42.   **42.3**

> Half-title page adds 'Old-Lore Series, vol. xiii'.

4. Diplomatarium Katanense et Sutherlandense. Caithness and Sutherland records. Collected and edited by Alfred W. Johnston and Amy Johnston. With introduction, notes and index by Donald Beaton. Vol. i. 1909–28.   **42.4**

> Half-title page adds 'Old-Lore Series, vol. x'. Mainly Latin, with English translations. Miscellaneous docs., mid-12th century–1449.

---

* Between 1907 and 1946 the Viking Society (until 1912 the Viking Club) issued its 'Old Lore' Series in 75 pts., making up ten vols., the first titled *Orkney and Shetland Miscellany*, the rest *Old Lore Miscellany of Orkney, Shetland, Caithness and Sutherland*. The materials which were later assembled to form 42.1–4 were issued at first as appendices to pts. 1 to 8, and then as separate pts. in the series. The rest of the 75 pts. comprise mainly secondary articles and therefore (though they include some additional docs.) they are not listed here. The Old Lore Series vol. numbers given on the half-title pages of the *Record* vols., as detailed above, are highly confusing; there are also vols. numbered vii and x in the original *Old Lore Miscellany* series, and vols. are numbered xii and xiii though no vol. xi exists. For guides to the Society's publications see J. A. B. Townsend, *Index to Old-Lore series* (1966) and *Index to Saga-Book* (1977). Matheson, *Catalogue*, began listing the Society's 'Translation' series, but this has been omitted here as works in it all concern Iceland. The later 'Text' series is omitted for the same reason.

43. WODROW SOCIETY

Place of publication: Edinburgh.

1. The Wodrow Society, for the publication of the works of the fathers and early writers of the reformed Church of Scotland. By James Pitcairn. 1841.

43.1

Prospectus, with list of works suggested for publication, etc.

2. Laws and list of members of the Wodrow Society. Instituted May, 1841. 1842.

43.2

3. The autobiography and diary of Mr James Melvill, minister of Kilrenny, in Fife, and professor of theology in the University of St Andrews. With a continuation of the diary. Edited from manuscripts in the libraries of the Faculty of Advocates and University of Edinburgh, by Robert Pitcairn. 1842.

43.3

The 'diary' *is* the autobiography, 1556–1602. The continuation, 'A true narratioune of the declyneing aige of the Kirk of Scotland', covers 1596–1610. Also Melville's will, 14 Jan. 1614; account of his illness and death, 1614; and verses on his death by Thomas Melville. For another edition see **6.37**.

4. The history of the Kirk of Scotland, from the year 1558 to August 1637. By John Row, minister of Carnock: with a continuation to July 1639, by his son, John Row, principal of King's College, Aberdeen. [Edited by David Laing.] 1842.

43.4

The history and 'Coronis' to the history are from a ms. in the hand of John Row younger dated 1650 (though both are by John Row elder), and the same date is on the ms. of the continuation or supplement. Also 'Additions to the Coronis', probably by William Row, minister of Ceres, *c.* 1670; extracts from the kirk session minutes of Carnock, 1642–50; and miscellaneous docs. relating to the Rows. See also **15.57**.

5. The correspondence of the Rev. Robert Wodrow, minister of Eastwood, and author of the History of the sufferings of the Church of Scotland. Edited from manuscripts in the Library of the Faculty of Advocates, Edinburgh, by Thomas M'Crie. 3 vols. 1842–3.

43.5

A few of Wodrow's letters are slightly abridged; some later ones are omitted, as are many of those addressed to him. Also a few miscellaneous docs. For earlier letters by Wodrow see **26.24.**
i : [1709–14.]
ii : [1715–22.]
iii: [1723–31.]

6. Sermons by the Rev. Robert Bruce, minister of Edinburgh. Reprinted from the original edition of MDXC and MDXCI. With collections for his life, by the Rev. Robert Wodrow. Now first printed from the manuscript in the Library of the University of Glasgow. Edited by William Cunningham. 1843.

43.6

Sixteen sermons and an exhortation. The latter and six of the sermons are dated 1589. One of the sermons was printed in 1740.

7. The history of the Kirk of Scotland. By Mr David Calderwood, some time minister of Crailing. Edited from the original manuscript preserved in the British Museum, by Thomas Thomson. [Vol. viii edited by David Laing.] 8 vols. 1842–9.

43.7

From a ms. completed by 1627. Vols. ii–v also contain appendices of miscellaneous docs.
i   : [1513–60, with preamble.]
ii : [1560–70.]
iii : [1570–83.]
iv : [1584–8.]
v   : [1589–99.]
vi : [1600–8.]
vii : [1609–25.]
viii: Appendix and general index. [Includes Calderwood's testament, 1650, and verses on his death. Thomson's life of Calderwood, which follows the index, was meant to be transferred to vol. i but usually remains in viii.]

8. Select works of Robert Rollock, principal of the University of Edinburgh. Reprinted from the original editions. Edited by William M. Gunn. 2 vols. 1844–9.

43.8

Vol. i is dated 1849, vol. ii, 1844.
i : [*A treatise of Gods effectval calling* from the London 1603 edition, which is translated from the Latin of the Edinburgh 1597 edition; sermons from the 1599, 1616 and 1634 editions; and *De aeterna mentis* . . . from the Edinburgh 1593 edition. Also memorial of Rollock (d. 1599) by Henry Charteris. (Latin, with English translation).]
ii : [*Lectvres vpon the history of the passion* from the Edinburgh 1616 edition.]

9. Select biographies. Edited for the Wodrow Society, chiefly from manuscripts in the Library of the Faculty of Advocates. By W. K. Tweedie. 2 vols. 1845–7.

43.9

i : The history of Mr John Welsh, minister of the gospel at Ayr. [From the Edinburgh 1703 edition. Welsh d. 1622. Probably written by James Kirkton, d. 1699. Also extracts from kirk session minutes of Ayr, 1603–5.]

A true record of the life and death of Master Patrick Simsone. [Written by his brother Archibald Simsone, minister of Dalkeith. Patrick (1556–1618) was minister of Stirling.]

A sermon on John, cap. v, verse 35. By the Rev. A. Simson, minister at Dalkeith. [1618. Preached on the death of his brother Patrick.]

A brief historical relation of the life of Mr John Livingstone, minister of the gospel. . . . Written by himself, during his banishment in Holland, for the cause of Christ. [Written 1666–9.]

The substance of a discourse had by Mr John Livingstone, to his paroch at Ancrum, foreseeing his separation from it. [1662.]

Ane accompt of what past when Mr John Livingstone appeared before the councill in the lower council-house at Edinburgh, December 11, 1662, at which time they banished him.

A letter from Mr John Livingstone to his paroch. [1663.]

A letter written by that famous and faithfull minister of Christ, Mr John Livingstone, unto his parishoners of Ancrum. [1671.]

Letters of Mr John Livingstone relating to the public events of his time. [1641, 1650–1, and n.d.]

Sayings and observations of Mr John Livingstone . . . to which are added, remarks at two communions, December 1634.

Remarks on preaching and praying in publick, by Mr John Livingstone. Observations by Mr John Livingstone, previous to his death. [1672.]

Memorable characteristics, and remarkable passages of divine providence . . . collected by Mr John Livingstone.

Letters from Elizabeth, daughter of Sir James Melvill of Halhill, and wife of John, Lord Colvill of Culross, to Mr John Livingstone. [1620s and 1630s.]

The last and heavenly speeches, and glorious departure, of John, Viscount Kenmure. [From the first edition, Edinburgh 1649. Attributed to Samuel Rutherford. Kenmure d. 1634.]

The memoirs of Walter Pringle of Greenknow, or some few of the free mercies of God to him, and his will to his children, left to them under his own hand. [Written 1662–5. From the first edition, Edinburgh 1723.]

An account of the particular soliloquies and covenant engagements, past betwixt Mrs Janet Hamilton, the defunct lady of Alexander Gordon of Earlstoun. [Written 1687–95.]

ii: A short account of the life of the Rev. David Dickson. By the Rev. Robert Wodrow. [From an 18th century edition of Dickson's *Truth's victory over error*. Also addresses by Dickson to the 1638 and 1639 General Assemblies. Dickson d. 1663.]

Memoirs of the life and character of Mr William Guthrie, minister at Fenwick. By the Rev. William Dunlop. With additions by Rev. Robert Wodrow, and Rev. Robert Trail. [From an 18th century edition of Guthrie's *The Christian's great interest*. Guthrie d. 1665.]

A sermon on sympathie. By the Rev. William Guthrie, minister at Fenwick.

Memoirs of the Rev. James Fraser of Brea, minister of the gospel at Culross. Written by himself. [From the Edinburgh 1738 edition. The memoirs cover 1639–83.]

A true relation of the life and sufferings of John Nisbet in Hardhill, his last testimony to the truth; with a short account of his last words on the scaffold, December 4 MDCLXXXV. [From the second edition, Edinburgh 1719. Written by James Nisbet.]

A rare soul-strengthening and comforting cordial for old and young Christians: being an exact account of the author's experience. . . . By John Stevenson, land-labourer in the parish of Daily in Carrick, who died in the year 1728. [From the Glasgow 1729 edition. Compiled by William Cupples, minister of Kirkoswald.]

Memoir of Mrs Goodal, written by herself. [1670s–1690.]

The last words of the Lady Coltness, who died, or rather entered into eternal life and glory, June 8, 1675. [With a verse epitaph by William Vilant, minister of Cambusnethan.]

A relation of my Lady Anne Elcho, about her being burnt February 17, 1700. By the Rev. Thomas Halyburton. [The burning was accidental.]

10. An apologetical narration of the state and government of the Kirk of Scotland since the Reformation. By William Scot, minister of Cupar. Certaine records touching the estate of the kirk in the years MDCV & MDCVI. By John Forbes, minister of Alford. Edited by David Laing. 1846.   43.10

Scot d. 1642; his *Narration* covers 1560–1633. Forbes d. 1634; his work begins with a brief narrative, 1560–1605.

11. The miscellany of the Wodrow Society: containing tracts and original letters, chiefly relating to the ecclesiastical affairs of Scotland during the sixteenth and seventeenth centuries. Selected and edited by David Laing. Vol. i. 1844.   43.11

The Confession of Faith of the churches of Switzerland; translated from the Latin, by George Wishart, 1536. [From London c. 1548 edition. The date 1536 is that of the original confession. Also printed in 11.11.]

Certamen cum Lutheranis, Saxoniae habitum, per Jacobum Melvil, Scotum. [From the Bologna 1530 edition.]

A historie of the estate of Scotland from July MDLVIII to April MDLX. [Ms. dated 1663, but the date of composition is unknown.]

Ane compendius tractive. By Mr Quintin Kennedy, abbot of Crossraguell. MDLVIII. [From Edinburgh 1558 edition.]

Ane answer to the compendius tractive of Mr Quintine Kennedy, abbot of Crossraguell, by John Davidson. MDLXIII. [From Edinburgh 1563 edition.]

Letter from the abbot of Crossraguell to James, Archbishop of Glasgow; together with the correspondence of the abbot and John Willock. MDLIX.

Letters to Robert Campbell of Kinyeancleuch, Ayrshire, MDLXIV–MDLXXIV.

The forme and maner of buriall used in the kirk of Montrois. [Late 16th century.]

Roberti Pontani parvus catechismus. MDLXXIII. [From St Andrews 1573 edition.]

Register of ministers and readers in the Kirk of Scotland. From the book of the assignation of stipends. MDLXXIV. [Abstract.]

The supplication of the General Assembly to the Regent Earl of Morton, April MDLXXVIII. [On presentation of the Second Book of Discipline.]

The presbytery of Hadington's subscription to the Second Book of Discipline, 30th September MDXCI.

Act of presbytery, appointing two ministers to attend the lords at Falkirk. August MDLXXVIII. [By the presbytery of Edinburgh; the lords were those opposed to the Regent Morton.]

Letters and papers of Mr James Carmichael, minister of Haddington. MDLXXXIV–MDLXXXVI.

An account of the death and funeral of Mr James Lawson, minister of Edinburgh. MDLXXXIV. [Lawson d. 12 October 1584 in London.]

Visitations of the kirk of Holyroodhouse, by the presbytery of Edinburgh, MDLXXXIII–MDXCVIII. [1583, 1588, 1593, 1596, 1598. Also an act of the Privy Council, 13 Sept. 1672.]

Vindication of the Church of Scotland, in reply to Dr Bancroft's sermon, at Paul's Cross, London, MDLXXXIX. [Reprint of John Davidson's *D. Bancrofts rashnes in rayling against the Church of Scotland*, Edinburgh 1590. Also extracts from Bancroft's sermon, 9 Feb. 1589, and miscellaneous docs.]

Ane forme of sindrie materis to be usit in the eldership. MDLXXXIX–MDXCII. [Late 16th century ms. collection of forms, from papers of presbytery of Haddington. Also prayers and graces by John Davidson, minister of Prestonpans.]

Letters of Mr John Welsch to Robert Boyd of Trochrig. MDCVII–MDCXIX. [Partly French.]

Ane afold admonitioun to the ministerie of Scotland. By Mr Alexander Hume, minister of Logie. MDCIX. [Written 1608 or 1609. For other editions see **6.44** and **31.23**.]

The forme and maner of ordaining ministers, and of consecrating archbishops and bishops, used in the Church of Scotland. [From Edinburgh 1620 edition.]

12. The works of John Knox; collected and edited by David Laing. 6 vols. 1846–64.   **43.12**

Vols. i and ii were issued by the Wodrow Society and also as **6.115**.
Vols. iii–vi are uniform with i and ii and were made available to members of the two bodies, but were not published by them. See **6.115** for details.

13. The life of Mr Robert Blair, minister of St Andrews, containing his autobiography, from 1593 to 1636, with supplement to his life, and continuation of the history of the times to 1680, by his son-in-law, Mr William Row, minister of Ceres. Edited for the Wodrow Society from the original manuscript. By Thomas M'Crie. 1848.   **43.13**

Supplement, 1593–1666, written 1676. Continuation, 1666–80. Also contains a continuation of Blair's life attributed to his sons James and David, 1636–c. 1666, and letters by Blair, 1651, 1657, 1659.

14. A logical analysis of the Epistle of Paul to the Romans, by Charles Ferme, translated from the Latin by William Skae,   **43.14**

A.M.; and a commentary on the same epistle by Andrew Melville, in the original Latin. Edited, with a life of Ferme, by William L. Alexander. 1850.

Ferme (or Fairholm) wrote his *Analysis* while minister of Fraserburgh (1598–1617), and it is here translated from the Edinburgh 1651 edition. Melville's *Commentary* is printed from a ms. copy dated 1601—Melville lived 1545–1622. The pagination of the two works is continuous, but the title page of Melville's work is dated 1849.

APPENDIX

44. ROYAL COMMISSION ON THE ANCIENT AND HISTORICAL MONUMENTS OF SCOTLAND, INVENTORIES*

Place of publication: Edinburgh.

1. The Royal Commission on the Ancient and Historical Monuments and Constructions of Scotland. First report and inventory of monuments and constructions in the county of Berwick. 1909.   **44.1**
   See **44.6** below for a revised edition.

2. . . . . Second report. . . . county of Sutherland. 1911.   **44.2**

3. . . . . Third report. . . . county of Caithness. 1911.   **44.3**

4. . . . . Fourth report. . . . in Galloway. Vol. i: county of Wigtown. 1912.   **44.4**

5. . . . . Fifth report. . . . in Galloway. Vol. ii: county of the stewartry of Kirkcudbright. 1914.   **44.5**

6. . . . . Sixth report. . . . county of Berwick (revised issue). 1915.   **44.6**

7. The Royal Commission on Ancient and Historical Monuments and Constructions of Scotland. Seventh report with inventory of monuments and constructions in the county of Dumfries. 1920.   **44.7**

8. . . . . Eighth report. . . . county of East Lothian. 1924.   **44.8**

9. . . . . Ninth report. . . . Outer Hebrides, Skye and the Small Isles. 1928.   **44.9**

10. . . . . Tenth report. . . . counties of Midlothian and West Lothian. 1929.   **44.10**

---

* Strictly speaking these inventories do not qualify for inclusion, being neither texts nor calendars. But Mullins, *T & C*, listed the inventories of the English and Welsh Commissions, so this appendix, devoted to rectifying the omissions relating to Scotland in his 'Part 1: Official Bodies', lists the Scottish equivalents.

11. . . . . Eleventh report. . . . counties of Fife, Kinross, and   **44**.11
Clackmannan. 1933.

12. The Royal Commission on the Ancient Monuments of   **44**.12
Scotland. Twelfth report with an inventory of the ancient
monuments of Orkney and Shetland. 3 vols. 1946.
> i : Report and introduction.
> ii : Inventory of Orkney.
> iii: Inventory of Shetland.

13. . . . . An inventory of the ancient and historical monuments   **44**.13
of the city of Edinburgh, with the thirteenth report of the
commission. 1951.

14. . . . . Roxburghshire, with the fourteenth report. . . .   **44**.14
2 vols. 1956.

15. . . . . Selkirkshire, with the fifteenth report. . . . 1957.   **44**.15

16. Stirlingshire. An inventory of the ancient monuments. 2   **44**.16
vols. 1963.
> Includes 16th report.

17. Peeblesshire. . . . 2 vols. 1967.   **44**.17
> Includes 17th report.

18. Argyll. . . . Vol. i: Kintyre. 1971.   **44**.18
> Includes 18th report.

19. Argyll. . . . Vol. ii: Lorn. 1975.   **44**.19
> Includes 19th report.

20. Lanarkshire. An inventory of the prehistoric and Roman   **44**.20
monuments. 1978.
> Includes 20th report.

21. Argyll. . . . Vol. iii: Mull, Tiree, Coll and Northern Argyll   **44**.21
(excluding the early medieval and later monuments of Iona).
1980.
> Includes 21st report.

22. Argyll. An inventory of the monuments. Vol. iv: Iona. 1982.   **44**.22
> Includes 22nd report.

23. Argyll. . . . Vol. v: Islay, Jura, Colonsay and Oronsay. 1984.   **44**.23
Includes 23rd report.

**WORKS UNIFORM WITH BUT NOT PART OF THE
INVENTORY SERIES**

A. Late medieval monumental sculpture in the West Highlands.   **44**.24
By Kenneth A. Steer and John W. M. Bannerman, with a
contribution by G. H. Collins. 1977.

A study intended to supplement the descriptions of individual monuments in
the inventories. Includes texts (Latin, with English translations) of all
inscriptions.

45.   SCOTTISH RECORD OFFICE*

Place of publication: Edinburgh.

1. States of the annual progress of the linen manufacture, 1727–1754. From the records of the Board of Trustees for Manufactures etc. in Scotland preserved in the Scottish Record Office. Edited by Roy H. Campbell. 1964.   **45.1**

Facsimiles.

2. Reports on the Annexed Estates, 1755–1769. From the records of the Forfeited Estates preserved in the Scottish Record Office. Edited by Virginia Wills. 1973.   **45.2**

Reports by factors, 1755–6, and by Archibald Menzies, the general inspector, 1765–9.

3. Statistics of the Annexed Estates, 1755–1756. From the records of the Forfeited Estates preserved in the Scottish Record Office. 1973.   **45.3**

4. Registrum secreti sigilli regum Scotorum. The register of the privy seal of Scotland. Vol. viii: 1581–1584. Edited by Gordon Donaldson. 1982.   **45.4**

Abridged transcripts and abstracts.

5. Accounts of the masters of works for building and repairing royal palaces and castles. Vol. ii: 1616–1649. Edited by John Imrie and John G. Dunbar. 1982.   **45.5**

Transcripts, slightly abridged.

---

* Works omitted in Mullins, *T & C* or published since the second volume of that work was completed. Two Scottish Record Office series deliberately omitted from both Mullins and the present volume, as consisting of neither texts nor calendars, are the 'Indexes' and 'Lists'. The 'Indexes' comprise indexes to the register of deeds, 1661–96 (36 vols., 1916–75); to the secretary's register of sasines, 1599–1609 and the particular registers of sasines, 1617–1780 (33 vols., 1924–75); and to the general register of sasines, 1701–20 (1917). The 'Lists' comprise the *Descriptive list of plans in the Scottish Record Office* (3 vols., 1966–74); the *Lists of gifts and deposits in the Scottish Record Office* (2 vols., 1971–6); and the *List of American documents* (1976).

INDEX

USE OF THE INDEX

To facilitate reference to particular items the index makes use of the figures given in the right-hand margins of the *Guide*: bold figures denote the section or series, ordinary figures after the full point denote the number of the item within the section; sections can be identified from the table of contents, pp. xi–xii above. An asterisk following the item number in the index shows that the entry for that item contains more than one reference to the subject required.

Abbreviations are used for some common Christian names, and for a few other terms, i.e. archbishop (archbp.), archbishopric (archbpric.), bishop (bp.), bishopric (bpric.), college (coll.), Episcopalian (Epis.), minister (min.), presbytery (pres.), professor (prof.), Protestant (Prot.), Roman Catholic (Cath.), university (univ.).

Names of places come before names of persons, and titles of nobility in order of precedence come before surnames. Titles of nobility contain cross-references to entries under the noble's surname; and in the surname sequence nobles are placed according to their Christian names. Lairds normally referred to according to territorial designation are indexed under surname followed by designation, after the sequence of plain surnames. Thus a notional sequence would be: 'Douglas (Lanarkshire)'; 'Douglas, Marquis of, *see* Douglas, Jas.'; 'Douglas, Earl of, *see* Douglas, Will.'; 'Douglas, Gavin'; 'Douglas, Geo., Earl of Morton'; 'Douglas, Jas., Marquis of'; 'Douglas, Jas.'; 'Douglas, Rob.'; 'Douglas, Will., Earl of'; 'Douglas family'; 'Douglas of Dalkeith, Sir Jas.'

When an item was issued in more than one series the *Guide* only gives one full entry describing the item, normally that to the item as it occurs in the series listed earliest in the *Guide*. The index gives only a reference to the full entry, where a cross-reference to the other series in which the item appears will be found.

Texts, etc., by unknown or unspecified authors are indexed by shortened titles in italics. Italics have also been used when it seemed desirable to index items under their printed title-page descriptions. Names of editors and others concerned in the publication of the items listed in the *Guide* have not been indexed.

Abbotsford, library at, **6**.63
Abbotsford Club:
  garlands, **1**.34
  members, publications, rules, **1**.33
Abercorn, Earl of, *see* Hamilton, Jas.
Aberdeen, burgh:
  advocates, **37**.41
  arms, **37**.48
  castle, **37**.48
  cathedral, *see* Old Aberdeen
  chronicle, **36**.6
  churches:
    St Nicholas:
      cartulary, **37**.2, 7
      description, **37**.7
      needlework, **38**.10
    St Paul's Chapel, **37**.35
  commissary court, **40**.37
  description, **36**.5, **37**.37
  Episcopalians, **22**.3, **37**.35
  friars, **2**.2, **36**.3

grammar school, **36**.24
losses, **36**.23
magistrates, **36**.16
music school, **16**.4
poets, **37**.9, **16**.38
protocols, **29**.63
records:
  accounts, **36**.24
  birth brieves, **36**.24, **38**.10
  burgesses, **37**.6, 35
  charters, **36**.5, **37**.49
  council & court, **21**.8, 9, **26**.49, **36**.12, 19, 24
  inventories, **37**.49
  letters, **36**.24
  witchcraft, **36**.3
Aberdeen, commissariot, **29**.6, **40**.37
Aberdeen, diocese:
  bishops, **2**.4, **6**.12, **37**.13
  description, **36**.9
Aberdeen, kirk session, **36**.15

Aberdeen, pres., **36**.15, 16
Aberdeen, synod, **36**.15
Aberdeen, univ.:
  bibliography, **37**.12, **38**.1
  bodies delivered to, **36**.6
  colleges:
    King's:
      bursaries, **36**.43
      dinner account, **38**.10
      graduates, **37**.11
      lectures, **40**.26
      Nova fundatio, **37**.11
      orations, **2**.7
      records, **36**.26, **37**.20
      staff, **37**.11
    Marischal, records, **37**.4, 19, 20
Aberdeen, Earl of, *see* Gordon, Geo.
Aberdeenshire:
  annual renters, **36**.16
  antiquities, **36**.17, 29, 32, 37
  bibliography, **37**.12, **38**.1
  castles, **38**.7
  Catholics, **36**.11
  cess roll, **38**.3
  collections for history, **36**.9
  descriptions, **36**.9
  fiars prices, **37**.35
  loan and tax, **36**.16
  mair of fee, **26**.12
  place names, **37**.22, **38**.18
  poll tax, **36**.39
  protocols, **29**.63
  sheriff court, **37**.29, 32, 33
  roads & bridges, **38**.6
  topography, **36**.17, 29, 32, 37
  valuation, **38**.4
  wadsetters, **36**.16
Aberdour, Lord, *see* Douglas, Jas.
Abernethy, protocols, **29**.37
Aboyne, Lady, *see* Hay, Sophia
Aboyne, records of, **37**.14
Account of the proceedings of the estates
  (1689–90), **26**.22, 46, 47
Accounts (account books; household
  books):
  burgh:
    Aberdeen, **36**.24
    Ayr, **26**.28
    Dumfries, **9**.1
    Edinburgh, **21**.3, 33, 34, 43, 46, 47
    Glasgow, **15**.16, **21**.11, 12, 16
    Irvine, **5**.15
    Old Aberdeen, **37**.21
    Peebles, **21**.10, 24
    schools, **15**.53
    Stirling, **21**.31
  central government:
    army, **25**.16, 17
    chamberlains, **6**.82
    comptroller, **26**.50
    king's pursemaster, **27**.2
    masters of work, **15**.59, **45**.5
    treasurers, **6**.62, **15**.36, **35**.1
  customs, Dumfries, **9**.1

Accounts (account books; household
  books)—*cont.*:
  ecclesiastical:
    Angus, **6**.1
    Brechin, **6**.105
    Dunkeld, **6**.1, **25**.10
    St Andrews:
      archbpric., **25**.4
      Archbp. Sharp, **15**.53
    See also Church of Scotland, *post-*
      Reformation: Thirds of Benefices
  personal:
    Earl of Angoulême. **1**.3
    Lady Grisell Baillie, **25**.1
    Jas. Beattie, **2**.9, **38**.15
    Duchess of Buckingham, **1**.3
    Duke of Buckingham, **1**.3
    Cunningham of Craigends, **24**.2
    Erskine of Carnock, **24**.14
    Foulis of Ravelston, **24**.16
    John Home, **26**.52
    James V, **6**.57
    Lauder of Fountainhall, **24**.36
    Duke of Lennox, **15**.25
    Earl of Lothian, **6**.125
    Murray of Ochtertyre, **24**.55
    Alex. Rose, **24**.15
    Archbp. Sharp, **15**.53
    Earl of Strathmore, **24**.9
    David Wedderburne, **24**.28
  relating to:
    Aberdeen:
      King's College, **38**.10
    archers, **15**.25
    Assynt, **26**.52
    books, **6**.125
    Breadalbane, **6**.103
    bridges, **6**.1
    Dunnottar, **38**.10
    English army at Flodden, **26**.43
    English monastic treasures, **1**.5
    music, **6**.62
    North British Railway, **27**.14
    paintings, **6**.22, 125
    plays, **1**.2
    Scots Brigade in Netherlands, **24**.38
    tutor, **19**.5
    weavers of Coventry, **1**.2
  See also Rentals, rental books
Acta dominorum Concilii, **40**.9
Acta dominorum Concilii et Sessionis, **40**.15
Adair, John, geographer (d. *c.* 1722), **6**.21
Adamnan, Abbot of Iona (d. 704), **6**.106
Admiralty, Court of, **40**.1, 3
Advocates:
  Faculty of, Edinburgh:
    address to, **39**.3
    members, etc., **29**.76
    minutes, **40**.31, 34
  King's, as prosecutor, **40**.28, 37
  Society of, Aberdeen, **37**.41
Aeneid, in Scots, **4**.3, **6**.67, **33**.26, 28, 29, 31
Agriculture:
  cattle trade, **13**.1

Agriculture—*cont.*:
estate instructions, **27**.1
estate management, **27**.8, 9
farm papers, **26**.43
gardener, **24**.45
Gordon's Mill Farming Club, **2**.10
improvements, **24**.13
Monymusk estate, **26**.39, **38**.14
Society of Husbandmen,
Clackmannanshire, **24**.15
See also Surveys
Aikman, Wm. (d. *c.* 1707), **24**.3
Airlie, papers of Earl of, **36**.20, 24
Aitken, Jas., Bp. of Galloway (d. 1687),
25.19
Alba amicorum, **2**.5
Albany, Duchess of, *see* Stuart, Charlotte
Albemarle, Earl of, *see* Keppel, Wm. Anne
Albemarle papers, **37**.25, 26
Alberoni, Cardinal, **24**.19
Alesius (Alan), Alex., Lutheran divine
(d. 1565), **6**.20
Alexander, romance of, **1**.4
Alexander, Dr John (mid 17 cent.), **11**.14
Alexander, Sir Wm., Earl of Stirling
(d. 1640):
life, **11**.30
register of royal letters, **11**.34
verses to, **1**.11
works, **11**.30, **32**.11, 24
Alexander family, **11**.30
Alexander the Great, **6**.49, **32**.12, 17, 21, 25
Alford, exercise or pres., **37**.18
Alliance, bands of, **36**.6, 20
America:
documents relating to, **45** note
emigration to, **6**.22
See also East New Jersey; Nova Scotia;
& Virginia
Analecta, **15**.62
Ancram, Earl of, *see* Kerr, Sir Rob.
Ancrum, parish, **43**.9*
Anderson, Jas., min. of Stirling (d. 1603),
30.11
Anderson, Jas., printer (late 17 cent.),
39.3
Anderson, Pat., Cath. writer (d. 1624),
31.20
Andrewes, Launcelot, Bp. of Winchester
(d. 1626), **1**.11
Angus, *see* Forfar, shire
Angus, Dean of Christianity of, **6**.1
Angus, Dowager Countess of, *see*
Grahame, Gille
Annan:
censuses, **30**.4
ships, **28**.1
tax roll, **30**.4
Anne, Queen (d. 1714), reign of, **25**.11
Anne of Denmark, Queen (d. 1619):
coronation, **6**.29
last moments, **1**.11
letters by, **15**.36
marriage, **6**.29

Annexed Estates:
commissioners, **27**.15
reports, **45**.2
statistics, **45**.3
See also Forfeited Estates
Annualrenters, **36**.16
Anstruther, Sir Rob. (early 17 cent.), **39**.4
Antiquities:
Aberdeenshire & Banffshire, **36**.17, 29,
32, 37
essays on, **36**.40
Fermartyn (Formartine), **37**.51
Howe of Cromar, **38**.2
Scottish, **24**.1
See also Monuments
Antwerp, **2**.4
Appin:
murder, **26**.22
sorcery, **25**.20
Apprentices, Edinburgh registers, **29**.28,
60, 61, 92
Arbroath Abbey, **6**.89
Arbuthnot, Alex., scholar & poet (d. 1583),
32.9
Arbuthnot (de Aberbuthenoth), Duncan
(early 13 cent.), **36**.24
Arbuthnot family, papers, **36**.6
Arbuthnott missal, **15**.69
Archers, **15**.25, 37
Ardchattan Priory, **11**.12
Argyll, commissariot, **29**.9, 33
Argyll, diocese, **6**.100
Argyll & the Isles, justiciary court, **40**.13,
27
Argyll, synod, **26**.37, 38
Argyll, estates:
inhabitants, **29**.91
instructions, **27**.1
Argyll, Dukes of, *see* Campbell, John
Argyll, Earl of, *see* Campbell, Arch.
Argyll family, *see* Campbell of Argyll
family
Argyllshire, monuments, **44**.18, 19, 21–23
Armies:
English, in Scotland:
(1296), **6**.20
(1547), **6**.11
(1650s), **6**.104
French, in Scotland:
(1553), **24**.44
Scottish:
(1640s), **25**.16, 17
general (1640), **15**.59
pay:
(1684), **15**.59
(1702), **15**.59
Armour, Highland, **13**.1
Arms & ammunition, **25**.16
Arthour and Merlin, **1**.12
Articles and ordinances of warre (1644), **25**.16
Ascanius, **17**.22
Asloan ms., **32**.8, 14, 16
Assignation of stipends, books or register
of, **6**.81, **15**.5, **43**.11

Association, band of, **15**.59
Assumption, books or register of, **6**.89, 92, **35**.2
Assynt, **26**.52
Atholl family, *see* Murray of Atholl family
Atkinson, Stephen, metallurgist (early 17 cent.), **6**.15
Aubrey, John, antiquarian (d. 1697), **38**.21
Auchinleck, Jas., poet (late 15 cent.), **6**.21, **19**.2, **33**.4
Auchinleck chronicle, **32**.14
Auchinleck ms., **1**.4, 12, 18, 28, 29, **15**.45, **31**.6
Auchterarder, **15**.59
Autobiographies:
 Rob. Blair (1593–1636), **43**.13
 Jas. Fraser of Brea (1639–83), **43**.9
 Mrs Goodal (1670s–1690), **43**.9
 Pat. Gordon (1635–99), **36**.31
 Alex. Jaffray (1614–61), **36**.42
 Alex. Jaffray (1755–1800), **38**.6
 Field Marshal Jas. Keith (1714–34), **36**.8
 John Livingstone (1603–69), **43**.9
 John McAdam (1806–80), **27**.16
 Maj. Gen. Hugh Mackay (1689–91), **6**.48
 John Macky (1690s), **17**.14
 Earl Marischal (1740s), **26**.21
 Jas. Melville:
  (1556–1601), **6**.37
  (1556–1610), **43**.3
 Sir Jas. Melville of Halhill (1549–93), **6**.19
 John Murray of Broughton (*c.* 1737–48), **24**.27
 Jas. Nimmo (1654–*c.* 1705), **24**.6
 Earl of Perth (1657), **36**.6
 Chas. Rogers (1825–76), **11**.10
 Sir Walter Scott, **3**.10
 Jas. Turner (1632–70), **6**.31
 See also Diaries, journals, etc.
Autograph books, **2**.5
Avignon:
 Jacobite papers, **26**.21
 letters of popes, **27**.12, 13
Ayr, burgh:
 friars, **5**.11
 protocols, **5**.6–9
 records:
  accounts, **26**.28
  charters, **5**.12
  council & court, **5**.6, **15**.40
  gild court, **5**.1
Ayr, kirk session, **43**.9
Ayrshire:
 memories, **26**.33
 military report, **5**.4
 protocols, **5**.6–9, **11**.8
Ayton (Aytoun), Sir Rob., poet (d. 1638), **6**.20, **11**.38, **34**.1
Ayton family, **34**.1

Babington Plot, **26**.3
Badenoch, **36**.6

Bagimond's Roll:
 Moray, **27**.2
 Scotland, **26**.33
 Teviotdale, **26**.21
Baillie, Alex., Cath. writer (early 17 cent.), **31**.20
Baillie, Lady Grisell (d. 1746), **25**.1
Baillie, Rob., divine (d. 1662), **6**.76
Baillie of Jerviswood, Geo. (early 18 cent.), **6**.75
Baillie of Jerviswood, Rob. (d. 1684), **25**.1
Bain family, **11**.24
Bairnie, epis. chapel, **29**.30
Balcarres, Earl of, *see* Lindsay, Colin
Balcarres mss., **1**.13
Balcarres papers, **26**.4, 7
Balfour, Sir Wm. (d. 1660), **8**.1
Balfour of Denmylne, Sir Jas., historian (d. 1657), **34**.1
Balfour of Denmylne mss., *see* Denmylne mss.
Balfour of Pittendreich, Sir Jas., Lawyer (d. 1583), **40**.23, 24
Balgair, court book of lands of, **29**.87
Ballad of good counsel, **19**.2, **31**.1, **32**.1
Ballads, **4**.1, 2, **6**.10, 121, **18**.1–3, **19**.2:
 Crawfurd collection, **34**.9
 on the Gordons, **37**.34
 Greig collection, **2**.6
 Gude and godlie, **31**.16
Balmerino Abbey, **1**.22, **26**.43
Balnaves of Halhill, Hen., protestant reformer (d. 1579), **11**.9
Balrinnes, battle of, **39**.3
Bancroft, Rich., Archbp. of Canterbury (d. 1610), **43**.11
Bands (bonds):
 alliance, **36**.6, 20
 association, **15**.59
 calps, **6**.103
 friendship, **31**.1*, **15**.53, **36**.6, 20
 maintenance, **13**.1*
 manrent, **6**.103, **13**.1*, **36**.6, 20
Banff, burgh, **37**.8, 10
Banff, kirk session, **37**.10
Banff, pres., **37**.10
Banff, synod, **37**.10
Banffshire:
 antiquities, **36**.17, 29, 32, 37
 bibliography, **37**.12, **38**.1
 collections for history of, **36**.9
 description, **36**.9
 records, **37**.43
 sheriff court, **36**.16
 topography, **36**.17, 29, 32, 37
Bannatyne (Bellenden), Adam, Bp. of Aberdeen (d. 1648), **36**.21
Bannatyne, Geo., poet (d. 1608?), **6**.5, 38, **24**.16
Bannatyne, Rich., secretary (d. 1605), **6**.20, 54
Bannatyne Club:
 garlands, **6**.121
 members, **6**.119

Bannatyne Club—*cont.*
  notices, **6.**122
  publications:
    catalogues, **6.**119
    notes, **6.**118
    proposed, **6.**120
  president, **6.**98, 102
Bannatyne ms.:
  contents, **6.**38
  editions, **12.**1, **32.**22, 23, 26, **33.**5
  extracts, **6.**5, **31.**15, **33.**2
Baptisms, registers & lists of:
  Aberdeen, **36.**6:
    St Paul's (Epis.), **37.**35
  Bairnie (Epis.), **29.**30
  Canisbay, **29.**48
  Canongate, **29.**90
  Dunfermline, **29.**44
  Durness, **29.**38
  Kilbarchan, **29.**41
  Kingarth, **7.**2
  Leith (Epis.), **29.**81
  Melrose, **29.**45
  Rothesay, **7.**1
  St Andrews (Epis.), births, **29.**49
  Scots Brigade in Netherlannds, **24.**38
  Tillydesk (Epis.), **29.**30
  Torphichen, **29.**40
Barbary, captives in, **39.**3, 4
Barbour, John, poet (d. 1395):
  Alexander, **6.**49, **32.**12, 17, 21, 25
  The Bruce, **31.**14, **34.**12, 13, **36.**28
Barclay, Wm., writer (d. *c.* 1630), **36.**3
Bargany, Lords, *see* Hamilton, John and Wm.
Barnard, Lady Anne, poet (d. 1825), **6.**10
Barnes, Father John (early 17 cent.), **1.**11
Baron courts:
  history, **29.**29
  records:
    on Breadalbane estates, **6.**103
    Carnwath, **26.**29
    on Chisholm estates, **25.**12
    Corshill, **5.**4
    Fintray, **38.**6
    Forbes, **25.**19
    history of, **26.**29
    Leys, **36.**24
    on Seaforth estates, **25.**12
    Skene, **36.**24
    Stitchill, **24.**50
    Urie, **24.**12
    Whitehaugh, **36.**24
Baronets of Nova Scotia, **6.**117
Barony, burghs of, *see* Burghs
Barrhead, **16.**14
Basilicon doron, **17.**11, **33.**17, 19
Bath, **25.**1
Baynes, Capt. Adam (d. 1670), **6.**104
Battle, trial by, **36.**6, **40.**37
Beaton, Cardinal David, Archbp. of St Andrews (d. 1546), **6.**20, **25.**4
Beaton, Jas., Archbp. of Glasgow (d. 1603), **11.**8, **15.**27*, **43.**11

Beattie, Jas., poet & philosopher (d. 1803), **2.**9, **38.**15
Beaugué, Jean de, writer (mid 16 cent.), **15.**2
Beauly Priory, **11.**12, **35.**2
Beaumanoir, Philippe de, Seigneur de Remi (d. 1296), **6.**71
Bee keeping, **1.**11
Beith, parish, **26.**33
Bell family (Dumfriesshire), **9.**2
Bellenden, Adam, *see* Bannatyne
Bellenden, John, poet and translator (mid 16 cent.):
  translation of Boece, **31.**18, **33.**10, 11, 16, 18
  translation of Livy, **31.**22
Bellenden of Auchinoul, John, lawyer (mid 16 cent.), **6.**6, **40.**37
Bellièvre, Pomponne de & Pierre de, diplomats (mid 17 cent.), **24.**29, 30
Benedict XIII of Avignon, Pope, **27.**13
Benefices, valuations of:
  Bagimond's Roll, **26.**21, 33, **27.**2
  See also Church of Scotland:
    pre-Reformation: Thirds of Benefices
Bentinck, Hans W., Earl of Portland (d. 1709), **6.**48
Bermuda, **4.**2
Berteville, Sir John (mid 16 cent.), **6.**11
Berwickshire:
  monuments, **44.**1, 6
  protocols, **6.**87, **29.**39
Bethune, Mary (mid 16 cent.), **15.**25
Bethune of Creich, Rob. (mid 16 cent.), **15.**25
Beza, Theodore, theologian (d. 1605), **26.**43
Bibliographia Aberdonensis, **38.**1
Bibliographies:
  Aberdeen, Banff & Kincardine, **37.**12, **38.**1
  Middle Scots poets, **31.**27
  Scottish topography, **25.**14, 15
Binns papers, **29.**70
Birth brieves, *see* Brieves
Bisset, Habakkuk, legal writer (early 17 cent.), **32.**10, 13, 18
Bisset (Byset), John (early 13 cent.), **11.**12
Bisset, John, min. of Aberdeen (d. 1756), **36.**3
Blackhalls of that Ilk & Barra family, **37.**30
Black Book of Paisley, **16.**8
Black Book of Taymouth, **6.**103
Blackford, **15.**59
Blackwell, Thos., prof. of divinity (d. 1728), **36.**3
Blackwood, Adam, Cath. writer (d. 1613), **15.**32
Blaeu, Joannis, cartographer (mid 17 cent.), **36.**9
Blair, David, min. of Edinburgh (d. 1710), **43.**13
Blair, James, min. of Dysart (d. 1655), **43.**13

Blair, Robert, min. of St Andrews (d. 1666), **43**.13
Blakhal, Gilbert, priest (mid 17 cent.), **36**.11
Blandford, Marquis of, *see* Godolphin, Wm.
Blind Harper, *see* Morison, Roderick
Blind Hary, *see* Hary
Boece, Hector, scholar (d. 1536):
  description of Scotland, **6**.35
  history by, **31**.18, **33**.10, 11, 16, 18
  lives of bps. of Aberdeen, **6**.12, **37**.13
Bonds, *see* Bands
Bontine of Ardoch, Rob. Cunninghame (early 19 cent.), **27**.2
Book (buik, buke):
  of Alexander the Grit, **32**.12, 17, 21, 25
  of batailles, **1**.27, **31**.19
  of Common Order, **6**.115, **23**.11
  of Deer, **36**.36
  of Dean of Lismore, **23**.1, 3
  of Discipline, Second, **43**.11*
  of Dunvegan, **38**.9
  of Glenbuchat, **38**.12
  of the governance of princes, **1**.27, **31**.19
  of the howlat, **6**.3, **31**.13
  of the order of knyghthood, **1**.27, **31**.19
  of Paisley, **16**.8
  of Taymouth, **6**.103
  of the universal kirk, **6**.84, **15**.50, 51
Books, *see* Libraries
booksellers:
  Jas. Cathkin, **6**.20
  in Edinburgh, **6**.21
  Rich. Lawson, **6**.22
Borgue, parish, **29**.17
Borthwick, Sir John (mid 16 cent.), **6**.20
Boston, Mass., **8**.1
Boswell, Jas., writer (d. 1795), **4**.4, **11**.7
Boswell of Glasmont, David (early 16 cent.), **15**.53
Bothwell, Earls of, *see* Hepburn, Jas. & Pat.
Bothwell, Countess of, *see* Sinclair, Agnes
Bowie, Wm. (late 16 cent.), **6**.103
Boyd, Rob., Lord Boyd (d. 1628), **15**.25
Boyd, Zachary, min. of Glasgow (d. 1653), **15**.53
Boyd family, papers, **5**.3
Boyd of Kilmarnock family, papers, **1**.11
Boyd of Trochrig, Jas., Archbp. of Glasgow (d. 1581), **15**.33
Boyd of Trochrig, Rob., divine (d. 1627), **6**.20, **15**.33, **43**.11
Breadalbane, **6**.103
Brechin, commissariot, **29**.13
Brechin, diocese, **6**.105
Breviaries, *see* Liturgies
Breviarum Aberdonense, **5**.1, **6**.99
Bridges:
  Aberdeenshire, **38**.6
  Dunkeld, **6**.1, **25**.10
Brieves:
  birth, **29**.31, **36**.24, **38**.10
  general, **10**.2, **40**.11, 37

Bristol, **25**.1
Brodie of Brodie, Alex., lawyer (d. 1680), **36**.33
Brodie of Brodie, Jas. (late 17 cent.), **36**.33
Broken men, **36**.21
Brosse, Jacques de la, diplomat (mid 16 cent.), **26**.36, 50
Broughton, regality, **7**.9
Broun, Rob., notary (early 17 cent.), **5**.7
Brown, Hen., manufacturer (early 19 cent.), **27**.14
Brown, Jas., min. of Glasgow (d. 1714), **5**.2
Brown, Thos. (late 16 cent.), **40**.28
Bruce, The, **31**.14, **34**.12, 13, **36**.28
Bruce, Alex., Earl of Kincardine (d. 1680), **39**.4
Bruce, Rob., min. of Edinburgh (d. 1631), **6**.20, **43**.6
Brulart, M. (late 16 cent.), **6**.25
Bryson, Jas., printer (d. 1642), **39**.3
Bryson, Rob., printer (d. 1645), **39**.3
Buchan, Maj. Gen. Thos. (d. 1720), **17**.8
Buchanan, David, writer (d. c. 1652), **6**.21, 58, **24**.52
Buchanan, Geo., scholar (d. 1582), **6**.21, **15**.8, **31**.12
Buckingham, Duke of, *see* Stafford, Humphrey
Buckingham, Dowager Duchess of, *see* Stafford, Anne
Buke, see Book
Bunyan, John, writer (d. 1688), **4**.3
Burgesses, lists & registers of:
  Aberdeen, **37**.6, 35
  Canongate, **29**.83
  Dumbarton, **29**.73
  Dumfries, **9**.4
  Edinburgh, **29**.59, 62, 68
  Glasgow, **29**.56, 66
Burghley, Lord, *see* Cecil, Wm.
Burghs:
  of barony, **21**.13, **26**.53
  commissioners, **15**.59
  Convention of Royal, **21**.13*, 52–59
  courts, **40**.1, 22
  See also Burghs: records
  laws & customs, **21**.1, 25, [**21**.22]
  records:
    Aberdeen, **21**.8, 9, **26**.49, **36**.5, 12, 19, 24*, **37**.49
    Ayr, **5**.12, **15**.40, **26**.28
    Canongate, **7**.9, **15**.53
    Crail, **15**.40
    Culross, **15**.40
    Dundee, **21**.28
    Dysart, **15**.75
    Edinburgh, **15**.40, 53, **21**.2–7, 33, 34, 43–51
    Elgin, **37**.28, 36
    Glasgow, **15**.16, 40, 67, **21**.11, 12, 14–17, 19, 23, 27, 36–41
    Inverness, **21**.55, **37**.39, 44
    Irvine, **5**.15
    Kirkcudbright, **7**.10, 15, 16

Burghs: records—*cont.*:
  Kirkintilloch, **26**.53
  Kirkwall, **38**.19
  Lanark, **21**.32
  Old Aberdeen, **37**.21, 37
  Paisley, **21**.35
  Peebles, **21**.10, 24
  Prestwick, **15**.28
  Rothesay, **7**.6, 7
  Selkirk, **29**.89
  Stirling, **21**.29–31
  See also Accounts: burgh &
    Charters: burgh
 of regality, **21**.13
 schools, **15**.53
 setts, **21**.13, 55
 state (1692), **21**.13, 55
 See also Burgesses
Burgundia (Burdeus), John de, *see*
  Mandeville, Sir John
Burgundy, Duke of (late 15 cent.), **26**.43
Burials, forms of, in Montrose, **43**.11
Burials or deaths, lists & registers of:
 Aberdeen, **36**.6
 Borgue, **29**.17
 Edinburgh, Greyfriars, **29**.26
 Holyrood, **29**.25
 Melrose, **29**.45
 Restalrig, **29**.32
 See also Monuments: inscriptions:
  churchyard
Burne, Nicol, Cath. writer (late 16 cent.),
  31.20
Burnes family, *see* Burns
Burnet, Father David (late 17 cent.), **6**.26
Burnet, Gilbert, Bp. of Salisbury (d.
  1715), **2**.3, **6**.22, **17**.14, 16, **24**.44
Burnet, Lady Margaret (late 17 cent.),
  6.27
Burnet, Rob., Lord Crimond, lawyer (d.
  1661), **24**.44
Burnet, Sir Thos. (d. 1753), **17**.16,
  37.53
Burnett mss., **37**.53
Burnett of Leys family, **37**.23, 50, 53
Burns, Rob., poet (d. 1796), **11**.23, 29
Burns, Wm. (mid 18 cent.), **11**.23
Burns (Burnes) family, **11**.23, 29
Bute, witchcraft in, **25**.20
Bute, Earl of, *see* Stuart, John
Butler, Jas., Duke of Ormond (d. 1745),
  24.19
Byron, Lord, *see* Gordon, Geo.
Byset, *see* Bisset

Cairncross charters, **25**.13
Caithness, commissariot, **29**.10
Caithness, diocese, **6**.22, 100
Caithness, shire:
 monuments, **44**.3
 records, **42**.4
 tour, **41**.1
Calderwood, Mrs, *see* Steuart, Margaret

Calderwood, David, historian (d. 1650),
  6.20, 84, **39**.3, **43**.7
Caldwell, Sir Jas. (mid 16 cent.), **40**.37
Caldwell papers, **15**.73
Caledonia, **16**.9
Callander, Earl of, *see* Livingstone, Jas.
Calps, **6**.103
Calvin, John, theologian (d. 1564), **23**.7
Cambuskenneth Abbey, **11**.4
Cambusnethan, kirk session, **15**.26
Cameron, Archibald, Jacobite (mid
  18 cent.), **17**.22
Cameron, John, theologian (d. 1625),
  1.11, **15**.33
Cameron clan, history, **1**.24
Cameron of Ffasfern, John (mid 18 cent.),
  25.20
Cameron of Lochiel, Sir Ewen (d. 1719),
  1.24, **39**.3
Campbell, Agnes (Mrs Anderson), printer
  (d. 1716), **39**.3
Campbell, Alex. (mid 18 cent.), **26**.9
Campbell, Arch., Earl of Argyll (d. 1685),
  6.36, **24**.14
Campbell, Dioness, Dean of Limerick
  (late 16 cent.), **15**.69
Campbell, John, banker (early 18 cent.),
  24.15
Campbell, John, Duke of Argyll (d. 1743),
  25.11
Campbell, John, Duke of Argyll (d. 1806),
  27.1
Campbell family, **25**.5, 12
Campbell of Argyll family, **15**.52
Campbell of Auchinbreck family, **26**.22
Campbell of Calder (Cawdor), John (d.
  1592), **25**.5
Campbell of Calder (Cawdor) family, **25**.5,
  36.30
Campbell of Craignish family, **26**.9
Campbell of Glenorchy family, **6**.103
Campbell of Glenure, Colin (d. 1752),
  26.22
Campbell of Kinyeancleuch, Rob. (late
  16 cent.), **43**.11
Campbell of Shawfield, Daniel (early
  18 cent.), **1**.11
Campbell of Strachur family, **26**.22
Campbeltown, **25**.5
Campvere, staple at, **26**.11
Candlemas day, **1**.1
Canisbay, parish, **29**.48
Canisius, St Pierre, Cath. writer (d. 1597),
  31.20
Canongate, burgh:
 burgesses, **29**.83
 council & court records, **7**.9, **15**.53
 privileges, **29**.85
 protocols, **29**.74
Canongate, kirk session, **29**.90
Canongate (Holyrood), parish, **29**.46, 90,
  43.11:
 baptisms, **29**.90
 marriages, **29**.46, 90

Canongate (Holyrood), parish—*cont.*:
  See also Holyrood Abbey &
    Holyroodhouse
Cant, Andrew, min. of Aberdeen (d. 1663),
  36.23
Cantelmi, Don Rostaino, Duke of Popoli
  & Prince of Petterano (late 17 cent.),
  39.4
Captain Ward and the Rainbow, **6.121**
Carbisdale, battle of, **24.15**
Cardross, Lord, *see* Erskine, Hen.
Carey, Hen., Lord Hunsdon (d. 1596),
  6.20
Carleton, Geo., Bp. of Chichester
  (d. 1628), **1.11**
Carmichael, Jas., min. of Haddington
  (d. 1628), **43.11**
Carmichael of Arthurstone, Peter
  (d. 1891), **27.6**
Carnock, kirk session, **43.4**
Carnwath, barony, **26.29**
Carrick, **5.4**
Carruthers, Mark, notary (mid 16 cent.),
  29.86
Carswell, John, Bp. of the Isles (d. 1572),
  15.33, **23.11**
Cartularies (registers), **40.1**:
  ecclesiastical:
    Aberdeen:
      bpric., **15.65**
      St Nicholas, **37.2, 7**
    Arbroath, **6.89**
    Balmerino, **1.22**
    Brechin, bpric., **6.105**
    Cambuskenneth, **11.4**
    Coldstream, **11.18**
    Coupar Angus, **11.17**
    Crail, **11.15**
    Dryburgh, **6.86**
    Dunfermline, **6.77**
    Edinburgh, St Giles, **6.108**
    Glasgow:
      bpric., **6.78**
      Our Lady College, **15.67**
    Inchaffray, **6.88**
    Kelso, **6.85**
    Lindores, **1.22, 24.42**
    Melrose, **6.59**
    Moray, bpric., **6.61**
    Newbattle, **6.92**
    Paisley, **15.17**
    St Andrews, **6.72**
    Scone, **6.81**
    Stirling, Chapel Royal, **11.20**
  secular:
    Lennox, **15.24**
    Morton, **6.97**
  See also Charters
Casaubon, Meric (d. 1671). **1.11**
Cassillis, Earl of, *see* Kennedy, John
Cassillis estates, rental, **9.4**
Castle Fraser, **38.21**
Castlewalls Farm, Renfrewshire,
  26.43

Catalogues:
  Abbotsford Library, **6.63**
  Hamilton archives, **15.69**
  Perth Museum, **14.1**
  property of Mary Queen of Scots, **6.114**
  publications:
    Abbotsford Club, **1.33**
    Bannatyne Club, **6.119**
    Grampian Club, **11.19**
    HMSO, **2.1**
    Hunterian Club, **12.9**
    Maitland Club, **15.39**
    Scottish clubs & societies, **2.1**
    Spalding Club, **36.38**
  seal impressions, **15.70**
Catechisms:
  Peter Canisius, **31.20**
  Rob. Forbes, **22.2**
  Gaelic, **23.7**
  Rob. Pont, **43.11**
Catholics in Scotland (*post*-1560):
  Aberdeenshire, **36.11**
  appeal to, **24.44**
  lists, **15.59**
  policy towards, **24.15, 25.20**
  tractates, **31.20**
Cathkin, Jas., bookseller (d. 1631), **6.20**
Cattle trade, **13.1**
Cavendish (née Bruce), Christian,
  Dowager Duchess of Devonshire
  (d. 1675), **15.59**
Cavendish, Wm., Earl of Newcastle
  (d. 1676), **8.1**
Cawdor, thanes of, **36.30**
Cecil, Dr John (late 16 cent.), **24.15**
Cecil, Wm., Lord Burghley (d. 1598), **8.2**
Censorship, **15.53**
Censuses:
  Annan, **30.4**
  Portpatrick, **30.8**
  Scottish, **26.44**
Cessolis, Jacobus de, **32.14**
Cess roll, Aberdeenshire, **38.3**
Chalmers, Alex., writer (d. 1834), **4.4**
Chalmers, David, Lord Ormond, lawyer
  (d. 1592), **15.8**
Chalmers, Geo., antiquary (d. 1825), **16.9**
Chaloner, Thos. (d. 1661), **8.2**
Chancellors of Scotland, **40.22**
Chapel royal, *see* Holyroodhouse & Stirling
Character of a modern Whig (1681), **8.2**
Charlemagne, history of, **1.4**
Charles I, King (d. 1649):
  last advice, **4.4**
  letters by, **15.36, 52**
  memoir of reign, **14.1**
  message by, **8.1**
  trial & execution, **4.1**
Charles II, King (d. 1685):
  declaration by, **24.25**
  letters by, **15.52**
  negotiations with Irish (1647), **8.2**
  portrait, **6.22**
  proclaimed, **8.1**

Charles II, King—*cont.*:
  & Scotland (1650), **24**.17
  warrants by, **6**.73, **39**.4
Charles X, King of France, formerly
  Comte d'Artois (d. 1836), at
  Holyrood, **40**.28
Charlotte Augusta, Princess (d. 1817), **4**.2
Charteris, Hen., printer (d. 1599), **6**.17,
  22, **33**.1, **43**.8
Charteris, Rob., printer (d. 1610), **6**.53
Charters:
  burgh:
    Aberdeen, **36**.5, **37**.49
    Ayr, **5**.12
    Dumfries, **9**.1
    Dundee, **21**.28
    Edinburgh, **21**.2, 6, 7
    Elgin, **37**.36
    Glasgow, **15**.67, **21**.14, 15, 17, 23, 27,
      36–41
    Irvine, **5**.15
    Kirkwall, **38**.19
    Lanark, **21**.32
    Old Aberdeen, **37**.21, 37
    Paisley, **21**.35
    Peebles, **21**.10, 24
    Rothesay, **7**.7
    Stirling, **21**.29, 30
  composition, **40**.28
  ecclesiastical:
    Aberdeen, Bp. Gordon, **15**.27
    Ayr, friars, **5**.11
    Balmerino, **26**.43
    Beauly, **11**.12, **35**.2
    Brechin, bpric., **6**.105
    Caithness, bpric., **6**.22
    Coldstream, **11**.18
    Coupar Angus, **11**.17, **26**.40, 41
    Crail, **11**.15
    Crossraguel, **5**.13
    Dryburgh, **6**.86
    Dunbar, **26**.33
    Edinburgh:
      St Giles, **6**.108
      Sciennes, **1**.21
      Soultra, **6**.112
      Trintiy, **6**.112, **21**.18
    Glasgow:
      bpric., **6**.78
      Blackfriars, **15**.67
      cathedral, **15**.13
    Glenluce, **5**.5
    Holyrood, **6**.73
    Inchaffray, **24**.56
    Inchcolm, **26**.32, 43
    Kilwinning, **5**.1
    Kinloss, **35**.2
    May, Isle of, **35**.1
    Melrose, **6**.59
    Moray, bpric., **6**.61
    Newbattle, **6**.92
    North Berwick, **6**.87
    Scone, **26**.43
    Stirling, Chapel Royal, **11**.20

Charters—*cont.*:
  family etc.:
    Aboyne, **37**.14
    Airlie, **36**.20, 24
    Blackhall, **37**.30
    Bothwell, **6**.22
    Boyd, **5**.3
    Breadalbane, **6**.103
    Cairncross, **25**.13
    Campbell of Cawdor, **36**.30
    Campbell of Strachur, **26**.22
    Dundonald, **29**.36
    Errol, **36**.6
    Erskine of Dun, **36**.20
    Sir Wm. Fraser (collection of), **26**.9,
      21
    Gordon, **36**.20
    Gordon of Auchleuchries, **36**.31
    Grierson of Lag, **29**.88
    Hepburn of Waughton, **6**.22
    Innes, **29**.79, **36**.34
    Lords of the Isles, **27**.22
    Lag, **29**.88
    Lennox, **15**.24
    Macnaughton, **25**.5
    Monymusk, **36**.6
    Morton, **6**.97
    Munro of Foulis, **29**.71
    Panmure, **36**.24
    Pitfirrane, **29**.67
    Pittodrie, **36**.6
    Wedderburne, **24**.28
    Wigtown, **29**.36
    Yester, **29**.55
  misc., **5**.4, **6**.22*, **25**.13, **39**.4
  relating to:
    Aberdeen Society of Advocates, **37**.41
    Aberdeenshire, **36**.17, 29, 32, 37
    Banffshire, **36**.17, 29, 32, 37
    Highlands, **26**.22
    Lanarkshire, **15**.12
    Nova Scotia, **6**.117
    Renfrewshire, **15**.12
    Wigtownshire, **26**.51
  as sources, **40**.1, 28
  univ.:
    Aberdeen:
      King's College, **36**.26, **37**.20
      Marischal College, **37**.4, 20
    Glasgow, **15**.16, 71, 74
  See also Cartularies
Chartier, Alain, writer (early 15 cent.),
  32.14
Chartists, **27**.16
Chattan, clan, **24**.41
Chepman, Walter, printer (d. *c.* 1528),
  31.28
Cheriton, battle of, **8**.1
Chess, **4**.2, **32**.14
Chisholm of Strathglass, Roderick (early
  18 cent.), **25**.12
Christianity, antiquity of, in Scotland,
  24.44
Christie family, **11**.32

Chronicles & histories of Scotland:
anonymous:
(–1513), **32.**14
(1558–60), **43.**11
Auchinleck (1420–60), **32.**14
Rob. Baillie (1637–62), **6.**76
Earl of Balcarres (1688–90), **6.**74
Rich. Bannatyne (1569–73), **6.**54
Hector Boece (–1437), **31.**18, **33.**10, 11,
16, 18
John Colville (1566–1617), **6.**14
Diurnal of remarkable occurrents (1513–
75), **6.**46
extracts:
Chronicle of Scotland in a part, **6.**22
Extracta e variis cronicis Scocie
(–1575), **1.**23
Fordun, **37.**2, **40.**37
misc., from Panmure mss., **6.**22
Nomina regum Scotorum (–Rob. III),
6.22
Jas. Gordon (1637–41), **36.**1, 2, 4
Pat. Gordon of Ruthven (1639–49),
36.10
Hen. Guthry (1625–49), **14.**1
Lord Herries (1542–71), **1.**6
Holyrood (–1356), **6.**23, **26.**30
Thos. Innes (–818), **36.**25
James I (1406–37), **15.**43
of kings of Scots (–1611), **15.**8
John Knox (1494–1567), **6.**115
Lanercost (1201–1346), **6.**68
Lauder of Fountainhall:
(1661–88), **6.**90
(1668–76), **24.**36
(1680–6), **6.**69
John Leslie:
(–1561), **31.**4
(1437–1561), **6.**41
John Major (–*c.* 1515), **24.**10
Melrose (*c.* 731–1270), **6.**52
David Moysie (1577–1603), **6.**42
John Nicoll (1650–67), **6.**55
Pitscottie (1437–1576), **31.**18
Chronicon rythmicum (741–1093), **6.**52
Scalachronica (1066–1362), **15.**41
John Spalding (1624–45), **6.**28, **36.**21,
23
Vraie cronique d'Escoce (–1463), **17.**5
Jas. Wilson (1625–49), **14.**1
Wyntoun (–1408), **31.**24
See also Church of Scotland: histories &
under names of places & persons for
local chronicles & histories
Chrystall, Thos., Abbot of Kinloss
(d. 1535), **6.**66, **35.**2
Church of England, mins. ejected from,
8.3
Church of Scotland:
histories:
David Calderwood (1513–1625), **43.**7
John Forbes (1560–1606), **43.**10
Rob. Keith (1524–68), **39.**1
John Knox (1494–1567), **6.**115

Church of Scotland: histories—*cont.*:
John Row (1558–1637), **15.**57, **43.**4
John Row (1637–9), **15.**57, **43.**4
Wm. Scot (1560–1633), **43.**10
John Spottiswoode (203–1625), **6.**96
post-Reformation:
commissioners, **30.**11
conflict with state (17 cent.), **3.**11
courts, **40.**1, 22
See also Kirk sessions; Presbyteries;
Synods; & General Assembly
fasti, **6.**124, **30.**1
forms of ordination etc., **43.**11★
ministers:
consultations (1652–60), **26.**1, 16
declaration by, **15.**59
deprived, **38.**21
fasti, **6.**124
Fermartyn (Formartine), **37.**51
lists (including readers and
exhorters), **15.**5, **26.**42, **30.**3, **43.**11
stipends (including readers and
exhorters), **15.**5, **26.**42, **43.**11
papers on affairs of (1603–25), **6.**95
proceedings concerning (1637–8), **6.**40
Protesters–Resolutioner dispute,
24.39, **26.**1, 16
records, **29.**94
Thirds of Benefices:
accounts, **6.**89, 92, **11.**17, **26.**8, 42
assignation of stipends, books or
register of, **6.**81, **15.**5, **43.**11
assumption, books or register of
(valuations), **6.**89, 92, **35.**2
visitations, **30.**11
pre-Reformation:
ancient, **39.**3
benefices, *see* Benefices, valuations of;
& Thirds of Benefices
councils, **6.**116, **24.**54
fasti, **30.**1
organization, **32.**10, 13, 18
parish clergy, **30.**3
records, **40.**1
statutes, **6.**116, **24.**54
See also Liturgies; Prayers; & Sermons
Churchyard, Thos., poet (d. 1604), **31.**11
Ciudad Rodrigo, **39.**3
Civil list (1655), **21.**13
Clackmannanshire:
monuments, **44.**11
Society of Husbandmen, **24.**15
Clan Chatttan, **24.**41, **36.**6
Clans:
genealogies, **13.**1★
lists, **13.**1
See also Families & clans
Clariodus, **15.**9
Clarke, Peter (early 18 cent.), **24.**15
Clement VII of Avignon, Pope, **27.**12
Clerk, Duncan, alias Terig (mid 18 cent.),
6.43
Clerk of Eldin, John, etcher (d. 1812), **6.**9,
101

Clerk of Penicuik, Sir John (d. 1755), 24.13, 27.2
Clerk of Penicuik family, 24.13
Cleutin, Henri, Seigneur d'Oysel, diplomat (mid 16 cent.), 26.50
Clothes:
　Highland, 13.1
　Mary Queen of Scots, 6.114
Clyde burghs, 21.20
Clyde Navigation Trust, 21.20
Cochrane, Andrew, provost of Glasgow (mid 18 cent.), 15.38
Cochrane (Cochran), Sir John (d. c. 1650), 24.15
Cockburn of Ormistoun, John (early 18 cent.), 24.45
Coinage, 8.1
Coke, John, of Holkham (d. 1644), 39.4
Colchesters teares (1648), 8.1
Coldstream Priory, 11.18
Coll, 44.21
College of Justice, senators of, 6.21
　See also Session, Court of
Collegiate churches:
　Crail, 11.15
　Dunbar, 26.33
　Edinburgh:
　　St Giles, 6.108
　　Trinity, 6.112, 21.18, 26
　Glasgow, Our Lady, 15.67
　Leith, St Anthony's, 11.14
　Lincluden, 5.10
　Midlothian, 6.112
Colonies, see Darien; East New Jersey; & Nova Scotia
Colonsay, 44.23
Colt family, 11.33
Coltness, Lady, see Eliot, Margaret
Coltness collections, 15.60
Colville, John, lawyer (d. 1605), 6.20, 107
Combats for lyfe, Order of, 36.6
Commissariots:
　Argyll, reg. of inventories, 29.33
　courts, see Commissary courts
　Edinburgh, processes & decreets, 29.34
　Kirkcudbright, executry papers, 29.17
　miscellaneous, executry papers, 29.24
　See also Testaments, registers of
Commissary (consistory) courts:
　Aberdeen, 40.37
　Caithness, 29.10
　Edinburgh, 40.7
　St Andrews & Lothian, 1.25, 40.36
　See also Commissariots; & Testaments, registers of
Commissioners of the kirk, see General assembly: commissioners of
Committees:
　for dispatches, 27.18
　of estates, 27.18
　for managing the affairs of the army, 27.18
Common good, see Accounts: burgh
Commons, House of (1641), 8.1

Commonties:
　directory, 30.2
　Hassendean, 40.28
Commonwealth:
　satire, 4.5, 8.2
　Scotland under, 24.18
Communication of trade, 21.13
Communion rolls:
　Canongate, 29.90
　Scots Brigade in Netherlands, 24.38
Company of Scotland trading to Africa & the Indies, 6.93, 26.6
Compassio Beate Marie, 6.99
Complaynt of Scotland, 34.11
Confessions:
　Catholic, 31.20
　Helvetian, 11.11, 43.11
Confirmations, Leith (Epis.), 29.81
Consistory courts, see Commissary courts
Constable family, 11.35
Constable of Scotland, 36.6
Convention of Estates, see Estates: Convention of Royal
Convention of Royal Burghs, see Burghs: Convention of Royal
Conversion of Saul, 1.1
Conveyancing, early Scottish, 40.38
Coombe, Thos., poet (late 18 cent.), 4.4
Cope, Sir John (d. 1760), 17.21
Copenhagen, 6.22
Copie of the king's message (1644), 8.1
Corbet, Sir Wm., notary (mid 16 cent.), 29.39
Cordara, Padre Giulio Cesare (mid 18 cent.), 26.9
Coronation, of Anne of Denmark, 6.29
Corshill, barony, 5.4
Cotton mss., 1.20
Council & Session, lords of:
　acts, 40.9, 15
　jurisdiction in heritage, 40.37
　records, 40.1
　See also Privy Council, & Session, Court of
Councils, ecclesiastical, see Church of Scotland (pre-Reformation)
Counties, electoral system in, 40.37
Coupar Angus Abbey, 11.17, 26.40, 41
Courcelles, M., diplomat (late 16 cent.), 6.25
Courland, Jas., Duke of (mid 17 cent.), 24.15
Courts, see under Scots law and particular courts
Courts martial, 17.3, 25.19
Coutts family, 11.33
Covenants:
　National:
　　declaration against, 15.59
　　& events in N. Scotland, 11.14
　　satirical reply to, 4.2
　Solemn League &:
　　army of, 25.16, 17
　　declaration against, 15.59

Covenants: Solemn League &—*cont.*:
  Kilbarchan, **16.**12
  refusal to sign, **24.**44
Covenanters, government under, **27.**18
Coventry, **1.**2
Cowper, Wm., Bp. of Galloway (d. 1619), **6.**20
Cox, Capt. Hiram (late 18 cent.), **4.**2
Craft gilds (incorporations):
  Canongate, **29.**85
  Edinburgh, **21.**21
  Melrose, weavers, **25.**13
  Old Aberdeen, **37.**21
  Coventry, weavers, **1.**2
Craig, Geo. (early 17 cent.), **2.**5
Craig, Sir Thos., lawyer (d. 1608), **24.**60
Craig of Riccarton, Sir Wm. Gibson,
  lawyer (d. 1878), **40.**37
Craig of Rose-Craig, Alex., poet (d. 1627),
  12.2.
Craignish, **26.**9
Crail, burgh:
  collegiate church, **11.**15
  records, **15.**40
Craufurd of Craufurdland, John W. (mid
  18 cent.), **5.**2
Craufurd of Craufurdland family,
  correspondence, **5.**2
Crawford, Geo. (early 18 cent.), **39.**3
Crawfurd, Andrew, collector of ballads (d.
  1854), **34.**9
Credulity, accounts of, **39.**4
Creighton, Wm., Jesuit (late 16 cent.),
  24.15
Crichton, Mr Jas. (mid 16 cent.), **25.**10
Crichton, Rob., Lord Sanquhar (d. 1612),
  1.11
Crieff, **15.**59
Cristisone, Sir John, notary (mid 16 cent.),
  29.63
Cromar:
  antiquities, **38.**2
  plundering, **36.**16
Cromwell, Thos. (d. 1540), **6.**20
Cromwellian occupation, **6.**104, **24.**18, 31,
  40, **25.**19
Cromwellian Union, **24.**40
Croo, Rob., writer (mid 16 cent.), **1.**2
Crossraguel Abbey, **5.**13
Cullen, Walter (late 16 cent.), **36.**6
Culross, burgh, **15.**40
Cumming, Thos. (early 17 cent.), **2.**5
Cuningham, Thos., conservator at
  Campvere (d. 1670), **26.**11
Cuninghame & Co., W., **27.**20
Cunningham, **5.**4, **15.**76
Cunningham, Alex., Earl of Glencairn (d.
  1574), **11.**9
Cunningham (Dr Fian), John (d. 1591),
  17.1
Cunningham of Barns, Jas. (d. 1716), **38.**5
Cunningham of Craigends, Wm. (16–17
  cents.), **24.**2
Cupar, pres., **1.**7

Cupar Angus, *see* Coupar Angus
Cupples, Wm., min. of Kirkoswald (d.
  1751), **43.**9
Customs duties, **6.**8, **21.**13*:
  Dumfries, **9.**1
  Edinburgh, **21.**2
  Glasgow, **21.**20, 41
  Irvine, **15.**76

Dalgarno, Geo., writer (d. 1687), **15.**30
Dalreoch, **15.**59
Dalrymple, David de (mid 15 cent.), **6.**22
Dalrymple, Father Jas., translator (late
  16 cent.), **31.**4
Dalrymple of Hailes, Sir David (d. 1721),
  39.4
Dalrymple of Stair, Sir Jas., Lord Stair
  (d. 1695), **6.**13, **40.**35
Dalrymple of Stair family, papers, **5.**7
Dalyell of the Binns family, papers, **29.**70
Darien papers, **6.**93
Darien venture, **6.**93, **24.**14, **26.**6
Darlington, **1.**3
David II, King (d. 1371), **26.**50
Davidson, John, regent at Glasgow Univ.
  (mid 16 cent.), **43.**11
Davidson, John, min. of Prestonpans
  (d. 1604), **11.**9, **43.**11
Davidson, John, poet (d. 1909), **3.**2, 3
Davis, Arthur, soldier (mid 18 cent.), **6.**43
Dawes, Sir Wm., Archbp. of York
  (d. 1724), **24.**15
Deaths, *see* Burials or deaths
De composicione cartarum, **40.**28
Debtors, **40.**28
Decreet of spulzie, **36.**6
Deeds:
  index to register of, **45** note
  Kirkcudbright sheriff court, **7.**12–14
  Melrose regality court, **25.**6
Deer, Book of, **36.**36
Delaware Bay, **8.**1
Dempster, Thos., Cath. writer (d. 1625),
  6.24
Denham, Lady, *see* Wemyss, Frances
Denham of Coltness & Westfield, Sir
  Arch. Stewart (d. 1773), **15.**60
Denham of Coltness & Westfield, Sir Jas.
  (d. 1780), **15.**60
Denmark:
  ambassador to, **5.**14
  attempts to recover Orkney & Shetland,
    40.37
  Earl of Bothwell in, **6.**32
  dogs sent to, **15.**59
  relations with, **31.**2
  treaty with, **38.**19
Denmylne (Balfour of Denmylne) mss.,
  1.9, **11***, 13, **25.**20
Derby, Earls of, *see* Stanley, Jas. & Wm.
Deskford, Lord, *see* Ogilvy, Jas.
Devereux, Rob., Earl of Essex (d. 1646),
  8.1*

Devill and the parliament (1648), **8**.1
Devonshire, Dowager Duchess of, *see* Cavendish, Christian
Devotional pieces in verse and prose, **33**.24
Dialogue between a Whig and a Jacobite (1716), **8**.2
Diaries, journals, etc:
  kept by:
    Rob. Baillie (1637–62), **6**.76
    Jas. Beattie (1773), **2**.9
    John Bisset (1745), **36**.3
    Alex. Brodie (1652–80), **36**.33
    Jas. Brodie (1680–5), **36**.33
    Brosse, Jacques de la (1560), **26**.36
    John Campbell (1745), **24**.15
    Peter Clark (1715), **24**.15
    Clerk of Penicuik (1676–1754), **24**.13
    Thos. Cuningham (1640–54), **26**.11
    Cunningham of Craigends (1673–1715), **24**.2
    Drummond of Hawthornden (1657–9), **26**.35
    Edward VI (1537–49), **8**.2
    Lord Elcho (1744–6), **17**.22
    Erskine of Carnock (1683–7, 1701), **24**.14
    John Forbes (1640, 1642–6), **36**.21, 23
    John Grant (1771), **38**.6
    Jas. Gordon (1692–1710), **38**.16
    Pat. Gordon (1635–99), **36**.31
    Hay of Craignethan (1559–60), **24**.39
    Sir Thos. Hope of Craighall (1633–45), **6**.79
    Sir Jas. Hope of Hopetoun:
      (1646), **26**.50
      (1646–54), **25**.19
    Hume of Crossrigg (1700–7), **6**.30
    Alex. Jaffray:
      (1614–61), **36**.42
      (1644), **36**.23
    Johnston of Wariston:
      (1632–4, 1637–9), **24**.61
      (1639–40), **24**.26
      (1650–4), **25**.18
      (1655–60), **26**.34
    Hen. Kalmeter (1719–20), **27**.14
    Lauder of Fountainhall (1665–76), **24**.36
    John Lamont (1649–71), **15**.7
    Bp. John Leslie (1571), **6**.22
    Geo. Leyburn (1647), **8**.2
    Jas. Melville:
      (1556–1602), **6**.37
      (1556–1610), **43**.3
    John Mill (1740–1803), **24**.5
    Wm. Mitchell (1717), **36**.3
    John Nicoll (1650–67), **6**.55
    Jas. Nimmo (1654–*c*. 1705), **24**.6
    Geo. Ridpath (1755–61), **26**.2
    Earl of Strathmore (*c*. 1682–9), **24**.9
    Geo. Turnbull (1657–1704), **24**.15
    Rob. Wodrow (1697–1701), **15**.62

Diaries, journals, etc—*cont*.:
  relating to:
    Edward I (1296), **6**.20, 50
    1745 rising, **24**.20–2
    See also Autobiographies
Dick (Dickson), David, divine (d. 1663), **43**.9
Dictionaries:
  painters, **30**.7
  places, **16**.9
  Scots, **16**.5
Digby mss., **1**.1
Dingwall, pres., **24**.24
Directories:
  commonties, **30**.2
  landownership, **30**.5
  Neilston, Barrhead & Grahamston, **16**.14
Discours particulier d'Escosse, **6**.6, **40**.37
Diurnal of remarkable occurrents (1513–75), **6**.46
Doddridge, John, lawer (d. 1628), **27**.21
Dogs, **15**.59
Donne, John, poet (d. 1631), **6**.125
Dornoch Cathedral, **6**.22
Douai, Scots College at, **24**.44, **37**.31
Douglas, Anne, Lady Elcho (d. 1700), **43**.9
Douglas, Geo., Earl of Morton (d. 1738), **15**.53
Douglas, Gavin, Bp. of Dunkeld, poet (d. 1522):
  description of Isle of May, **4**.3
  poems, **6**.18, **32**.7, 20, **34**.3
  translation of the *Aeneid*, **6**.67, **33**.26, 28, 29, 31
Douglas, Jas., Earl of Morton, regent (d. 1581), **31**.11, **43**.11*
Douglas, Jas., Lord Aberdour, Earl of Morton (d. 1768), **15**.53
Douglas, Rob., Bp. of Dunblane (d. 1716), **6**.22
Douglas, Field-Marshal Rob. (d. 1662), **39**.4
Douglas, Wm., Earl of Morton (d. 1648), **15**.25, 59
Douglas of Auchintulloch, Rob. (mid 17 cent.), **25**.20
Douglas of Dalkeith, Sir Jas. (d. 1420), **6**.21, **40**.37
Douglas family, **6**.3
D'Oysel, *see* Cleutin, Henri
Drebbel, Cornelius Van (early 17 cent.), **1**.11
Dress, *see* Clothes & Vestments
Drummond, Geo., provost of Edinburgh (d. 1766), **1**.11
Drummond, John (mid 18 cent.), **1**.24
Drummond, John, Duke of Melfort (d. 1714), **39**.4
Drummond, John, Earl of Perth (d. 1662), **36**.6

Drummond of Hawthornden, Wm., poet
 (d. 1649):
  diary, **26.**35
  letters, **6.**125
  works, **3.**6, **15.**18, **32.**3, 4
Dryburgh Abbey, **6.**86
Duart estates, **25.**5
Duckett, Geo. (d. 1732), **17.**16
Ducks, ecclesiastical, **36.**20
Dudley, Rob., Earl of Leicester (d. 1588),
 6.20
Dumbarton, burgh, **21.**20, **29.**73
Dunavertie, massacre at, **25.**12
Dumfries, burgh:
  accounts, **9.**1
  burgesses, **9.**4
  charters etc., **9.**1
  customs accounts, **9.**1
  history, **9.**1
  protocols, **29.**86
  ships, **28.**1
  stent roll, **9.**4
Dumfries, commissariot, **29.**14
Dumfriesshire:
  Bell family in, **9.**2
  coalmining in (Nithsdale), **9.**3
  monuments, **44.**7
  protocols, **29.**86
Dunbar, burgh:
  French garrison (1553), **24.**44
  collegiate church, **26.**33
Dunbar, Earl of, *see* Murray, Jas.
Dunbar, Lord, *see* Murray, Jas.
Dunbar, Wm., poet (d. *c*. 1530), **31.**2,
 32.7, 20
Dunblane, burgh, library, **6.**22*
Dunblane, diocese, visitation, **30.**11
Dunblane, commissariot, **29.**15
Duncan, Rev. Hen. (d. 1846), **11.**23
Duncan family, **37.**52
Dundee, burgh:
  hospital, **21.**28
  courts martial, **25,**19
  records, **21.**28
  shipping dispute, **27.**2
  shipping lists, **24.**28
  textile industry, **27.**6
Dundee, Lord, *see* Graham of Claverhouse
Dundonald, earldom of, **29.**36
Dundonald, kirk session, **7.**8
Dundrennan Abbey, **5.**10
Dunfermline, parish:
  baptisms, **29.**44
  marriages, **29.**44
Dunfermline, Earl of, *see* Seton, Alex.
Dunfermline Abbey, **6.**77
Dundas (née Graham), Elizabeth (early
 19 cent.), **27.**3
Dunkeld, commissariot, **29.**16
Dunkeld, diocese:
  accounts, **6.**1, **25.**10
  lives of bps., **6.**1, **14.**1, **25.**10
Dunlop, Wm., principal of Glasgow Univ.
 (d. 1700), **43.**9

Dunning, **15.**59
Dunnottar:
  castle, **24.**26
  chamberlain account, **38.**10
Dun papers, **36.**20
Dunrossness, parish, **24.**5
Dunvegan, Book of, **38.**9
Durness, parish:
  baptisms, **29.**38
  marriages, **29.**38
Dury, Sir Wm. (mid 16 cent.), **6.**20
Dyer, Mary, Quaker (d. 1660), **4.**3
Dysart, burgh, **15.**75

East Lothian:
  contributions to French church, **25.**19
  monuments, **44.**8
East New Jersey, **6.**22
Eastwood, parish, **16.**11
Easy Club, **34.**7
Eden, Rich., translator (d. 1576), **4.**3
Edgar, Jas., secretary (mid 18 cent.), **11.**5
Edgar, Rob., clerk (d. 1759), **9.**1
Edgar family, **11.**5
Edinburgh, burgh:
  churches:
    Greyfriars, burials, **29.**26
    St Cuthbert's, inscriptions, **29.**47, 51
    St Giles, **6.**108
    Trinity, **6.**112, **21.**18, 26
  descriptions, **6.**20, 21
  Easy Club, **34.**7
  guilds & crafts, **21.**21
  hospitals:
    Soultra, **6.**112
    Trinity, **6.**112, **21.**18, 26
  Jacobite occupation, **17.**22
  magistrates, **6.**21
  marriages, **29.**27, 35, 53
  ministers, consultations, **26.**1, 16
  monuments, **44.**13
  printers & booksellers, **6.**21
  protocols, **29.**43, 64, 72, 74, 75, **30.**10,
   40.3
  records:
    accounts, **21.**3, 33, 34, 43, 44, 46, 47
    apprentices, **29.**28, 60, 61, 92
    burgesses, **29.**59, 62, 68
    charters, **21.**2, 3, 7
    council & court, **15.**40, 53, **21.**2–6,
     43–51
    poll tax, **29.**82
  survey, **6.**21
  trades council, **27.**5
  visit to, **38.**6
Edinburgh, commissariot:
  consistory court, **40.**7
  processes & decreets, **29.**34
  register of testaments, **29.**1–3
Edinburgh, diocese, official's court, **40.**36
Edinburgh, kirk sessions:
  general, **15.**25
  St Cuthbert's **25.**19

Edinburgh, pres., **43**.11*
Edinburgh, shire, *see* Midlothian
Edinburgh, univ.:
  Clement Little's library, **15**.26
  graduates & staff, **6**.109
Edinburgh Castle, sieges of, **6**.21, 26,
  31.11
Edmestoun, John (early 17 cent.), **1**.11
Education:
  in W. Highlands & Isles, **13**.1
  See also Schools
Edward I, King of England (d. 1307):
  expedition (1296), **6**.20, 50
  reign, **15**.58
Edward III, King of England (d. 1377),
  37.2
Edward VI, King of England (d. 1553),
  8.2
Edward, Prince (son of Malcolm III), **6**.20
Egerton, Sir Thos., Lord Ellesmere
  (d. 1617), **1**.11
Elcho, Lord, *see* Wemyss, David
Elcho, Lady, *see* Douglas, Anne
Elder, Adam, monk of Kinloss (mid
  16 cent.), **35**.2
Elder, John, redshank (mid 16 cent.),
  6.20, **13**.1
Elections, parliamentary:
  county, **40**.37
  Midlothian, **27**.11
  Renfrewshire, **27**.2
Elgin, burgh:
  hotel bill, **38**.6
  records, **37**.28, 36
Elgin, kirk session, **37**.36
Elgin, pres., **37**.36
Eliot, Margaret, Lady Coltness (d. 1675),
  43.9
Elizabeth, Queen of Bohemia (d. 1662),
  4.2, **15**.36, **39**.4
Elizabeth, Queen of England (d. 1603),
  15.52, **24**.43
Ellesmere, Lord, *see* Egerton, Sir Thos.
Elliot family, **20**.2
Elphinstone, Wm., Bp. of Aberdeen
  (d. 1514), **12**.5
Elphinstone of Balmerino, family, **11**.17
England:
  declaration of sports, **34**.14
  French ambassadors to, **6**.70, **24**.29, 30
  household account, **1**.3
  journeys in, **1**.3, **4**.1, **15**.60
  monasteries, **1**.5
  officers of army:
    (1648), **8**.2
    (1650s), **6**.104
    (1660), **8**.2
  ordinance on preachers (1653), **8**.2
  plays, **1**.1, 2, 10
  pretensions of, to French crown, **17**.5
  relations with Scotland, **24**.10, 11
    negotiations: **6**.21*, **24**.43
  See also Union
  romances, *see* Romances: English

England—*cont.*:
  sermon, **1**.11
  Scots armies in, **24**.44, **25**.16, 17
  Scots commissioners in:
    (1484), **6**.21
    (1644–6), **17**.18
  state of (1641), **8**.1
  succession to crown, **17**.10
Epics of the ton, **4**.2
Epigrams, **15**.31, **37**.16
Episcopalians:
  Aberdeen, St Paul's chapel, **37**.35
  Aberdeenshire, mins. deprived, **38**.21
  Bairnie, **29**.30
  complaints about, **25**.20
  grievances of, **39**.4
  Leith, **29**.81
  North East, **22**.1–3
  St Andrews, **29**.49
  Tillydesk, **29**.30
Epitaph on the Duke of Grafton, **4**.2
Errol papers, **36**.6
Erskine, Hen., Lord Cardross (d. 1693),
  24.14
Erskine, Jas., Lord Grange (d. 1754),
  1.11, **36**.16
Erskine, John, Earl of Mar (d. 1634),
  15.59
Erskine, John, Earl of Mar (d. 1732),
  24.26
Erskine, Rob., physician (17–18 cents.),
  24.44
Erskine, Sir Thos. (d. 1404). **40**.37
Erskine, Thos., Lord Erskine (d. 1766),
  24.26
Erskine of Carnock, John (d. 1743), **24**.14
Erskine of Dun, John (d. 1591), **15**.33
Erskine of Halton, Sir Thos. (mid
  16 cent.), **36**.6
Essex, Earl of, *see* Devereux, Rob.
Estates, the Three:
  commission by (1640), **15**.59
  committee of, **27**.18
  Convention of:
    (1678), **6**.69
    (1689), **26**.46, 47
  See also Parliament of Scotland
Etchings, **6**.9, 101
Ettrick Forest, **40**.37
Eure, Sir Wm. (mid 16 cent.), **33**.2
Excise duties:
  Banffshire, **37**.43
  commissioners, **6**.8, **21**.13
  officials, **21**.13
  settlement (1656), **6**.8, **21**.13
Exchequer, **5**.11, **6**.82, **37**.28, **40**.28
Expenses, of an unknown earl (1274),
  1.3

Fairfax, Ferdinando, Lord (d. 1648), **8**.1*
Faithful memorial (1659), **8**.2
Falkirk, meeting at, **43**.11
Falmouth, Virginia, **27**.20

Families & clans; histories & genealogies:
  collected:
    clans, **13**.1*
    Lyon Office, **29**.31
    by W. McFarlane, **24**.33, 34
    Mearns, **38**.10
  individual:
    Alexander, **11**.30
    Ayton, **34**.1
    Bain, **11**.24
    Bannatyne, **6**.38, **24**.16, **33**.5
    Bell, **9**.2
    Bisset, **11**.12
    Blackhall, **37**.30
    Burnet of Leys etc., **37**.23, 50, 53
    Burns (Burnes), **11**.23, 29
    Cameron, **1**.24
    Campbell, **25**.12
    Campbell of Auchinbreck, **26**.22
    Campbell of Calder, **25**.5, **36**.30
    Campbell of Craignish, **26**.9
    Campbell of Glenorchy, **6**.103
    Campbell of Strachur, **26**.22
    Christie, **11**.32
    Clerk of Penicuik, **24**.13
    Colt, **11**.33
    Constable, **11**.35
    Coutts, **11**.33
    Duncan, **37**.52
    Edgar, **11**.5
    Elliot, **20**.2
    Erskine of Dun, **36**.20
    Farquharson, **24**.41
    Farquharson of Invercauld, **37**.24
    Ferguson, **37**.52
    Forbes, **38**.8
    Forbes of Forbesfield, **37**.52
    Forbes of Waterton, **36**.44
    Foulis of Ravelston & Woodhall,
      24.16
    Fraser, **24**.47
    Glen, **11**.36
    Gordon, **37**.27, 34, 40
    Gourlay, **11**.37
    Haldane of Barmony, **11**.28, 35
    Haliburton, **11**.13
    Hume of Wedderburn, **1**.15
    Innes, **36**.34
    Knox, **11**.16
    MacDonald, **13**.1, **25**.5
    MacGregor (Gregor), **13**.1
    Mackenzie, **25**.12
    MacLea, **26**.22
    Maclean of Duart, **25**.5
    MacLeod, **38**.9
    Macnaughton, **25**.5
    Macpherson, **24**.41
    Macrae, **25**.5
    Masterton, **24**.15
    Maxwell of Pollock, **16**.15
    Morgan, **37**.52
    Mure of Caldwell, **15**.73
    Mure of Rowallan, **31**.17
    Oliphant of Gask, **11**.2

Families & clans; histories & genealogies:
  individual—*cont.*:
    Playfair, **11**.25, 28, 35
    Roger, **11**.25, 28, 35
    Rose of Kilravock, **36**.18
    Scott (Scot), **11**.13, **20**.2
    Seton (Seytoun), **6**.34
    Sinclair, earls of Orkney, **6**.22
    Skene, **37**.1, 47
    Spottiswoode, **39**.3
    Stewart of Allanton, **15**.60
    Stewart of Coltness, **15**.60
    Stewart of Goodtrees, **15**.60
    Strachan, **11**.31
    Strachan of Thornton, **11**.27
    Urquhart, **15**.31
    Wallace, **11**.22
    Wedderburn, **24**.28
    Wise, **11**.27, 31
    Wishart, **11**.11
    Wyse of Lunan, **11**.27
Farne Island, ducks, **36**.20
Farquharson, John, surveyor (mid
  18 cent.), **26**.27
Farquharson family, **24**.41
Farquharson of Invercauld family, **37**.24
Fasti Aberdonenses, **36**.26
Fasti Academiae Mariscallanae, **37**.4, 19,
  20
Fasti Ecclesiae Scoticanae, **6**.124
Fasti Ecclesiae Scoticanae medii aevi,
  30.1
Fees, of officials, **15**.59
Fencible men, **6**.103
Fénelon, Sieur de la Mothe, *see* Salignac
  de la Mothe Fénelon
Fergus, **1**.19
Ferguson family, **37**.52
Fergusson, David, min. of Dunfermline
  (d. 1598), **6**.113, **32**.15
Fergusson, Geo., Lord Hermand, lawyer
  (d. 1827), **40**.7
Fergusson, Rob., poet (d. 1774), **3**.4,
  33.22, 25
Fermartyn (Formartine), thanes of, **37**.51
Ferme (Fairholm), Chas., min. of
  Fraserburgh (d. 1617), **43**.14
Ferrerius, John (mid 16 cent.), **6**.66, **35**.2,
  37.34
Fian, Dr, *see* Cunningham, John
Fiars prices, Aberdeenshire, **37**.35
Fife, shire:
  chronicle, **15**.7
  monuments, **44**.11
  protocols, **29**.37
  sheriff court, **26**.12
  tax roll, **26**.12
Fife, synod:
  minutes, **1**.8
  superintendent, **6**.20, **24**.4
Findlater & Seafield, Earls of, *see* Ogilvy,
  Jas.
Finnie, Agnes, witch (mid 17 cent.), **39**.4
Fintray, barony, **38**.6

Fisheries:
in W. Highlands & Isles, **13.1**
on Ythan, **26.5**
FitzRoy, Hen., Duke of Grafton (d. 1690),
4.2
Flagellum parliamentarium, **4.1**
Flanders, war in (1701–11), **24.38**
Fletcher, Andrew, Lord Milton (d. 1766),
37.26
Fletcher of Saltoun, Andrew (d. 1716),
27.2
Fletcher of Saltoun family, **27.2**
Flodden, battle of, **26.43**
Flodden papers, **26.20**
Florice and Blauncheflour, **1.29**
Fontenelle, Bernard le Bovier de, writer
(d. 1757), **4.4**
Forbes, barony, **25.19**
Forbes, Alex., Lord Pitsligo (d. 1762),
26.31
Forbes, John, min. of Alford (d. 1634),
43.10
Forbes, John, theologian (d. 1648), **36.21,
23**
Forbes, John, printer (mid 17 cent.), **16.4**
Forbes, Pat., Bp. of Aberdeen (d. 1635),
39.5
Forbes, Rob., Bp. of Ross & Caithness
(d. 1775), **22.2, 24.20–2**
Forbes, Wm. Bp. of Edinburgh (d. 1634),
36.21, 39.3
Forbes, Wm., Lord Forbes (d. 1697),
37.15
Forbes family, **38.8**
Forbes of Culloden, Duncan (d. 1704),
36.34
Forbes of Reres, Arthur (mid 16 cent.),
40.37
Forbes of Forbesfield family, **37.52**
Forbes of Foveran, Sir Sam. (early
18 cent.), **36.9**
Forbes of Waterton family, **36.44**
Fordoun, monuments, **6.91**
Fordun (Fordoun), John of (late 14 cent.),
37.2, 40.37
Forest law, **40.37**
Forestar of Skipinch, Sir Duncan,
comptroller (late 15 cent.), **26.50**
Forfar (Angus), shire:
description, **39.3**
monuments, **6.91**
tax roll, **6.105**
Forfeited Estates, **24.57**
See also Annexed Estates
Forgery, **40.28**
Formartine (Fermartyn), thanes of, **37.51**
Formularies (books of styles), **10.2, 40.8,
10, 11, 28, 38**
Forth & Brentford, Earl of, *see* Ruthven,
Pat.
Fortirgal, Chronicle of, **6.103**
Fosterage, **13.1**
Foular, John, notary (early 16 cent.),
29.64, 72, 75, 30.10

Foulis, Jas., notary (mid 16 cent.), **29.57**
Foulis of Ravelston, Sir John (d. 1707),
24.16
Foulis of Woodhall, Wm. (d. 1737), **24.16**
Fowler, Wm., poet (d. 1612), **32.6, 33.7,
14**
*Fowler's Neilston, Barrhead, Grahamston &
neighbourhood directory*, **16.14**
France:
Agents from, in Scot., **17.7, 8, 26.36, 50**
Alliances with Scot., **15.37, 26.20**
Ambassadors from:
in Eng., **6.70, 24.29, 30**
in Scot., **6.20, 25, 70, 24.29, 30**
Earl of Bothwell, **6.22**
contributions to church in, **25.19**
docs. in relating to Scot., **1.14**
forces of in Scot., **24.44**
Mary Queen of Scots in, **15.26**
plays performed in, **4.2**
popular credulity, **39.4**
pretensions of English, to crown of, **17.5**
Scots ambassador, **15.27**
Scots College in, **1.6, 15.27**
Scots guards in, **15.37**
Scots privileges, **15.37, 21.53**
Scots relations with, **6.70, 110, 123,
15.26*, 17.5, 26.4, 7, 10, 20**
Francis II, King of France (d. 1560), **17.2**
Fraser, Dr Jas. (d. 1731), **36.24**
Fraser, Jas., min. of Wardlaw (d. 1709),
24.47
Fraser, John (late 17 cent.), **39.4**
Fraser, Simon, Lord Lovat (d. 1747),
26.5, 36.6, 39.3
Fraser, Sir Wm., antiquary (d. 1898),
26.5, 9, 21
Fraser of Beaufort, Thos. (late 17 cent.),
26.5
Fraser of Brea, Jas., min. of Culross
(d. 1699), **43.9**
Fraser of Inverallochy, Chas. (mid
18 cent.), **36.6**
Fraser of Powis family, papers, **38.17**
Frasers, Chronicles of the, **24.47**
Frederick V, Elector Palatine, King of
Bohemia (d. 1632), **4.2, 15.36**
Frederick Henry, Prince (son of
Frederick V), **15.36**
Freeholders:
Banffshire, **37.43**
Berwickshire, **39.3**
Frendraught, tower, **36.21**
Friars:
Aberdeen, **2.2, 36.3**
Ayr, **5.11**
Glasgow, **15.67**
Friendship, bands of, **13.1*, 15.53, 36.6,
20**
Fuller, Wm., imposter (d. *c.* 1717), **8.1**
Funerals:
Field-Marshal Rob. Douglas, **39.4**
escutcheons, **29.31**
John Erskine of Carnock, **24.14**

Funerals—*cont.*:
Bp. Pat. Forbes, **39**.5
Jas. Lawson, **43**.11
Marquis of Montrose, **8**.1
Furniture:
Mary Queen of Scots, **6**.114
Murray of Ochtertyre, **24**.55

Gaelic:
texts in, 2.8. **13**.1*, **23**.1–15, **36**.36,
40.37
translations from, **4**.1, **13**.1*, **23**.1–4, 8,
9, 11–15
Gaffney, **8**.2
Galbraith of Balgair family, **29**.87
Gallienus redivivius (1695), **8**.2
Galloway:
churches, **5**.10
miscellany, **28**.5
monuments, **44**.4, 5
Old Galloway Papers, **28**.4–7
shipping, **28**.1
Galloway, Pat., min. of Perth, & later
Edinburgh (d. 1626), **6**.20*
Galt, John, novelist (d. 1839), **3**.5, 8, 14
Garden, Geo., scholar (d. 1733), **38**.5
Garden (Gardyne), Alex., poet & lawyer
(d. 1642), **1**.26, **12**.5
Garden, Jas., theologian (d. 1726), **38**.21
Gardener, **24**.45
Garibaldi, Giuseppe (d. 1882), **27**.16
Garioch, coroners & foresters of, **37**.30
Gascoigne, Geo. (d. 1577), **4**.4
Gates, Sir Thos. (d. 1621), **4**.2
Gau, John, translator (d. *c.* 1553), **6**.22,
31.8
Gaw, Sir Alex., notary (mid 16 cent.),
29.37
Geddy, John, bee keeper (late 17 cent.),
1.11
Genealogies, *see* Families & clans
General Assembly of the Church of
Scotland, **6**.84, **15**.50–1:
(1618), **39**.3
(1638–9), **43**.9
(1640), **36**.4
(1650), **24**.25
(1692), **15**.6
commissioners of:
(1627), **6**.22
(1646–53), **24**.11, 25, 58
(1701–5), **15**.59
(*c.* 1703, 1714), **25**.20
& Caths., **15**.59, **25**.20
& Epis., **25**.20
Geographical descriptions, *see*
Topographical descriptions
Ghost, The, **4**.2
Gibson, Walter, merchant (late 17 cent.),
6.22
Gilbert de Moravia, Bp. of Caithness (d.
c. 1245), **6**.22
Gilderoy, *see* MacGregor, Pat.

Gillespie, Geo., min. of Edinburgh (d.
1648), **36**.23
Gilmour, Sir John, lawyer (d. 1671), **26**.21
Girthon, parish, **9**.4
Gilds (guilds), *see* Craft gilds; *&* Merchants
Gladstanes, Geo., Archbp. of St Andrews
(d. 1615), **15**.33
Glamis, Lord, *see* Lyon, John
Glamis Castle & estate, **24**.9
Glanvill, Ranulf de (d. 1190), **40**.12
Glasgow, burgh:
address to Wm. II, **15**.59
affairs of, **15**.38
churches:
cathedral, **15**.13
Our Lady College, **15**.67
friars, **15**.67
Jacobite occupation, **15**.38
Memorabilia, **15**.40
records:
accounts, **15**.16, **21**.11, 12, 16
burgesses, **29**.56, 66
charters, **21**.14, 15, 17, 23, 27, 36–41
council & court, **15**.16, 40, **21**.11, 12,
16, 19, 23, 27, 36–41
relations with other burghs, **15**.14
tobacco trade, **27**.20
writers, **15**.14
Glasgow, commissariot, **29**.7
Glasgow, diocese:
parishes, **6**.100
protocols, **11**.8
rental book, **11**.8
Glasgow, pres., **15**.25, 26
Glasgow, univ.:
band supporting Wm. II, **15**.59
charter, **15**.16
records, **15**.71, 74
Glasgow & Ayr, synod, **15**.69
Glassarie, lands of, **25**.12
Glebes, **7**.7
Glenaven, forest of, **38**.22
Glenbuchat, Book of, **38**.12
Glencairn, Earl of, *see* Cunningham, Alex.
Glencoe, massacre, **8**.2
Glen family, **11**.36
Glenkindie, **38**.10
Glenlivet, battle of, **39**.3
Glenluce Abbey, **5**.5, 10
Godolphin, Wm., Lord Rialton, Marquis
of Blandford (d. 1731), **8**.1, **39**.3
Godolphin, Sidney, Earl of (d. 1712),
25.11
Gold mines, **6**.15
Goodal, Mrs (late 17 cent.), **43**.9
Goodal, Walter, historian (d. 1766), **11**.26
Gordon, Alex., Bp. of Galloway (d. 1575),
15.33
Gordon, Geo., Marquis of Huntly
(d. 1636), **36**.20
Gordon, Geo., Marquis of Huntly
(d. 1649), **36**.10
Gordon, Geo., Earl of Aberdeen (d. 1720),
36.22

Gordon, Geo., Earl of Huntly (d. 1576), **36**.16
Gordon, Geo., Lord Byron (d. 1824), **17**.20
Gordon, Henrietta, Madame de Gordon (mid 17 cent.), **36**.11
Gordon, Jas., min. of Banchory-Devenick (d. 1714), **22**.1
Gordon, Jas., min. of Foveran (d. 1732), **38**.16
Gordon, Jas., min. of Rothiemay (d. 1686):
  descriptions by:
    Aberdeen, **36**.5, **37**.37
    misc., **24**.52
  history by, **36**.1, 2, 4
  plan of St Andrews, **6**.22
Gordon, John, Lord Kenmure (d. 1634), **43**.9
Gordon, Lord Lewis (d. 1754), **36**.3
Gordon, Maj. Nathaniel (d. 1646), **39**.3
Gordon, Wm., Bp. of Aberdeen (d. 1577), **15**.27
Gordon Castle, papers, **36**.20
Gordon family, **37**.27, 34, 40, **38**.22
Gordon letters, **36**.16
Gordon's Mill Farming Club, **2**.10
Gordon of Auchleuchries, Gen. Pat. (d. 1699), **36**.31
Gordon of Glenbuchat, John (mid 18 cent.), **17**.21
Gordon of Gordonstoun, Sir Rob. (d. c, 1685), **37**.34
Gordon of Gordonstoun, Sir Rob. (d. 1704), **37**.34
Gordon of Ruthven, Pat., historian (mid 17 cent.), **36**.10
Gordon of Straloch, Rob., topographer (d. 1661):
  correspondence, **36**.3
  descriptions by:
    Aberdeenshire & Banffshire, **36**.9
    misc., **24**.52
  genealogy by, **37**.34
Gordon of Straloch family, papers, **36**.3
Gospel book: *Book of Deer*, **36**.36
Gourlay family, **11**.37
Gowrie, Earls & Masters of, *see* Ruthven, Jas., John, & Wm.
Gowrie Conspiracy, **6**.20, 118, **14**.1, **17**.15
Government of Scotland; *see under* Scotland
Graeme (Graham), Geo., Bp. of Dunblane & Orkney (d. 1643), **24**.44
Grafton, Duke of, *see* FitzRoy, Hen.
Graham, Gille, Dowager Countess of Angus (late 16 cent.), **1**.11
Graham, Jas., Marquis of Montrose (d. 1650):
  declarations by, **24**.25
  funeral, **8**.1
  papers relating to, **15**.53, 68, **24**.15
  rising, **36**.10

Graham, Pat., Archbp. of St Andrews (d. 1478), **25**.19
Graham of Claverhouse, Lord Dundee (d. 1689), **6**.16, **24**.3
Grahame, Simion, traveller & soldier (d. 1614), **6**.39
Grahamston, **16**.14
Grameid, **24**.3
Grampian Club, publications etc., **11**.19
Grange, Lord, *see* Erskins, Jas.
Grant, John, min. of Dundurcas (d. 1814), **38**.6
Grant of Laggan, Mrs Anne (early 19 cent.), **24**.26
Gray, John (mid 16 cent.), **15**.5
Gray, Pat., Master of, Lord (d. 1611), **6**.20, 51
Gray, Sir Thos., chronicler (d. 1369?), **15**.41
Gray ms., **31**.28
Greenock, burgh, **21**.20
Greig, Gavin, ballad collector (d. 1914), **2**.6
Grey, Mary (late 17 cent.), **8**.1
Grierson of Lag family, charters, **29**.88
Grote, Gilbert, notary (mid 16 cent.), **29**.43
Guards:
  in France, **15**.37
  Mary Queen of Scots, **15**.25
Gude and godlie ballatis, **31**.16
Guild, Thomas, monk of Newbattle (mid 16 cent.), **6**.22
Guilds, *see* Craft gilds; & Merchants
Guillaume le Clerc (13 cent.), **1**.19
Guise, Duke of (mid 16 cent.), **24**.43
Gustavus Adolphus, King of Sweden (d. 1632), **39**.4
Guthrie, Wm., min. of Fenwick (d. 1665), **43**.9*
Guthry, Hen., Bp. of Dunkeld (d. 1676), **6**.31, **14**.1
Gypsies, **4**.4, **36**.16

Haddington, pres., **6**.22, **43**.11*
Haddington, Earl of, *see* Hamilton, Thos.
Haddingtonshire, *see* East Lothian
Haggart of Cairnmuir, David (mid 18 cent.), **40**.37
Hailes, Master of, *see* Hepburn of Bolton, Pat.
Haldane of Barmony (Bermony) family, **11**.28, 35
Haldenstone, Jas., prior of St Andrews (early 15 cent.), **19**.4
Haliburton family, **11**.13
Halket of Pitfirrane family, writs, **29**.67
Halyburton, Thos., min. of Ceres (d. 1712), **43**.9
Hamilton, burgh, **15**.25
Hamilton, Lady Anne, poetess (early 19 cent.), **4**.2
Hamilton, Jas., Duke of Hamilton (d. 1649), **24**.44

Hamilton, Jas., Earl of Abercorn
(d. 1670), **15.**25
Hamilton, Janet (late 17 cent.), **43.**9
Hamilton, John, Archbp. of St Andrews
(d. 1571), **6.**22
Hamilton, John, Lord Bargany (d. 1658),
5.7
Hamilton, John, Lord Bargany (d. 1693),
5.7
Hamilton, John, Cath. writer (d. 1609),
31.20, **33.**7
Hamilton, Thos., Earl of Melrose &
Haddington (d. 1637), **1.**9
Hamilton, Thos., Earl of Haddington
(d. 1640), **15.**59
Hamilton, Wm., Lord Bargany (d.
c. 1712), **5.**7
Hamilton Palace, archives, **15.**69
Hamilton of Wishaw, Wm. (d. 1724),
15.12
Hamilton & Campsie, commissariot, **29.**5
Hannay, Pat., poet (d. *c.* 1629), **12.**4
Harington, Sir John, writer (d. 1612),
17.10
Harisone, John (early 17 cent.), **39.**3
Hary (Henry) the Minstrel (Blind Hary),
(15 cent.), **6.**22, **31.**5, 13, **33.**13, **34.**4,
5
Hassendean, **40.**28
Hatton, Lord, *see* Maitland, Chas.
Hawes, Stephen, poet (early 16 cent.),
1.32
Hay, Alex., Lord Easter Kennet, lawyer
(d. 1594), **11.**6
Hay, Sir Geo., Earl of Kinnoull (d. 1634),
39.4
Hay, Sir Gilbert, poet (15 cent.), **1.**27,
31.19
Hay, Lady Isabel (mid 17 cent.), **36.**11
Hay, John, Earl of Tweeddale (d. 1697),
26.33
Hay, John, Cath. writer (d. 1607), **31.**20
Hay, Father Rich. Augustine, antiquarian
(d. 1736), **39.**3*
Hay, Sophia, Lady Aboyne (d. 1642),
36.11
Hay, Wm., lawyer (d. 1542), **40.**26
Hay of Craignethan, Andrew (d. 1689),
24.39
Hay of Errol family, papers, **36.**6
Hay of Yester family, writs, **29.**55
Hearth tax, *see* Taxation
Hebrides, *see* Isles
Helvetian Confession, **11.**11, **43.**11
Henrietta Maria, queen (d. 1669), **17.**12
Henry II, King of France (d. 1559), **15.**26,
53
Henry III, King of France (d. 1589), **6.**20,
25
Henry VIII, King of England (d. 1547):
coronation, **1.**32
proposal for union made to, **6.**20, **13.**1
monastic treasures, **1.**5
reign, **15.**58

Henry, Prince of Wales (d. 1612), **15.**36,
33.7
Henry the Minstrel, *see* Hary
Henryson, Rob., poet (d. *c.* 1506), **6.**7,
15.15, **31.**25, **32.**7, 20
Hentzner, Paul (d. 1623), **4.**1
Hepburn, Earls of Bothwell, **6.**22*
Hepburn, Jas., Earl of Bothwell (d. 1578),
6.32
Hepburn, Pat., Earl of Bothwell (d. 1556),
6.22
Hepburn of Bolton, Master of Hailes
(d. 1576), **6.**22
Hepburn of Humbie, Sir Adam (mid
17 cent.), **25.**16, 17
Hepburn of Wauchton family, **6.**22
Heriot, Geo., goldsmith (d. 1624), **15.**59
Heritors, Old Aberdeen, **37.**37
Hermit of Warkworth, **4.**2
Herok (Herock), Arch., Bp. of Caithness
(d. 1278?), **6.**22
Herries, Lords, *see* Maxwell, John & Wm.
Heywood, Thos., dramatist (d. 1650?), **4.**2
Higden, Ralph, chronicler (d. 1364), **32.**14
Highlands & Islands:
clans & landlords, **13.**1*
depredations, **37.**15
letters concerning, **24.**26
Medieval sculpture, **44.**24
monuments, **44.**2, 3, 9, 18, 19, 21–4
papers on, **13.**1*, **15.**59, **25.**5, 12, 20,
26.22
reports on, **37.**17
state of, **15.**59, 66
See also Gaelic; Isles; & Jacobites
Historie of Judith, **33.**15
Histories, *see* Chronicles & histories
Hogg, Jas., min. of Caputh (d. 1752),
40.37
Hogg, Jas., novelist (d. 1835), **3.**1, 12,
28.3
Holinshed, Raphael, chronicler (d.
c. 1580), **6.**21
Holland, *see* Netherlands
Holland, Sir Rich., poet (15 cent.), **6.**3,
31.13
Holyrood, parish, *see* Canongate
Holyrood Abbey, **6.**21, 73, **29.**25, **40.**28
Holyrood chronicle, **6.**23, **26.**30
Holyroodhouse, **6.**22, 29:
chapel royal, **29.**25
See also Canongate, parish
Homage, Ragman Rolls, **6.**50
Home, John, surveyor (late 18 cent.), **26.**52
Homer, **2.**8
Honours (regalia) of Scotland, **6.**33,
24.26
Hooke, Col. Nathaniel, agent (d. 1738),
17.7, 8
Hope of Craighall, Sir Thos., lawyer
(d. 1646), **6.**79, **24.**15, **40.**4, 5
Hope of Hopetoun, Sir Jas. (d. 1661),
25.19, **26.**50
Horn et Rimenhild, **6.**83

Horne, Donald (mid 19 cent.), **27**.11
Horse races, **15**.25
Hoskins, John, lawyer (d. 1638), **1**.11
Sixtus IV, Pope (d. 1484), **25**.19
Hospitallers (Knights of St John of
    Jerusalem), **27**.19, **39**.4
Hospitals:
  Dundee, **21**.28
  Edinburgh:
    Soutra, **6**.112
    Trinity, **6**.112, **21**.18, 26
  Leith, St Antony's, **6**.112, **21**.18, 26
Household, royal (14 cent.), **24**.44
Household books, *see* Accounts
Howard, Theophilus, Lord Walden, Earl
    of Suffolk (d. 1640), **6**.22
Howell, Jas., writer (d. 1666), **1**.11
Howie, Rob., scholar (d. *c.* 1645), **19**.6
Hudson, Hen., navigator (d. 1611), **8**.1
Hudson, Thos., poet (16–17 cents.),
    33.15
Hull, siege of, **8**.1
Humbie, kirk session, **15**.26
Hume, Alex., min. of Logie & poet
    (d. 1609), **6**.44, **31**.23, **43**.11
Hume, David, lawyer (d. 1838), **40**.6, 14,
    16, 18–21
Hume-Campbell, Hugh, Earl of
    Marchmont (d. 1794), **26**.21
Hume of Crossrigg, Sir David, lawyer
    (d. 1707), **6**.30
Hume of Godscroft, David (early
    17 cent.), **1**.15
Hume of Wedderburn family, **1**.15
Hunsdon, Lord, *see* Carey, Hen.
Hunter of Hunterston family, papers,
    29.58
Hunterian Club, publications, **12**.9
Huntly, lordship, **36**.20
Huntly, regality, **15**.26
Huntly, Marquis of, *see* Gordon, Geo.
Huntly, Earls of, *see* Gordon, Geo.
Hymns:
  Gude & godlie ballatis, **31**.16
  by Alex. Hume, **6**.44

Iliad, in Gaelic, **2**.8
Inchaffray Abbey, **6**.88, **24**.56
Inchcolm Abbey, **26**.32, 43
Incorporations, *see* Craft gilds
Industries:
  chemical, **27**.14
  mining:
    coal, **9**.3
    gold, **6**.15
    lead, **25**.19, **26**.50
  miscellaneous, **27**.14
  textile:
    Dundee, **27**.6
    Galashiels, **27**.14
    linen, **45**.1
    New Mills, **24**.46
Innes, Thos., antiquary (d. 1744), **36**.6, 25

Innes family:
  papers, **36**.6
  writs, **29**.79
Inscriptions, *see* Monuments
Inventories:
  charters, papers, writs:
    Aberdeen burgh, **37**.49
    Balmerino family, **11**.17
    Breadalbane, **6**.103
    Cairncross family, **25**.13
    Crail collegiate church, **11**.15
    Dundee burgh, **21**.28
    Dundonald earldom, **29**.36
    Innes barony, **29**.79
    Lamont family, **29**.54
    Leith, St Anthony's hospital, **11**.14
    Paris, **1**.14
    Pitfirrane, Halkets of, **29**.67
    Scots in France, **21**.53
    Scrymgeour family, **29**.42
    South Leith kirk session, **11**.14
    Wigtown earldom, **29**.36
  goods:
    Argyll commissariot, **29**.33
    Geo. Heriot, **15**.59
    Mary Queen of Scots, **6**.114
    Orkney commissariot, **30**.6
  jewels, ornaments:
    Coupar-Angus, **11**.17
    Glasgow, cathedral, **15**.13
    Holyrood, **6**.21
    St Andrews, St Salvator's College,
      15.59
    Stirling, chapel royal, **15**.27*
  misc.:
    books, *see* Libraries
    eccl. records of NE, **37**.6
    furniture, **24**.55
    monuments, **44**.1–22
Invercauld, **37**.24
Inverness, burgh:
  records, **37**.39, 44
  sett, **21**.55
Inverness, commissariot, **29**.4
Inverness, pres., **24**.24
Iona (Hy, Icolmkill), **6**.106, **13**.1*, **44**.22
Ireland:
  campaign in (1691), **6**.48
  Leyburn's mission in (1647), **8**.2
  papers relating to, **1**.11
  popular credulity, **39**.4
Irish annals, **13**.1
Irland, John, divine & diplomat (late
    15 cent.), **32**.14, 19, **34**.2
Irvine, burgh, **5**.15, **15**.76, **21**.20
Irvine of Drum, Sir Alex. (mid 17 cent.),
    36.16
Islay, **44**.23
Isles (Hebrides):
  description, **39**.4
  lords of the, **27**.22
  monuments, **44**.9, 19, 21, 22
  observations, **15**.69
Isles, commissariot, **29**.11

Isles, diocese, **6**.100, **13**.1★
Italy:
  popular credulity, **39**.4
  Stuarts in, **26**.35
Itineraries:
  Edward I (1296), **6**.20, 50
  Prince Charles Edward (1745–6), **24**.23
Irvine, burgh:
  customs books, **15**.76
  history, **21**.20
  protocols, **11**.8
  records, **5**.15

Jacobites:
  conspiracies, **25**.11
  correspondence, **1**.17, **17**.7, 8, **24**.27
  court, in Rome, **26**.31
  Locharkaig treasure, **26**.35
  papers, **37**.15
  risings:
    (1715–16):
      account, **8**.1★
      dialogue, **8**.2
      & Glasgow, **15**.38
      letters, **26**.25
      narrative, **1**.30
      papers, **24**.15
      prisoners, **39**.4
      villages burnt, **15**.59
    (1719), **24**.19
    (1745–6):
      history, **17**.21
      letters, **26**.21, **36**.20
      march of army, **36**.3
      narratives, **15**.55, **26**.9, 50
      origins, **25**.2
      papers, **17**.22, **24**.15, 20–3, **36**.3★,
        39.4★
      persons concerned in, **24**.8
      in Perth, **39**.4
      prisoners, **26**.13–15
      songs, **23**.15
      trials, **37**.17
  See also James VII; Stuart, Prince Charles;
    Stuart, Prince James; & Stuarts
Jaffray, Alex. (d. 1673), **36**.23, 42
Jaffray, Alex. (d. *c*. 1826), **38**.6
James I, king (d. 1437):
  chronicle, **15**.43
  death, **15**.43
  life, **10**.1, **15**.43
  poems, **11**.39, **19**.2, **31**.1, **32**.1
James III, King (d. 1488), **6**.22, **26**.43
James IV, King (d. 1513):
  letters, **26**.45
  work composed for, **32**.19, **34**.2
James V, King (d. 1542):
  confessor, **6**.34
  household books, **6**.57
  letters by, **15**.53
  secretary, **36**.6
  strena to, **6**.21
  work presented to, **33**.10, 11, 16

James VI & I, King (d. 1625):
  & Catholics, **24**.15
  commissions by, **30**.11
  conference with, **6**.20
  coronation, **6**.29
  death, **14**.1
  & English throne, **17**.10
  favourites, **1**.11
  letters by, **11**.11, **15**.25, 52, 59, **17**.10
  letters to, **1**.11★, **6**.20, **15**.36, **39**.3
  letters & papers of reign, **1**.11★, 13,
    6.95, **15**.27
  library, **15**.25, **24**.15
  marriage, **6**.29
  narratives of life & reign, **1**.6, **6**.14
  plots against, **6**.20★, **17**.1
  See also Gowrie conspiracy
  sayings, **24**.15
  submission to, **39**.4
  works:
    Basilicon doron, **17**.11, **33**.17, 19
    poems, **1**.11, **6**.20, **33**.23, 27
    prose, **34**.14
James VII & II, King, formerly Duke of
  York (d. 1685):
  devotional papers, **17**.19
  letters by, **39**.4
  memoir of, **8**.2
  papers, **17**.12
  portrait, **6**.22
  warrants, **6**.73
  work presented to, **6**.74
Jamesone, Mary (mid 17 cent.), **38**.10
Jamieson, John, lexicographer (d. 1838),
  16.5
Jenkin, Valentine, painter (early 17 cent.),
  15.59
Jewels & ornaments, **6**.21, 114, **11**.17,
  15.13, 27, 59
Johnsoun, Thos., notary (16 cent.), **29**.52
Johnston, Arthur, poet (d. 1641), **37**.9, 16
Johnston (Johnstoun), John, poet &
  scholar (d. 1611), **15**.26, **19**.6
Johnston of Standingstones, Gilbert (late
  16 cent.), **40**.28
Johnston of Wariston, Sir Archibald,
  lawyer (d. 1661), **24**.26, 61, **25**.18,
  26.34
Jones, Sir Wm. (d. 1794), **4**.2
Journeys, tours, travels, visits:
  to Bath & Bristol, **25**.1
  Darlington to Usk, **1**.3
  Dundurcas to Edinburgh, **38**.6
  Edinburgh to Glasgow, **24**.44
  in England, **15**.60, **24**.36
  Holland & Low Countries, **15**.60, **26**.50
  foreign, **25**.1
  France, **24**.36
  Kirkwall to Edinburgh, **15**.53
  to London, **38**.10
  Rome to Paris, **17**.22
  in Scotland, **24**.1, 36, **27**.14
  in Sutherland & Caithness, **41**.1
  See also Topographical descriptions

Juries, **40**.25
Justice clerks, Lord, **40**.22
Justice courts, *see* Justiciary, courts of
Justices of the peace:
  Banffshire, **37**.43
  Lanarkshire, **26**.17
Justiciary, courts of (Justice courts):
  collected trials:
    (1488–1624), **6**.45
    (1624–50), **40**.17, 29, 30
    (1661–78), **24**.48, 49
  history, **40**.1, 22
  individual trials, **1**.11, **6**.43, **24**.17,
    39.4*, **40**.37
  local:
    Argyll, **40**.13, 27
    raid on Glenkindie, **38**.10
    Highlands, **14**.1
    Orkney, **15**.53
    Shetland, **15**.53, **29**.84

Kalmeter, Hen., industrial spy (early
    18 cent.), **27**.14
Keith, Alex. (mid 18 cent.), **36**.9
Keith, Geo., Earl Marischal (d. 1778),
    26.21, **38**.6
Keith, Jas., physician (d. 1726), **38**.5
Keith, Field-Marshal Jas. (d. 1758), **36**.8,
    37.53
Keith, Rob., primus of Epis. Church (d.
    1756), **39**.1
Kelso Abbey, **6**.20, 85
Kenmure, Lord, *see* Gordon, John
Kennedy, Jas., Bp. of St Andrews
    (d. 1465), **6**.3
Kennedy, John, Earl of Cassillis (d. 1615),
    5.5, **15**.25
Kennedy, Lady Margaret, *see* Burnet,
    Lady Margaret
Kennedy, Quintin, Abbot of Crossraguel
    (d. 1564), **43**.11*
Kennedy of Brunston, Hugh (early
    17 cent.), **15**.25
Kennedy of Cassillis, estate, **9**.1
Kennedy of Cullean, Sir Thos. (d. 1602),
    15.25
Keppel, Wm. Anne, Earl of Albemarle
    (d. 1754), **37**.25
Keppoch, bard of, *see* MacDonald,
    John
Kerr, Sir Rob., Earl of Ancram (d. 1654),
    6.125
Kerr, Rob., Earl of Roxburgh (d. 1650),
    6.20
Kerr, Sir Wm., Earl of Lothian (d. 1675),
    6.125
Kilbarchan, parish:
  baptisms & marriages, **29**.41
  history, **16**.12
Kilmacolm, parish history, **16**.10
Kilwinning Abbey, **5**.1
Kincardine, Earl of, *see* Bruce, Alex.
Kincardine papers, **39**.4

Kincardineshire (the Mearns):
  barons, **38**.10
  bibliography, **37**.12, **38**.1
  papers, **26**.5
  protocols, **29**.63
King, Adam, Cath. writer (late 16 cent.),
    31.20
King and no king (1716), **8**.1
Kingis quair, **19**.2, **31**.1, **32**.1
Kingarth, kirk session, **7**.2
Kingston, Lord, *see* Seton, Alex.
Kingswells, recollections of, **38**.6
Kinloss Abbey:
  chronicle, **35**.2
  lives of abbots, **6**.66, **35**.2
  records, **35**.2
Kinross-shire, monuments, **44**.11
Kintyre:
  monuments, **44**.18
  papers, **25**.20
Kippis, Andrew, biographer (d. 1795),
    15.60
Kirkcudbright, burgh:
  descriptions, **28**.4
  records, **7**.10, 15, 16
  ships, **28**.1
Kirkcudbright, commissariot, **29**.17
Kirkcudbright, sheriff court deeds, **7**.12–
    14
Kirkcudbright, stewartry, monuments,
    44.5
Kirkintilloch, burgh, **26**.53
Kirklands, temporalities of:
  Arbroath, **6**.89
  Inchaffray, **6**.88
  Newbattle, **6**.92
Kirk sessions, minutes etc.:
  Aberdeen, **36**.15
  Ayr, **43**.9
  Banff, **37**.10
  Cambusnethan, **15**.26
  Canongate, **29**.90
  Carnock, **43**.4
  Dundonald, **7**.8
  Dunrossness, **24**.5
  Elgin, **37**.36
  Edinburgh:
    general, **15**.25
    St Cuthbert's, **25**.19
  Humbie, **15**.26
  Kingarth, **7**.2
  Melrose, **29**.45
  Minnigaff, **7**.11
  Old Aberdeen, **37**.37
  Penninghame, **7**.3, 4
  Perth, **15**.10
  Rothesay, **7**.1
  Rothiemay, **36**.1
  St Andrews, **6**.20, **15**.59, **24**.4, 7
  Sanday, **1**.11
  South Leith, **11**.14
  Stirling, **15**.25, 26
Kirkton, Jas., historian (d. 1699),
    43.9

Kirkwall, burgh:
journey from, to Edinburgh, **15**.53
records, **38**.19
cathedral chapter, **6**.22
Kirriemuir, parish, **22**.4
Kisses, **4**.2
Kneller, Sir Godfrey, painter (d. 1723), **6**.22
Knox, John, min. of Edinburgh (d. 1572):
family, **11**.16
testament, **6**.54
works, **6**.115
Knox family, **11**.16
Kossuth, Lajos (d. 1894), **27**.16
Kyle, **5**.4

Lag charters, **29**.88
Laideus (MacGregor), Duncan (16 cent.), **6**.103
Lamont, Donald, Gaelic writer (d. 1958), **23**.6
Lamont family, papers, **29**.54
Lamont of Newton, John, chronicler (mid 17 cent.), **15**.7
Lanark, burgh, **21**.32
Lanark, commissariot, **29**.19
Lanark, pres., **1**.16
Lanarkshire:
descriptions, **15**.12
Justices of the peace, **26**.17
monuments, **44**.20
protocols, **29**.29
Upper Ward, **28**.2
Lancelot du Lak, **15**.49, **32**.2
Lanfine papers, **5**.2
Landowners, directory of, **30**.5
Lanercost Chronicle, **6**.68
Lauder, commissariot, **29**.18
Lauder, Geo., poet (mid 17 cent.), **6**.121
Lauder, John, lawyer (early-mid 16 cent.), **40**.8
Lauder, Rob., notary (mid 16 cent.), **6**.87
Lauder of Fountainhall, Sir John (d. 1722), **6**.69, 90, **24**.36
Lauderdale, Duke of, *see* Maitland, John
Lauderdale, Duchess of, *see* Murray, Elizabeth
Lauderdale, Earls of, *see* Maitland, Chas. & John
Lauderdale, John, poet (late 18 cent.), **28**.6
Law, *see* Scots law
Law, Jas., Archbp. of Glasgow (d. 1632), **15**.12
Lawson, Jas., min. of Edinburgh (d. 1584), **43**.11
Lay patronage, **36**.3
Lead mining, **25**.19, **26**.50
Leases, *see* Tacks
Leibnitz, Gottfried, philosopher (d. 1716), **37**.53
Leicester, Earl of, *see* Dudley, Rob.

Leighton, Rob., Archbp. of Glasgow (d. 1684), **6**.22, **15**.69, **24**.44
Leith, burgh:
Epis. congregation, **29**.81
siege of, **26**.36
St Anthony's hospital, **6**.21, **11**.14
Leland (Leyland), John, antiquary (d. 1552), **15**.41
Lennox, earldom of, **15**.24
Lennox, Dukes of, *see* Stuart, Jas. & Ludovic
Leslie, Sir Alex., Earl of Leven (d. 1661), **15**.59
Leslie, John, Earl of Rothes (d. 1640), **6**.40
Leslie (Lesley), John, Bp. of Ross (d. 1596), **6**.20, 22, 41, **31**.4
Leslie of Powis family, papers, **38**.17
Leslie of Wardhouse, John (late 16 cent.), **40**.28
Letters of fire & sword, **36**.6
Leven, Earl of, *see* Leslie, Sir Alex.
Leven & Melville, earls of, archives, **15**.59
Leven & Melville papers, **6**.80
Lewis:
account of, **39**.4
chemical works, **27**.14
troubles, **25**.12
Lex talionis (1647), **8**.2
Leyburn, Geo., agent (d. 1677), **8**.2
Leys, barony, **36**.24
Libraries & other lists of books:
Abbotsford, **6**.63
Dunblane, Leightonian, **6**.22*
Edinburgh Univ., Clement Little, **15**.26
Glasgow, cathedral, **15**.13
James VI, **15**.25, **24**.15
Duke of Lauderdale (mss.), **6**.21
Lauder of Fountainhall, **24**.36
Earl of Lothian, **6**.125
Mary Queen of Scots, **6**.114, **15**.25
Salton, **6**.22
St Andrews:
St Salvator's College, **15**.59
univ., **15**.26
Lincluden, collegiate church, **5**.10
Lindores Abbey, **1**.11, 22, **24**.42
Lindsay, Colin, Earl of Balcarres (d. *c*. 1722), **6**.74
Lindsay, David, min. of Leith, Bp. of Ross (d. 1613), **30**.11
Lindsay, David, Bp. of Brechin (d. 1641), **39**.3
Lindsay, Pat., Lord (d. 1589), **6**.20
Lindsay, Pat., Archbp. of Glasgow (d. 1644), **15**.53
Lindsay, Wm., (early 17 cent.), **27**.2
Lindsay of Menmuir, John, Lord Menmuir (d. 1598), **1**.13
Lindsay of the Mount, Sir David, poet (d. 1555), **33**.1, 2, 6, 8
Lindsay of Pitscottie, Rob., historian (early-mid 16 cent.), **31**.18
Linen industry, **45**.1

Linlithgow:
  palace, **39**.3
  protocols, **29**.52, 57
Linton, protocols, **29**.39
Lisbon, **1**.11
Lithgow, Wm., traveller (early 17 cent.),
  14.1
Little, Clement, lawyer (d. 1580), **15**.26
Liturgies:
  Aberdeen breviary, **6**.99
  Arbuthnott missal, **15**.69
  Book of Common Order, **6**.115, **23**.11
  epistolary, **2**.4
  offices:
    St Kentigern (St Mungo), **15**.69
    St Wynnyn, **5**.1
  prayer book, **27**.2
Livingstone, Jas., Earl of Callander
  (d. 1674), **25**.17
Livingstone, John, min. of Ancrum
  (d. 1672), **43**.9*
Livingstone, Wm. (mid 17 cent.), **25**.17
Livy, **31**.22
Locharkaig Treasure, **26**.35
Lochleven Castle, **15**.26, 27
Lochtayside, survey, **26**.27
Lockhart, John G., writer (d. 1854), **3**.7
Lodge, Thos., writer (d. 1625), **12**.7
Logan, Jas., antiquary (early 19 cent.),
  37.7, 37, **38**.11
Logan charter, **5**.4
Logan of Restalrig, Rob. (early 17 cent.),
  17.15
London:
  descriptions, **4**.2, 4
  executions in, **1**.11*, **4**.1
  journey to, **38**.10
  Scots commissioners in, **17**.18
  Tower of, **1**.11
  visit to, **2**.9
London's remains (1667), **4**.4
Lothian, archdeaconry, official's court,
  1.25, **40**.36
Lothian, Earl of, *see* Kerr, Sir Wm.
Lothian & Tweeddale, synod, **40**.32
Louis XIV, King of France (d. 1715),
  17.8
Lovat, Lord, *see* Fraser, Simon
Low Countries, *see* Netherlands
Ludlow, Edmund, regicide (d. 1692), **4**.1
Lundie, John, scholar (early 17 cent.),
  1.26
Lupton, Donald, writer (d. 1676), **4**.2
Lutherans, **43**.11
Lyon, John, Lord Glamis (d. 1578),
  26.43
Lyon, Pat., Earl of Strathmore (d. 1695),
  24.9
Lyon, King at Arms (Lyon Office):
  officials, **29**.77
  records, **29**.31
Lyon in mourning, **24**.20–3
Lyoun of Auldbar, John (early 17 cent.),
  6.4

McAdam, John, radical (d. 1883), **27**.16
McArthur, John, surveyor (late 18 cent.),
  26.27
MacCodrum, John, Gaelic poet (d. 1779),
  23.2
McConnel, James I, mine owner (d. 1957),
  9.3
McConnel, John [*sic*] Anne (d. 1917), **9**.3
Macdonald, Alex. Bane (mid 18 cent.),
  6.43
MacDonald, Donald, servant (early
  18 cent.), **14**.1
Macdonald, Flora (d. 1790), **17**.22
Macdonald, Hugh (mid-late 17 cent.),
  25.5
MacDonald, John (Iain Lom), bard of
  Keppoch (17 cent.), **23**.8
Macdonald, Sir John, Jacobite (mid
  18 cent.), **17**.22
MacDonald, Sileas (Julia), Gaelic poet
  (d. *c*. 1729), **23**.13
MacDonald clan, **13**.1, **25**.5
MacDonald of Islay, Angus (16–17 cents.),
  39.4
MacDonald of Islay clan, **25**.20
MacDonnell of Glengarry, Alex. (mid
  18 cent.), **24**.23
MacDonnell of Lochgarry, Donald (mid
  18 cent.), **24**.23
MacDougall clan, **25**.12
MacDougall of Dunollie, Duncan
  (d. 1620), **40**.37
M'Eacharne, Colein (mid 17 cent.) **25**.12
Macfarlane, Walter, antiquary (d. 1767):
  genealogical collections, **24**.33, 34
  geographical collections, **24**.51–3,
  39.4
McGill of Nether Rankeilor, Jas., lawyer
  (mid 16 cent.), **6**.6, **40**.37
MacGregor (Laideus), Duncan (16 cent.),
  6.103
MacGregor, Jas., Dean of Lismore
  (d. 1551), **6**.103, **23**.1, 3
McGregor, Pat. (Gilderoy, outlaw (mid
  17 cent.), **36**.21
MacGregor clan, **13**.1, **15**.59
Machiavelli, Niccolo (d. 1527), **33**.7
Macintosh, Lauchlane (early 16 cent.),
  36.6
Macintosh clan (Clan Chattan), **24**.41
MacIntyre, Donald, Gaelic poet (d. 1964),
  23.10
Macintyre, Duncan Ban, Gaelic poet
  (d. 1812), **23**.4
Mackay, Maj. Gen. Hugh (d. 1692), **6**.48,
  56
Mackenzie, Alex., student (early 18 cent.),
  19.5
Mackenzie, Sir Geo., Lord Tarbat, Earl of
  Cromarty (d. 1714), **25**.11
Mackenzie, Kenneth, student (early
  18 cent.), **19**.5
Mackenzie, Thos., student (early
  18 cent.), **19**.5

INDEX

Mackenzie, Wm., Earl of Seaforth (d. 1740), **25**.12
M'Kenzie of Applecross, John (mid 17 cent.), **25**.12
Mackenzie clan, **25**.12
Mackenzie of Delvine, John (d. 1722), **19**.5, **26**.21
MacKinnon, Donald, Gaelic writer (d. 1914), **23**.5
Macky, John, agent (d. 1726), **17**.14
Macky, Spring (early 18 cent.), **17**.14
MacLachlan, Ewen, Gaelic poet (d. 1822), **2**.8
McLea family, **26**.22
Maclean, Sir Allan (late 18 cent.), **25**.5
Maclean, Eachann (Hector) Bacach, Gaelic poet (18 cent.), **23**.14
Maclean of Duart family, **25**.5
Maclean poets, **23**.14
MacLeod, Mary, Gaelic poet (17 cent.), **23**.9
McLeod of Assynt, Neil (17 cent.), **24**.17
Macleod of Dunvegan, Wm. (d. 1553), **13**.1
Macleod of Lewis clan, **25**.12
Macleod of Macleod family, papers, **38**.9
MacNaughtan, Alex. (early 17 cent.), **25**.5
Macnaughtan clan, **25**.5
Macpherson, Jas., fiddler (d. 1700), **36**.16
Macpherson, Jas., poet (d. 1796), **4**.1
Macpherson clan (Clan Chattan), **24**.41
Macpherson of Cluny, Ewen (mid 18 cent.), **36**.6
Macpherson of Invereshie, Sir Aeneas (d. 1705), **24**.41
Macpherson's rant, **36**.16
Macrae (MacRa), John, min. of Dingwall (d. 1704), **25**.5
Macrae (Macra) clan, **25**.5
Macrae (MacRa) of Inverinate, Farquhar (d. 1789), **25**.5
Macro ms., **1**.10
Madrid, Scots College in, **15**.27, **37**.31
Maintenance, bands of, **13**.1*
Mair (Major), John, historian (d. 1550), **24**.10
Maitland, Chas., Lord Hatton, Earl of Lauderdale (d. 1691), **24**.15
Maitland, Jas. (16–17 cents.), **24**.44
Maitland, John, Earl & Duke of Lauderdale (d. 1682):
  letters by, **24**.15, **26**.21, 33
  letters to, **6**.27, 36
  library, **6**.21
Maitland, John, Lord, see Maitland of Thirlestane
Maitland, Thos. (d. 1572), **15**.4
Maitland of Lethington, Sir Rich., poet (d. 1586), **15**.4, **32**.7, 9, 20
Maitland of Lethington, Wm. (d. 1573), **15**.27, **24**.43, 44
Maitland of Thirlestane, Sir John, Lord (d. 1595), **15**.4, 54

Maitland Club:
  article on, **16**.6
  autographs of members, **15**.79
  history, **15**.80
  proposed publications, **15**.11
  publications, members, rules, **15**.39, 80
  reports, **15**.78, 80
Maitland folio ms., **32**.7, 20
Maitland quarto ms., **32**.9
Major, John, see Mair, John
Makculloch ms., **31**.28
Malcolm III, King (d. 1093), **6**.20
Malcolm, John, min. of Perth (d. 1634), **6**.20
Malmö, Sweden, **6**.22
Malvoisine, Wm., Bp. of St Andrews (d. 1238), **36**.24
Man, Jas., philologist (d. 1761), **36**.1
Mandeville, Sir John (John de Burgundia; John de Burdeus), traveller (d. 1372), **16**.8
Manners, **20**.1
Manrent, bands of, **6**.103, **13**.1*, **36**.6, 20
Mansfeld (Mansfield), Ernst, Count von (d. 1626), **39**.4
Manufactories, see Industry
Manufactures, Board of Trustees for, **45**.1
Maps, papers relating to, **6**.21
Mar, Earls of, see Erskine, John
March Laws, **40**.28
Marchmont, Earl of, see Hume-Campbell, Hugh
Marie Hamilton, **4**.1
Marischal, Earl, see Keith, Geo.
Maritime law, **33**.4, **40**.1, 3
Marriages:
  contract, **15**.25
  individual, **4**.2, **6**.29, **15**.25, **17**.2
  lectures on, **40**.26
  lists & registers of:
    Aberdeen, **36**.6
    Canisbay, **29**.48
    Canongate, **29**.90
    Dunfermline, **29**.44
    Durness, **29**.38
    Edinburgh, **29**.27, 35, 53
    Gretna Hall, **29**.80
    Holyrood, **29**.46
    Kilbarchan, **29**.41
    Kingarth, **7**.2
    Leith (Epis.), **29**.81
    Melrose, **29**.45
    St Andrews (Epis.), **29**.49
    Scots Brigade in Netherlands, **24**.38
    South Leith (irregular), **29**.95
    Torphichen, **29**.40
    Unst, **29**.78
Marsh, Geo. (late 18 cent.), **24**.15
Marvell, Andrew, poet (d. 1678), **4**.1
Mary, Queen (d. 1694), **15**.59
Mary, Queen of Scots (d. 1587):
  & Babington Plot, **26**.3
  execution, **8**.2
  guards, **15**.25

218

Mary, Queen of Scots (d. 1587)—*cont.*:
  imprisonment, **15**.26, 27
  inventories, **6**.114
  letters by, **15**.26, 52, 59, **24**.43
  letters & papers of reign, **15**.27, 42
  library, **15**.25
  marriage, **17**.2
  meditation, **6**.20
  narratives of life & reign, **1**.6, **15**.32
  protection by, **15**.53
  report to, **6**.6
Mary, Princess of Orange (d. 1660), **39**.4
Mary of Lorraine (Guise), Dowager Queen
    of Scots (d. 1560), **6**.6, **15**.26*, **26**.4,
    7, 10
Mary Magdalene, **1**.1
Mary of Modena, Queen (d. 1718), **17**.12
Mason, John, notary (16–17 cents.), **5**.6
Mason, Sir John (mid 16 cent.), **40**.37
Masters of work, **15**.59, **45**.5
Masterton, Chas. (early 18 cent.), **24**.15
Masterton, Francis (17–18 cents.), **24**.15
Masterton family, **24**.15
Mathematics, **6**.65, **15**.31
Maxfield, Thos., Cath. martyr (d. 1616),
    1.11
Maxwell, John, Lord Herries (d. 1677),
    1.6
Maxwell, Wm., Lord Herries (d. 1603),
    1.6
Maxwell, Wm., Lord Herries (d. 1631),
    1.6
Maxwell of Kirkconnell, Jas. (d. 1762),
    15.55
Maxwell of Pollok family, **16**.15
May, Isle of, **4**.3, **35**.1
May, Peter, surveyor (d. 1795), **27**.15
Mazzini, Giuseppe (d. 1872), **27**.16
Mearns, *see* Kincardineshire
Medicine:
  bodies for dissection, **36**.6
  physicians, **24**.44
  tracts, **6**.111
Meigle, monuments, **6**.91
Melfort, Duke of, *see* Drummond, John
Melrose, Earl of, *see* Hamilton, Thos.
Melrose, parish, **29**.45
Melrose, regality, **25**.6, 8, 13
Melrose, weavers, **25**.13
Melrose, Wm., tea merchant (d. 1863),
    27.10
Melrose Abbey, **6**.59
Melrose chronicle, **6**.52
Melvill, Elizabeth (early 17 cent.), **43**.9
Melville, Andrew, scholar (d. 1622), **6**.29,
    43.14
Melville, David (early 17 cent.), **17**.17
Melville, Geo., Earl of (d. 1707), **6**.80
Melville, Jas., Cath. writer (mid 16 cent.),
    43.11
Melville, Jas., min. of Kilrenny (d. 1614),
    6.37, **17**.17, **43**.3
Melville (Melvill), Sir Rob., Lord (d.
    1621), **15**.59

Melville, Thos., poet (early 17 cent.), **43**.3
Melville of Halhill, Sir Jas.,
    autobiographer (d. 1617), **6**.19
Melville (Mailuill, etc) of the Raith, Sir
    John (early 16 cent.), **15**.53
Memoirs of Scotish affairs (1624–51), **36**.1
Menzies, Archibald, inspector of Annexed
    Estates (mid 18 cent.), **45**.2
Mercer, John, burgh clerk of Perth (mid
    17 cent.), **15**.10
Merchants:
  accounts, **24**.28
  gilds:
    Ayr, **5**.1
    Edinburgh, **21**.21
    Old Aberdeen, **37**.21
    Stirling, **21**.31, 42
  letter book, **25**.9
  tea, **27**.10
Mercurius Caledonius (1661), **8**.1
Mercurius Politicus (1652–4), **39**.4
Merlin, **1**.12
Merton, protocols, **29**.39
Midlothian (Edinburghshire):
  collegiate churches, **6**.112
  electoral politics, **27**.11
  monuments, **44**.10
  taxation, **6**.22
Military report, Ayrshire, **5**.4
Mill, John, min. of Dunrossness (d. 1805),
    24.5
Mind, will and understanding, **1**.1, 10
Ministers, *see* Church of Scotland (*post-*
    Reformation)
Minnigaff, kirk session, **7**.11
Minnigaff, parish, list of inhabitants,
    29.50
Mitchell, Jas., fanatic (d. 1678), **24**.49
Mitchell, John, secession min. (d. 1844),
    26.33
Mitchell, Wm., min. of Edinburgh
    (d. 1727), **36**.3
Moir of Stonywood, Jas. (mid 18 cent.),
    36.3
Monasteries:
  English, **1**.5
  Scottish, **8**.1
  See also Accounts; Cartularies; Charters;
    Friars; Nuns; & *under names of
    particular houses*
Monck, Geo., Duke of Albemarle
    (d. 1670), **8**.2
Moncreiff of Carnbee (16–17 cents.),
    15.7
Monfries, Alex., biographer (late
    19 cent.), **27**.6
Monro, Alex., principal of Edinburgh
    Univ. (d. 1698), **26**.21
Montereul, Jean de, diplomat (mid
    17 cent.), **24**.29, 30
Montgomerie, Alex., poet (d. 1598), **31**.7,
    26
Montrose, parish, burials in, **43**.11
Montrose, Marquis of, *see* Graham, Jas.

Monuments:
ancient & historical, inventories, **44**.1–24
inscriptions:
churchyard:
Edinburgh, St Cuthbert's, **29**.47, 51
Girthon, **9**.4
Scottish, **11**.3
Pictland, **38**.13
W. Highland, **44**.23
sculptured:
Angus, **6**.91
Scotland, **36**.27, 35
W. Highland, **44**.23
See also Antiquities
Monymusk:
estate, **26**.39, **36**.6, **38**.14
protocols, **29**.63
Morals, poems on, **33**.12
Moray, commissariot, **29**.20
Moray, diocese:
Bagimond's Roll, **27**.2
cartulary, **6**.61
rental, **6**.61
Moray, Earl of, *see* Stewart, Jas.
Morer, Thos. (late 17 cent.), **36**.15
Morgan family, **37**.52
Morice, Jas., tutor (early 18 cent.), **19**.5
Morison, D., foreman (mid 19 cent.), **27**.14
Morison, Roderick (the Blind Harper), Gaelic poet (d. *c*. 1714), **23**.12
Morisone, John (late 17 cent.), **39**.4
Morraye, Angus, slave in Barbary (early 17 cent.), **39**.4
Mortcloth dues, Torphichen, **29**.40
Morton, earldom of, **6**.97
Morton, Earls of, *see* Douglas, Geo., Jas., & Wm.
Morvern, **27**.1
Mosman, John, notary (mid 16 cent.), **40**.3
Moulin, Pierre du, Huguenot (d. 1658), **1**.11
Moysie, David, clerk (16–17 cents.), **6**.42
Muir of Auchindrain, John (early 17 cent.), **15**.25
Mull, **27**.1, **44**.21
Munro of Foulis family, writs, **29**.71
Munster, Sebastian, cosmographer (d. 1552), **6**.20
Mure of Caldwell, Wm., baron of exchequer (d. 1776), **15**.73
Mure of Caldwell, Wm. (d. 1821), **15**.73
Mure of Caldwell family, **15**.73
Mure of Rowallan, Sir Wm., poet (d. 1657), **31**.17, **33**.4
Mure of Rowallan family, **31**.17
Murray, Elizabeth, Duchess of Lauderdale & Countess of Dysart (d. 1698), **24**.15
Murray, Jas., Earl of Dunbar (d. 1770), **17**.22
Murray, John, Earl of Annandale (d. 1640), **1**.11

Murray, John, Earl of Tullibardine (d. 1703), **14**.1
Murray, Munro (mid 17 cent.), **1**.11
Murray (Moray) of Abercairnie, Sir Rob. (late 17 cent.), **6**.88
Murray of Atholl family, correspondence, **1**.17
Murray of Broughton, John, Jacobite (d. 1777), **24**.27
Murray of Gorthy, Sir David, poet (d. 1629), **6**.2
Murray of Kilbaberton, Sir Jas., master of works (d. 1634, **15**.59
Murray of Ochtertyre, Sir Pat. (mid 18 cent.), **24**.55
Murray of Ochtertyre, Wm. (mid 18 cent.), **24**.55
Musa Latina Aberdonensis, **37**.9, 16, 38
Muscovy Company, **8**.1
Music:
hymns, **6**.44, **31**.16
organ, **24**.9
notes on, **11**.20
roundels, **17**.17
St Andrews music book, **19**.3
schools, **16**.4, **38**.10
Skene ms., **6**.62
songs:
Aberdeenshire, **2**.6
Gaelic, **23**.2, 4, 8, 9, 10, 12, 13, 15
Galloway, **28**.5
Scots, **11**.40, **16**.4
Musgrave, Sir Philip (d. 1678), **24**.44
Musselburgh, battle of, *see* Pinkie
Muster rolls:
French at Dunbar (1553), **24**.44
Gordons, **37**.40
territorials of North East, **37**.42
Muthill, **15**.59
Myll, G., translator (late 15 cent.), **6**.21, **32**.14
Myllar, Andrew, printer (early 16 cent.), **31**.28
Myln, Alex., Abbot of Cambuskenneth (d. 1548), **1**.23, **6**.1, **14**.1, **25**.10
Mylne, Rob., writer (late 17 cent.), **1**.11
Mysteries, *see* Plays
Mystery of the good old cause (1660), **4**.2
Mystics, of the North East (18 cent.), **38**.5

Napier of Merchiston, John, mathematician (d. 1617), **6**.65
Needlework, **38**.10
Neilston, parish history, **16**.14
Netherlands:
journeys to, **15**.60, **26**.50
Scots Brigade in, **24**.32, 35, 38
Newbattle Abbey, **6**.92
Newburgh, Fife, **1**.11
Newcastle, Duke of, *see* Pelham-Holles, Thos.
Newcastle, Earl of, *see* Cavendish, Wm.
New England, **4**.3, **8**.1

Newes from Scotland, **17**.1
Newhaven, **11**.14
New Mills, cloth manufactory, **24**.46
Newport, Capt. Chris. (d. 1617), **4**.2
New Spalding Club:
  history, **38**.10
  members, **37**.45
  reports, **37**.46
  rules, **37**.45
Newspapers, **15**.53
New Testament, in Scots, **31**.21
Niccols, Rich., poet (d. 1616), **12**.3
Nicoll, John, diarist (mid 17 cent.), **6**.55
Nicolson, Wm., Bp. of Carlisle (d. 1727), **24**.15
Nimmo, Jas., covenanter (d. 1709), **24**.6
Nisbet, Jas. (late 17 cent.), **43**.9
Nisbet, John, in Hardhill (d. 1685), **43**.9
Nisbet, Murdoch, translator (early 16 cent.), **31**.21
Nithsdale, coal mining in, **9**.3
Nobility:
  English, **17**.14
  Scottish:
    character, **17**.14
    declaration by, **15**.59
    lists, **11**.6
    precedency, **15**.26
    state, **6**.20
Noltland Castle, **38**.19
Norsemen, **13**.1*
North Berwick:
  priory, **6**.87
  protocols, **6**.87
North British Railway, **27**.14
Norway, **6**.22
Notaries public:
  records, **40**.1
  Rob. Wedderburn, **33**.4
  See also Protocols, protocol books
Nottingham, **6**.21
Nova Scotia, **6**.117, **11**.34
Novels, **3**.1, 5, 7, 14
Nuns:
  North Berwick, **6**.87
  Sciennes, **1**.21

Obits (obituaries):
  by Rob. Boyd, **6**.20
  of Erskines of Dun, **36**.20
  of Franciscan friary, Aberdeen, **36**.3
  of St Anthony's, Leith, **6**.21, **11**.14
Ochterlony of Guynd, John (late 17 cent.), **39**.3
Ochtertyre House, **24**.55
Octavian, **4**.1
Officers of state, **11**.26, **15**.59, **17**.14
Officials, courts of:
  general, **40**.36
  records, **40**.1
  St Andrews & Lothian, **1**.25, **40**.36
Ogilvie, Geo., min. of Kirriemuir (d. 1771), **22**.4

Ogilvie, John, Cath. martyr (d. 1615), **15**.27
Ogilvie of Barras, Sir Geo. (d. 1679), **6**.33
Ogilvy, Jas., Earl of Findlater & Seafield (d. 1730), **25**.3, 11
Ogilvy, Jas., Earl of Findlater & Seafield (d. 1770). **27**.15
Ogilvy, Jas., Lord Deskford, Earl of Findlater & Seafield (d. 1764), **38**.5
Ogilvy, Jas., commendator of Dryburgh (early 16 cent.), **36**.6
Ogilvy of Airlie family, papers, **36**.20, 24
Ogilvy of Boyne, Alex. (mid 16 cent.), **15**.25
Ogilvy of Powrie, John (late 16 cent.), **24**.15
Ogilvy of Stratherne, John (early 16 cent.), **36**.6
Old Aberdeen, burgh:
  cathedral:
    description, **37**.37
    effigies, **38**.11
    epistolary, **2**.4
    heraldic ceiling, **37**.3
    roof, **38**.6
  description, **36**.5, **37**.37
  Gordon's Mill Farming Club, **2**.10
  King's College, *see* Aberdeen, Univ.
  music school, **38**.10
  records:
    accounts, **37**.21
    council & court, **37**.21
    list of inhabitants, **37**.21
    miscellaneous, **37**.37
Old Aberdeen (Old Machar), kirk session, **37**.37
Old extent, memorial on, **40**.11
Old Machar, *see* Old Aberdeen, kirk session
Oliphant, Carolina, Lady Nairne, poetess (d. 1845), **11**.40
Oliphant, Caroline, poetess (d. 1831), **11**.40
Oliphant, Margaret, novelist (d. 1897), **3**.15
Oliphant of Gask family, history, **11**.2
Organ, musical, **24**.9
Oriental mss., **38**.20
Orkney, commissariot, **29**.21, **30**.6
Orkney, diocese, **6**.22
Orkney, earldom & shire:
  complaints, **1**.31
  courts, **15**.53, **27**.4
  Danish claim to, **40**.37
  law, **40**.37
  oppressions, **1**.31
  papers, **36**.24, **42**.1, 3
  parishes, **15**.53
  sasines, **42**.3
  sheriff court, **1**.11, **15**.53, **27**.4
  sovereignty, **40**.37
  witchcraft, **1**.11
Orkney, Earls of, *see* Sinclair, Wm.
Orkneyinga saga, **25**.7
Orléans, Jean d', Earl of Angoulême (mid 15 cent.), **1**.3

Orléans, Scots nation in Univ. of, **24.44**
Ormond, Duke of, *see* Butler, Jas.
Oronsay, **44.23**
Orrok of that Ilk, Rob. (early 16 cent.), **15.53**
Otuel, **1.4**
Overbury, Sir Thos., poet (d. 1613), **12.3**

Painters:
 dictionary, **30.7**
 Valentine Jenkin, **15.59**
 Sir Godfrey Kneller, **6.22**
 Jacob de Wet (Witte), **6.22, 24.9**
Paintings:
 belonging to Mary Queen of Scots, **6.114**
 of Earl of Lothian, **6.125**
 of Scots kings, **6.22**
Paisley Abbey, **15.17, 16.2**
Paisley, burgh, **21.20, 35**
Paisley Union Bank robbery, **40.28**
Pali tablets, **14.1**
Panmure House, **36.24**
Panmure mss., **6.22*, 72**
Papacy:
 negotiations with, **24.37**
 relations with, **25.19**
 Scottish letters by, **27.12, 13**
 Scottish supplications to, **26.23, 48, 27.7**
Parfre, Jhan (early 16 cent.), **1.1**
Paris:
 papers relating to Scot., **1.14**
 Scots College in, **1.6, 15.27**
Parishes:
 antiquities, **6.100**
 clergy, **30.3**
 histories:
  Eastwood, **16.11**
  of Formartine, **37.51**
  Kilbarchan, **16.12**
  Kilmacolm, **16.10**
  Kirriemuir, **22.4**
  Neilston, **16.14**
 Medieval, **29.93**
 ministers, *see* Church of Scotland (*post-Reformation*)
 origins, **6.100**
 Orkney & Shetland, **15.53**
 plantation of kirks, **15.35**
 registers, *see* Baptisms; Burials; & Marriages
 See also Kirk sessions
Parliament of England, **4.1, 2*, 8.1*, 2**
Parliament of Great Britain:
 elections to, **27.2, 11**
 & Porteous Riot, **15.53**
Parliament of Scotland:
 acts:
  burghs, **21.25**
  Edinburgh, **21.3**
  Forfeited Estates, **24.57**
  misc., **6.88, 37.21**
  schools, **15.53**
 commissioners to, **15.25, 37.43**

Parliament of Scotland—*cont.*:
 order in, **15.59***
 Parliament House, **40.22**
 petition to, **39.3**
 proceedings in:
  (1689–90), **26.46, 47**
  (1700–7), **6.30**
 riding, **15.59**
Passionate remonstrance made by his holiness (1641), **4.2**
Paterson, Andrew, lawyer (early 19 cent.), **27.2**
Peebles, burgh, **21,10, 24**
Peebles, commissariot, **29.12**
Peeblesshire, **44.17**
Pelham-Holles, Thos., Duke of Newcastle (d. 1768), **17.16, 37.25**
Penni worth of witte, **1.29**
Penninghame, kirk session, **7.3, 4**
Pensions, **15.59**
Percy, Thos., Bp. of Dromore (d. 1811), **4.2**
Perpetuities, in Scots law, **40.33**
Perth, burgh:
 chronicle, **15.10**
 Jacobite army in, **39.4**
 & St Andrews Univ., **14.1**
Perth, Earl of, *see* Drummond, John
Perth, kirk session, **15.10, 39.4***
Perth, Literary & Antiquarian Society, museum, **14.1**
Perth, sheriff court, **15.10**
Perth, synod, **36.24**
Perthshire, protocols, **29.37**
Peter the Great, Czar of Russia (d. 1725), **24.44**
Petrie, Adam, writer (mid 17 cent.), **20.1**
Philip of Almerieclose, Jas., poet (17–18 cents.), **24.3**
Philotus, **6.53, 33.4**
Pictland, inscriptions, **38.13**
Pinkie (or Musselburgh), battle of, **6.11**
Pitcairne, Arch., physician & poet (d. 1713), **15.6**
Pitfirrane writs, **29.67**
Pitsligo, Lord, *see* Forbes, Alex.
Pittodrie, **36.6**
Place names:
 Aberdeenshire, **38.18**
 W. Aberdeenshire, **37.22**
Plans, lists of, **45 note**
Plantation of kirks, **15.35**
Playfair family, **11.25, 28, 35**
Playing cards, **4.5, 8.2**
Plays:
 by Sir Wm. Alexander, **32.11**
 French, **4.2**
 mysteries, English, **1.1, 10**
 pageant of Coventry weavers, **1.2**
 Philotus, **6.53, 33.4**
 Satyre of the thrie estaitis, **33.2, 8**
Plundering, in Cromar, **36.16**
Pluscarden Priory, **11.12, 36.6**

Poems, verses:
  alliterative, **6**.47, **31**.13
  ancient English, **1**.29
  by:
    Sir Wm. Alexander, Earl of Stirling,
      32.11, 24
    Alex. Arbuthnot, **32**.9
    Jas. Auchinleck, **6**.21, **19**.2, **33**.4
    Sir Rob. Ayton, **6**.20, **11**.38, **34**.1
    Geo. Bannatyne, **6**.5, 38, **12**.1, **32**.22,
      23, 26, **33**.5
    John Barbour, **31**.14, **34**.12, 13, **36**.28
    Lord Byron, **17**.20
    Thos. Coombe, **4**.4
    Alex. Craig of Rose-Craig, **12**.2
    John Davidson, **3**.2, 3
    Gavin Douglas, **4**.3, **6**.18, 67, **32**.7,
      33.26, 28, 29, 31, **34**.3
    Wm. Drummond of Hawthornden,
      3.6, **15**.18, **32**.3, 4
    Wm. Dunbar, **31**.2, **32**.7
    John Edmestoun, **1**.11
    Rob. Fergusson, **3**.4, **33**.22, 25
    Wm. Fowler, **32**.6
    Alex. Garden, **1**.26, **12**.5
    Simion Grahame, **6**.39
    Lady Anne Hamilton, **4**.2
    Pat. Hannay, **12**.4
    Blind Hary, **31**.5, 13, **33**.13, **34**.4, 5
    Rob. Henryson, **6**.7, **15**.15, **31**.25,
      32.7
    Sir Rich. Holland, **6**.3, **16**.6
    John Hoskins, **1**.11
    Thos. Hudson, **33**.15
    Alex. Hume, **31**.23
    John Irland, **32**.19, **34**.2
    James I, **11**.39, **19**.2, **31**.1, **32**.1
    James VI, **1**.11, **33**.23, 27
    Arthur Johnston, **37**.9, 16
    Geo. Lauder, **6**.121
    John Lauderdale, **28**.6
    John Leslie, Bp. of Ross, **6**.20
    Sir David Lindsay, **33**.1, 2, 6, 8
    Wm. Lithgow, **14**.1
    Thos. Lodge, **12**.7
    John Lyon of Auldbar, **6**.4
    John MacCodrum, **23**.2
    John (Iain Lom) MacDonald, **23**.8
    Julia (Sileas) MacDonald, **23**.13
    Donald MacIntyre, **23**.10
    Duncan Ban Macintyre, **23**.4
    Ewen MacLachlan, **2**.8
    Hector Maclean, **23**.14
    Maclean poets, **23**.14
    Mary Macleod, **23**.9
    Sir John Maitland, **15**.4
    Sir Rich. Maitland, **15**.4. **32**.7, 9
    Thos. Maitland, **15**.4
    Alex. Montgomerie, **31**.7, 26
    Roderick Morison, **23**.12
    Sir Wm. Mure of Rowallan, **31**.17,
      33.4
    Sir David Murray of Gorthy, **6**.2
    Rich. Niccols, **12**.3

Poems, verses: by—*cont*.:
    Jas. Philip of Almerieclose, **24**.3
    Arch. Pitcairne, **15**.6
    Allan Ramsay, **3**.4, **33**.20, 21, 30,
      34.6–8
    John Rolland, **6**.60, **31**.3, **33**.3
    Alex. Ross, **33**.9
    Sam. Rowlands, **12**.6, 8
    John Scot, **24**.38
    Walter Scot of Satchells, **20**.2
    Alex. Scott, **31**.15
    John Stewart of Baldynneis, **32**.5
    Geo. Whetston, **4**.4
    Andrew of Wyntoun, **31**.24
  dating from:
    15 cent., **15**.43
    15–16 cents., **31**.28
  devotional, **33**.24
  from:
    Asloan ms., **32**.14, 16
    Bannatyne ms., **6**.5, 38, **12**.1, **32**.22,
      23, 26, **33**.5
    Book of Dean of Lismore, **23**.1, 3
    Maitland mss., **32**.7, 9, 20
    Jas. Watson collection, **34**.10
  Gaelic poems, *see under* Gaelic
  Galloway, **28**.5
  Makgregouris testament, **6**.103
  Musa Latina Aberdonensis, **37**.9, 16, 38
  on:
    Sir Wm. Alexander, Earl of Stirling,
      1.11
    Rob. Burns, **11**.23
    '45 rising, **23**.15
    Duke of Grafton, **4**.2
    General Assembly, **15**.6
    James V, **6**.21
    James VI, **14**.1
    morals, **33**.12
    Reformation, **31**.11
    Rob. Rollock, **6**.17
    Earl of Roxburgh, **6**.20
    St Katherine, **1**.20
    saints, **1**.20, **31**.9
  Ossianic, **4**.1
  political squibs (17 cent.), **4**.2
  prophecies, **6**.47
  Ratis raving, **33**.12
  Rymour Club, **18**.1–3
  Thre prestis of Peblis, **32**.8
  See also Ballads; Music: Songs; Plays;
    Psalms; Romances; & Satires
Pococke, Rich. Bp. of Meath & Ossory
  (d. 1765), **24**.1, **41**.1
Poland:
  invaded (1563), **4**.2
  Scots in, **24**.59
Poll tax, *see* Taxation
Pollokshaws, burgh history, **16**.15
Pont, Rob., min. of St Cuthbert's,
  Edinburgh (d. 1606), **15**.33, **27**.21,
  43.11
Pont, Timothy, topographer (d. *c*. 1614),
  15.76, **24**.52

Poor relief:
  Minnigaff, **7**.11
  Old Aberdeen, **37**.37
  Penninghame, **7**.3, 4
  Wigtown, **7**.5
Population statistics, **26**.44
Port Glasgow, **21**.20
Porteous Riot, **15**.53
Portland, Earl of, *see* Bentinck, Hans W.
Portpatrick:
  censuses, **30**.8
  ships, **28**.1
Powis papers, **38**.17
Practicks, **40**.1, 4, 5, 23, 24
Prayers:
  John Davidson, **43**.11
  Rob. Forbes, **22**.2
  James VII & II, **17**.12
  St Anthony's, Leith, **11**.14
Presbyteries:
  Aberdeen, **36**.15, 16
  Alford, **37**.18
  Banff, **37**.10
  Cupar, **1**.7
  Dingwall, **24**.24
  Edinburgh, **43**.11*
  Elgin, **37**.36
  Glasgow, **15**.25, 26
  Haddington, **6**.22, **43**.11*
  Inverness, **24**.24
  Lanark, **1**.16
  Rothesay, **7**.7
  St Andrews, **1**.7
  Strathbogie, **36**.7
  Stirling, **27**.17
Present state of Europe (1715), **8**.1*
Presentation in the temple, **1**.2
Prestonpans, battle of, **26**.50
Prestwick, burgh, **15**.28
Prince Charles, ship, **17**.22
Pringle, Magdalen (mid 18 cent.), **17**.22
Pringle of Greenknow, Walter (mid
    17 cent.), **43**.9
Printers:
  censorship, **15**.53
  in Edinburgh, **6**.21
  in Glasgow, **15**.14
  individual:
    Jas. Anderson, **39**.3
    Jas. Bryson, **39**.3
    Rob. Bryson, **39**.3
    Agnes Campbell, **39**.3
    Hen. Charteris, **6**.17, 22, **33**.1, **43**.8
    Rob. Charteris, **6**.53
    Walter Chepman, **31**.28
    John Forbes, **16**.4
    Andrew & Rob. Foulis, **15**.14
    Andrew Hart, **15**.15
    Andrew Myllar, **31**.28
    Rob. Saunders, **39**.3
    Rob. Waldegrave, **6**.47, **31**.23
    Rob. Young, **39**.3
  of early newspapers, **15**.53
Privateering, **1**.11

Privy Council of England, **6**.20
Privy Council of Scotland:
  Catholics, **15**.59
  Glasgow Univ., **15**.59
  Highlands, **15**.59
  letters to, **15**.25, **39**.4
  misc. acts, **36**.6, 16, **37**.28, **43**.11
  parliament, **15**.59*
  proceedings (1700–7), **6**.30
  proclamation, **15**.25
  records, **40**.1
  schools, **15**.53
  See also Council & Session, Lords of
Privy seal, register of, **45**.4
Prize of wisdom, **4**.4
Proper lessons for the Tories (1716), **4**.2
Prophecies, **6**.47
Protectorate, papers concerning, **24**.31
Protocols, protocol books:
  by:
    Rob. Broun, **5**.7–9
    Mark Carruthers, **29**.86
    Sir Wm. Corbet, **29**.39
    Sir John Cristisone, **29**.63
    John Foular, **29**.64, 72, 75, **30**.10
    Jas. Foulis, **29**.57
    Sir Alex. Gaw, **29**.37
    Mr Gilbert Grote, **29**.43
    Thos. Johnsoun, **29**.52
    Rob. Lauder, **6**.87
    John Mason, **5**.6
    John Mosman, **40**.3
    Sir Rob. Rollock, **29**.65
    Gavin Ros, **29**.29
    Cuthbert Simon, **11**.8
    Nicol Thounis, **29**.57
    Jas. Young, **29**.74
  relating to:
    Abernethy, **29**.37
    Aberdeen, **29**.63
    Aberdeenshire, **29**.63
    Ayr, **5**.6–9, **29**.29
    Ayrshire, **5**.6–9, **11**.8, **29**.29
    Berwickshire, **6**.87, **29**.39
    Canongate, **29**.74
    Dumfries, **29**.86
    Dumfriesshire, **29**.86
    Edinburgh, **29**.43, 64, 72, 74, 75,
      30.10, **40**.3
    Fife, **29**.37
    Glasgow, diocese, **11**.8
    Irvine, **11**.8
    Kincardineshire, **29**.63
    Lanarkshire, **29**.29
    Linlithgow, **29**.52, 57
    Linton, **29**.39
    Merton, **29**.39
    Monymusk, **29**.63
    North Berwick, **6**.87
    Perth, **29**.65
    Perthshire, **29**.65
    Roxburghshire, **29**.37, 39
    Stirling, **21**.30, 31
Proverbs, **32**.15, **34**.7

Provincial councils, *see* Church of
Scotland: *pre*-Reformation; & Synods
Psalms:
Earl of Ancram, **6**.125
James VI, **6**.20. **33**.27
in metre (1565), **6**.115
Murray of Gorthy, **6**.2
Purvey, John, translator (d. *c.* 1428),
31.21

Quakers, **4**.3, **36**.42
Quair of jelousy, **6**.21, **19**.2, **33**.4
Quoniam attachiamenta, **40**.11, 12

Radicals, **27**.16
Ragman Rolls, **6**.50
Railway, North British, **27**.14
Ramsay, Allan, poet (d. 1758), **3**.4, **33**.20,
21, 30, **34**.6–8
Ramsay, Edward B., Dean of Edinburgh
(d. 1872), **11**.41
Ramsay of Abbotshall, Sir Andrew (mid
17 cent.), **6**.36
Ramsay of Ochtertyre, John (d. 1814),
27.3
Rangoon, **14**.1
Ratis raving, **33**.12
Ratisbon, Scots College at, **37**.31
Reade, Thos., secretary (d. 1669), **24**.44
Readers, **15**.5, **43**.11
Reever's penance, **6**.121
Regalia, *see* Honours
Regality, courts of:
Broughton, **7**.9
Huntly, **15**.26
Melrose, **25**.6, 8, 13
Spynie, **36**.6
Regiam majestatem, **37**.1, **40**.1, 12
Registers (of charters, *see* Cartularies
Reid, Rob., Abbot of Kinloss (d. 1558),
35.2
Reid, Thos., philosopher (d. 1796), **2**.7
Relics, **15**.13
Rembrun, **1**.18
Remonstrance of the state of the kingdom
(1641), **8**.1
Renfrew, burgh, **21**.20
Renfrewshire:
election, **27**.2
descriptions, **15**.12
farm papers, **26**.43
freeholders, **24**.2
history, **16**.13
Rentals (rental books):
burgh:
Canongate, **29**.85
Dumfries, **9**.4
Glasgow, **21**.16
Rothesay, **7**.7
Stirling, **21**.30
ecclesiastical:
Aberdeen, St Nicholas, **37**.2, 7

Rentals (rental books): ecclesiastical—
cont.:
Arbroath, **6**,89
Brechin, **6**.105
Coupar Angus, **11**.17
Dunfermline, **6**.77
Dryburgh, **6**.86
Glasgow, **11**.8
Inchaffray, **6**.88
Inchcolm, **26**.32
Kinloss, **35**.2
Leith, St Anthony's, **6**.21, **11**.14
Moray, **6**.61
Newbattle, **6**.92
Paisley, **16**.2
Torphichen, **27**.19
secular:
Breadalbane, **6**.103
Cassillis, **9**.4
Craigends, **24**.2
Huntly (Strathbogie), **36**.20
Melrose, **25**.13
Strathavon, **38**.22
Urie, **24**.12
See also Accounts & Valuations
Restalrig, **29**.32
Revolution (1688–90), **6**.74, **26**.46, 47
Rich, Barnaby, writer (d. 1617), **6**.53
Rich, Rob., Earl of Warwick (d. 1658),
1.11
Richard III, King of England (d. 1485),
6.21
Richardinus, Rob. (early 16 cent.), **26**.26
Richmond, Viriginia, **8**.1
Ridpath, Geo., journalist (d. 1726), **1**.11
Ridpath, Geo., min. of Stitchel (d. 1772),
26.2
Roads, **38**.6, 10
Robert I, King (d. 1329), *see Bruce, The*
Robert of Dunhelm (Durham), monk of
Kelso (13 cent.), **6**.20
Robert Oig, **4**.1
Robertson, Geo., (16–17 cents.), **6**.17
Robes, of nobles, officials, etc., **15**.25
Robinson, Wm. (d. 1659), **4**.3
Robinson, Jas., tobacco factor (late
18 cent.), **27**.20
Robinson, Samuel, stonemason (d. 1875),
28.7
Rob Stene's dream, **15**.54
Roehenstart, Count, *see* Stewart, Chas.
Edward
Rogers, Chas., charlatan, & founder of
Royal Historical Society (d. 1890),
11.10, 41
Roger family, **11**.25, 28, 35
Rolland, John, in Dalkeith, poet (mid
16 cent.), **6**.60, **31**.3, **33**.3
Rollock, Sir Rob., notary (early 16 cent.),
29.65
Rollock, Rob., principal of Edinburgh
Univ. (d. 1599), **6**.17, **43**.8
Romances:
Anglo-Norman, **1**.19

Romances—*cont.*:
English, **1**.4, 12, 18, 28, **4**.1, **6**.64, 83, **15**.45
French, **6**.71, 83, **32**.12
Scots, **6**.49, 64, 83, **15**.9, 49, **31**.6, **32**.2, 12, 17
Roman de la manekine, **6**.71
Rome:
English traveller in (1721), **8**.1, **39**.3
Jacobite court, **26**.31
Scots College, **37**.31
See also Papacy
Ros, Gavin, notary (early 16 cent.), **29**.29
Rose, Alex. (early 18 cent.), **24**.15
Rose, Hew, min. of Nairn (d. 1686), **36**.18
Rose of Kilravock family, **36**.18
Ross, Alex., schoolmaster (d. 1784), **33**.9
Ross of Arnage, John, provost of Aberdeen (early 18 cent.), **36**.3
Ross, diocese, **6**.100
Rothesay, burgh, **7**.6, 7, **21**.20
Rothesay, kirk session, **7**.1
Rothesay, pres., **7**.7
Rothiemay, kirk session, **36**.1
Rouland and Vernagu, **1**.4
Roundheads, **6**.104, **8**.2
Routes, Kirkwall to Edinburgh, **15**.53
See also Journeys
Row, John, min. of Carnock (d. 1646), **15**.57, **43**.4
Row, John, principal of King's Coll., Aberdeen (d. 1672), **15**.57, **43**.4
Row, Wm., min. of Ceres (d. 1698), **15**.57, **43**.4, 13
Rowlands, Samuel, writer (d. 1630?), **12**.6, 8, 9
Roxburghshire:
Bagimond's Roll, **26**.21
families, **20**.2
monuments, **44**.14
protocols, **29**.39
services of heirs, **29**.69
Roy, David, cook (early 17 cent.), **15**.10
Royalists, executions of, **39**.3*
Russell, John, Scots lawyer? (d. 1613?), **27**.21
Russell, Wm., Lord (d. 1683), **8**.1
Russia:
Gen. Pat. Gordon in, **36**.31
Dr Rob. Erskine in, **24**.44
invades Poland (1563), **4**.2
Rutherford, Samuel, divine (d. 1661), **43**.9
Rutherglen, burgh, **21**.20
Ruthven, Jas., Master & Earl of Gowrie (d. 1588), **14**.1
Ruthven, John, Earl of Gowrie (d. 1600), **6**.20
Ruthven, Pat., Earl of Forth & Brentford (d. 1651), **17**.6
Ruthven, Wm., Earl of Gowrie (d. 1584), **6**.20
Ruthven correspondence, **17**.6
Rymour Club, history, **18**.3

Sadoleto, Cardinal, **6**.20
Sagas, **13**.1*, **25**.7
Sage, John, Epis. bp. (d. 1711), **39**.2
St Andrews, archdiocese:
accounts, **25**.4
official's court, **1**.25, **40**.36
St Andrews, burgh:
Epis. congregation in, **29**.49
plan, **6**.22
St Andrews, commissariot, **29**.8
St Andrews, kirk session, **6**.20, **15**.59, **24**.4
St Andrews, pres., **1**.7
St Andrews, Univ.:
colleges:
St Leonard's, bursars' diet, **19**.5
St Salvator's, books, jewels, etc., **15**.59
faculties, acts & statutes of:
arts, **19**.1, 7, **26**.54, 55
theology, **19**.1
graduation & matriculation rolls, **26**.8
library, **15**.26
move to Perth proposed, **14**.1
reform, **6**.21
students, **19**.5
St Andrews Priory, **6**.72, **19**.4
St Angustine, commentary on rule of, **26**.26
St Bartholomew's, massacre, **8**.3
St Columba, **6**.106
St Cuthbert's ducks, Farne Island, **36**.20
St Fillan, staff of, **36**.16
St Katherine of Alexandria, legend, **1**.20
St Katherine of Sienna, nunnery, *see* Sciennes
St Kentigern (Mungo), office of, **15**.69
St Wynnyn, life & office of, **5**.1
Saints, legends of the **31**.9
Salignac de la Mothe Fénelon, Bertrand de, French ambassador in Eng. & Scot. (d. 1599), **6**.20, 70
Salton, parish library, **6**.22
Sanday, kirk session, **1**.11
Sanderson, Sir Wm., historian (d. 1676), **4**.4
Sandilands, Jas., Lord Torphichen (Lord St John), (d. 1579), **39**.4
Sanquhar, barony, **1**.11
Sanquhar, Lord, *see* Crichton, Rob.
Sasines:
indexes to registers of, **45** note
Orkney, **42**.3
Shetland, **42**.2
Satires, concerning:
Jas. Boswell, **4**.4
Commonwealth, **4**.5, **8**.2
three estates, **33**.2
Bp. Jas. Kennedy, **6**.3
misc., **4**.4
Reformarion, **31**.11
Restoration, Parl. (Eng.), **4**.1
Scotland, **1**.11
Lord Thirlestane, **15**.54

Satire, concerning—*cont.*:
  Walpole, **4**.3
Saunders, Rob., printer (d. 1694), **39**.3
Savile, Sir Henry, classical scholar (d. 1622), **27**.21
Scalacronica, **15**.41
Schaw, Capt. & Ensign (early 18 cent.), **17**.3
Schaw, Sir John (early 18 cent.), **17**.3
Schools:
  Aberdeen, **36**.24
  acts relating to, **15**.53
  commissioners for visiting, **27**.2
  music, *see* Music: schools
Schoolmasters:
  acts relating to, **15**.53
  Rothesay, **7**.1
  teaching Latin, **27**.2
Sciennes Nunnery, **1**.21
Scone Abbey, **6**.81, **26**.43
Scot, John, soldier & poet (early 18 cent.), **24**.38
Scot, Wm., min. of Cupar (d. 1642), **43**.10
Scot of Satchells, Capt. Walter (late 17 cent.), **20**.2
Scot of Scotstarvet, Sir John (d. 1670), **11**.26, **24**.52
Scotichronicon, **16**.8
Scotland:
  descriptions, *see* Topographical descriptions
  discourse on, **6**.6, **40**.37
  etchings, **6**.9, 101
  government:
    covenanters, **27**.18
    discourse on, **24**.52
    military (1650s), **24**.18, 31
  life & manners, **11**.1
  maps, **6**.21
  records, **40**.28
  social life, **11**.21
  state of, **6**.21, **17**.8, **26**.50, **27**.2
  tours, **24**.1
Scots:
  kings of, lists & portraits, **6**.22*
  origins, **6**.22, **32**.14
Scots Colleges abroad:
  Douai, **24**.44, **37**.31
  Madrid, **15**.27, **37**.31
  Paris, **1**.6, **15**.27
  Ratisbon, **37**.31
  Rome, **37**.31
  Valladolid, **37**.31
Scots commissioners in London (1644–6), **17**.18
Scots dictionary, **16**.5
Scots law:
  brieves, **10**.2, **40**.11, 37
  courts, **6**.6
  See also under particular courts
  formularies, **40**.8, 10, 11
  general, **32**.10, 13, 18, **40** *passim*
  history, **40**.22
  maritime, **33**.4, **40**.1, 3

Scots law—*cont.*:
  sources & literature, **40**.1, 2
Scott, Alex., poet (mid 16 cent.), **31**.15
Scott, Sir Walter (d. 1832), **3**.10, **6**.38, 63, **11**.13
Scott of Balwery, Wm. (early 16 cent.), **15**.53
Scott (Scot) family, **11**.13, **20**.2
Scottish History Society, history, **26**.29, **27**.4
Scottish Record Office, indexes & lists, **45** note
Scottish soldiers:
  under Gustavus Adolphus (officers), **39**.4
  under Count Mansfeld, **39**.4
  shipped from Campbeltown, **25**.5
  See also Muster rolls
Scottish Text Society, history, **33**.4
Scrymgeour family, **29**.42
Sculpture, medieval, **44**.24
Seafield, Earls of, *see* Ogilvy, Jas.
Seafield correspondence, **25**.3
Seaforth, Earl of, *see* Mackenzie, Wm.
Seal impressions, **6**.94
Seals of cause, **29**.85
Secundus, Johannes (1511–36), **4**.2
Seditious preachers, ungodly teachers (1709), **8**.3
Selkirk, burgh, **29**.89
Selkirkshire:
  families, **20**.2
  monuments, **44**.15
  statistics, **28**.3
Semple, Col. Wm. (d. 1633), **15**.27
Sermons:
  burlesque (English), **1**.11
  funeral of Bp. Pat Forbes, **39**.5
  by:
    Rich. Bancroft, **43**.11
    Rob. Bruce, **43**.6
    Rob. Forbes, **22**.2
    Jas. Gordon, **22**.1
    Wm. Guthrie, **43**.9
    Arch. Simsone, **43**.9
    John Spottiswoode, **39**.3
Services of heirs:
  Aberdeenshire, **37**.27
  Roxburghshire, **29**.69
Session, Court of:
  case before, **40**.28
  early records, **40**.1
  events connected with (1668–76), **24**.36
  history, **40**.22
  presidents, **40**.22
  See also Council & Session, lords of
Seton, Alex., Earl of Dunfermline (d. 1622), **6**.4
Seton, Alex., Lord Kingston (d. 1691), **6**.34
Seton, Alex., friar (early 16 cent.), **6**.34
Seton (Seytoun) family, **6**.34
Setts, burgh:
  Inverness, **21**.55

Setts, burgh—*cont.*:
　royal burghs, 21.13
Seven sages, 6.60
Several declarations (1688), 8.2
Sharp, Jas., Archbp. of St Andrews
　(d. 1679), 15.53, 24.15, 49
Shaw, Lachlan, min. of Elgin, antiquarian
　(d. 1777), 25.5, 36.18
Shawfield Riots, 1.11
Shelley, Percy B., poet (d. 1822), 4.2
Sheridan, Gen. Philip H. (d. 1888), 8.1
Sheriff courts:
　history, 26.12, 40.22
　records, 40.1
　shires of:
　　Aberdeen, 37.29, 32, 33
　　Banff, 36.16
　　Fife, 26.12
　　Kirkcudbright, 7.12–14
　　Orkney, 1.11, 15.53, 27.4
　　Perth, 15.10
　　Shetland, 15.53, 27.4, 29.84
Sheriffmuir, battle of, 39.4
Sheriffs:
　Banffshire, 37.43
　history, 26.12
Shetland, commissariot, 29.21
Shetland, county:
　courts, 15.53
　Danish claim to, 40.37
　justice court, 29.84
　law, 40.37
　monuments, 44.12
　oppressions, 1.31
　papers, 24.5, 36.24, 42.1, 2
　parishes, 15.53
　sasines, 42.2
　sheriff court, 15.53, 27.4, 29.84
　sovereignty, 40.37
Ships:
　Darien venture, 26.6
　dispute over, Dundee, 27.2
　lists, 21.20, 24.28, 27.10, 28.1
　Spanish, 1.11
Shirley, John, transcriber (d. 1456), 15.43
Short stories, 3.8, 12, 15
Sibbald, Sir Rob., physician (d. 1722),
　6.22
Simon, Cuthbert, notary (15–16 cents.),
　11.8
Simsone, Arch., min. of Dalkeith
　(d. 1628), 43.9*
Simsone, Pat., min. of Stirling (d. 1618),
　43.9*
Sinclair, Agnes, Countess of Bothwell
　(d. c. 1574), 6.22
Sinclair, John, Master of (d. 1750), 1.30,
　17.3, 39.4
Sinclair, Mathew (d. 1611), 39.3
Sinclair (St Clair), Wm., Earl of Orkney
　(d. 1479–80), 6.22*
Sinclair, earls of Orkney, genealogy, 6.22
Sinclair of Roslin, Sir Wm. (mid 16 cent.),
　1.23

Sinclair of Swynbrocht, Sir David (early
　16 cent.), 6.22
Sir Beves of Hamtoun, 15.45
Sire Degarre, 1.28
Sir Gawain (Gawayne), 6.64
Sir Guy of Warwick, 1.18
Sir Tristrem, 31.6
Skene, barony, 36.24
Skene, Sir John, lawyer (d. 1617), 37.1,
　40.12, 28
Skene family, 37.47
Skene ms., 6.62
Skene of Belhelvie family, 37.1
Skene of Hallyards, John (early 17 cent.),
　6.62
Skene of Skene, Geo. (d. 1756), 38.10
Skene of Skene family, 37.1
Skeyne (Skene), Gilbert, physician
　(d. 1599), 6.111
Stene, Rob (late 16 cent.), 15.54
Slezer, Capt. John (d. 1714), 6.21
Skye, monuments, 44.9
Smith, John, secretary of Maitland Club
　(mid 19 cent.), 15.79, 80
Smyth, John, monk of Kinloss (d. 1557),
　chronicle of, 35.2
Snell, John (d. 1679), 40.37
Sommers, Sir Geo. (early 17 cent.), 4.2
Songs, *see* Music
Sophia, Electress of Hanover (d. 1714),
　17.14, 37.53
South Leith:
　marriages, 29.95
　writs, 11.14
Soutar of Russlo, Thos. (mid 18 cent.),
　40.37
Soutra, hospital, 6.112
Sovereignty, of Orkney & Shetland, 40.37
Spain:
　Scots Coll., 15.27, 37.31
　expedition to Scot. proposed, 24.19
　relations with Scot., 6.123
　ships of, 1.11
Spalding, John, historian (mid 17 cent.),
　6.28, 36.21, 23
Spalding Club:
　history, 38.10
　members, publications, reports, 36.38
Spectakle of luf, 6.21, 32.14
Spelman, Sir Henry, lawyer (d. 1641),
　27.21
Spottiswoode, Sir Hen., poet (mid
　17 cent.), 39.3
Spottiswoode, Jas., Bp. of Clogher
　(d. 1645), 39.3
Spottiswoode, John, superintendent of
　Lothian (d. 1585), 15.33
Spottiswoode, John, Archbp. of St
　Andrews (d. 1639), 6.96, 39.3*
Spottiswoode, Capt. John (d. 1650), 39.3
Spottiswoode, John (early 18 cent.),
　39.3*
Spottiswoode, Sir Rob., lawyer (d. 1646),
　39.3*

Spottiswoode of that Ilk, John (early 17 cent.), **39**.3
Spottiswoode family, **39**.3
Sprot, Geo. (early 17 cent.), **17**.15
Spynie, regality, **36**.6
Stafford, Anne, Duchess of Buckingham (d. *c*. 1480), **1**.3
Stafford, Humphrey, Duke of Buckingham (d. 1460), **1**.3
Stair, Lord, *see* Dalrymple, Sir Jas.
Stang, punishment, **15**.26
Stanley, Jas., Lord Strange, Earl of Derby (d. 1651), **4**.2
Starkey, John (mid 16 cent.), **6**.20
Stanley, Wm., Earl of Derby (d. 1642), **4**.2
State papers:
  and '45 rising, **26**.13–15
  Highland (1607–25), **25**.20
  Irish (1604–24), **1**.11
  Scottish:
    (1309–1759), **15**.69
    (*c*. 1578–1625), **1**.13
    (1599–1625), **1**.9
    (1603–25), **6**.95
    (1614–24), **1**.11
    (1615–35), **11**.34
    (1689–91), **6**.80
Statutes of the Church of Scotland (pre-Reformation), **6**.116, **24**.54
Stent rolls, *see* Taxation
Stephens (Stephenson), Andrew, poet (mid 17 cent.), **39**.3
Stephenson, Marmaduke (d. 1659), **4**.3
Steuart, John, merchant (mid 18 cent.), **25**.9
Steuart, Margaret, Mrs Calderwood (d. 1774), **15**.60
Steuart of Allanton, Hen. (early 19 cent.), **24**.26
Stevenson, John, labourer (d. 1728), **43**.9
Stewart, Jas., Earl of Moray, Regent of Scotland (d. 1570), **6**.20*, **36**.16
Stewart, Jas. (mid 18 cent.), and Appin Murder, **26**.22
Stewart of Baldynneis, John, poet (late 16 cent.), **32**.5
Stirling, burgh:
  castle, **15**.59
  chapel royal, **11**.20, **15**.27*
  James VI surprised at, **6**.20
  records, **21**.29–31, 42
Stirling, commissariot, **29**.22
Stirling, kirk session, **15**.25, 26
Stirling, pres., **27**.17
Stirling, Earl of, *see* Alexander, Sir Wm.
Stirlingshire, monuments, **44**.16
Stitchill, barony, **24**.50
Strachan, Geo., Oriental scholar (early 17 cent.), **2**.5, **38**.20
Strachan family, **11**.31
Strachan of Thornton family, **11**.27
Straloch papers, **36**.3
Strange, Lord, *see* Stanley, Jas.

Stranraer, **28**.1
Strathavon, lordship, **38**.22
Strathbogie, lordship, **36**.20
Strathbogie, pres., **36**.7
Strathearn, earldom of, **6**.88
Strathmore, Earl of, *see* Lyon, Pat.
Stuart, Anne, Duchess of York (d. 1671), **17**.19
Stuart, Chas. Edward, Count Roehenstart (d. 1854), **26**.43
Stuart, Prince Chas. Edward, 'the Young Pretender', (d. 1788):
  army, **36**.3
  grandson, **26**.43
  itinerary (1745–6), **24**.23
  & '45 rising, **15**.55, **17**.22*, **24**.20–3, **26**.9
  wanderings, **17**.22
Stuart, Charlotte, Duchess of Albany (d. 1789), **24**.44
Stuart, Hen., Cardinal of York (d. 1807), **25**.2
Stuart, Jas., 'the Old Pretender' or Chevalier de St George (d. 1766):
  birth, **8**.1, 2
  intrigues, **39**.4
  letters by, **24**.26
  letters to, **17**.21
  meeting with, **8**.1, **39**.3
  memoirs, **8**.2
  secretary, **11**.5
Stuart, Jas., Duke of Lennox (d. 1655), **8**.1
Stuart, Capt. Jas. (mid 18 cent.), **36**.3
Stuart, John, Earl of Bute (d. 1792), **27**.15
Stuart, Ludovic, Duke of Lennox (d. 1624), **1**.11, **15**.25
Stuart papers, **17**.12
Stuart of Inchbreck, John, scholar (d. 1827), **36**.40
Stuarts in exile, **17**.4, 12, **26**.31, 35
Styles, books of, *see* Formularies
Suffolk, Earl of, *see* Howard, Theophilus
Supplications, to Rome, **26**.23, 48, **27**.7
Supply, commissioners of, Banffshire, **37**.43
Surveyors:
  John Farquharson, **26**.27
  John Home, **26**.52
  John MacArthur, **26**.27
  Peter May, **27**.15
Surveys:
  Assynt, **26**.52
  Lochtayside, **26**.27
  misc., **27**.15
Sutherland:
  estate management, **27**.8, 9
  monuments, **44**.2
  records, **42**.4
  tour, **41**.1
Sutherland, Wm., Earl of (d. 1306–7), **6**.22

Sutherland, Wm., Earl of (d. 1750), 5.2
Sutherland of Dunbeath, Alex. (mid
    15 cent.), 6.22
Sweden:
    industrial spy from, 27.14
    Montrose in, 24.15
    Scots officers in, 39.4*
    work printed in, 6.22
Sweetheart Abbey, 5.10
Swynton, Sir Geo. (d. 1630), 6.121
Sydserf, Thos., Bp. of Galloway (d. 1663),
    39.6
Sydserf, Thos., comedian (late 17 cent.),
    1.11
Synods:
    post-Reformation:
        Aberdeen, 36.15
        Argyll, 26.37, 38
        Banff, 37.10
        Fife, 1.8
        Glasgow & Ayr, 15.69
        Lothian & Tweeddale, 40.32
        Perth, 36.24
    pre-Reformation, 6.116, 24.54

Tacks (leases):
    Breadalbane, 6.103
    Coupar Angus, 11.17
    Gaelic, 40.37
    St Andrews Priory, 19.4
Talbot, Capt. Geo. A. (mid 18 cent.),
    17.22
Tarbolton, parish, 5.2
Taxation:
    cess, Aberdeenshire, 38.3
    hearth tax:
        Rothesay, 7.7
        Scotland, 30.9
        W. Lothian, 30.9
    land tax:
        committee, Aberdeeenshire, 36.16
        tax or stent rolls:
            Annan, 30.4
            Canongate, 29.85
            Dumfries, 9.4
            Dryburgh Abbey, 6.86
            Fife, 26.12
            Forfarshire, 6.105
            Holyrood Abbey, 6.73
            Inchaffray Abbey, 6.88
        warrant for, Midlothian, 6.22
        See also Valuations
    poll tax:
        commissioners, Banffshire, 37.43
        rolls:
            Aberdeenshire, 36.39, 37.27
            Edinburgh, 29.82
            Kilbarchan, 16.12
            Kilmacolm, 16.10
            Neilston, 16.14
            Old Aberdeen, 37.21
Taymouth, Black Book of, 6.103
Templars, Knights, 39.4*

Tea, 27.10
Terig, Duncan, *see* Clerk, Duncan
Territorial soldiering, in the North East,
    37.42
Testaments:
    of individuals:
        Duchess of Albany, 24.44
        Rich. Bannatyne, 6.54
        Archbp. Jas. Beaton, 11.8, 15.27
        David Buchanan, 6.58
        Gilbert Burnet, 17.14
        Thos. Burnet, 17.16
        David Calderwood, 43.7
        Sir Jas. Douglas of Dalkeith, 6.21
        David Fergusson, 6.113
        Geo. Heriot, 15.59
        John Johnston, 15.26
        John Knox, 6.54
        Archbp. Jas Law, 15.12
        Rich. Lawson, 6.22
        Rob. Logan of Restalrig, 17.15
        Jas. Melville, 43.3
        Col. Wm. Semple, 15.27
        Sir David Sinclair of Swynbrocht,
            6.22
        John Snell, 40.37
        Sir Alex. Sutherland of Dunbeath,
            6.22
    registers:
        Aberdeen, 29.6
        Argyll, 29.9
        Brechin, 29.13
        Caithness, 29.10
        Dumfries, 29.14
        Dunblane, 29.15
        Dunkeld, 29.16
        Edinburgh, 29.1–3
        Glasgow, 29.7
        Hamilton & Campsie, 29.5
        Inverness, 29.4
        Isles, 29.11
        Lanark, 29.19
        Lauder, 29.18
        Moray, 29.20
        Orkney, 29.21
        Peebles, 29.12
        St Andrews, 29.8
        Shetland, 29.21
        Stirling, 29.22
    relating to:
        Bannatyne family, 6.38
        Cunningham, 15.76
        Orkney, 30.6
        printers & booksellers, 6.21
        Wigtown, 29.23
Teviotdale, archdeaconry, Bagimond's
    Roll, 26.21
Textiles, *see* Industry
Thanes:
    Cawdor, 36.30
    Fermartyn (Formartine), 37.51
Third Spalding Club, history, 38.10
Thirds of Benefices: *see* Church of
    Scotland, *post*-Reformation

Thirlestane, Lord, *see* Maitland of
 Thirlestane, John
Thistle, Order of the, **11**.20
Thomas the Rhymer, poet (13 cent.), **18**.3
Thomson, Geo. (late 16 cent.), **24**.44
Thomson, Thos., antiquary (d. 1852):
 life, **6**.98, 102
 Memorial on old extent, **40**.11
Thounis, Nicol, notary (mid 16 cent.),
 29.57
Thre prestis of Peblis, **32**.8
Thrissels banner, **26**.11
Tillydesk, Epis. chapel, **29**.30
Tiree, **27**.1, **44**.21
Tobacco:
 trade, **27**.20
 treatises on, **34**.14, **36**.3
Toleration, religious, **36**.3
Tomintoul, **38**.22
Topographical descriptions, Scottish:
 by:
  John Adair, **6**.21
  Thos. Morer, **36**.15
  Rich. Pococke, **24**.1
  Sir Rob. Sibbald, **6**.22
  John Slezer, **6**.21
  Ubaldini, **6**.35
 Caledonia, **16**.9
 Macfarlane collections, **24**.51–3, **39**.4
 misc., **15**.69
 of:
  Aberdeenshire & Banffshire, **36**.17,
  37
  Cunningham, **15**.76
  Lanarkshire & Renfrewshire, **15**.12
Topography, bibliography of, **24**.14, 15
Torfaeus, Thormodus, writer (d. 1719),
 1.31, **6**.22
Tories, **4**.2
Torphichen, lordship & preceptory,
 27.19
Torphichen, parish, **29**.40
Tours, *see* Journeys
Trades council, Edinburgh, **27**.5
Trail, priory of the Isle of, **6**.21
Trail, Rob., divine (d. 1716), **43**.9
Treason, law of, **6**.6
Treasurer, accounts of, *see* Accounts:
 central government
Trimmer (1706), **39**.3
Tucker, Thos. (late 17 cent.), **6**.8,
 21.13
Tullibardine, Earl of, *see* Murray, John
Tulloch, Thos., Bp. of Orkney (mid 15
 cent.), **6**.22
Turnbull, Geo., min. of Alloa &
 Tyninghame (d. 1744), **24**.15
Turner, Sir Jas., soldier (d. *c.* 1686), **6**.31,
 25.12
Turpin, Archbp. of Reims, **1**.4
Tweeddale, Earl of, *see* Hay, John
Twenty lookes over all the Round-heads
 (1643), **8**.2
Twopenny faith (1559), **6**.22

Tynemouth Priory, **6**.20
Tyrebagger Hill, **38**.10
Tyrie, Jas., Cath. writer (late 16 cent.),
 31.20

Ubaldini, Petruccio (d. 1600?), **6**.35
Uniformity, act of (Eng.), **8**.3
Union of England & Scotland:
 negotiations:
  (1650–1), **24**.40
  (1669–70), **24**.40
 proposal, **6**.20, **13**.1
 tracts:
  (1604), **27**.21
  (1605), **24**.60
  (1706), **39**.3
Universal language, **15**.31
Universities, commissioners for visiting,
 27.2
 See also particular univs.
Unst, parish, **29**.78
Urban IV, Pope, (d. 1264), **36**.6
Urban VIII, Pope (d. 1644), **4**.2
Urquhart, Andrew, min. of Portpatrick (d.
 1890), **30**.8
Urquhart family, **15**.31
Urquhart of Cromarty, Sir Thos., writer
 (d. 1660), **3**.13, **15**.31
Urry (Hurry), Sir John, soldier (d. 1650),
 17.6
Usk, **1**.3

Valladolid, Scots College in, **37**.31
Valuations:
 benefices:
  Bagimond's Roll, **26**.21, 33, **27**.2
  books of assumption, **6**.89, 92, **35**.2
 directory of landowners compiled from,
  30.5
 old extent, **40**.11
 relating to:
  Aberdeenshire, **38**.4
  Kincardineshire, **26**.5
  Old Aberdeen, **37**.21
  Penninghame, **7**.3
  Wigtownshire, **5**.6
 See also Taxation
Vans of Barnbarrroch, *see* Vaus
Varthema, Lodovico de (Lewis
 Wertomannus), traveller (16 cent.),
 4.3
Vatican Archives, **26**.21, 22, **40**.1
Vaus (Vans, Waus) of Barnbarroch, Sir
 John (early 17 cent.), **5**.5
Vaus (Vans, Waus) of Barnbarroch, Sir
 Pat. (late 16 cent.), **5**.14
Vaus (Vans, Waus) of Barnbarroch family,
 correspondence, **5**.5, 14, **15**.26
Verses, *see* Poems
Vestments, **15**.13, 59
Vilant (Violent), Wm., min. of
 Cambusnethan (d. 1693), **43**.9

Vincentius (5 cent), **15**.34, **31**.10
Virginia:
  plantation, **4**.2
  tobacco trade, **27**.20
Visitation, of diocese of Dunblane, **30**.11
Volusenus (Wilson or Williamson?),
  Florentius (mid 16 cent.), **6**.20
Voyages:
  to Bermuda, **4**.2
  by Varthema, **4**.3

Wadsetters (Aberdeenshire), **36**.16
Wages, servants at Warthill, **36**.20
Wakefield, battle of (1643), **8**.1
Waldegrave, Rob., printer (d. 1604), **6**.47,
  31.23
Wallace, **6**.22, **31**.5, **33**.13, **34**.4, 5
Wallace, Sir Wm. (d. 1305), **6**.22, **11**.22,
  31.5, **33**.13, **34**.4, 5
Wallace family, **11**.22
Wallwood, John (early 17 cent.), **27**.2
Walpole, Sir Rob. (d. 1745), **4**.3
Walsingham, Sir Francis (d. 1590),
  6.20
Warren, Rich., Jacobite (mid 18 cent.),
  17.22
Warrender, Sir Geo., provost of
  Edinburgh (early 18 cent.), **26**.25
Warrender letters, **26**.25
Warrender papers, **26**.18, 19
Wars:
  in Flanders (1701–11), **24**.38
  in Ireland (1691), **6**.48, 56
  of Spanish succession (1706), **39**.3
  Russian–Polish (1563), **4**.2
  Scottish:
    civil:
      (1559–60), **26**.36, 50
      (1573), **6**.21
      (1639–50), **6**.28, **24**.15, **25**.17,
        36.10, 21, 23, **39**.3
      (1689–90), **6**.26, 48, 56, 74
      See also Jacobites: risings
    with England:
      (1296), **6**.20, 50
      (1514), **26**.43
      (1546), **6**.11
      (1548–9), **15**.2
      intervention in English civil, **25**.16,
       17
Warthill, **36**.20
Warwick, Earl of, *see* Rich, Rob.
Watson, Jas., printer (d. 1722), **34**.10
Watson, John, canon of Aberdeen (mid
  16 cent.), **15**.27
Waus of Barnbarroch, *see* Vaus
Weavers:
  Coventry, **1**.2
  Melrose, **25**.13
Webster, Alex., min. of Edinburgh
  (d. 1784), **26**.44
Webster, D., numismatist (mid 18 cent.),
  8.1

Wedderburn, Rob., notary & poet
  (d. 1611), **33**.4
Wedderburn, Rob., writer (d. *c*. 1557),
  34.11
Wedderburne, David, merchant (d. 1632),
  24.28
Weldon, Sir Anthony, writer (d. 1649?),
  1.11
Welsh, John, min. of Ayr (d. 1622), **43**.9,
  11
Welwood, Wm., lawyer (d. 1622), **33**.4
Wemyss, David, Lord Elcho (d. 1787),
  17.22
Wemyss, David, min. of Glasgow
  (d. 1615), **15**.33
Wemyss, Frances, Lady Denham
  (d. 1789), **15**.60
Wemyss of Pettincreif, Patrick (mid
  16 cent.), **40**.37
West Lothian:
  hearth tax, **30**.9
  monuments, **44**.10
Western Isles, *see* Isles
Wet, Jacob de (Witte, James de), painter
  (d. 1697), **24**.9
Whetstone, Geo., writer (d. 1587?), **4**.4
Whigs, **8**.2*
Whitehaugh, barony, **36**.24
Whitehead, Paul, satirist (d. 1774), **4**.4
Whithorn Priory, **5**.10
Whytelaw, Arch. (late 15 cent.), **6**.21
Wicked wayes of the cruell Cavaliers (1644),
  8.1
Wigtown, burgh, ships, **28**.1
Wigtown, commissariot, **29**.23
Wigtown, earldom, **15**.53, **29**.36
Wigtown, kirk session, **7**.5
Wigtownshire:
  charters, **26**.51
  list of inhabitants, **29**.50
  monuments, **44**.4
  reminiscences, **28**.7
  valuation, **5**.6
William I, King (d. 1214), **6**.66
William II & III, King (d. 1702):
  accepts government, **26**.47
  address to, **15**.59
  band supporting, **15**.59
  end of resistance to, **26**.22
  letters to, **6**.48
Williams, Sir John, Lord (d. 1559), **1**.5
Willock, John, min. of Edinburgh
  (d. 1585), **15**.33, **43**.11
Wills, *see* Testaments
Willy & Mary, **4**.1
Wilson, David (early 19 cent.), **28**.2
Wilson, Jas., plagiarist (mid 17 cent.),
  14.1
Windsor Castle, **8**.2
Winram, John, superintendent of Fife
  (d. 1582), **15**.33
Winzet, Ninian, Cath. writer (d. 1592),
  15.34, **31**.10
Wise family, **11**.31

Wise of Hillbank family, **11**.27
Wishart, Geo., Prot. reformer (d. 1546), **11**.11, **43**.11
Wishart, Geo., min. of Edinburgh (d. 1785), **8**.1
Wishart family, **11**.11
Witchcraft:
  novel on, **3**.1
  trials:
    Aberdeen, **36**.3
    Agnes Finnie, **39**.4
    Highlands, **25**.20
    James VI & I, **17**.1, **34**.14
    misc., **39**.4
    Orkney, **1**.11
    Isobel Young, **39**.4
Wodrow, Rob., min. of Eastwood (d. 1734):
  Analecta, **15**.62
  biographies, biographical collections, **15**.33, **37**.5, **43**.6, 9
  correspondence, **1**.11, **26**.24, **43**.5
  diary, **15**.62
  papers on church history of North East, **36**.6
  transcript by, **6**.20

Wodrow Society:
  laws & members, **43**.2
  prospectus, **43**.1
Woods, in Highlands & Isles, **13**.1
Writers:
  dictionary of, **6**.24
  Glasgow, **15**.14
  lives, **6**.58
Wycliffe, John, theologian (d. 1384), **31**.21
Wyngfield, Rob. (late 16 cent.), **8**.2
Wyntoun, Andrew of, chronicler (d. *c.* 1422), **31**.24
Wyse of Lunan family, **11**.27

Yester House, writs, **29**.55
York, Duke of, *see* James VII & II
Young, Isobel, witch (early 17 cent.), **39**.4
Young, Jas., notary (15–16 cents.), **29**.74
Young, Sir Peter, tutor (d. 1628), **24**.15
Young, Rob., printer (mid 16 cent.), **39**.3
Ythan, river, **26**.5

Zetland, *see* Shetland